CRUSH THE COMPOSITION

Transform the way you look at photography
to get the best images you've ever taken

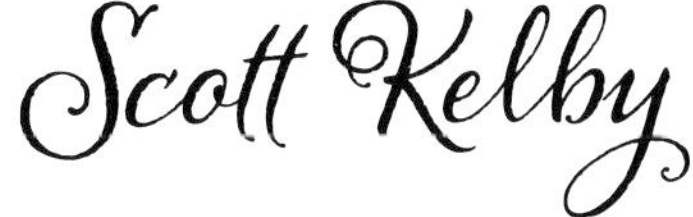

CRUSH THE COMPOSITION

Photography: Scott Kelby

Managing Editor: Kim Doty

Copy Editor: Cindy Snyder

Layout & Typography: Jessica Maldonado

Published by
Rocky Nook
1010 B Street, Suite 350
San Rafael, CA 94901

ISBN: 979-8-88814-249-3

10 9 8 7 6 5 4 3 2 1

Printed and bound in China

This book is printed on acid-free paper.

Distributed in the UK and Europe by Publishers Group UK

Distributed in the U.S. and all other territories by Publishers Group West

Library of Congress Control Number: 2024934879

kelbyone.com
rockynook.com

To Christina Sauer:

I'm so glad I get to work with you each day.

You've been a blessing to our company, our family,

your team, and everyone around you.

We got very lucky the day we found you!

ACKNOWLEDGMENTS

I start the acknowledgments for every book I've ever written the same way—by thanking my amazing wife, Kalebra. If you knew what an incredible woman she is, you'd totally understand why.

This is going to sound silly, but if we go grocery shopping together, and she sends me off to a different aisle to get milk, when I return with the milk and she sees me coming back down the aisle, she gives me the warmest, most wonderful smile. It's not because she's happy that I found the milk; I get that same smile every time I see her, even if we've only been apart for 60 seconds. It's a smile that says, "There's the man I love."

If you got that smile dozens of times a day for 35 years of marriage (in September of this year), you'd feel like the luckiest guy in the world, and believe me—I do. To this day, just seeing her puts a song in my heart and makes it skip a beat. When you go through life like this, it makes you one incredibly happy and grateful guy, and I truly am.

So, thank you, my love. Thank you for your kindness, your hugs, your understanding, your advice, your patience, your generosity, and for being such a caring and compassionate mother and wife. I love you.

Secondly, a big thanks to my son, Jordan. I wrote my first book when my wife was pregnant with him (27+ years ago) and he has literally grown up around my writing, so you can imagine how incredibly proud I was when he completed his first book (a 243-page fantasy novel) a few years ago. It has been a blast watching him grow up into such a wonderful young man, with his mother's tender and loving heart and compassion way beyond his years. As he heads into his life, with his wonderful wife Stephi, he knows his dad just could not be prouder or more excited for him. Throughout his life he has touched so many people, in so many different ways, and even though he's still a young man, he's already inspired so many people, and I just cannot wait to see the amazing adventure—and the love and laughter—this life has in store for him. This world needs more "yous!"

Thanks to our wonderful daughter, Kira, for being the answer to our prayers, for being such a blessing to your older brother, and for proving, once again, that miracles happen every day. You are a little clone of your mother, and believe me, there is no greater compliment I could give you. It is such a blessing to get to see such a happy, hilarious, clever, creative, and just awesome little force of nature dancing around the house each day—she just has no idea how happy and proud she makes us.

A special thanks to my big brother, Jeff. I have so much to be thankful for in my life, and having you as such a positive role model while I was growing up is one thing I'm particularly thankful for. You're the best brother any guy could ever have, and I've said it a million times before, but one more surely wouldn't hurt—I love you, man!

My heartfelt thanks go to my entire team at KelbyOne. I know everybody thinks their team is really special, but this one time—I'm right. I'm so proud to get to work with you all, and I'm still amazed at what you're able to accomplish day in, day out, and I'm constantly impressed with how much passion and pride you put into everything you do. Shout out to the world's best video team: Christina, Juan, Eric, Ron, and Jason.

A warm word of thanks goes to my in-house editor, Kim Doty. It's her amazing attitude, passion, poise, and attention to detail that has kept me writing books. When you're writing a book like this, sometimes you can really feel like you're all alone, but she really makes me feel that I'm not alone—that we're a team. It's often her encouraging words or helpful ideas that keep me going when I've hit a wall, and I just can't thank her enough. Kim, you are the best!

I'm equally as lucky to have the brilliant Jessica Maldonado designing my books. I just love the way Jessica designs, and all the clever little things she adds throughout. She's not just incredibly talented and a joy to work with, she's a very smart designer and thinks five steps ahead in every layout she builds. We hit the jackpot when we found you!

Also, a big thanks to our copy editor, Cindy Snyder, whom I feel very blessed to have still working with us on these books. Thank you, Cindy!

A big thanks to my dear friend, the "real rocket man," astro-awesome guy, professor of Tesla studies, master of the nighttime landscape, and Amazon Prime aficionado, Mr. Erik Kuna. You are one of the reasons I love still coming to work. You're always uncovering cool things, thinking outside the box, and making sure we always do the right thing for the right reasons. Thanks for your friendship, your hard work, and your invaluable advice.

Thanks to Kleber Stephenson for making sure all sorts of awesome things happen, doors open, and opportunities appear. I particularly enjoy our business trips together where we laugh too much, eat way too much, and have more fun on a business trip than was previously scheduled.

To Ted Waitt, my fantastic "Editor for life" at Rocky Nook: Thanks for being such a great friend, a world-class sounding board, and for helping these ideas become a reality. To my publisher Scott Cowlin: I'm so delighted I still get to work with you, and thankful for your open mind and vision.

Thanks to Manny Steigman for always believing in me, and for his support and friendship all these years. Thanks to Gabe, Rebecca, and all the wonderful folks at B&H Photo. Yes, it is the greatest camera store in the world, but it's so much more.

Thanks to these friends who had nothing to do with this book, but so much to do with my life, and I just want to give them the literary version of a hug: Fernando "Chicky Nando" Santos, Paul Kober, Jeff Revell, Kelly Jones, Moose Peterson, Larry Grace, Rob Foldy, Dave Clayton, Dobson Ayerule, Victoria Pavlov, Dave Williams, Larry Becker, Peter Treadway, Roberto Pisconti, Jeff Leimbach, Scott Berger, Marvin Derizen, Willey Peckham, Maxx Hammond, Joe McNally, Annie Cahill, Rick Sammon, Mimo Meidany, Claire Jones, Tayloe Harding, John Couch, Serge Ramelli, Miles Smith, Ryan Turner, Kathy Porupski, and of course, Vanelli. Thanks to my *Call of Duty: Warzone* teammates: Hans, Slaps, Geezer, Maxx, Robo, and Dobson for always reviving me when I'm downed.

I owe a debt of thanks to some awesome people at Adobe: Jeff Tranberry, Terry White, Julieanne Kost, and Russell Preston Brown. Gone but not forgotten: Barbara Rice, Rye Livingston, Jim Heiser, Tom Hogarty, Sharad Mangalick, Bryan Lamkin, Bryan Hughes, John Loiacono, Kevin Connor, Deb Whitman, Addy Roff, Cari Gushiken, Karen Gauthier, and Winston Hendrickson.

Thanks to my mentors, whose wisdom and whip-cracking have helped me immeasurably: John Graden, Jack Lee, Dave Gales, Judy Farmer, and Douglas Poole.

Most importantly, I want to thank God, and His Son Jesus Christ, for leading me to the woman of my dreams, for blessing us with two amazing children, for allowing me to make a living doing something I truly love, for always being there when I need Him, for blessing me with a wonderful, fulfilling, and happy life, and such a warm, loving family to share it with.

OTHER BOOKS BY SCOTT KELBY

Light It, Shoot It, Retouch It

Scott Kelby's Lightroom 7-Point System

The iPhone Photography Book

The Natural Light Portrait Book

Photoshop for Lightroom Users

The Travel Photography Book

The Flash Book

The Landscape Photography Book

How Do I Do That In Lightroom?

How Do I Do That In Photoshop?

The Digital Photography Book, parts 1, 2, 3, 4 & 5

Professional Portrait Retouching Techniques for Photographers Using Photoshop

The Adobe Photoshop Lightroom Classic Book

The Adobe Photoshop Book for Digital Photographers

The Photoshop Elements Book for Digital Photographers

It's a Jesus Thing: The Book for Wanna Be-lievers

Professional Sports Photography Workflow

ABOUT THE AUTHOR

Scott Kelby is President and CEO of KelbyOne, an online educational community for photographers. He is co-founder of *Photoshop User* magazine; host of *The Grid*, the influential, live, weekly talk show for photographers; and is founder of the annual Scott Kelby's Worldwide Photo Walk.™

Scott is an award-winning photographer, designer, and best-selling author of more than 100 books, including *The Flash Book*; *Light It, Shoot It, Retouch It*; *The Adobe Photoshop Lightroom Classic Book*; *Professional Portrait Retouching Techniques for Photographers Using Photoshop*; *The Landscape Photography Book*; *The Adobe Photoshop Book for Digital Photographers*; *The Travel Photography Book*; *How Do I Do That In Lightroom?*; *The Natural Light Portrait Book*; and his landmark, *The Digital Photography Book*, which has become the #1 top-selling book ever on digital photography.

His books have been translated into dozens of different languages, including Chinese, Russian, Spanish, Korean, Polish, Taiwanese, French, German, Italian, Japanese, Hebrew, Dutch, Swedish, Turkish,

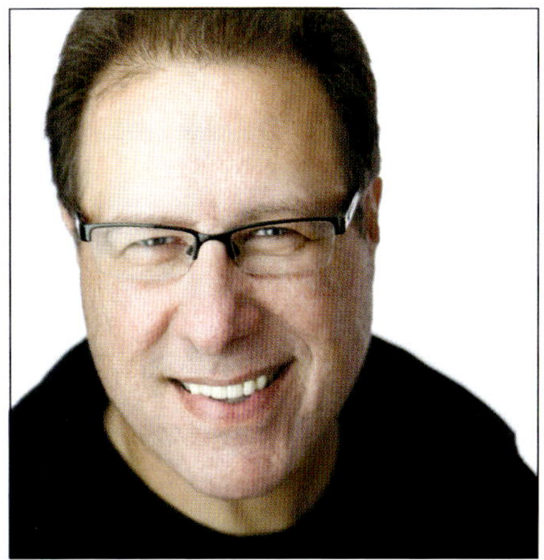

and Portuguese, among many others. He is a recipient of the prestigious ASP International Award, presented annually by the American Society of Photographers for "…contributions in a special or significant way to the ideals of Professional Photography as an art and a science," and the HIPA award, presented for his contributions to photography education worldwide.

Scott is Conference Technical Chair for the annual Photoshop World Conference and a frequent speaker at conferences and trade shows around the world. He is featured in a series of online learning courses at KelbyOne.com and has been training photographers and Photoshop users since 1993.

For more information on Scott, visit him at:

His daily Lightroom blog: lightroomkillertips.com

His personal blog: scottkelby.com

Twitter: @scottkelby

Facebook: facebook.com/skelby

Instagram: scottkelby

CONTENTS

CONTENTS

CONTENTS

CONTENTS

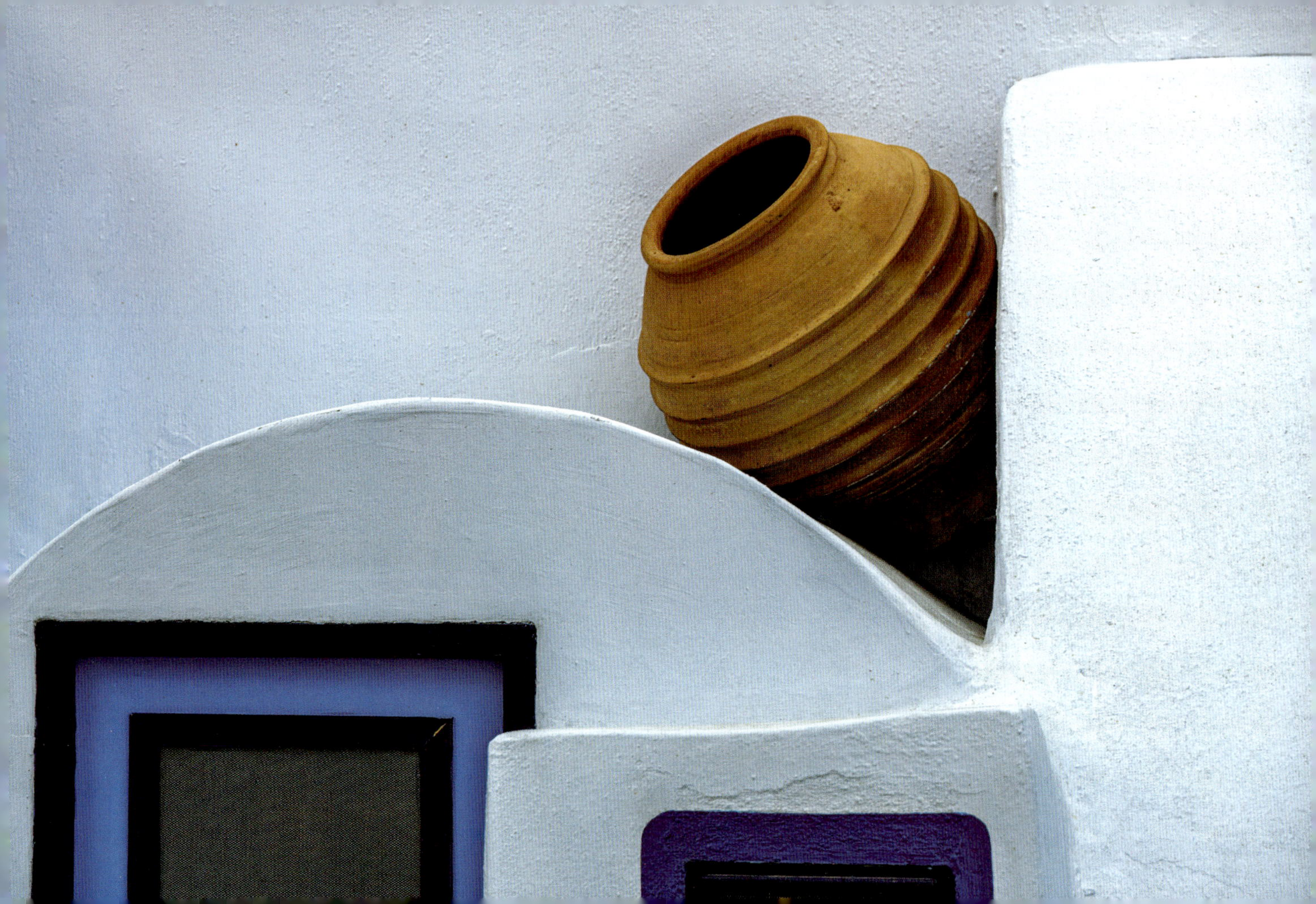

Read This First

DOES THE WORLD NEED ANOTHER BOOK ON COMPOSITION?

From time to time, book publishers will send me a copy of a book they've published in the hopes that I'll do a review on my blog or on social. One day a book about photography composition came across my desk, and I stopped to give it a look because the cover photo was really compelling. As I flipped through it, I noticed that all the photos were really great—this guy could shoot—but once I looked at the names of the chapters, I got really disappointed. There was yet another chapter on "The Rule of Thirds," and "Leading Lines," and "Repeating Patterns," and the same stuff they've been teaching forever. If you went back to the 1940s and bought a book on composition, I'd bet the chapters would be called "The Rule of Thirds," "Leading Lines," "Repeating Patterns," and so on. In fact, the rule of thirds was first referred to by John Thomas Smith back in 1797, yet this was the stuff that was in that book. If you're thinking, "There has got to be more to photographic composition than that!" you'd be right. That's what inspired this book. This isn't to say those "rules" of composition aren't valid; it's just that there's way more to composition than just those rules—there's something they're not telling you. That's what *this* book is all about, and I can't wait to share those techniques with you in the coming pages. Over the past few years, I've done a talk called "Crush the Composition" for keynote presentations at conferences and live seminars, and the feedback has been phenomenal, with the most common comment being, "Why didn't anyone tell me about this before?" One more thing: to my longtime readers, you'll notice that I'm going with a very different layout and design for this book than you've found in my previous books. The idea for it came from my book editor and dear friend Ted Waitt, who felt this should be a book with one leg in the classroom and one leg on the coffee table, and the marvelous Jessica Maldonado made it all come together with her keen sense of layout and design. I hope this book opens your mind to a new way of thinking, working, and seeing photographic composition in a fresh new way and that it helps you create your best images yet.

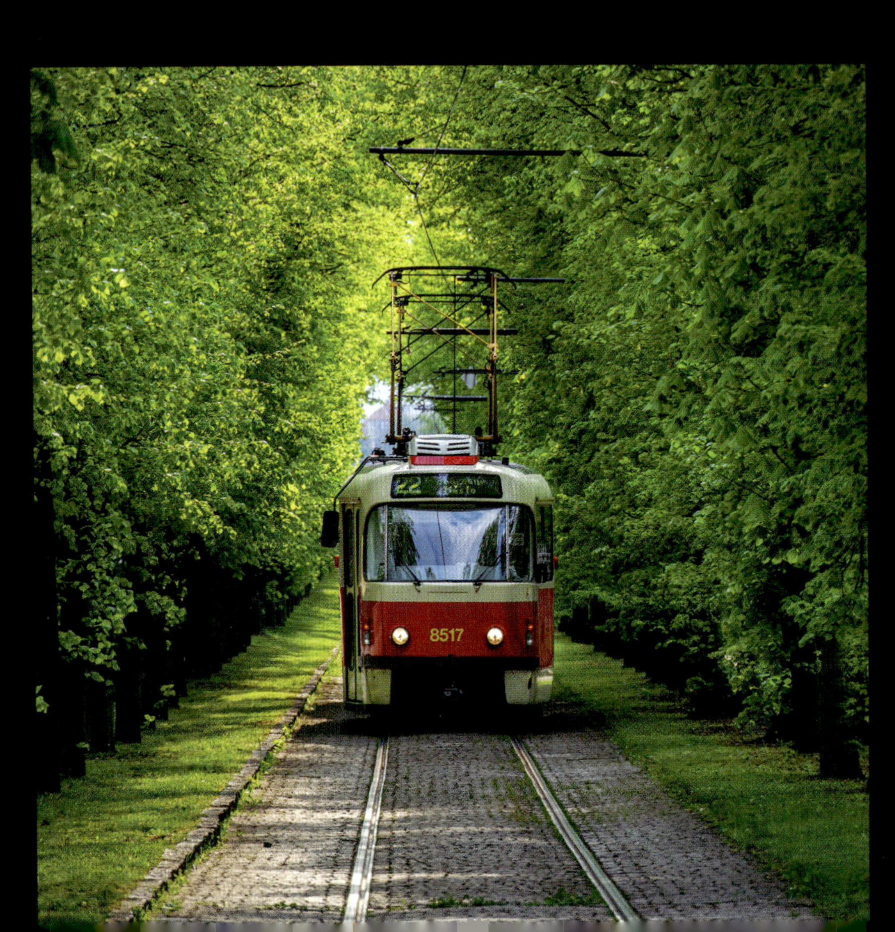

Chapter 01

SEEING DIFFERENTLY

The first two pages of this chapter are probably the two most important pages in this entire book. That's why I put them first. Okay, it's actually probably the first page that is the most important of the two, but those two pages together unlock the recipe for what actually determines whether you're going to have a great photo or just an "okay" or "meh" photo. When you read those two pages, you might think, "Well, yeah. That makes sense," and they may even seem kind of obvious, and if you finish those two pages and feel like that, read them again. Read them again because the concepts on those pages will single-handedly play the biggest role in how your images look and how people react to them. In the rest of this first chapter, we're going to tackle some of the things that are going to have the biggest impact on your photography, and not a single one of them is a camera setting or accessory to buy. It's the stuff that matters, and I'm going to be very frank about these topics—just like if I were sitting with a friend at a bar talking about what really matters in photography. After Chapter 1, the rest of the book is to help you better understand how to make the most of page 3 in this chapter and that takes us a whole book, but when you get to the end, you're going to have so many compositional tools and ideas at your disposal that there's probably not going to be a scene you're standing in front of with your camera where you don't know what to do. That's what everything from page 3 to page 247 is for. Okay, you ready to rock this thing? Let's go!

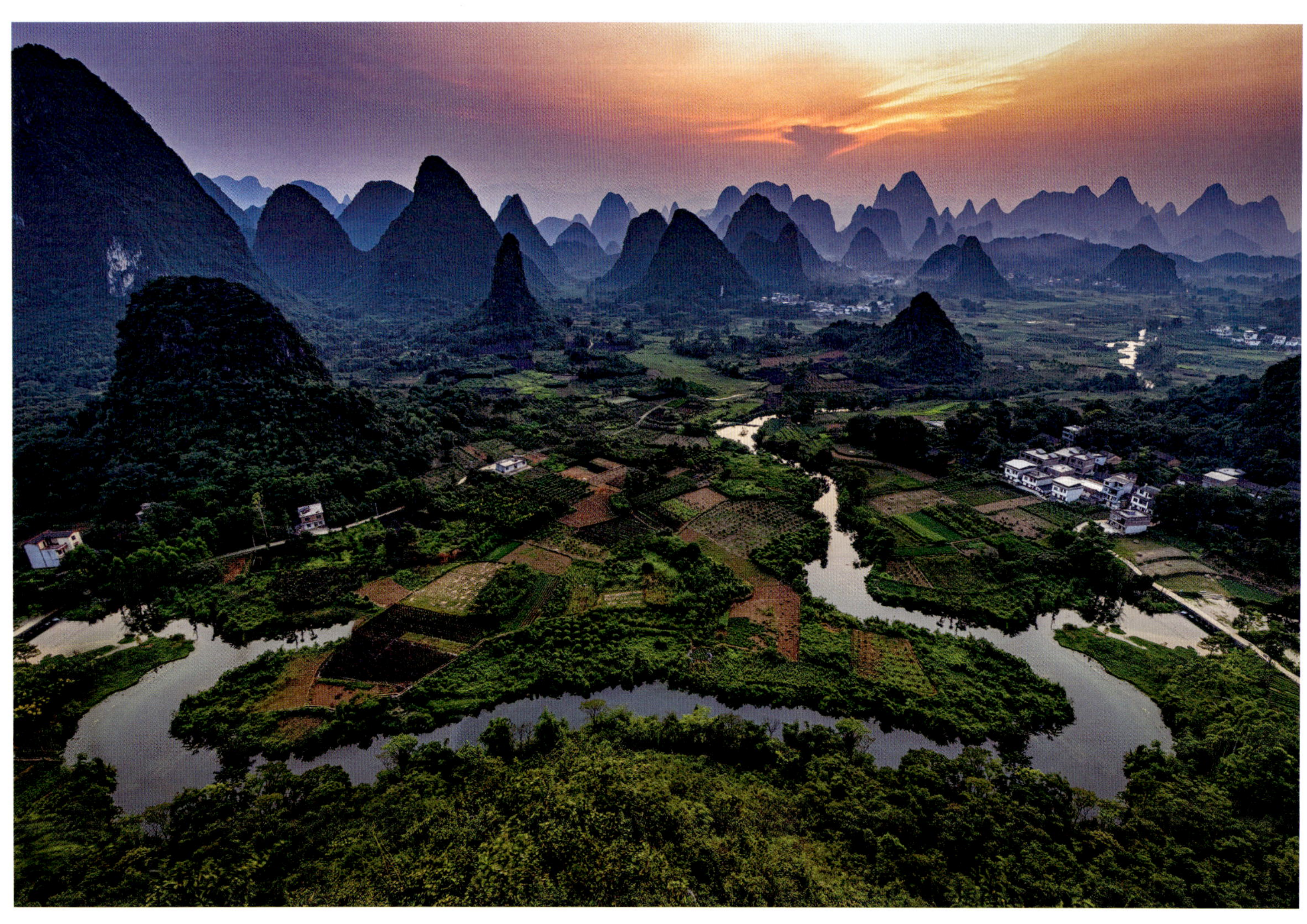

IT'S WHAT YOU'RE STANDING IN FRONT OF...

It was probably 15 years ago, maybe more now, when I was a guest speaker at a landscape photography workshop up in Vermont, and a guy I hadn't heard of until that workshop—Joe McNally was his name—was doing a presentation on his work, and his work was stunning. How I hadn't ever heard of this guy, I have no idea, but his photography and his presentation were both brilliant. Brilliant! About halfway through he said something that changed me and my photography forever. He was sharing something that one of his magazine editors once told him (I think it was his editor at *Life* magazine), which was: "Joe, if you want to take more interesting photos, stand in front of more interesting things." That hit me like a ton of bricks. I grabbed a notepad on the table in front of me and wrote that down. It made me want to stop buying lenses and more gear and accessories and start buying airline tickets, so when I aimed my camera I would be aiming at something interesting. It really comes down to this: does what you're standing in front of have a chance of making the person viewing your image say "Wow!"? Is it amazing, beautiful, awe-inspiring? If it's a person, are they intriguing, super-photogenic, stunning, fascinating? If it's a place, will seeing your shot make someone want to go there? The food you're about to shoot—is it beautifully presented and plated, with great light in a wonderful setting? Is the athlete you're about to photograph doing something incredible, are they at a peak moment of action, and is there a crowd on their feet cheering behind them, or are there a bunch of empty seats behind them in the stadium? Does the landscape you're standing in front of make you pause just to take it all in and count your blessings that you even get to see something like this—especially when it's bathed in magical early dawn light? If it doesn't, you're probably not standing in front of the right thing. If it's an "okay" landscape location, that's probably how your photo is going to come out. It's going to look "okay." But if you want it to look spectacular, if you want it to move people, and awe them, and make them say "Wow!" that's the landscape you need to be standing in front of. That's the first part of how great photos are made—standing in front of something, or someone, or somewhere that is more interesting. If you start there, where you're standing at that magical location, with your camera sitting quietly on your tripod, how hard would it be to make a great photo? Think about that. How much of a struggle would it be? Exactly. Now, add in the missing piece of this puzzle (on the next page, and the rest of this book), and that's when the magic happens, and I want you to make magic.

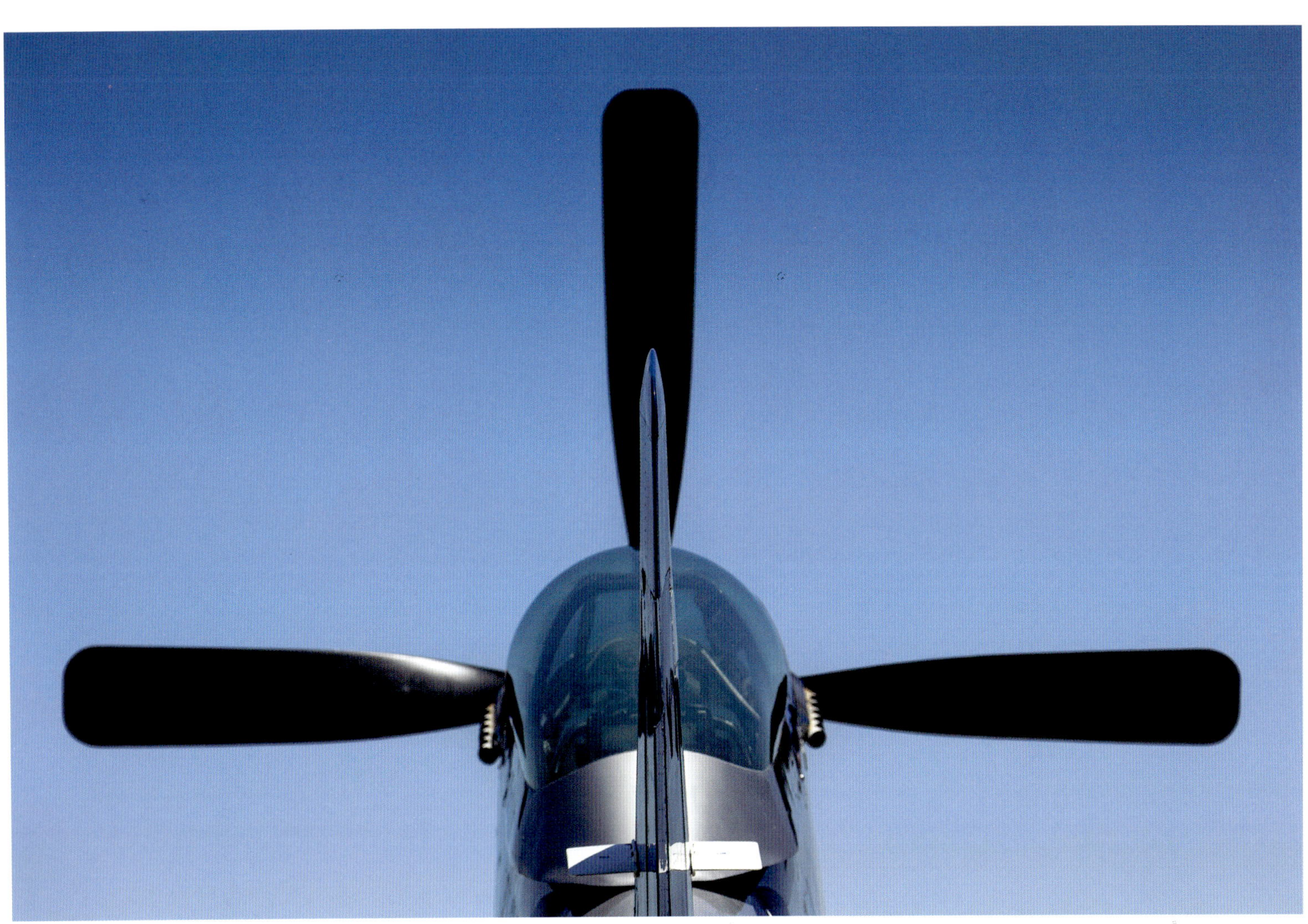

...AND THEN, HOW YOU FRAME IT

You've done everything right—you're on location in an incredible place and the light is stunning. You got lucky because Mother Nature showed up for you big time with the most beautiful sky you've seen in a while. Your gear is set, and you're ready to run the table. I've been in situations like this with groups of other photographers where we were all like: "Can you believe this sky? Can you believe this location? Can you believe how lucky we got?" But then later, when I looked at some of their images, it was like we weren't even in the same place. It made me want to ask them, "That's what you saw there?" That's because incredible images don't *just* come from incredible places or subjects. It's what you do next that is either going to make or break the shot, and that is quite simply how you frame the shot. How you compose it. What you decide to leave in, what you decide to leave out, which lens you decide to use, and, simply, where you aim your camera. So, am I saying that photography really all comes down to "what you're standing in front of and how you frame up the shot once you're there?" Yes. Yes, I am. It is the very essence of what we do. That doesn't mean that light and color and shape and texture and form and all that stuff don't play a role, but they are supporting roles. What you're standing in front of, and how you frame it are the stars, and that's why they get all of the attention. In case you were wondering, the shot here is a vintage World War II P-51 Mustang warbird, photographed from straight on behind the tail.

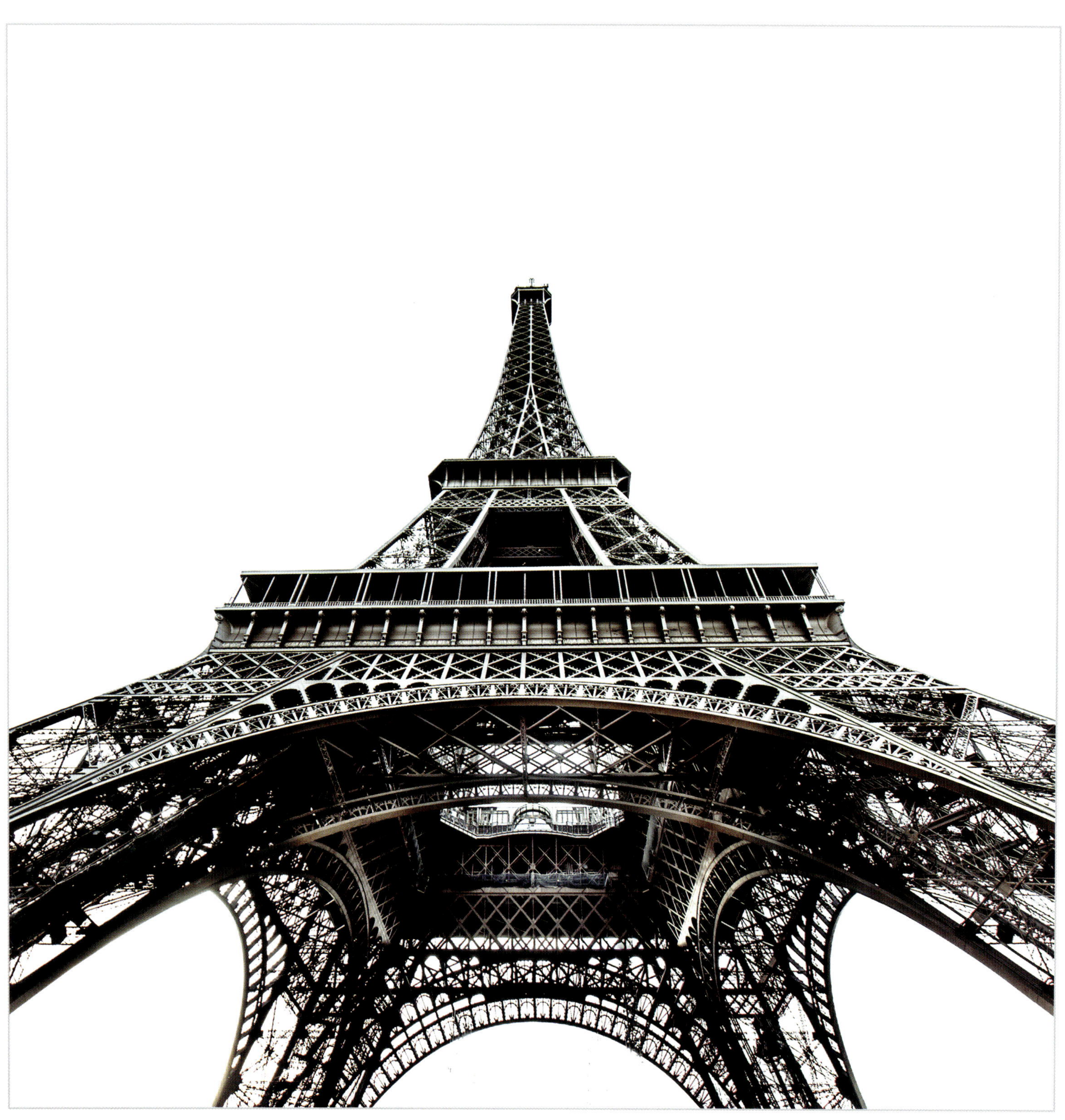

TAKING BAD PHOTOS
OF BEAUTIFUL THINGS

If you mention "Paris," what's the first image that pops into most folks' minds? The Eiffel Tower, right? Boom. It's instant. It's one of the most visited monuments in the world—people want to see it and experience it with their own eyes. It was built in 1889 for the World's Fair in Paris, and to this day it's considered by many to be one of the most beautiful architectural wonders on the planet. And I've seen some of the crappiest photos of it that you can imagine. Seriously bad photos of what is considered to be one of the most beautiful structures in the world. How is that possible? That's easy—bad composition. Of course, it could be bad light, too, but the problem usually isn't light. It's that they found a way to make something really good look really bad. So, if we can agree that it's possible to stand in front of something beautiful and make a really bad photo, is the opposite true? If you're really good at composition, can you take things that aren't all that interesting on the surface and make them look "Wow!"? Great composition has that superpower. You can take regular things and make them look awesome. So, if you can make regular things look interesting, what does great composition do when you're standing in front of something awesome? You know the answer.

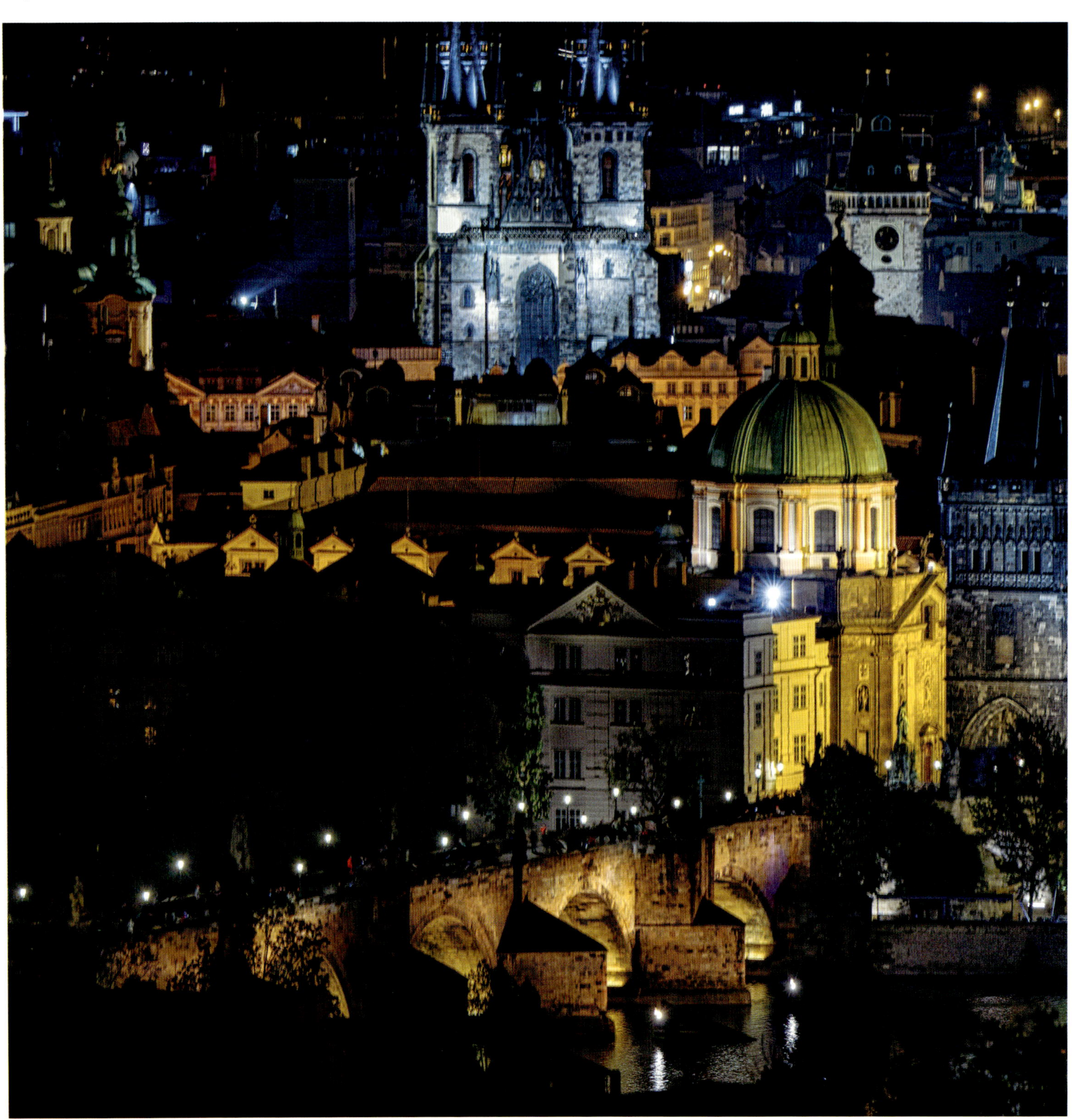

STOP LOOKING FOR
THE MAGIC MENU SETTING

I talk to so many photographers who tell me, "I just really need to learn how to use my camera." There are so many menus and categories of menus, six and seven levels deep, and they think buried in there is some menu or setting that the pros know about that they don't, and if they could just uncover that menu and start using those "pro" settings, a whole new world of photography would be unveiled. Of course, there is no magic menu, no hidden pro feature that will make your photos look better than the next guy's (or gal's). Your camera is a lot like your car. There are three things in your car that get you from point A to point B: the gas pedal, the brake, and the steering wheel. That's it. Those three are what drive your car. So what are the electric windows for? What's the stereo for? What about electric seats and air conditioning? They are all there to make your experience more enjoyable and more customized to your tastes, but again, they don't drive the car—they just make it more comfortable. Same thing with your camera. There are three settings that make photos: aperture (your f-stop), shutter speed, and ISO. Those three settings make your photos. All the stuff in the menus—the stuff that makes it easier and more comfortable— they don't make photos. They just make the process of taking photos more comfortable. But, there is one camera feature beyond those that does make a difference: it's what you aim your camera at and how you aim it when you do.

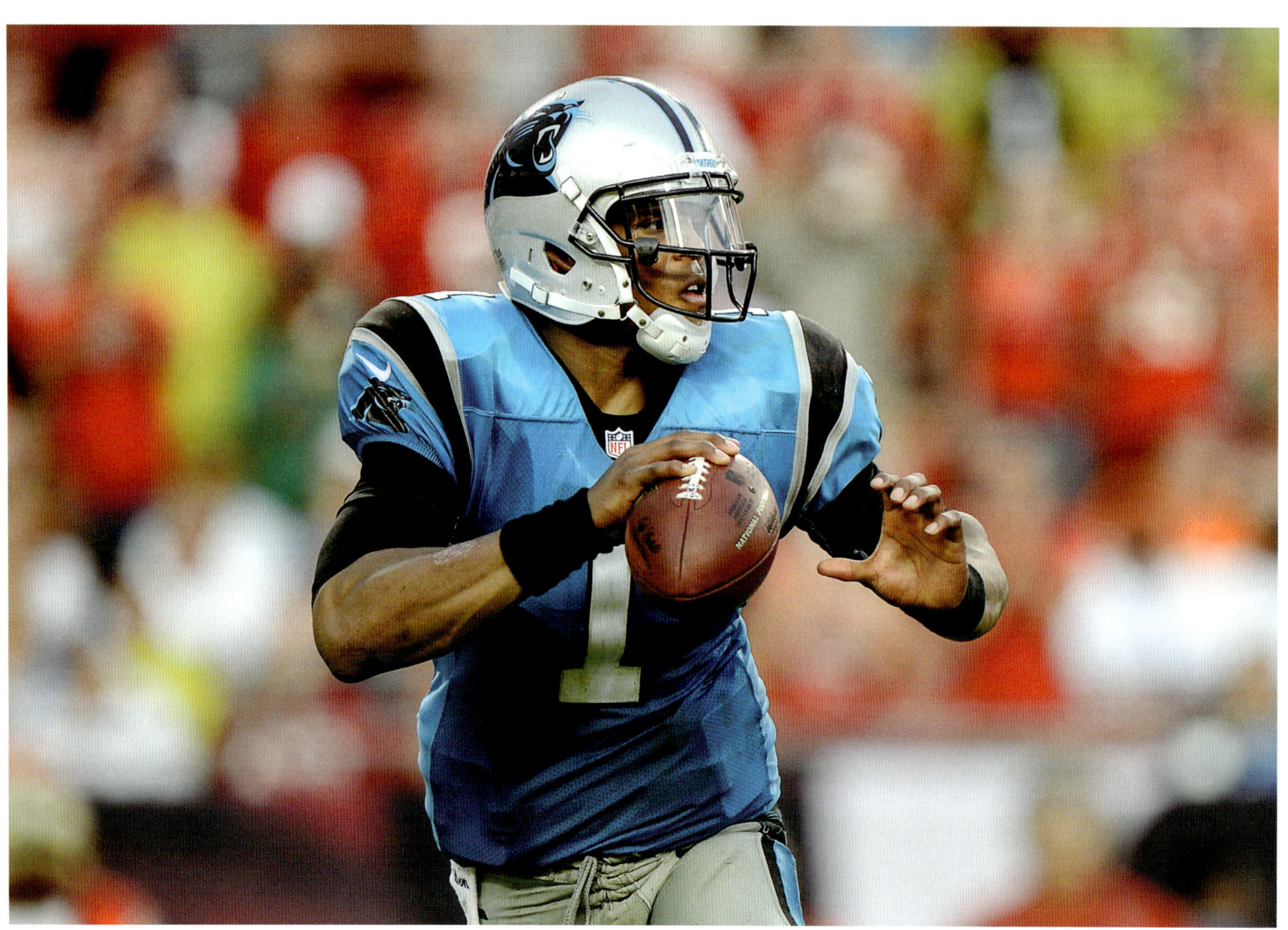

MY MOST-ASKED QUESTION

When I do full-day, in-person seminars, during the break in between sessions, I answer one-on-one questions from the photographers who are there. They always have lots of great questions on everything from which ink jet printer I recommend to things about Lightroom. But, by far, the most-asked question I get is about exposure: which metering mode do I use (it's matrix metering), when do I switch to spot metering (I don't), and every other metering and exposure question you can imagine. This is really unfortunate because I don't want to say it doesn't matter, but it really doesn't matter that much. Why? Because if you take a shot and look at the back of your camera and see that it's a bit underexposed, what could you possibly do? You could rotate a dial like 1/8 of an inch and make the photo brighter. What if you didn't notice it while you were shooting, so you didn't find out it was underexposed until later when you opened the image on your computer? What could you possibly do then? Move a slider in Lightroom or Photoshop 1/16 of a inch and it's fixed. But this is the thing we worry about. This is the thing we stand in line to ask about. I can tell you this: your phone isn't going to ring one day, and on the other end is a potential client who says, "I'm looking to hire a photographer and I need one that can take the shot and not make it too dark or too bright." It's not going to happen. Ever. But that's what we're worried about. Who will get hired? Someone who can take an image of a scene that isn't that interesting and make it really interesting.

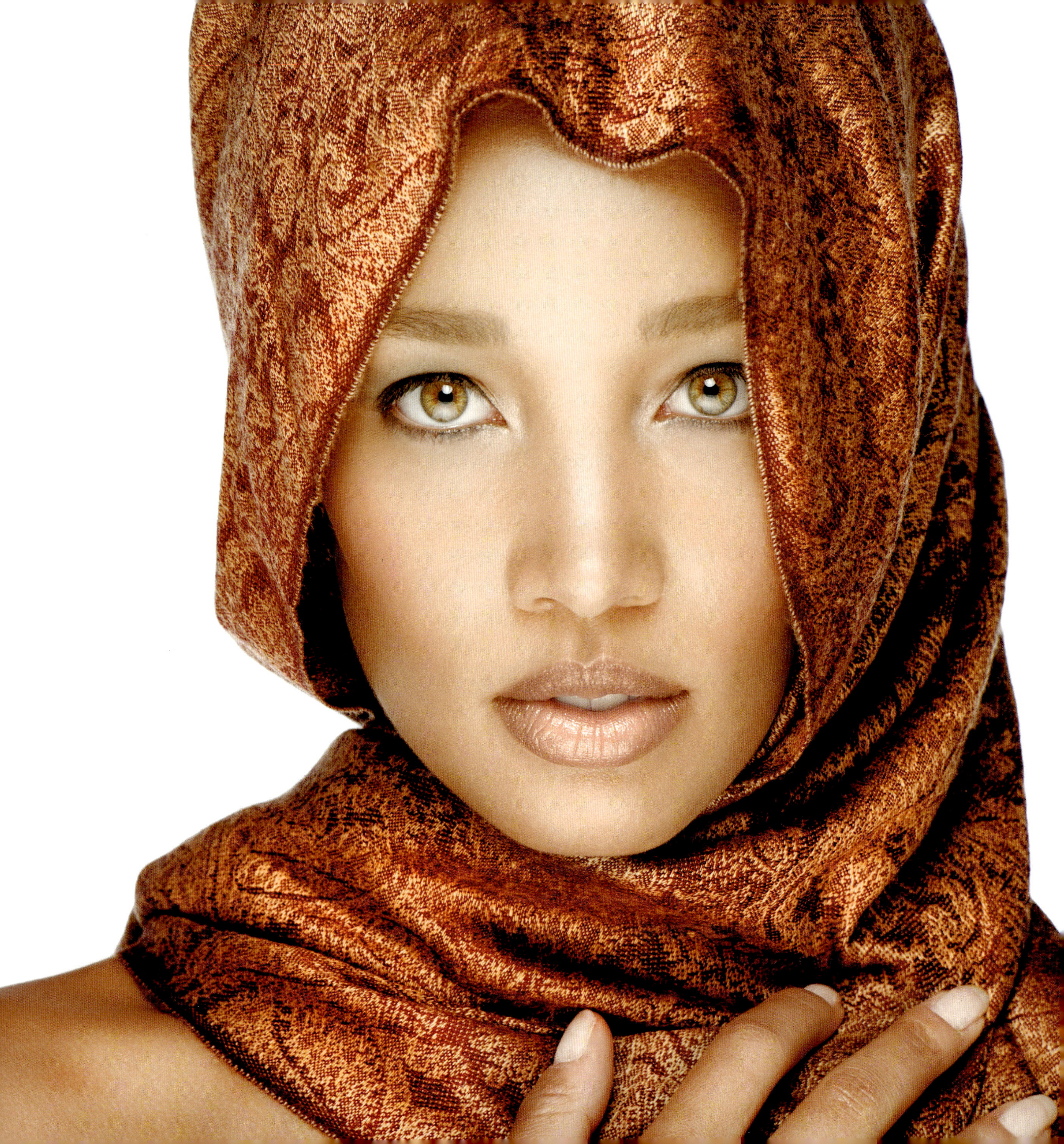

IF THEY NOTICE THE NOISE
THE PICTURE ISN'T WORKING

For years, toward the front of every issue of *Sports Illustrated* magazine, there was a section each week called "Leading Off," and on those pages were some of the greatest sports photos in the history of sports photography. Photos that really stuck with you because they gave you an intimate look into the games and athletes that you couldn't get any other way—even if you were at the game. Seriously incredible images. So, picture a group of people at work the day after the big game, and one of them has a copy of *Sports Illustrated*. They're looking through "Leading Off," and there's this incredible football image, really up close, where you can see the defender's hand wrapped around the front of the receiver's face mask, and he's literally ripping his helmet off, and sweat and dirt and grass are flying everywhere, but it's all frozen there in the air, and the shot is just incredible.

But then, one of the folks looking at the shot says, "Oh, but look at the noise. I can't enjoy this." It sounds ridiculous, right? That scenario doesn't happen because the only people who even notice noise are photographers. The rest of the world is asking us to show them something amazing. Something fascinating. Something they haven't seen before, and we're sitting around obsessing about noise. Noise has been a part of photography since it started. Inside Photoshop and Camera Raw, are a number of filters for adding noise and film grain to your photos, but we're scared to shoot at high ISOs because someone might see some noise. If the people looking at your image notice the noise, it's not a good enough image.

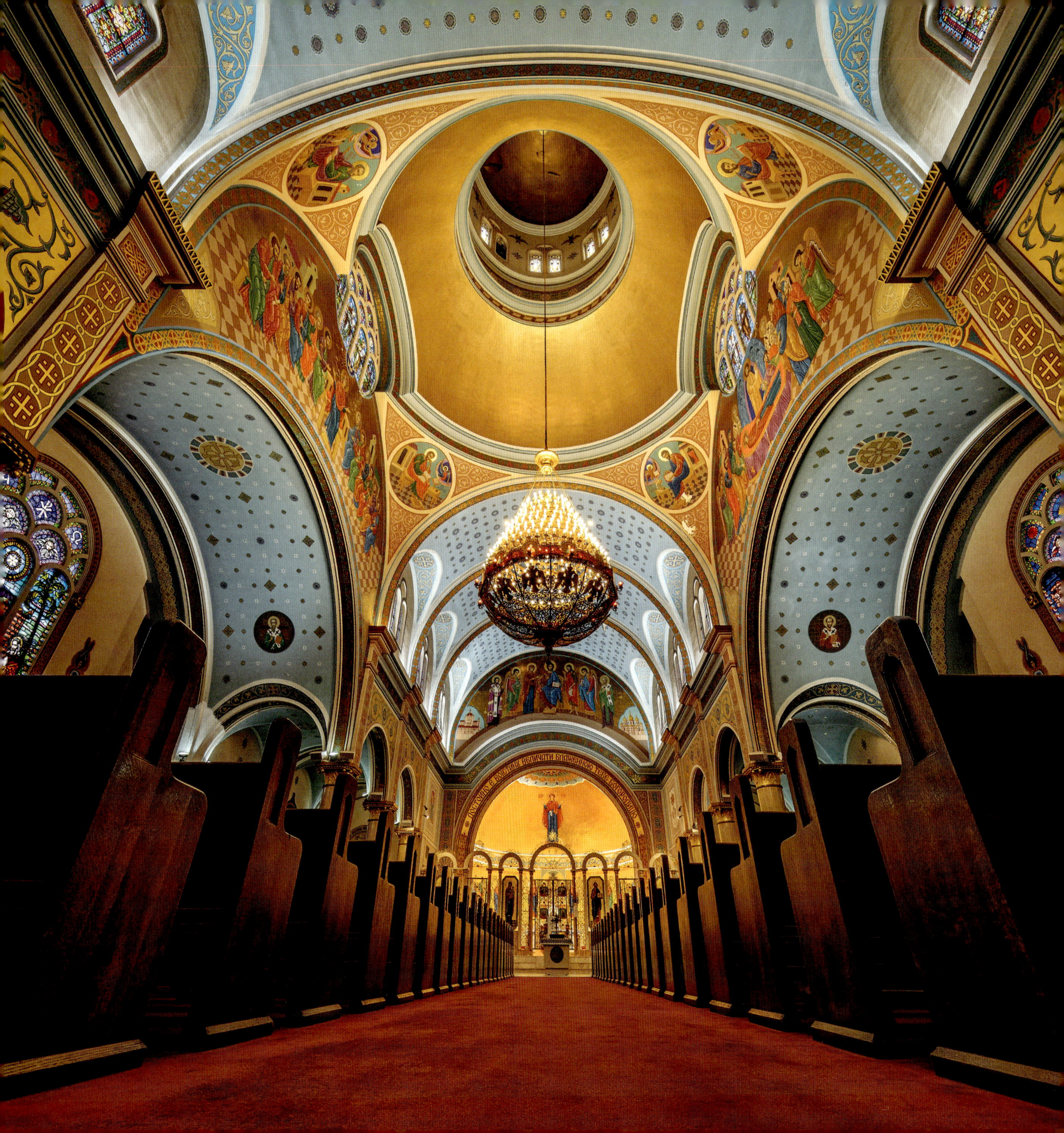

TECHNICAL VS. EMOTIONAL

I feel very fortunate that I get to sit on judging panels for many different photo contests, and I love it because I love looking at photos. Today, after the pandemic, most of the judging is done individually, online, with you looking at hundreds, maybe thousands, of images and trying to find the very best ones. But I really miss the days when all the judges would sit in a room and judge the images together. We'd sit around a long table with a large screen at the end. The names of the entrants were hidden, so all you could see were large images onscreen, one after another. We'd be viewing them and it would be pretty quiet, except every once in a while, an image would come up and you'd hear someone say, "I kind of like that one," or maybe, "That's kind of cool," and so on. But then, an image would come up onscreen, and within a split second, the entire room would erupt with "Ooooohhhh!" We knew right then we had a contest finalist—maybe a winner. In that split-second, when it came onscreen, everyone reacted immediately. We didn't have time to analyze whether there were technical issues or if rules of composition had been broken because that image had emotional impact. It swept over us. That type of image is what happens when a fascinating subject, great light, and great composition all come together. It creates magic that goes beyond just following a set of rules.

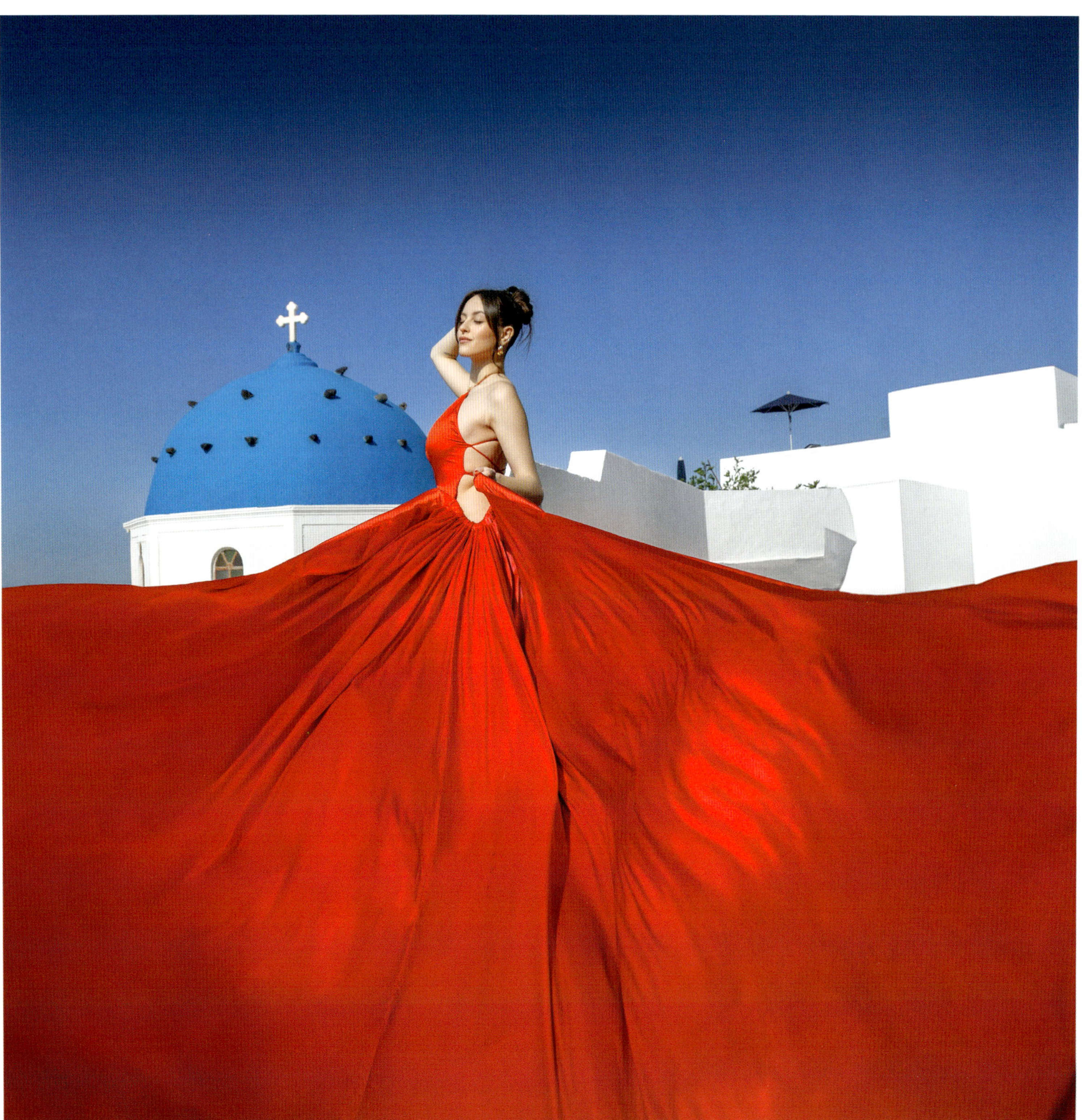

DO THE OLD RULES STILL APPLY?

The whole idea behind this book is to go beyond the time-honored, classic rules of composition—the rules that have been around since painters used them in the late 1800s and photographers started embracing them in the early 1900s. Photographer Cole Thompson described it in 2014 this way: "The rules of composition is [sic] an attempt to distill the creative process into a series of simple guidelines that if followed, will produce a good image." He went on to say it was kind of a "paint by numbers" way of taking photos. Ansel Adams had harsher words for it. He said, "The so-called rules of photographic composition are, in my opinion, invalid, irrelevant, immaterial." Ouch! I don't want to argue with Ansel, because…well…he's Ansel Freakin' Adams, but I think if we stop thinking of those as "rules" of composition, and more as just helpful tools we can use if we want to, they are way more helpful than harmful. That's why, at the end of this book, I included just one chapter on those time-honored "rules." Er, suggestions. Useful guides? Whatever you want to call them, they're there at the end of the book, but I wouldn't haven't written this book if I thought that they worked miracles because there's something big that's missing. Something the rules don't cover, and that's what the rest of the book is about, starting in Chapter 2.

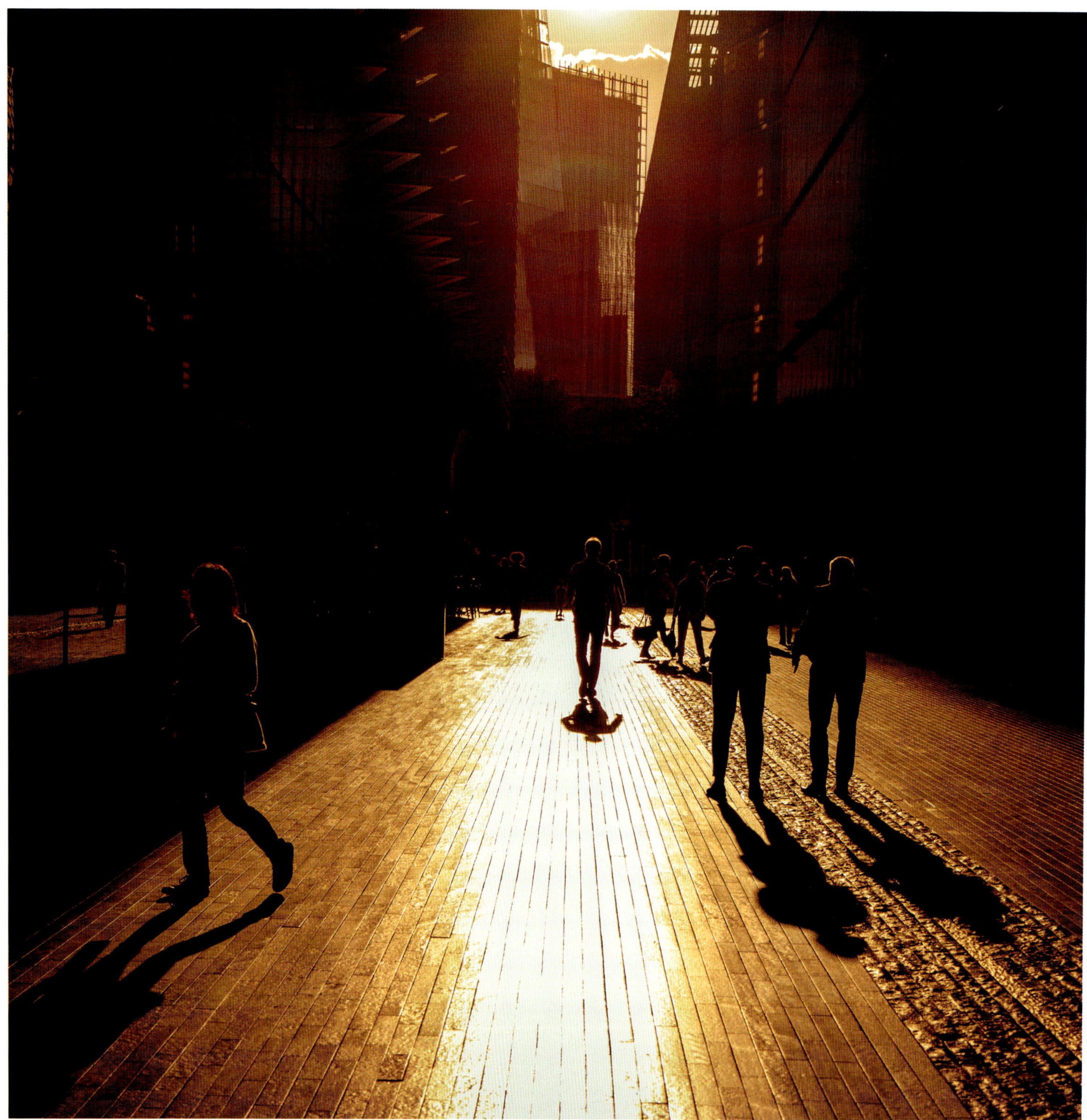

WHAT ROLE DOES LIGHT PLAY?

George Eastman, founder of Eastman Kodak, had a great quote about light. He said, "Light makes photography. Embrace light. Admire it. Love it. But above all, know light. Know it for all you are worth, and you will know the key to photography." He seemed to do pretty well for himself, but I would argue that light, as critical of a role as it plays, in a really boring photo is just that—a really boring photo with great light. However, what light can do is take a good or great image and make it pretty incredible. Great light makes everything look better. Landscapes become amazing with great light. Food photography? Looks its best in great light. Portraits? Great light is critical, but you'd have to agree that you've seen portraits that had awful light but with a brilliant expression, or intense emotion, that were still great shots— bad light and all. Sports shots look amazing with the right light, as do wildlife shots. Light is the icing on the cake. The thing that takes the shot over the top. But, by itself, it won't usually pull the wagon. If I had to boil it down to the three key things that make great photography it would be to start with a fantastic subject, improve it with great composition, and then add some wonderful light on top. We've all seen great images that didn't use that formula, but we've seen a whole lot more that do. Let's focus on that composition part.

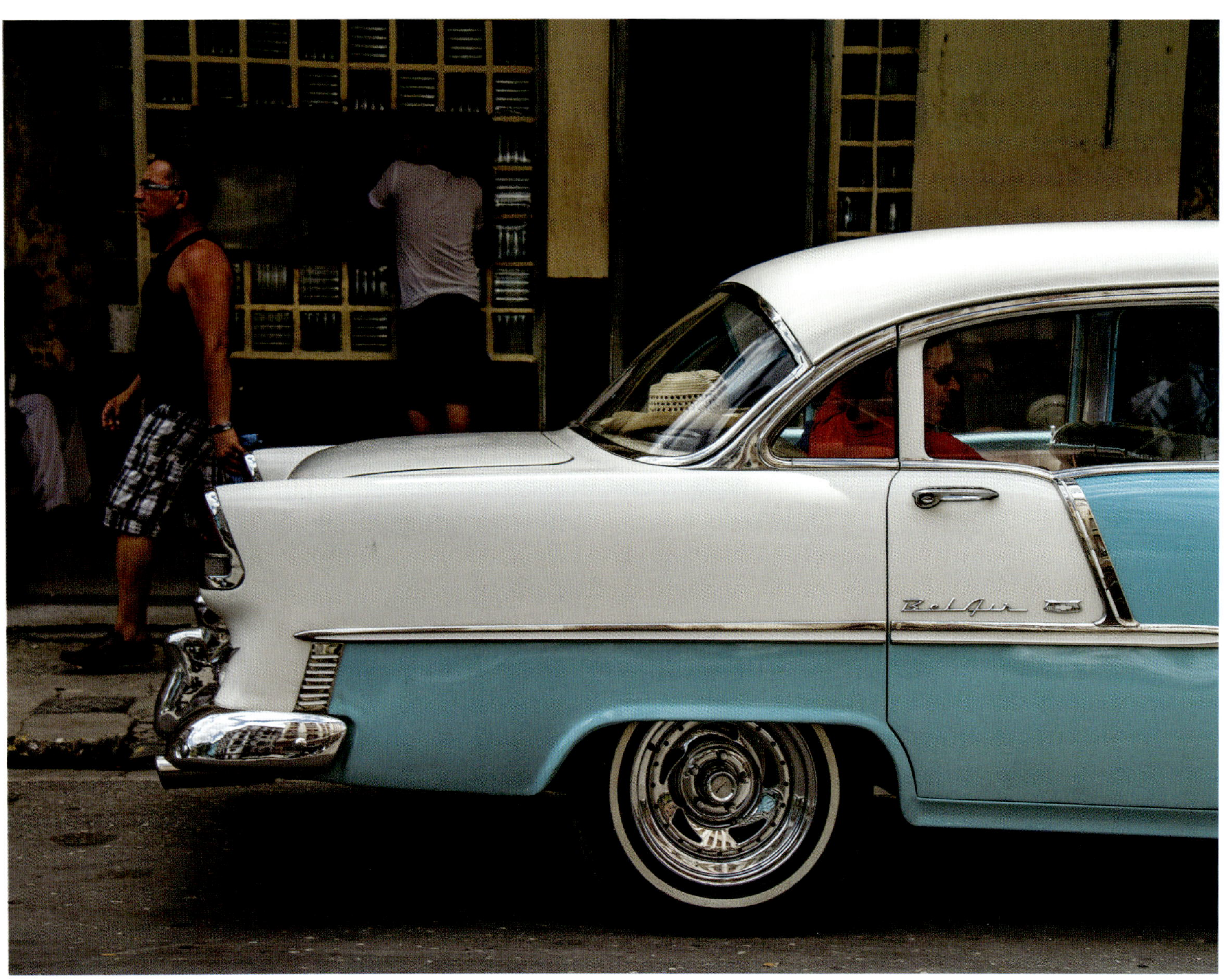

FRAMING TO TELL THE STORY YOU WANT TO TELL

Composition can be used to tell the story you want to tell with your image. You see this pretty often in news reporting where the photo matches the story the reporter wants to tell, whether it's really accurate or not. Let's say, for example, you come to one of my in-person seminars and you're there to do an article about the seminar for your photo club. How you frame the story of that day has a lot to do with how you frame up the shot of the ballroom where the seminar is being held— what you decide to include in the shot, and what you decide to ignore. You could stand in the back, in a corner of the ballroom where there are some empty seats, and you could frame up the shot from that angle showing those empty seats to support the headline "Disappointing Turnout for Scott's Seminar in Dallas This Week." Or, you could stand in a section where there are no empty seats, and frame up the shot to where it looks like there's a bunch of people there to support the headline "Packed House for Scott's Seminar in Dallas This Week." How you choose to frame the shot, and what you choose to include or ignore, gives you the power to tell the story you want to tell. Whether it's accurate or not is up to you. There's a lot of storytelling power there, even if you're not doing news.

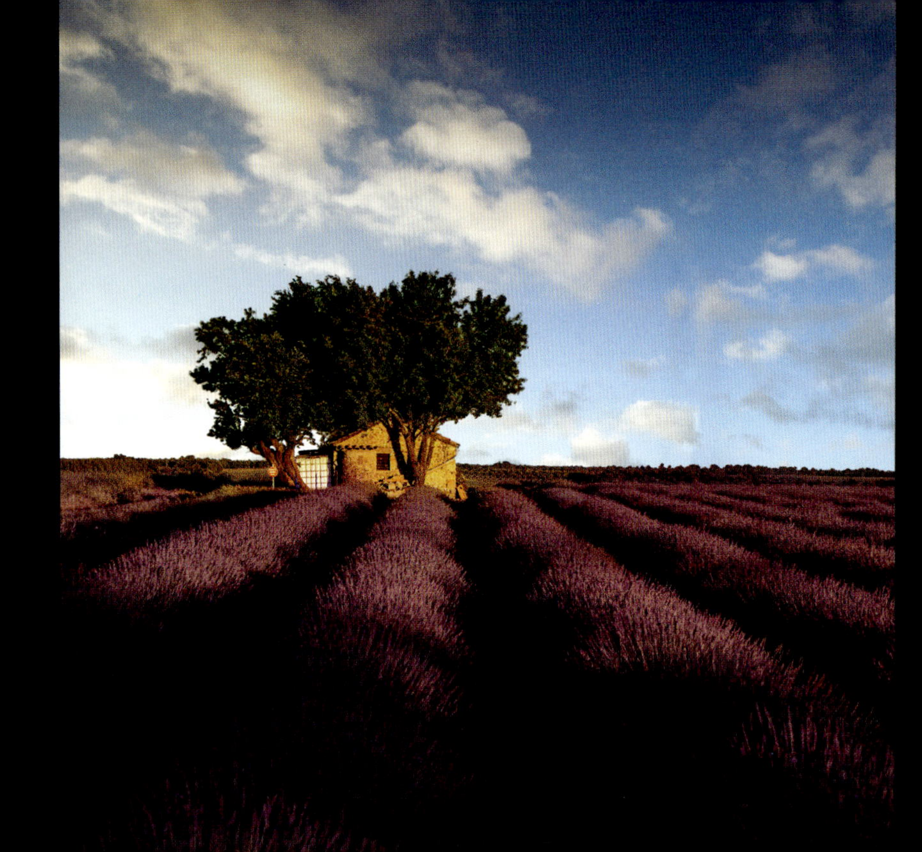

Chapter 02

WORK THE SCENE

Over the years, I've talked to a number of photographers who assume a top pro walks up to any given scene (landscape, cityscape, street photography, portrait, etc.), puts the camera up to their eye, takes one or two shots, looks at the back of the camera, and says out loud, "Nailed it." Then they walk over to another scene and do the same thing again and again, just nailing shot after shot after only pressing the shutter button once or twice. In reality, that's pretty much exactly the opposite of the way it happens. Instead of just snapping one or two quick shots, they literally "work the scene." The first thing that they do is slow down. They take a minute to really look at what's in front of them before they ever raise the camera to their eye. They're thoughtful about it. Then they start working the scene that's in front of them and maybe that means taking 20 shots, or maybe that means taking 100, but they keep doing it until they can look at the back of the camera and say, "Nailed it!" Only then do they move on to the next scene or location and start the process of seeing and experimenting all over again. Shots don't just fall into your lap that often. Instead, to get the type of results we're all looking for we have to work the scene, and that's what this chapter is all about—doing what it takes. Sometimes it comes easier than other times, but if you have a plan in place before you get to the shoot, or the scene, or the location, your chances of success go way up. "Hoping to get lucky" usually isn't a great strategy for coming back with something great. A solid plan is. Let's get to planning.

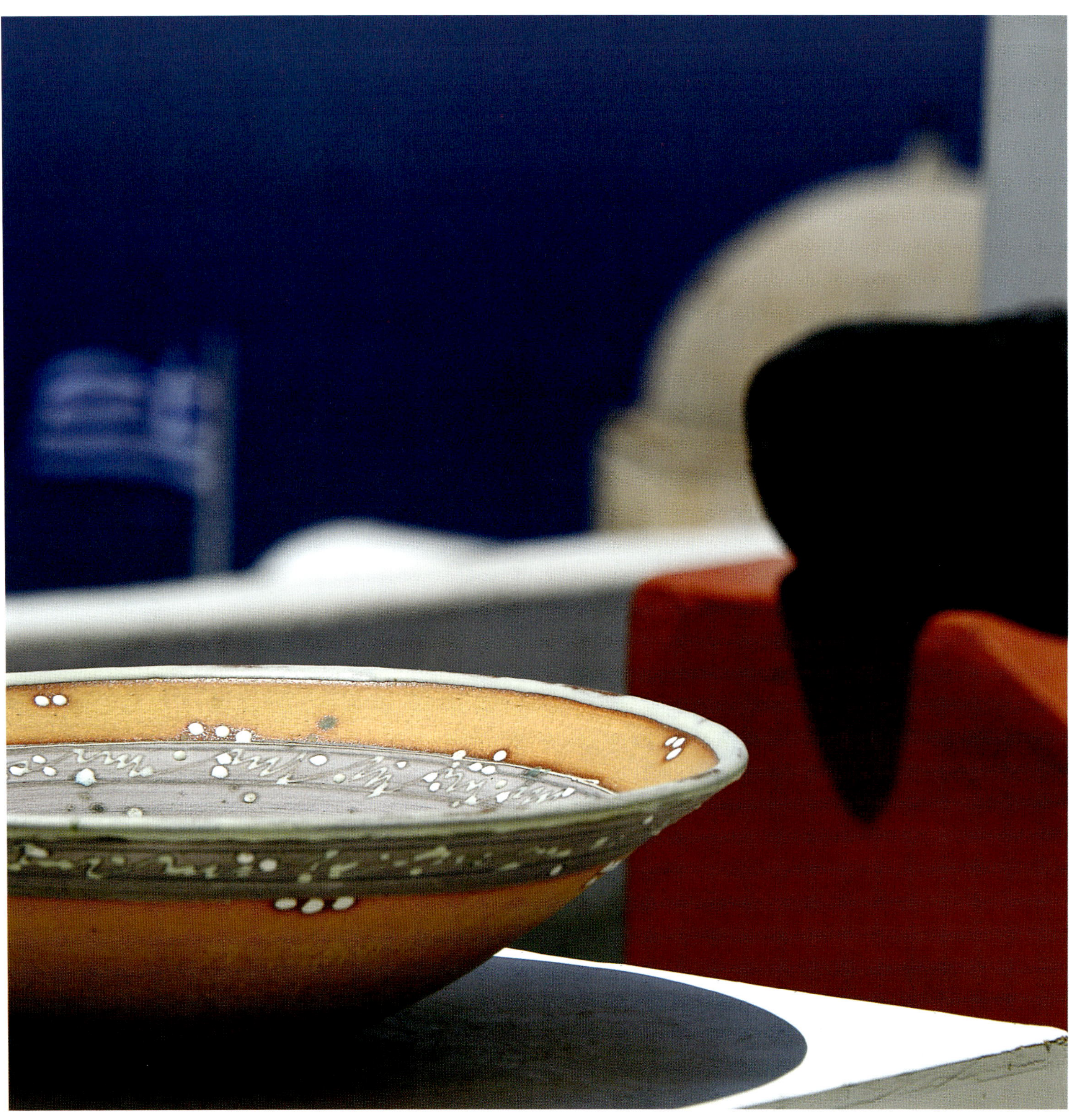

SOMETHING MADE YOU STOP

Let's say you're walking around a city and something catches your eye, so you stop and start shooting. You take a few shots, look on the back of your camera—"Nah. Nothing"—and you move on. Maybe that was the right call; maybe there was nothing there. Something did catch your eye and made you stop, though. But you only took a couple of shots, thought, "Nah. Nothing," and you moved on. There probably was something there, but you didn't work the scene. You didn't take the time, or try a number of shots from different angles, with different compositions, to see if there really was anything there. My guess is there was something there, but you'll never know if you don't work the scene. Don't rush off—don't speed over to the next thing. It's like living legend of photography Jay Maisel says: "Just stop. Wait. Most of us run around trying to cover as much ground as possible. But it's not about covering ground. It's about having something happen right in front of you, and nothing happens if you're running." Take the time to work the scene and see if that little voice in your head—that just a minute or two ago said there's something there—was right. There probably is something there, and it's your job to find it. Working the scene is the process to uncover it.

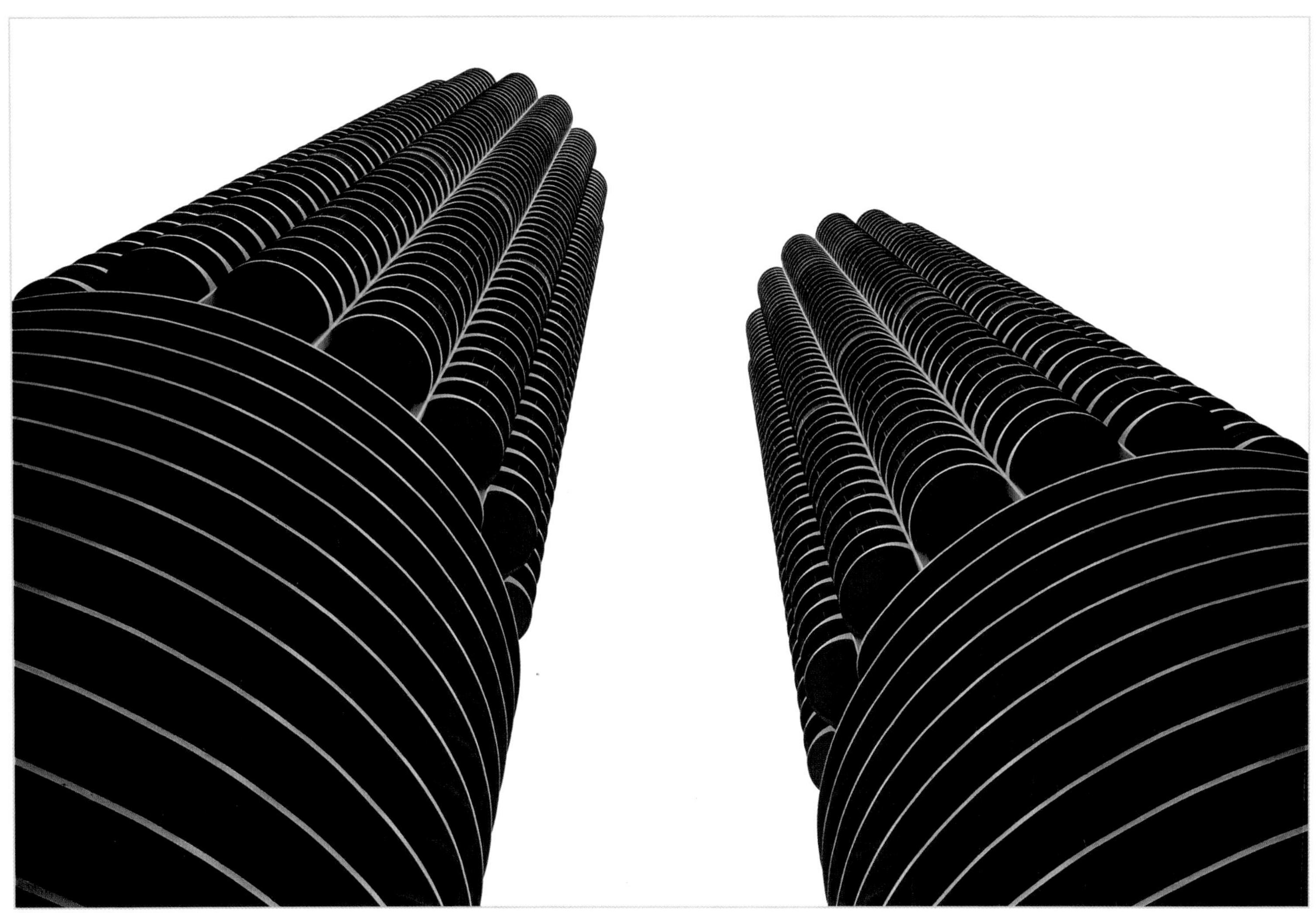

THERE'S AN ANGLE

I can't remember who said it, but I remember reading this years ago and as soon as I did, I was like, "Yes. That's it," and the "that's it" is a big part of composition (bigger than I've seen anyone give it since). It's this: There is a certain angle where whatever (or whomever) you're standing in front of looks its best. There is some angle where it all comes together and if you stop before you find that angle, you're going to wind up with anything from a "meh" photo to an okay photo. Unless you somehow get lucky, you're not going to come away with that killer shot. So, how do you find this angle? You work the scene by trying out different angles. Our general go-to is to stand directly in front of whatever we're shooting, but what if that magical angle is from one side or the other, or at a 45° angle? There's an angle where it looks better, and you know what I'm about to say—that's right, it's our job to try different angles to find out which one works best. It still might not make a killer image, but at least you'll know it isn't because you stopped before you found the right angle. It's because it's a boring shot. Hey, it happens.

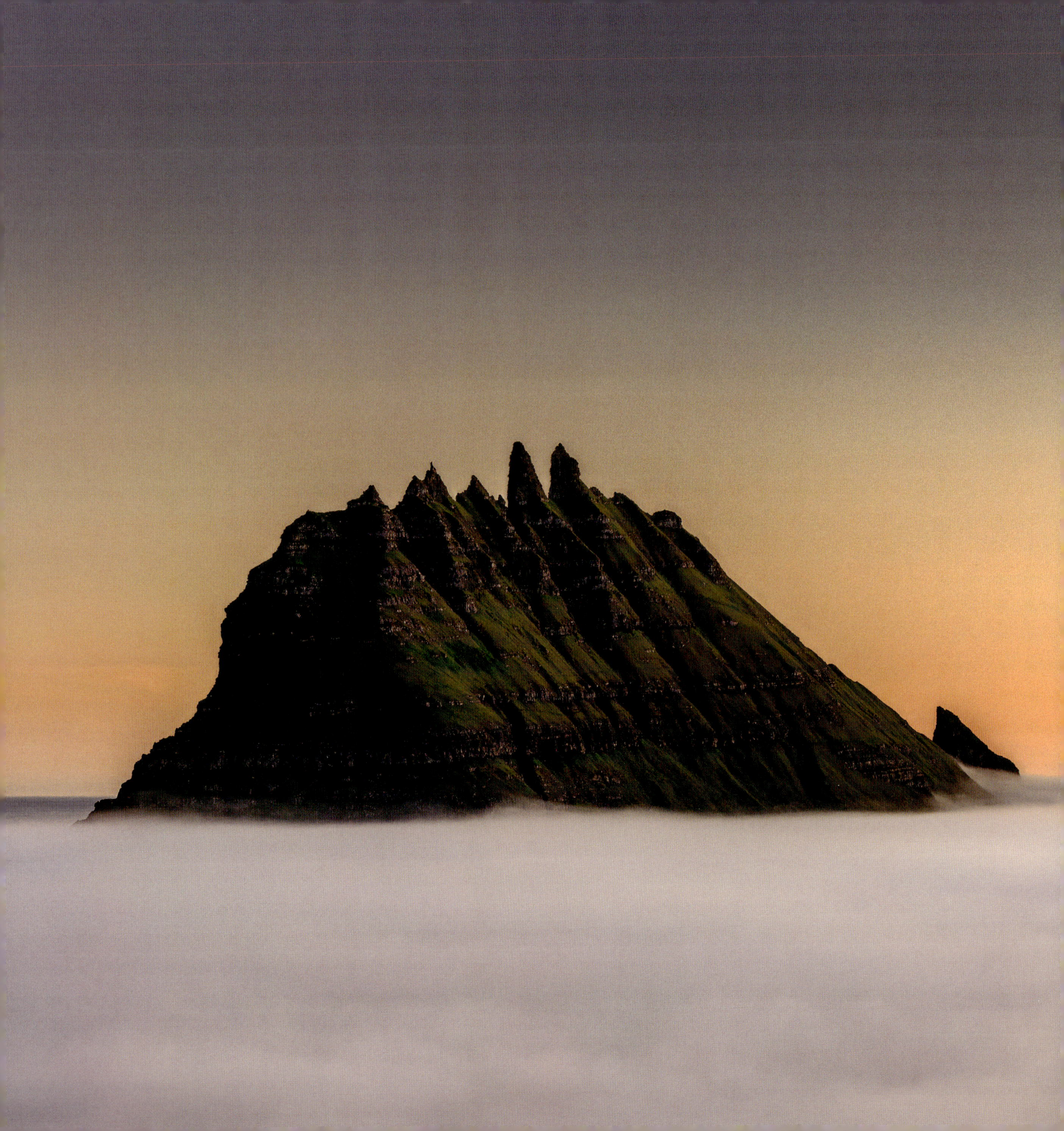

DON'T SET YOUR TRIPOD DOWN YET

Okay, picture this: It's 30 minutes before dawn, and you and a group of your photography friends arrive at an amazing landscape location. What's the first thing that happens? It's almost like a race to see who can find their spot and set up their tripod first. I've seen it so many times. But, if you see a top pro in these same situations, you'll probably notice something very different. They're walking around, checking out the scene, and carefully picking out where their first spot is going to be. They often don't even have their tripod out yet (it's still in the trunk) because where you set that tripod down is a very important composition decision, especially because when most photographers set up their tripods for a landscape shoot, it's almost like they set it down in wet concrete. That's their shooting location for the next hour. The top pro, however, sees that spot where they set up their tripod as the first one of many. This is them working the scene. The scene isn't just one place (the spot where you first parked your tripod). Think of that as a starting place (you have to start somewhere, right?). Take a few shots there, and then try someplace else. That could be as simple as a few feet to the left or the right, but you know how they say, "Photography is a game of inches"? Well, imagine what moving a few feet away might do.

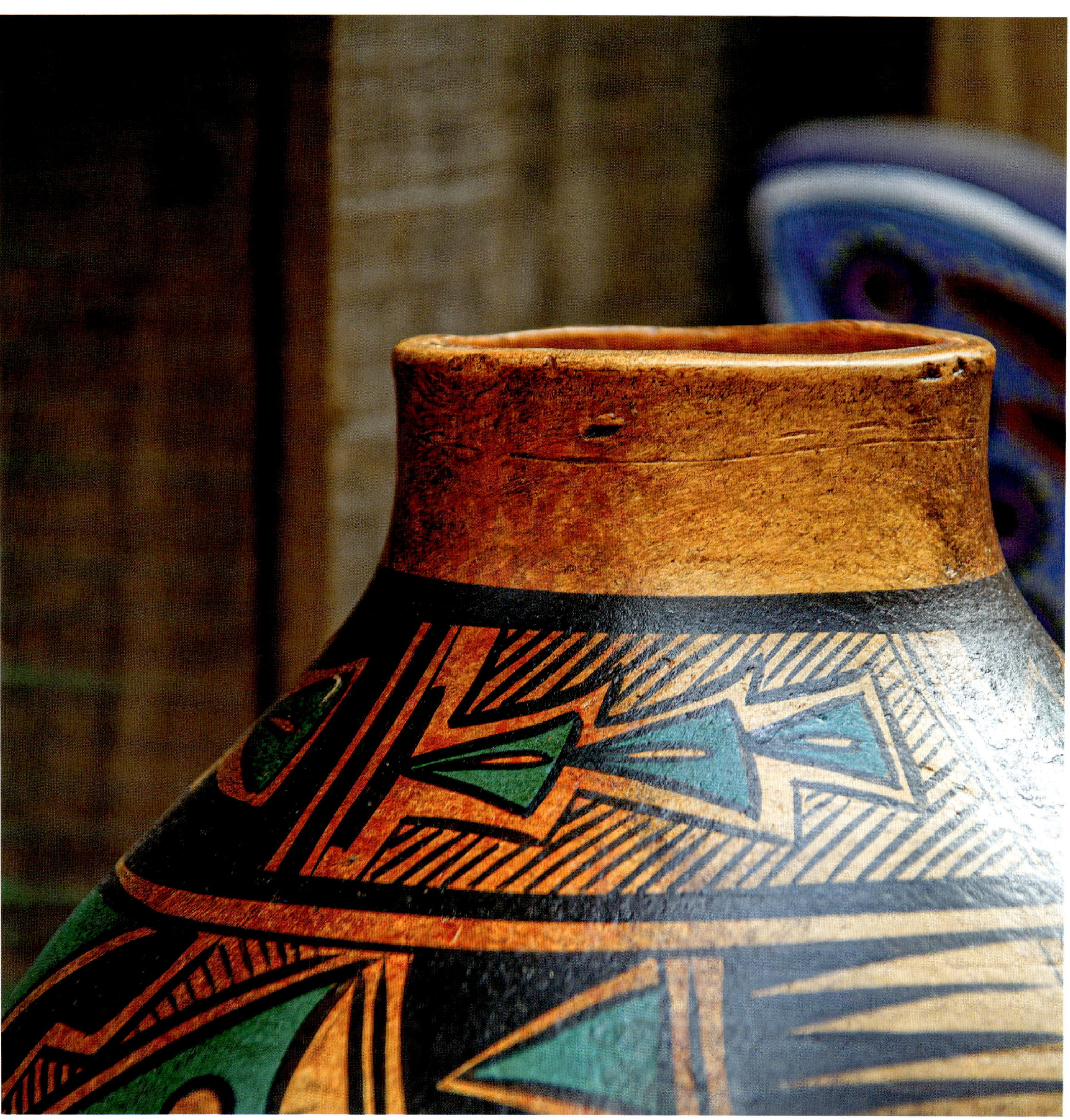

CUT THROUGH THE CLUTTER

This goes along with what I said earlier about getting to choose what we put in our frames. Take a look at the image on the facing page—that was taken in the gift shop you see on the right here. Yup, it's a fun, cluttered, glorious mess (well, that's what my wife called it, as she was shopping around in there). As I was standing there waiting for her, with a camera over my shoulder, I noticed that the ceiling had kind of a sunroof letting some natural light in (as you can see in the gift shop photo), and I noticed that for a gift shop, that was some pretty nice light. So, I started looking for something interesting to shoot. That's when I found the vase (on the facing page). If you look at the gift shop image, you can see it—it's about 1/4 of the way into the left side of the photo. You see that dark vase (I think it's a vase anyway) on the floor? Look at the shelves to its immediate left, up on the third shelf. Yup. That's it right there. I zoomed in tight so

pretty much only half the vase is showing in the shot. You'd never know it was taken in the busy, cluttered environment you see here because we get to decide what goes in the frame, right? I don't have to show the cluttered gift shop—I'm not reporting on it for a newspaper or magazine. We get to choose what goes in our frame. There's a lot of creative power in this process.

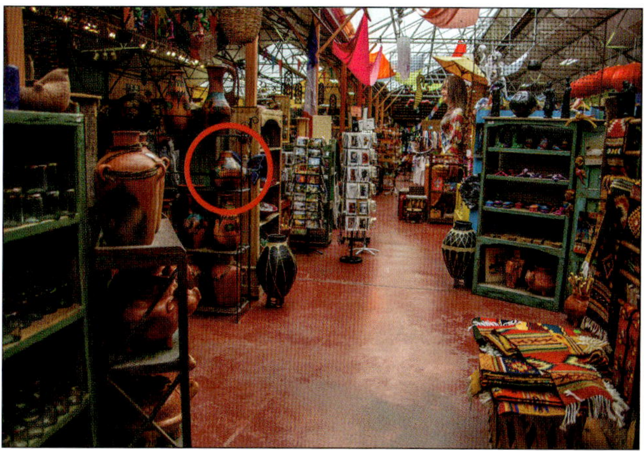

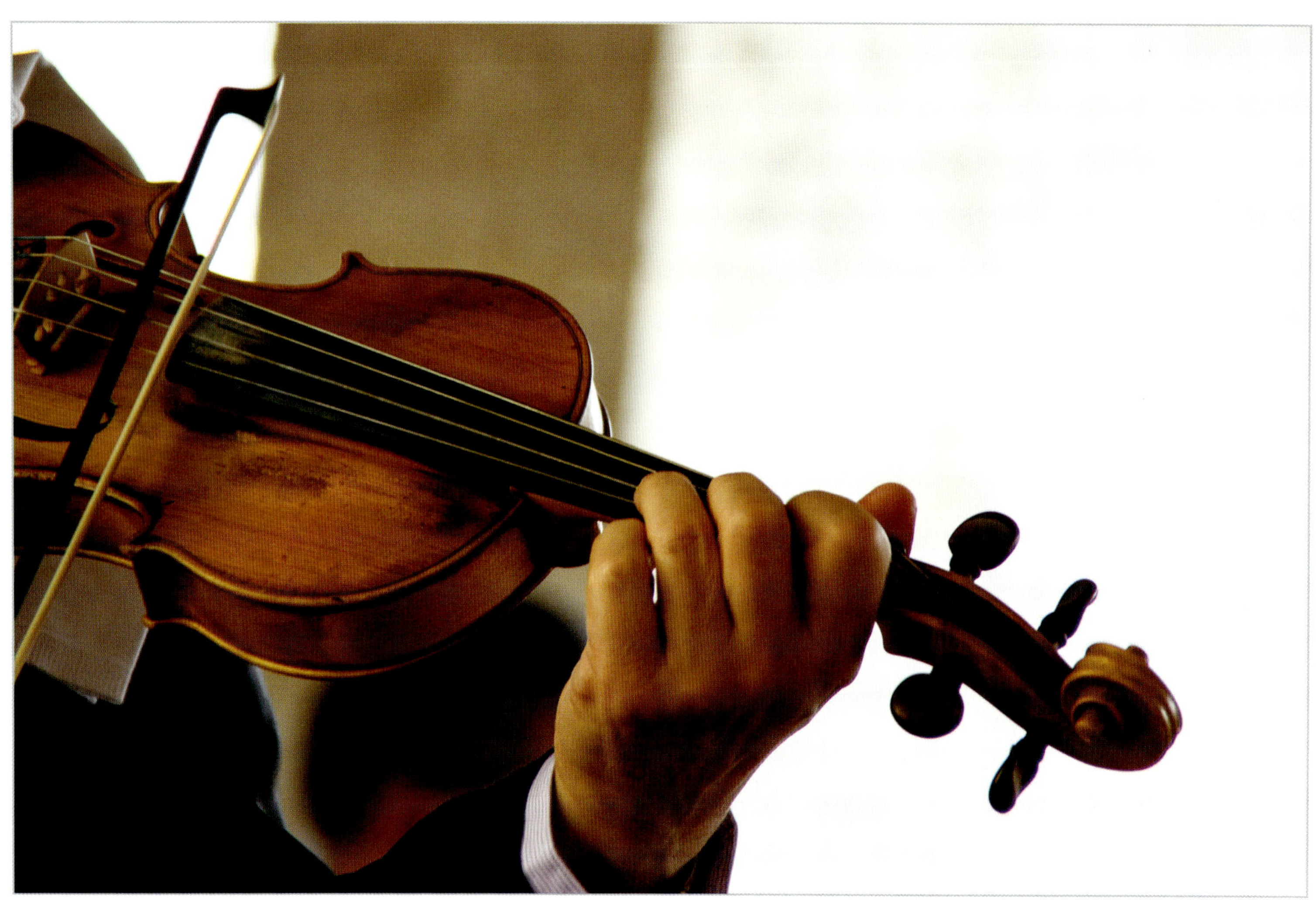

CHOOSE WHAT GOES IN YOUR FRAME

Photo journalists have a very strict set of rules that they have to follow because they're covering news and their job is to show the scene as it is. Luckily for the rest of us, we have zero obligation to show the scene as it is. In fact, our job is to cherry pick the best parts of a scene and use those as the focus of our images. Deciding what to show (and what to leave out) is a critical composition decision, but it's also one of the most fun parts of photography. We get to choose what goes in the frame and that's where the art of this lies. Take a look at the image on the facing page. This was taken in a busy restaurant packed with tourists, servers, and a strolling violinist in the heart of a tourist area in Budapest, Hungary. The scene I was standing in front of was a very busy one (you can see what it looked like here on the right), but we don't have to show all those tourists and servers, so I didn't. The thing that drew me to this scene was literally his violin, so I used a zoom lens to zoom in tight on the violin, his hand, and bow, leaving out all the parts that would have

made it just a snapshot. This composition decision, choosing what goes in your frame, is the heart of what we do. We don't have to show the messy scene. We are very fortunate that we get to choose what appears in our frame and what doesn't. Now, did I just take these two photos? Nope. I took a whole bunch, but see the next page for why I only showed this one.

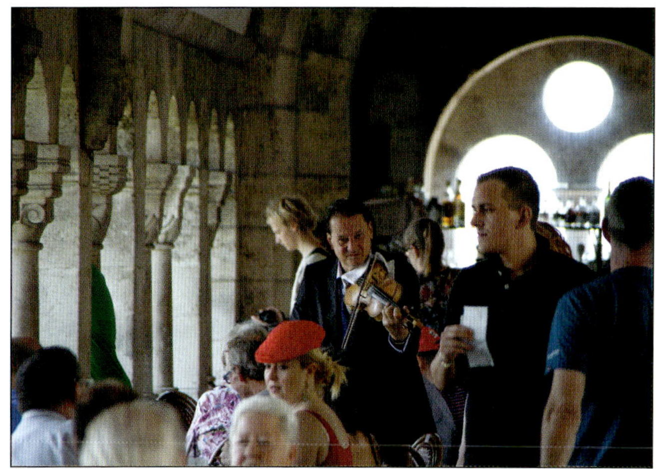

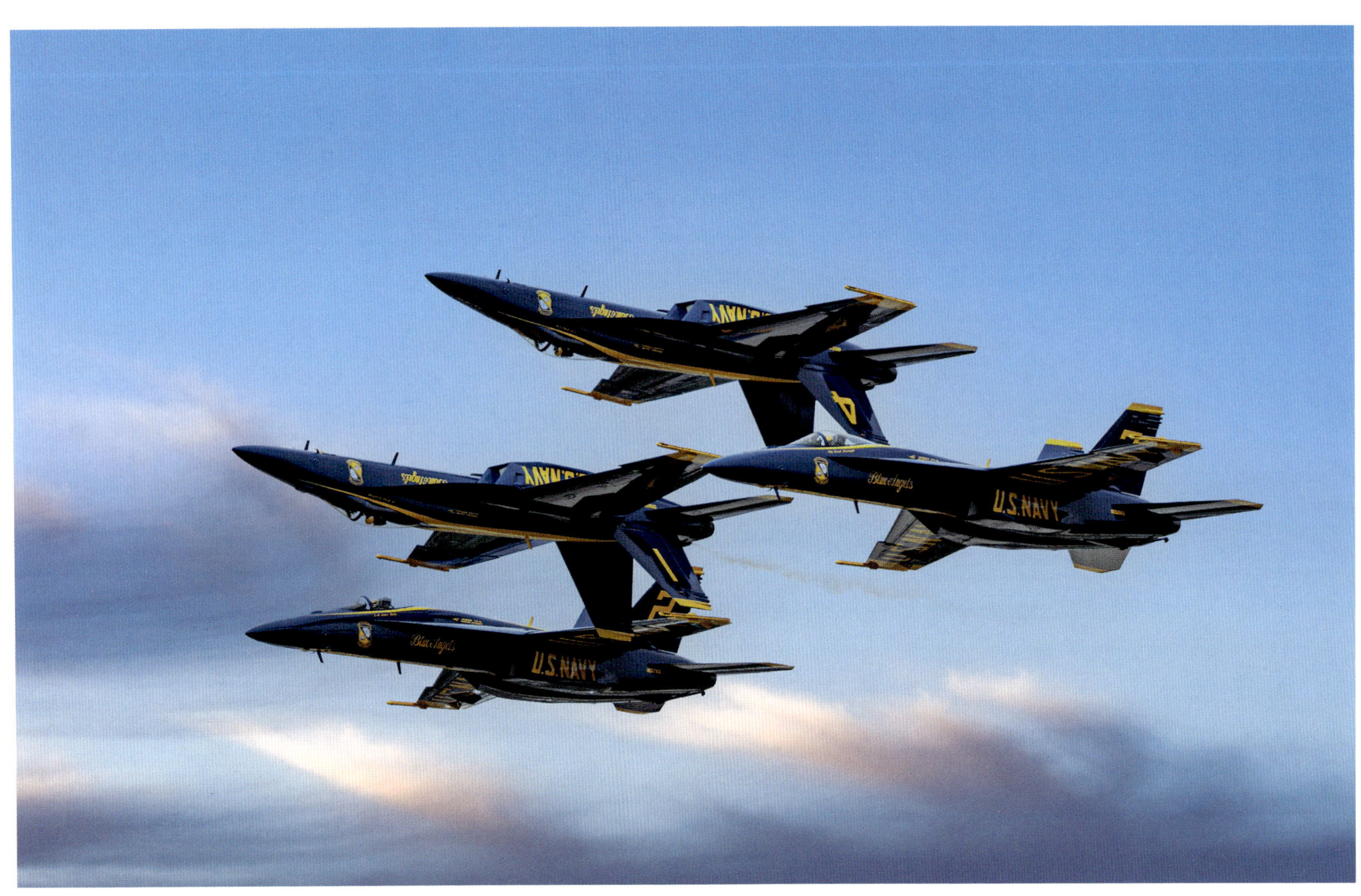

YOU ONLY NEED ONE

When I do a shoot of any kind (sports, portraits, landscape, travel), I'm going to wind up taking a lot of shots of the same thing—it's part of the "working the scene" concept. Let's say, for example, I'm photographing an air show and the highlight is an appearance by the US Navy's incredible Blue Angels flight demonstration squadron. I'm going to shoot literally hundreds of shots during their demo runs (it could easily be 500 or 600 shots), but how many am I actually going to show? Well, if I'm posting them on my Facebook page, I might show five or six of the best ones, or on Instagram, maybe two or three, but from any shoot, what am I really looking for? I'm looking for one really nice shot. That's all you need because after your social media post (which has a half-life of about 6 or 8 hours, and then it's buried down in most people's feeds), what do you have left for your portfolio or to print and hang on the wall? You just need that one. Think about it: If you get a killer shot of "The Blues," you might frame it and hang it in your home, right? Are you going to print and hang four shots? Five? Nope. You just need that one. You're going to take a lot of shots, from different angles and viewpoints, because you're on the hunt for that one where everything comes together—the light, the focus, the angle, the moment— and that's the one. Even when we shoot hundreds of shots, we have 30 or 40 "keepers" and a handful of what we call "selects" (ones we might share online), but if we can come away with that one killer shot, it was all worth it.

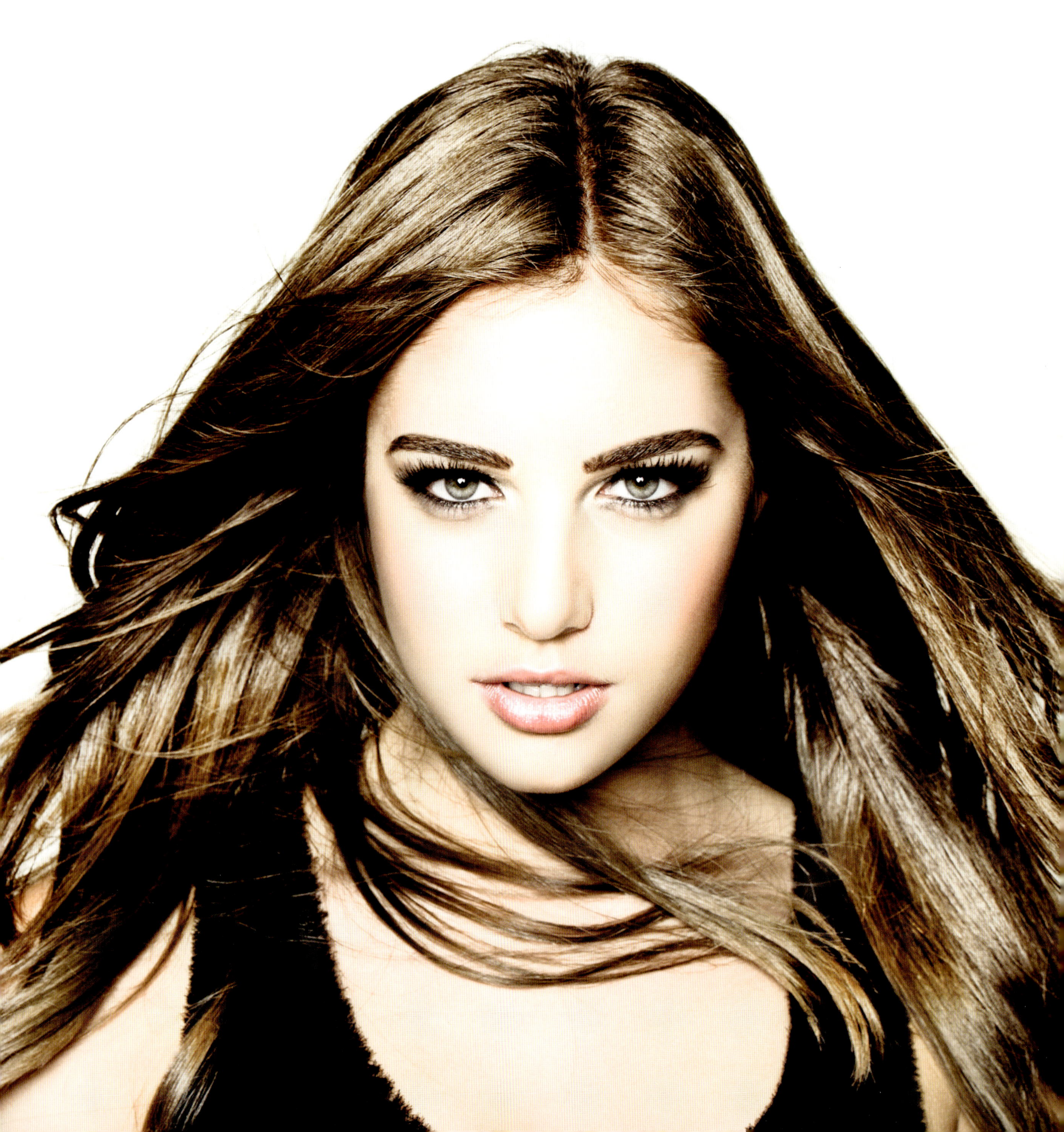

PAUSE AND REVIEW

When you're working the scene, it's very easy to get into a rhythm where you're just shooting and shooting and shooting (and the more you shoot, the greater chance you'll have of coming up with that one killer shot). But, if you break up the nonstop shooting and pause to review your shots, it'll help a lot. First, it'll help to see if you're heading in the right direction. If you take a few shots, and then stop to review them on the back of your camera, you'll be able to see if there's something not working, and maybe it just needs a change of angle, or maybe you need to move to a different spot and try from there. Don't just blindly shoot and shoot and shoot. Pause. Evaluate what you're getting and make an informed decision to stick or move. I find this really helpful when I'm doing a portrait shoot. About five minutes in, I take a break and start reviewing the shots, and where this really pays off is when you see something that can be corrected before it's too late. For example, let's say during this pause and review you notice that when your subject does a really big smile, you see a lot of their gums. They most likely already know they sometimes have a "gummy" smile and they're probably not going to pick any of the photos where they see their gums big-time in the photo. But, if you continue just shooting, you're going to wind up with a whole shoot of those—photos your client isn't going to pick (clients tend to avoid images that show something they're self-conscious about). Now that you saw that, just five minutes into the shoot, you can make adjustments without, of course, ever mentioning any of this to your subject. Instead, when you go back to continue the shoot, you can say, "Okay, let's do a few where we're not smiling." Then after a few of those, you can say, "Okay, now give me a little smile," and then, "Okay, a little bigger smile." Now you're controlling the amount of their smile and making sure that, for the most part, they don't do that big smile that shows their gums. You'll now have a huge number of shots that they're much more likely to choose from, rather than those that were never going to make the cut. I've had this happen so many times with different facial features. I've had subjects who thought they were smiling, but they were smirking instead, and when they saw the shots on my laptop, they were like, "I need to stop smirking." Keep an ear out for comments like that, so you can steer the shoot away from shots they are never going to want. Just remember, once the shoot is over, it's too late. Do this five or so minutes in, and repeat it fairly often, so you have a chance to make adjustments while you still can.

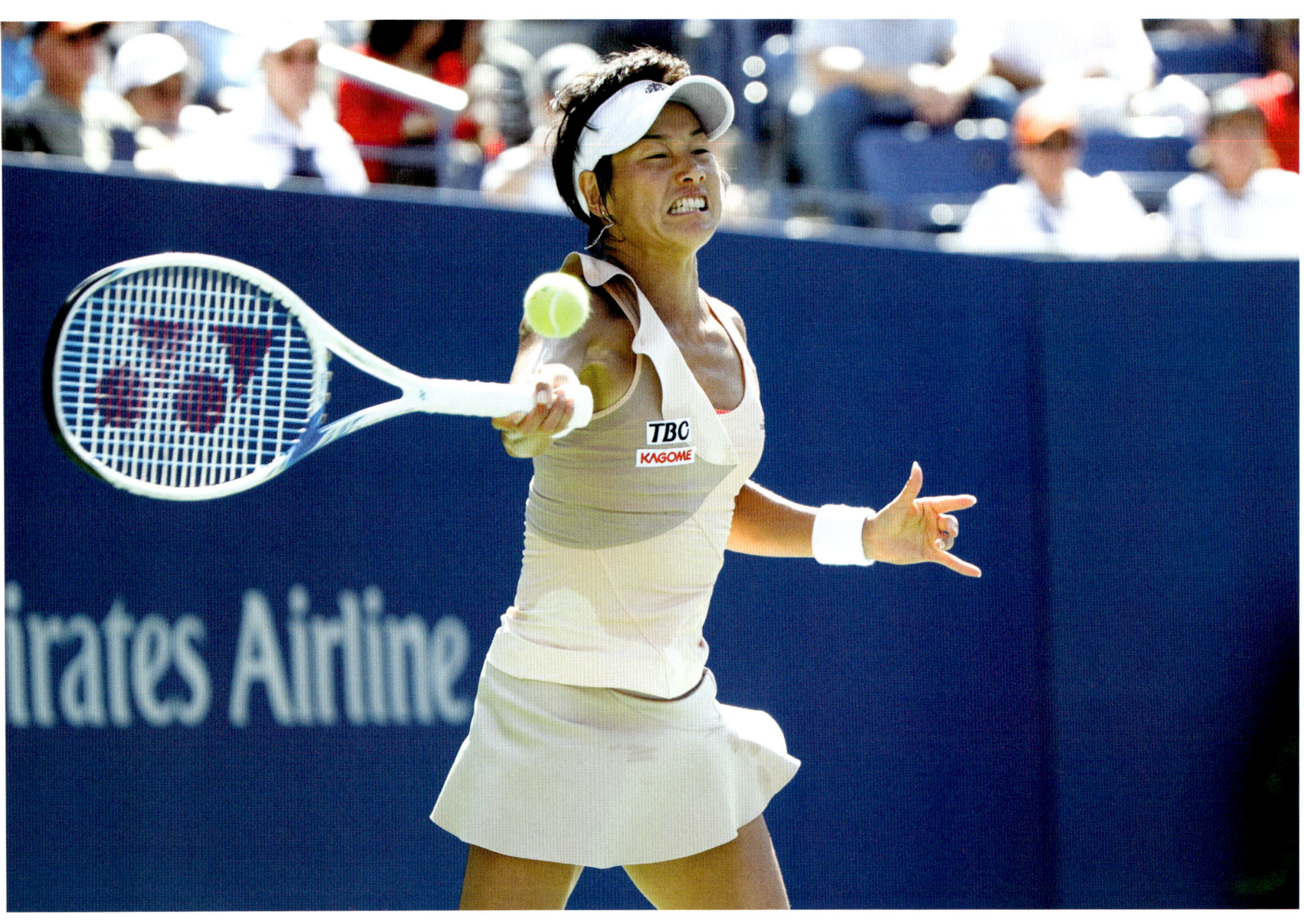
irates Airline
TBC
KAGOME

EXPECT BAD SHOTS

When you're working the scene, one thing you can absolutely count on is that when you're trying out different angles and different ideas, a bunch of them are just not going to work. You're going to wind up with a decent amount of what you'd call "bad shots." But, the thing is: don't sweat it. It's part of the process—the same process many top pros use. So even though you're doing everything right, and really working the scene, you can expect to see lots of bad shots along the way. Remember, we're searching for that angle where it all comes together, and getting to that angle takes a bit of detective work and a lot of trial and error. That means a lot of bad photos along the way and that's okay. Again, this is all part of the process, so don't let it throw you, and don't start having doubts about your abilities. This is how it's done. If you want to make a great omelet, you're going to have to crack some eggs, so get cracking.

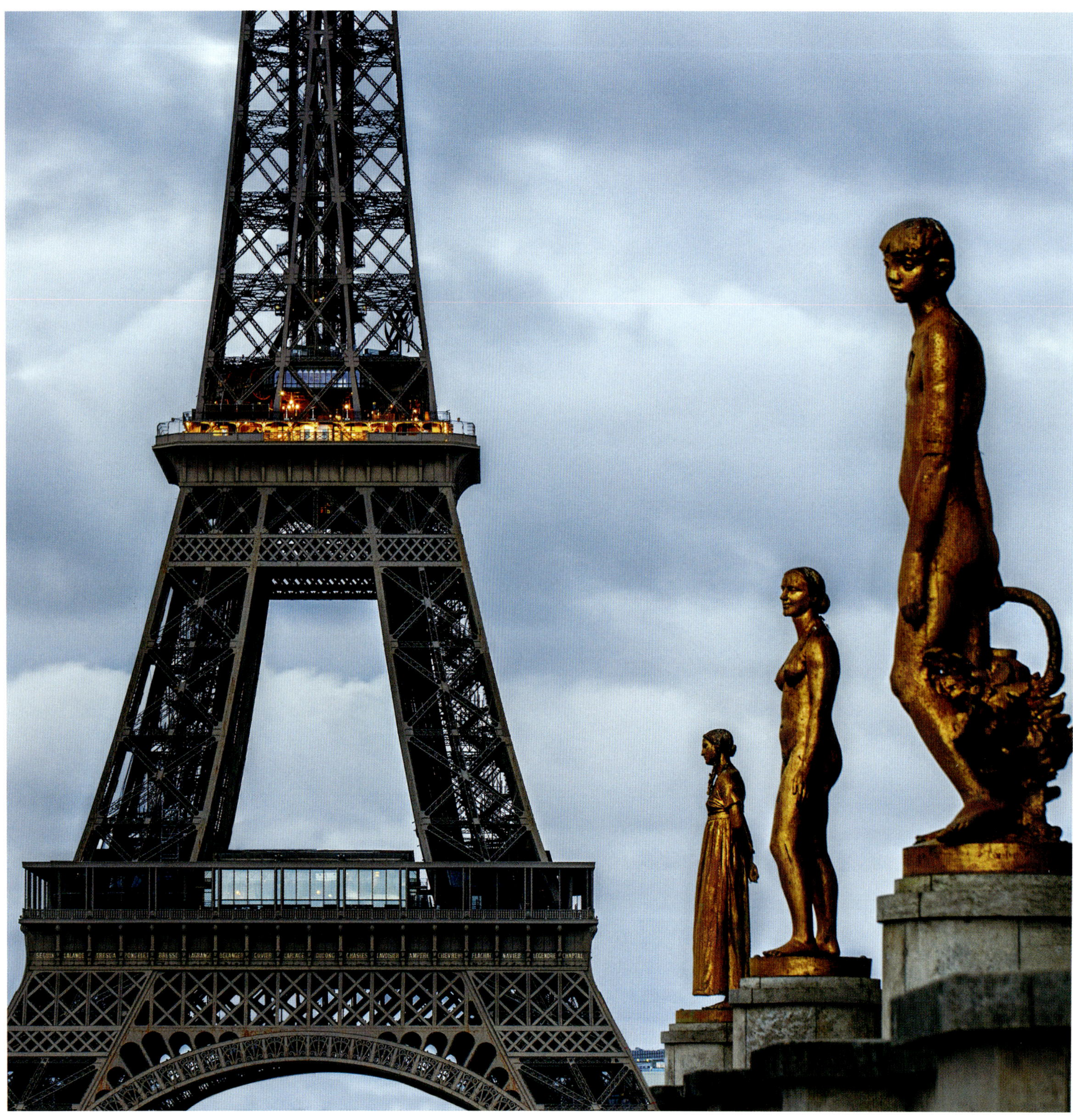

SEGUIN LALANDE TRESCA PONCELET BRESSE LAGRANGE BELANGER CUVIER LAPLACE DULONG CHASLES LAVOISIER AMPERE CHEVREUL FLACHAT NAVIER LEGENDRE CHAPTAL

LENS CHOICE IS
A COMPOSITION DECISION

Don't just reach into your camera bag and grab a lens. This is decision time because the lens you put on your camera will have a huge impact on your composition—and maybe not even in the way you're thinking. For example, when you choose a wide-angle lens, it takes the scene you're standing in front of and pushes everything in it away from you, so things in the background are even farther away. That's why many landscape photographers will often stay away from using super-wide-angle lenses (like a 16mm or a 14mm on a full-frame camera) because it takes mountains and pushes them farther away, making them seem less epic and more distant (many landscape pros consider a 24mm lens the sweet spot). So, what if you want something in the background to appear closer? That's when you reach for a long lens, like I did in the image you see here. This was taken from the popular Eiffel Tower viewing point called the Trocadéro. Although the tower itself is more than half a mile away, it seems much closer because of the compression you get when you zoom in with a long lens. It brings the background closer and compresses the distance between these statues and the tower. I took hundreds of shots that morning from this location (I worked the scene to death), using different lenses, different angles, and different perspectives to come up with one I really liked.

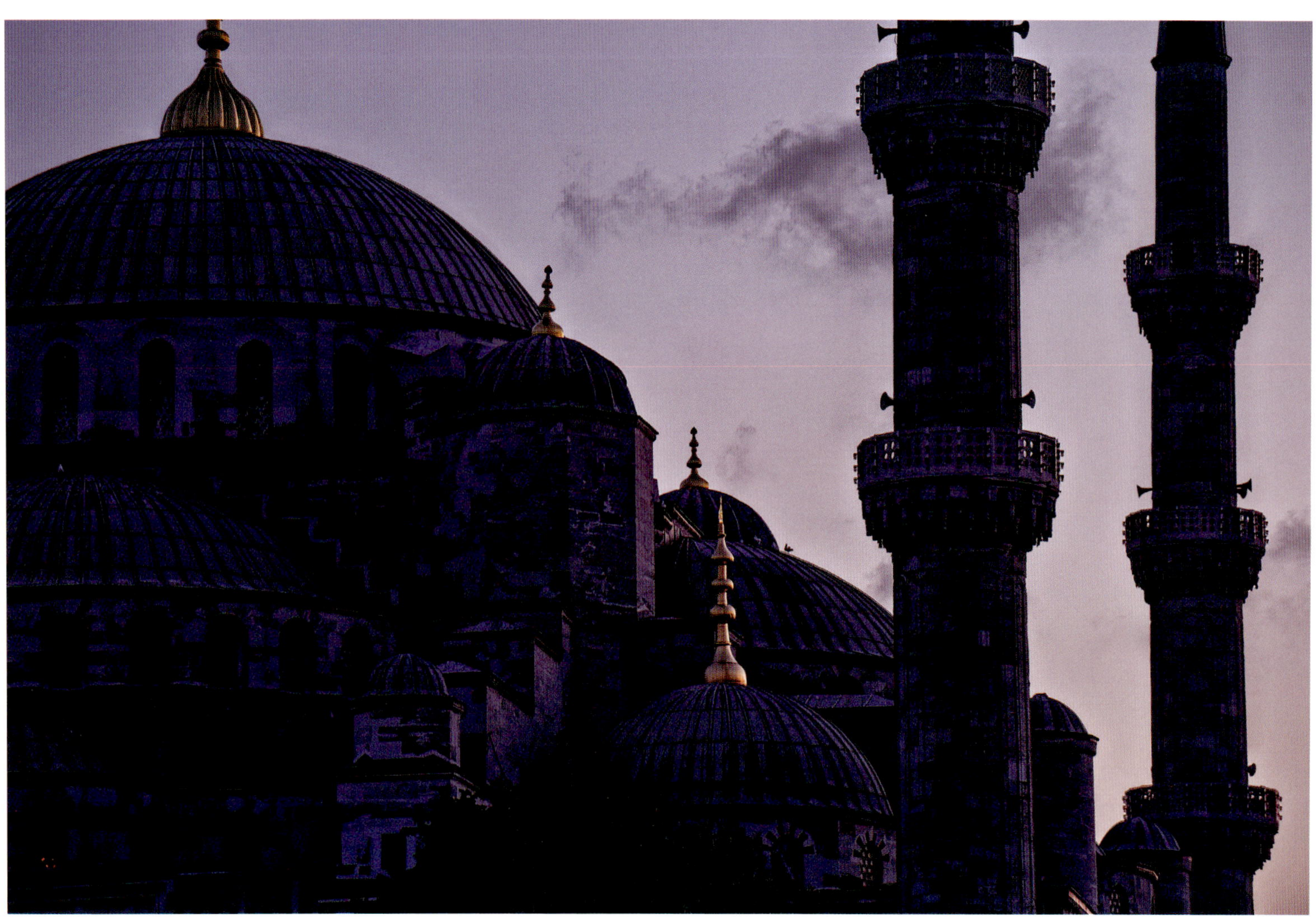

SUGGEST
THE WHOLE

It's hard to get a clean shot of just about any monument or cathedral or palace these days without capturing lots of junk surrounding them, like billboards, power lines, signage, security barriers—all sorts of distracting things that take the romance and timelessness away from the image. That's why one of my favorite composition techniques is to zoom in a bit tighter to show part of the building or monument—you don't have to show the entire thing (warts and all). You can shoot the detail areas and the viewer will get it—their mind will fill in the missing areas. The shot you see here is of Istanbul's famous Blue Mosque, and if you've ever seen it, you instantly recognized it in this image without seeing the whole thing. I have shots of the whole building (I worked the scene) and most of them are pretty bad, with tour buses in front, and light poles, and tourists, and signage, and all sorts of unnecessary things. By zooming in, you're showing some of the intricate details you wouldn't see if you were actually standing there. You're bringing the viewer something unique, and they still get the overall idea of how the building or the monument or the palace looked without having to include the distractions.

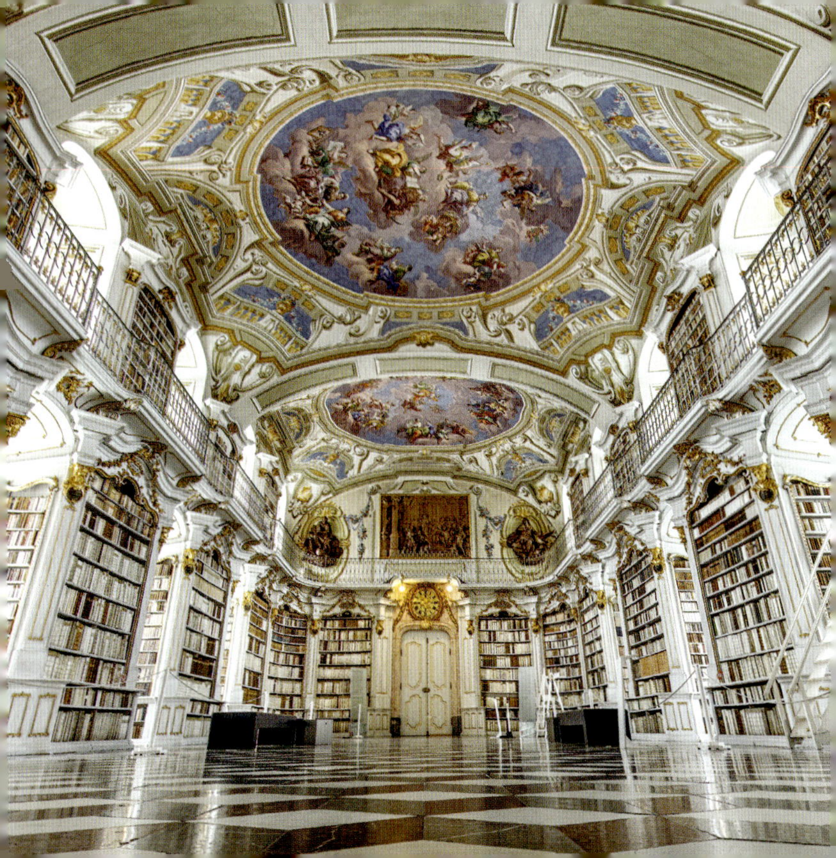

Chapter 03

CHANGE YOUR PERSPECTIVE

Picture a street photographer in your mind, camera to their eye. Now a travel photographer. Okay, now a portrait photographer. Picture each of these photographers in your mind because I have a prediction about your vision of them. I'll bet, in your mind, each of these photographers was standing, shooting their photos at eye level. I was right, right? That's because that is pretty much how the world takes photos—standing with their camera up to their eye, shooting at eye level. This is actually fantastic news for you and me because the easiest and most inexpensive thing we can do to have our photos stand out from the pack is simply to change our perspective. If we shoot at any other position other than just standing there at eye level, we're already showing the viewer something they're not used to seeing. Can it really be that easy? Yes, it's that easy. But, I guess it isn't really all that easy or everybody would already be doing it. I think we shoot from that standing, eye-level position because it's the easiest and most comfortable way for us to shoot, and I would agree. It's just not the most compelling. A few little changes, like the ones we're going to talk about in this chapter, can make all the difference in your composition.

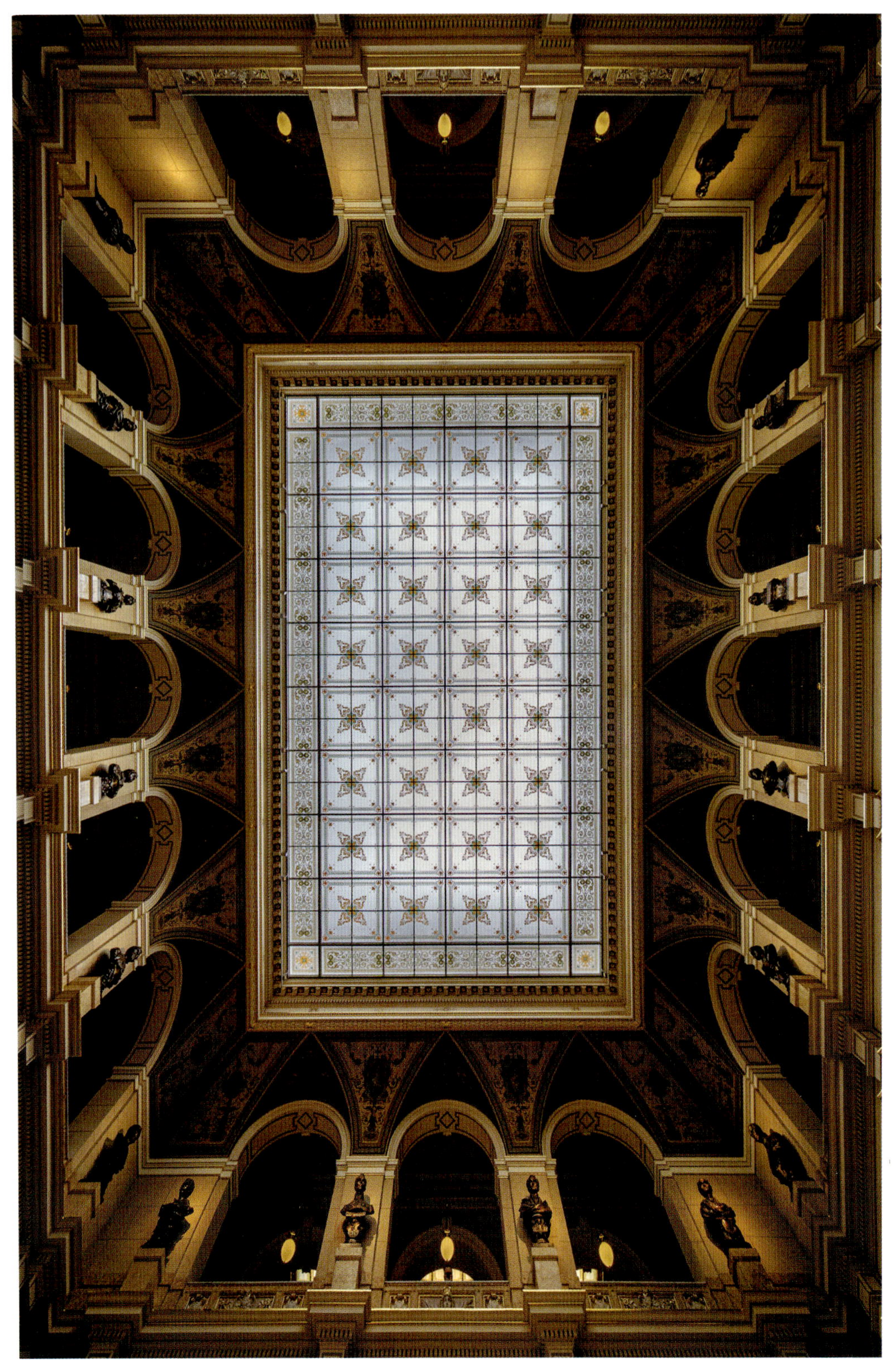

STRAIGHT UP

This is one you can do while you're standing (so it's still fairly comfortable), although I've also done this many times by setting my camera on the floor, setting the self timer to 2 seconds, and then firing off the shot using the remote camera app you can download for your phone, which lets you operate your camera wirelessly (Canon, Nikon, Sony, Fuji, and OM System all have these, and they're free). The ceiling shot you see on the facing page was taken in Prague's National Museum seen here on the right. I didn't put the camera on the floor this time; I stood directly under the ceiling, as close to being dead center as I could be. I looked up at the ceiling, rested my camera against my face (for added stability) with the viewfinder up to my eye, and took the shot. I took a burst of several shots as I figured at least one of them would be in sharp focus, and I was right (this burst mode tip is an old trick for anytime you're in kind of a low-light situation, so your shutter will be open a bit longer, but you're having to hand-hold your camera. You just fire off a bunch of shots, and some will be really blurry, but in almost every case, one of that burst of shots will be sharp

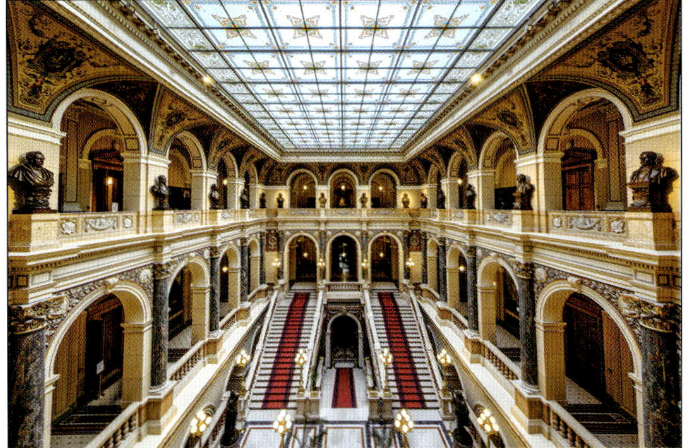

and crisp). Making this simple change in perspective—shooting straight up—can give you some really interesting shots, especially in places like cathedrals and palaces and, in this case, a museum. But, also when you're shooting in a forest among soaring trees, or downtown with buildings on all four sides. Keep an eye out for that straight-up shot. By composing your shot like this, you're bringing the viewer an angle and viewpoint that they don't normally see, so you're setting your shot up for success.

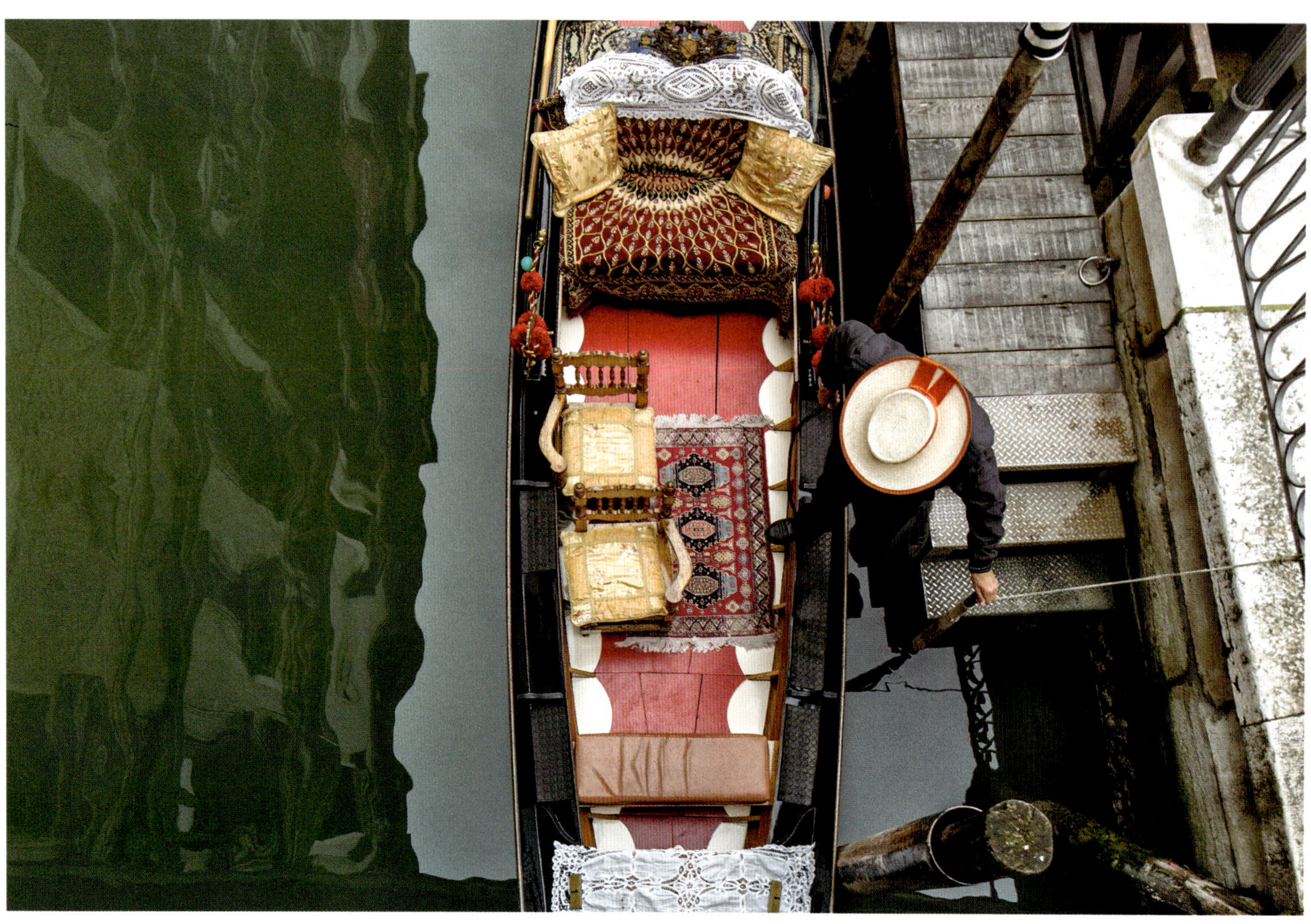

A HIGHER ANGLE

I love the overhead view—it's one of my favorites—and sometimes it's really easy to achieve. On the facing page, I was walking over one of the small bridges in Venice that go over the canals and I saw this gondolier stepping onto this gondola, so I leaned over the edge and held my camera out as far as I could (with the strap wrapped about my wrist in case I lost my grip). This is a view you normally don't see, and while it's not some kick-butt, awesome shot, it's different, and that adds the interest. In this case, it was a small walking bridge, but it could've just as easily been shooting down into a square from the second floor, or out a third or fourth story hotel window, or from on top of some steps—anything you can do to depart from the eye-level standard, everyday perspective will do the trick. Here's another place where shooting from a high angle really pays off: the tops of mountains. How do we usually shoot them? From street level. We pull our car off the road, maybe into an overlook, and shoot from there, or we shoot from wherever we pulled our car over.

But, if you want to show people a view they don't normally see, shoot the mountain tops from high up within the mountains. In fact, if you can be up in the mountains, shooting down on other mountains, that's a really compelling viewpoint, and something we're not used to seeing every day. Add the high viewpoint to your composition bag of tricks, and you'll be surprised at how easy it is to make a more interesting image using this simple little change.

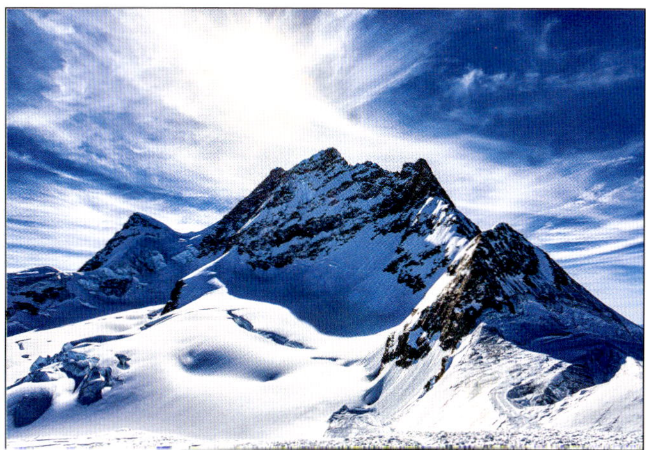

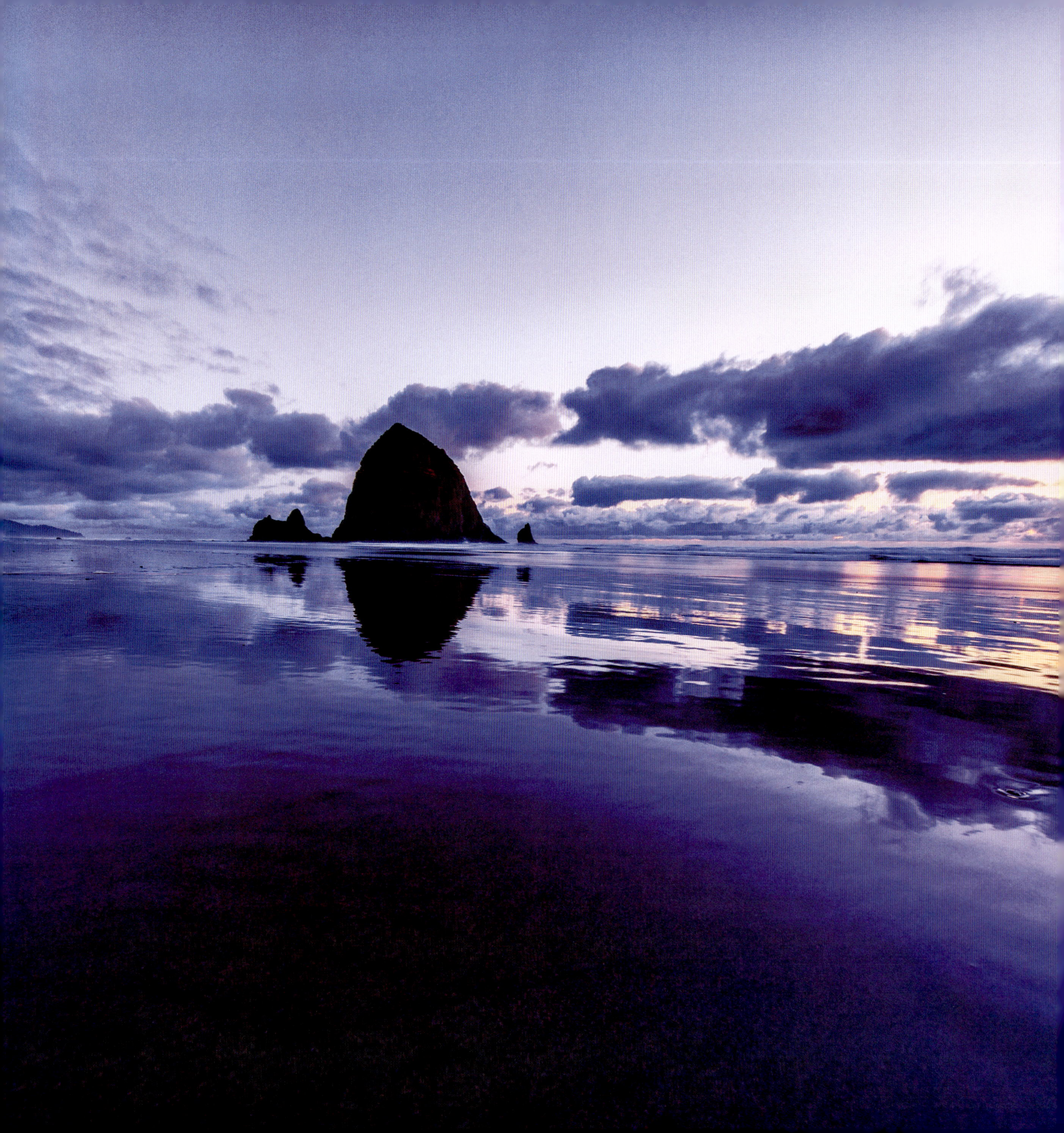

A LOWER ANGLE

This one is a little more of a pain in the butt to do, but the results
are usually worth it. Again, by changing your perspective like this
you get an entirely different feel to the image by shooting down low,
and you'll see this low perspective somewhat less often than you'll see
a higher one, so that's a bonus. In the image here, I'm shooting on a
tripod (it's a low-light situation), and I've retracted all the legs except
the top ones, so my tripod is only maybe two feet off the ground, if that.
This is when having a rotatable LCD panel on the back of your camera
is worth its weight in gold because you can tip it upward toward you
to see and compose the shot, so you're not having to get down on
your knees in the wet sand (in this instance). Most photographers
avoid going down low like this, so you've already got an advantage
and an opportunity for a more compelling composition just by the
sheer fact that you're down low and not at eye level.

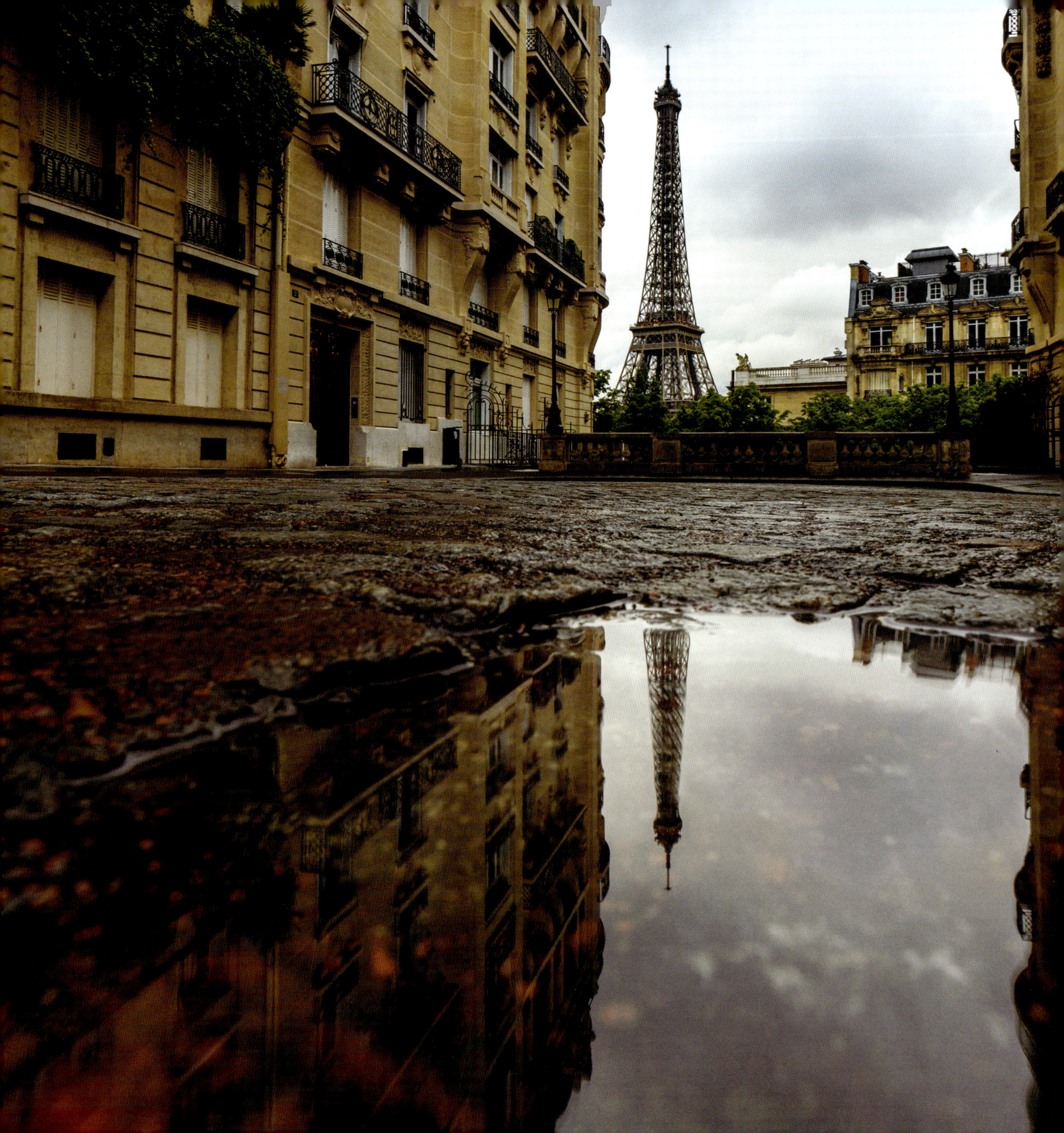

GET EVEN LOWER

This is one of my go-to compositional techniques: getting as low as possible. So much so that I now use a specialized tripod called the "Platypod Ultra." It's a flat plate made of lightweight aircraft aluminum that you screw a small ballhead onto, and then you put your camera onto it, so you can get crazy low perspectives like the one you see here below right. I wish I had my Platypod with me the day I took this shot in Paris; I had to set my camera down right on the wet cobblestone street to get this reflection shot from a tiny puddle of water in a missing section of cobblestones. See the impact that small puddle has on the look of the shot? You only get that type of reflection when you get really, really low like we're doing here. Another benefit of getting really low like this is that a floor (wood, tile, etc.) that doesn't look reflective when you're standing there, looks amazingly reflective when shot from that low perspective. This super-low angle is my go-to in cathedrals (right down the center aisle), or in palaces, in museums, or any place they won't

allow a regular tripod (one that has legs). For example, I'll sit in a pew in a cathedral and put my rig down on the floor and either press the shutter button manually, or I'll use a wireless app to trigger it. Nobody says a word—security doesn't intervene—and I get a shot that has a unique perspective, which is what it's all about.

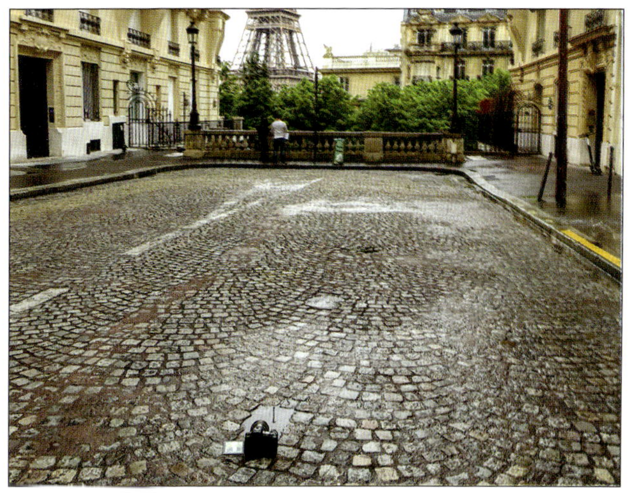

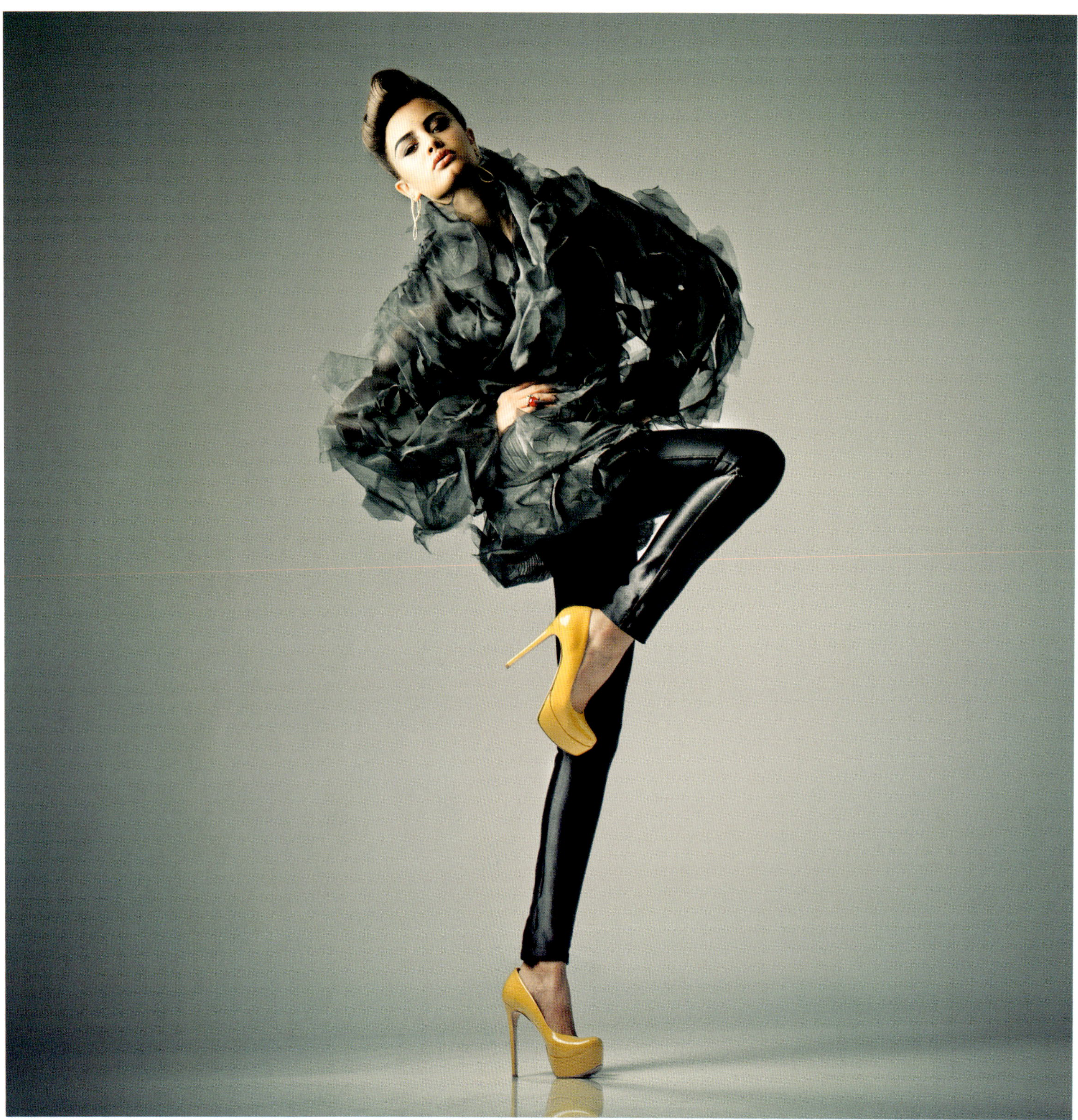

SHOOTING FULL LENGTH

If you're shooting full-length fashion or portraits, there's a simple trick to get your image looking more dynamic without creating some really unflattering body distortion, and that is to shoot from down low—ideally around waist level or slightly lower. The goal is to shoot straight on to your subject—without having to tilt the camera up—and that minimizes any body distortion that happens when you're shooting full-length from eye level. Changing your perspective like this is great compositionally because, again, most photographers would shoot a shot like this standing up at eye level (and have the accompanying body distortion that often comes along with it). But, by getting low, you get the bonus of removing distortion and making your subject appear slimmer and taller, and more majestic, with longer legs, so it's all the good stuff without any of the bad stuff. I took this image sitting right on the floor, cross-legged from the back of the room, so I have the minimum amount of distortion and I didn't have to tilt the camera up at my subject. You'll sometimes see pro fashion photographers either sitting in a low chair or even lying on the ground to get this style of perspective (the lower you go, the taller and more imposing you make your subject). This is also why sports photographers shoot the whole game down on one knee—that lower perspective makes the players look bigger than life and when they jump, it looks like they're jumping four feet into the air.

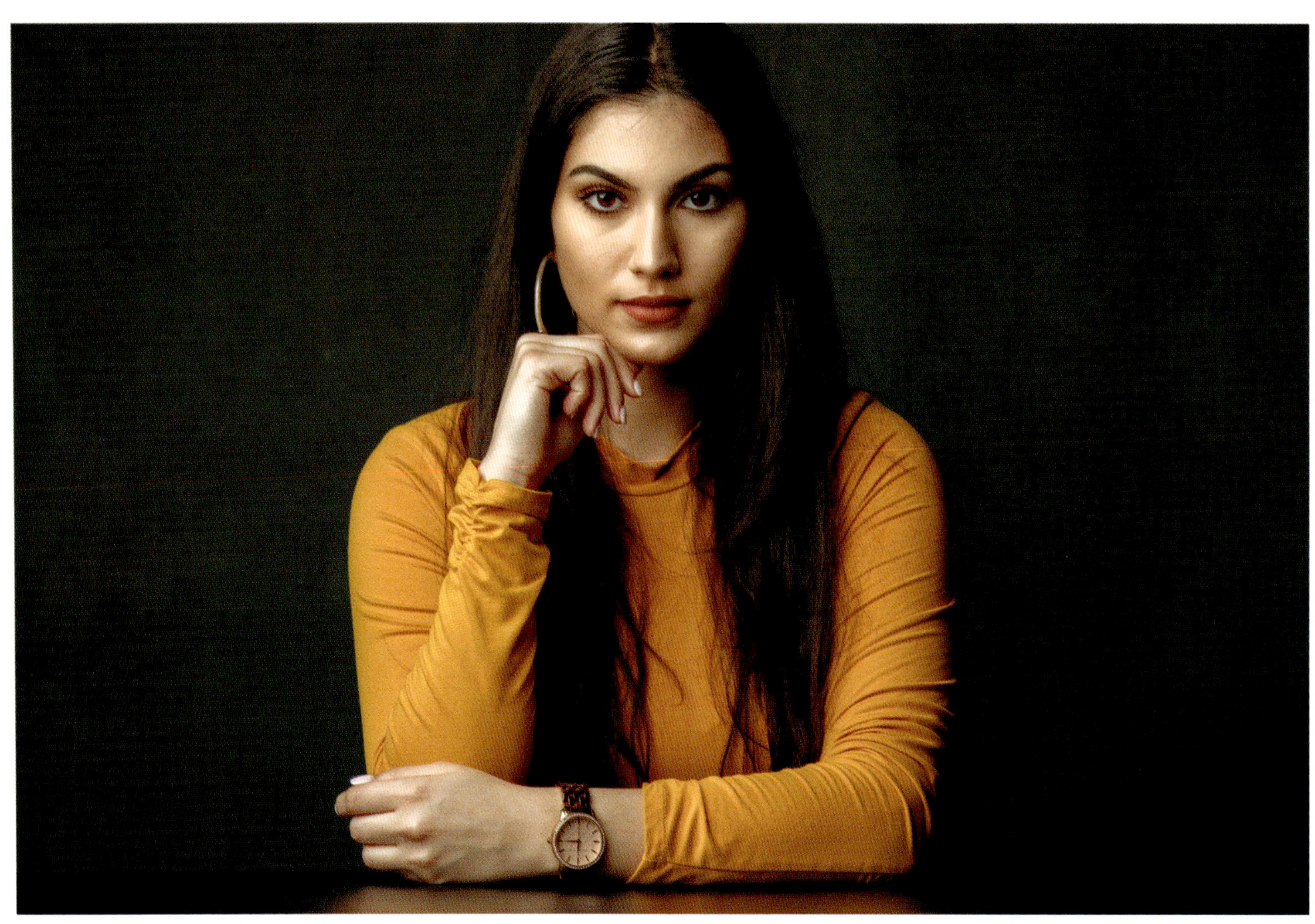

IF THEY SIT, YOU SIT

If you ever watch somebody who is really good at taking selfies, where do they position their phone when they're taking the selfie? Up a little above their head, aiming back down at them. Why? Because it makes them look better. That slightly higher angle creates a more flattering look, but if you take a portrait from too high a position, then it kind of works the opposite way, and you get distortion of their face. That's why, if we have our subject seated, we can sit as well, and ideally shoot from just above their eyes. Why? That slightly higher angle creates a more flattering look.

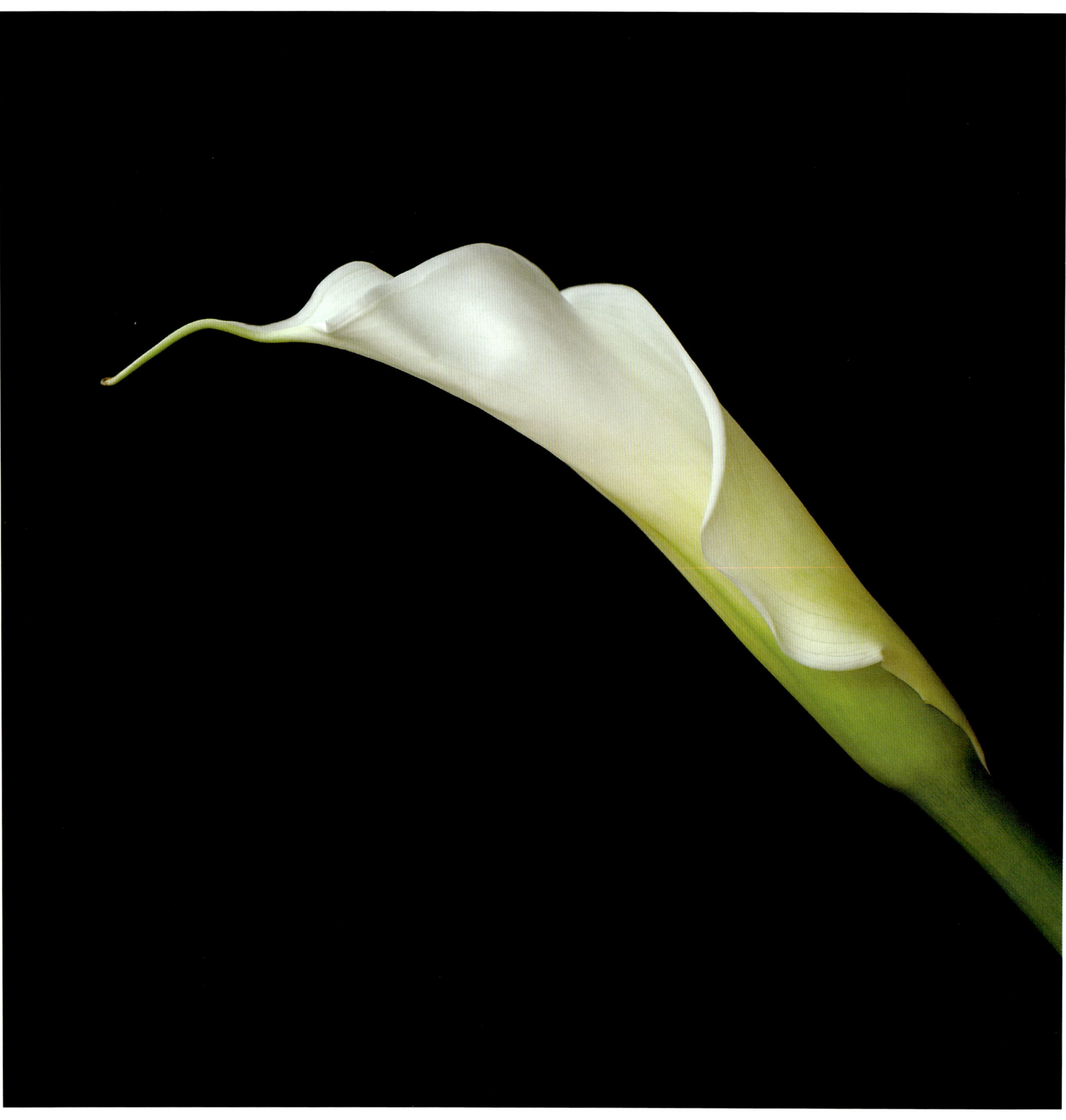

CHILDREN AND FLOWERS

These two are all about the shooting angle, and the goal is to not shoot down on either one because looking down at kids and flowers is the usual way we see them—when we're standing, both of them are down lower. So, when we get down to their level, we're bringing an angle most viewers never see. In the image here, rather than shooting down on the flower, I used a tripod (so the shot would be super-sharp), set it so I would be shooting perfectly level with the flower, and you get a very natural-looking view of the calla lily. Shooting down low like this, down at its level, rather than the common method of shooting down on it, gives it a much more intimate and delicate look.

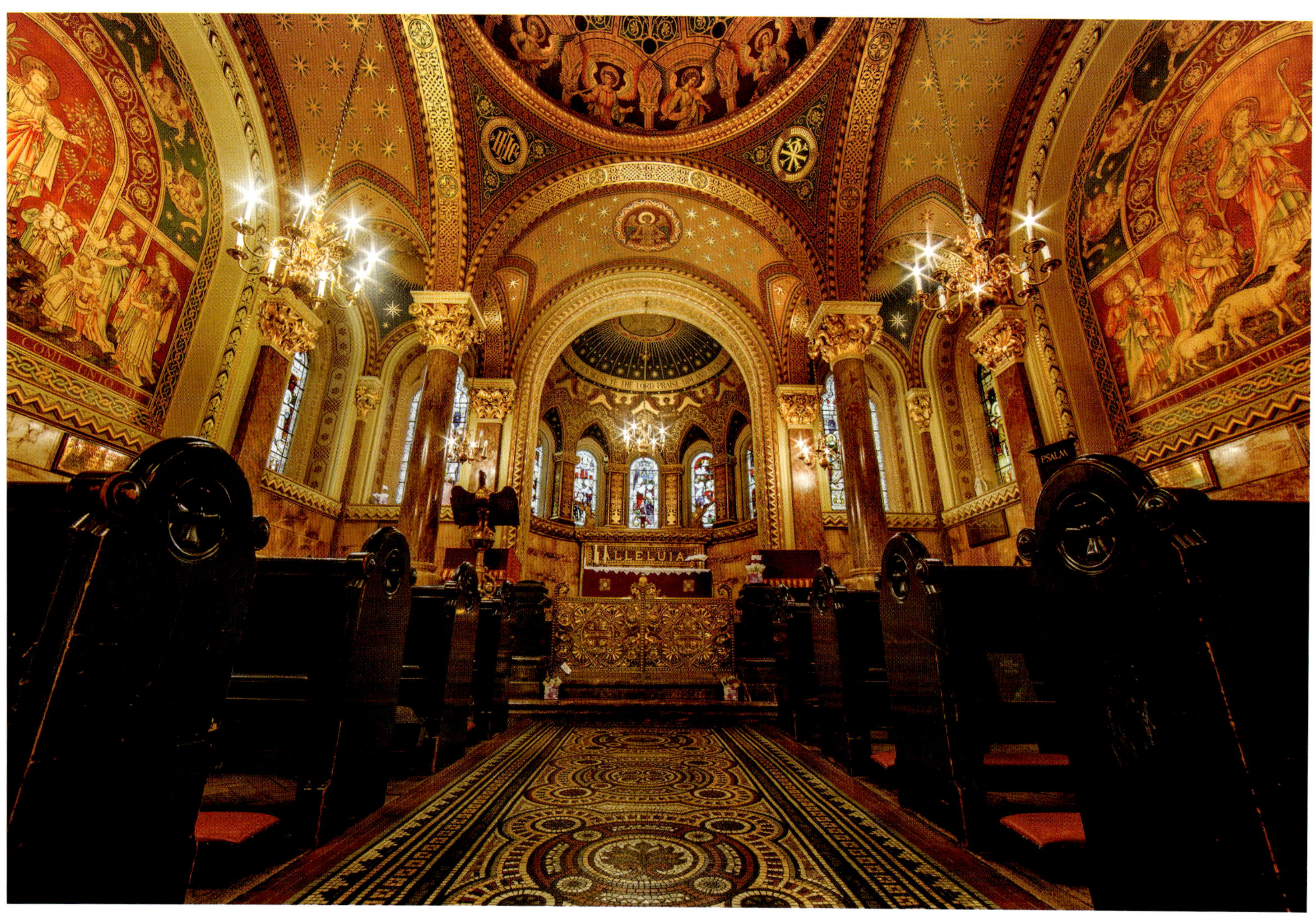

GO WIDE AND LOW

Tell me that title above wouldn't make a great name for a law firm. Anyway, there is a pretty magical combination of a particular type of lens and a particular type of composition that absolutely rocks. You use a super-wide-angle lens (so, a 14mm or 16mm on a full-frame camera, or a 10mm or 12mm on a crop-sensor body), and then you put it way down low. This combination takes a small space and makes it look absolutely epic! Take a look at the image shown here. It's a chapel so small that it's actually inside a children's hospital in London, and if you look carefully, you'll notice how small it really is—the entire chapel is only four pews deep. I took this shot standing in the doorway (it's as far back as you can go), so it's literally only about 12 feet from the back of the church to the altar. But, look at how big and epic that combination of a super-wide-angle lens and getting really low makes.

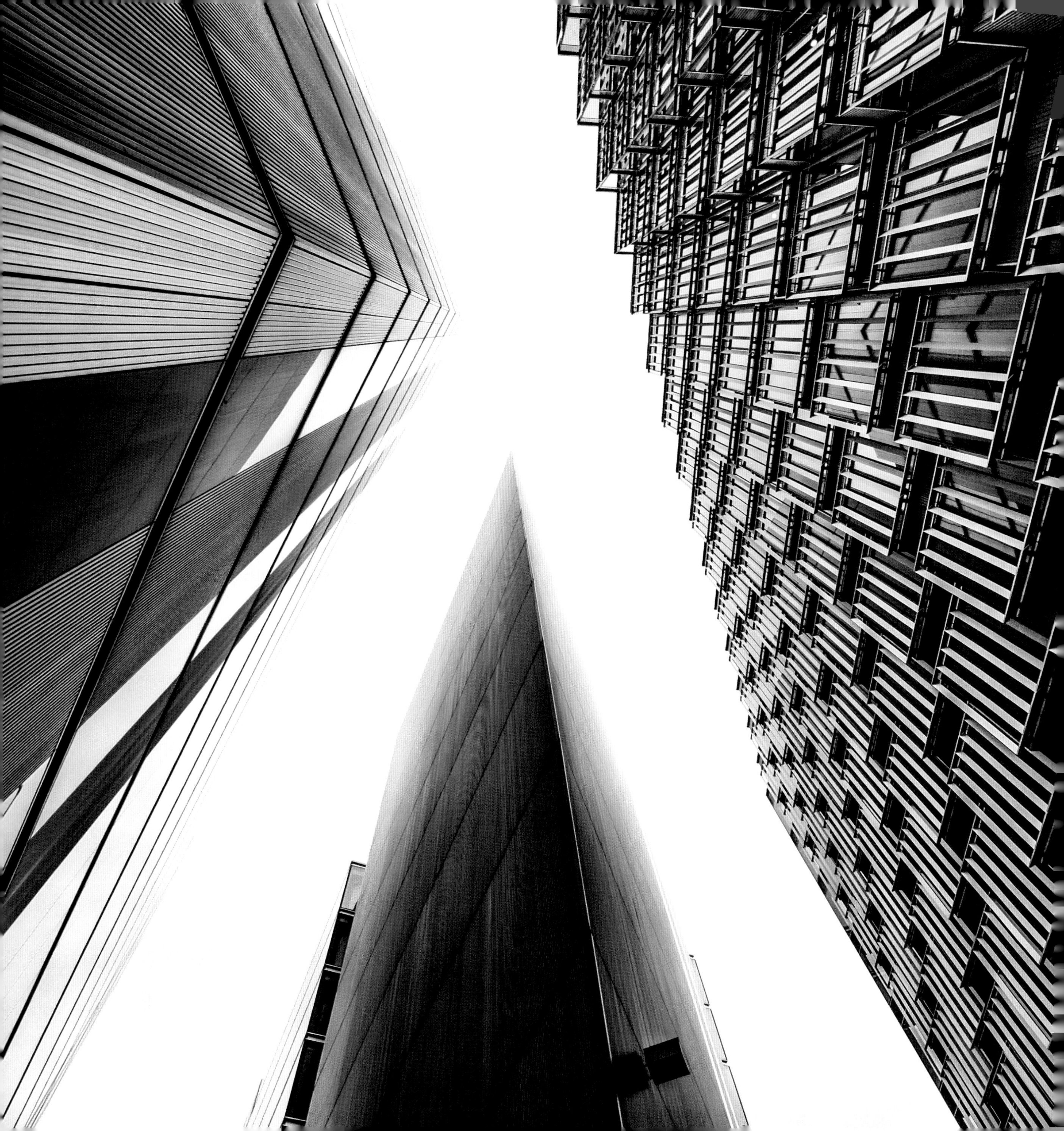

WORK THE LENS

Your choice of lens will change the perspective of the scene as well, so while you're shooting, it can help to ask yourself, "Is there another lens I should be trying now?" Or, "Is there a better focal length I should be using?" If you're shooting a portrait, are you using a lens that flatters the subject—that helps make them look their best—or is the lens you're using just your "go-to" lens, or your favorite lens? There's one great way to find out: try out some different focal lengths (easy to do if you're using a zoom lens, right?) or simply put on a different lens to see how it changes your image. How would a fish-eye lens look inside that opera house, or how would a landscape shot look if you zoomed in tight on those mountains? A different lens, with its different perspective and look, could be the thing that transforms your image, but you'll never know if you don't take just a few moments to give it a try. Think about it. How long does it really take to change lenses? Thirty seconds? Forty-five seconds? Isn't it worth investing less than a minute to see if it makes a difference? You could be 30 seconds away from everything suddenly coming together, but you'll never know if you don't give it a quick try.

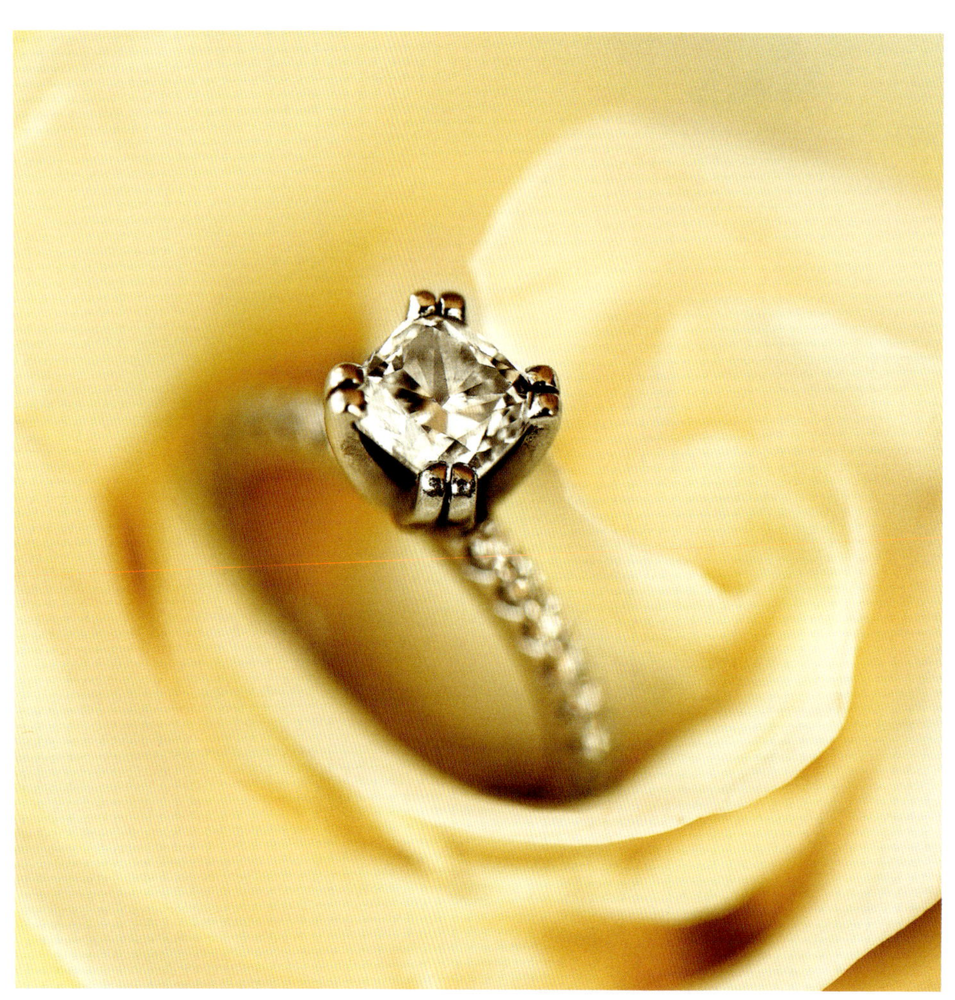

GO MACRO!

If you want to show your viewers a perspective they don't often see, get in really, really close with a close-up macro lens. First, check to see if one of the zoom lenses you already own has a built-in macro feature (many of them do), allowing you to zoom in incredibly close—closer than most regular lenses would ever allow you to focus. If you don't have a macro lens for your mirrorless or DSLR, then it's time to pull out your phone's camera. Most smartphone cameras today have a built-in macro feature (Samsung phones and Apple's iPhone kick into Macro mode automatically when you position your camera just a few inches from your subject). Getting in super-close like this gives an entirely different perspective. Like the wedding ring you see here, which was sitting with the bride's bouquet. When shot with a macro lens, you're getting a super-up-close and detailed view you wouldn't get normally, even if you took the ring and stuck it right up to your face because your eye can't focus that close. But, your macro lens can. Want to show a different perspective? This is an easy way to get there (well, for the right type of subject, right?).

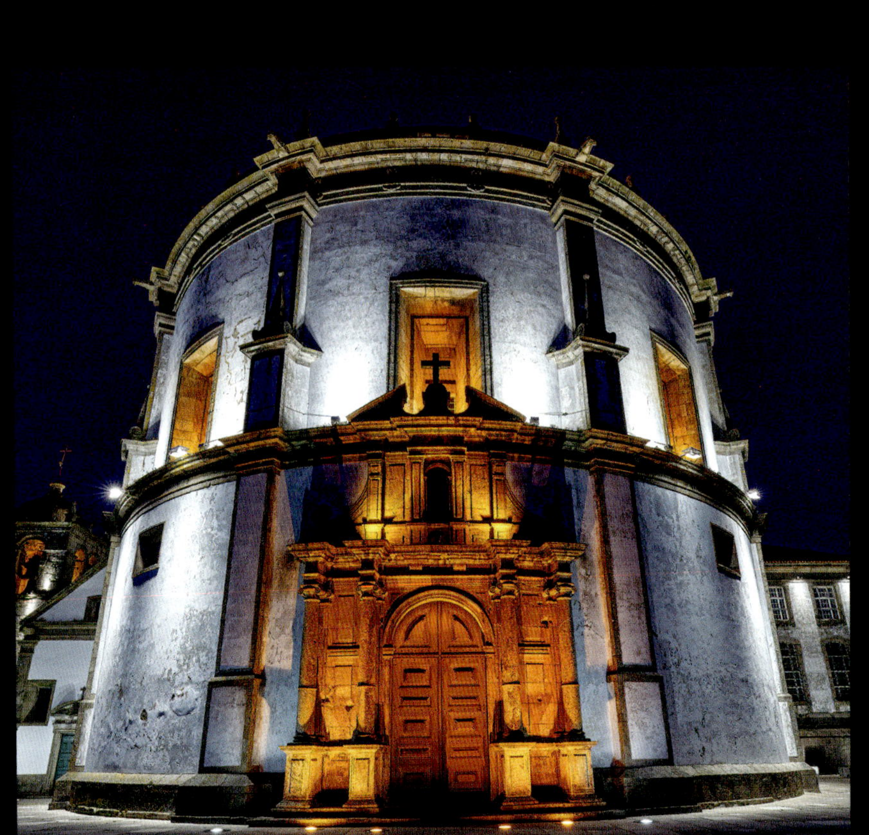

Chapter 04

WORK THE SHARPNESS

A super-important part of "working the scene" is making sure the shots we're working are in super-sharp focus, so this entire chapter is about strategies to do just that. The reason sharpness is such an important part of the process is this: If you get a great shot and it's "soft," most likely you're going to throw it away. It never makes the light of day, you don't share it online, and it seems like it happens a lot on what would have been an awesome shot, so it's really worth taking seriously. Now, all that being said, I don't worry about the sharpness so much when I'm starting to work the scene—when I'm just scouting the location and trying different perspectives and angles and such. But once I know I'm onto something, or I'm getting close, that's when I get serious about the sharpness. There are a number of things we can do once we get to that point—where sharpness becomes "a thing"—and while there are dozens of methods and techniques, I'm going to focus on the ones I actually use in my own photography (the same ones I'd tell to a friend).

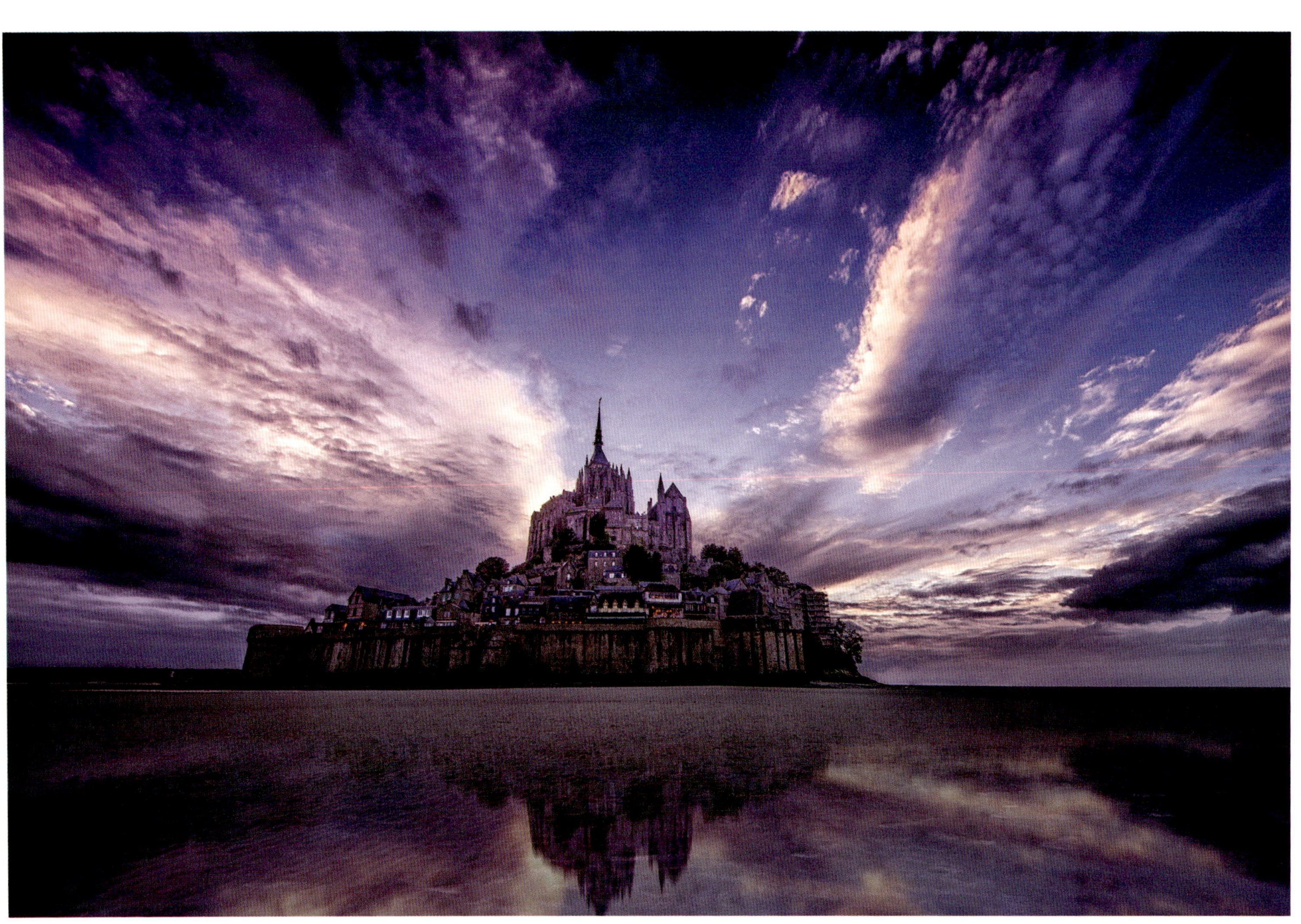

SHOULD YOU USE A TRIPOD?

The enemy of sharp shots is camera movement. If your camera moves, even the slightest amount, while you're taking the photo, that movement will make your image anywhere from a little blurry to a lot blurry. Now, that doesn't mean you need to use a tripod for every shot (even though it would pretty much guarantee your shots would be sharp) because it's not only not practical (and lots of places won't allow you to shoot with a tripod at all), it's also not necessary. For example, if you're shooting outside in bright daylight, there's so much light that your shutter speed will be super-fast (probably thousandths of a second)—so fast, in fact, that even if you moved the camera a little while shooting (which we all do while hand-holding our cameras), it would still be really sharp. So, if you're doing street or travel photography during the day, not only is it impractical (or impossible) to use a tripod, you just don't need one. However, when we're shooting in lower light, as in landscape photography when the light is the best around dawn and dusk, it's a must if we want to make the kind of shots we really want.

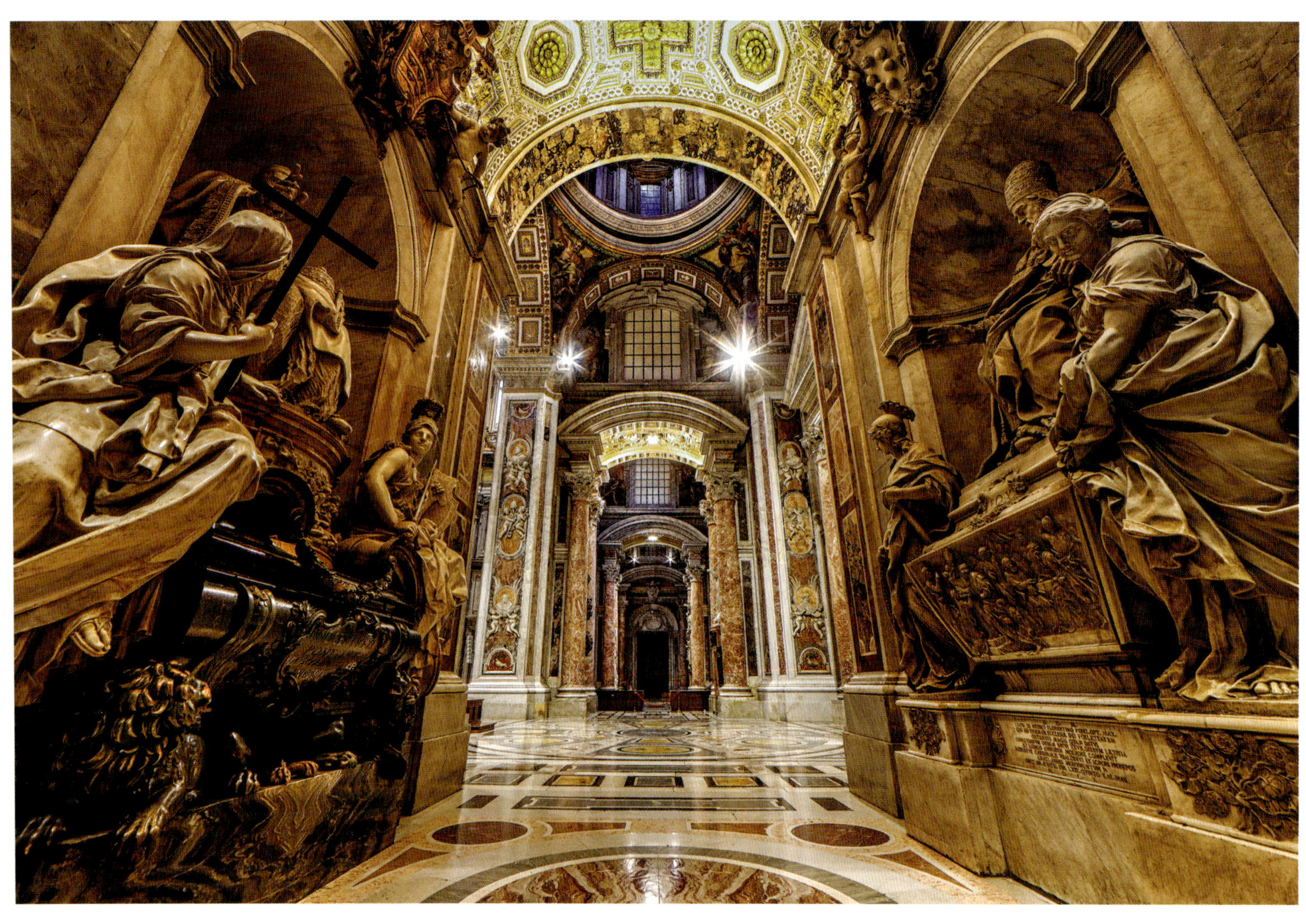

A TRIPOD ALTERNATIVE

Besides having to lug them around, there's another big downside to using a tripod. Unless you're out in nature, tripods have become the natural enemy of security guards everywhere, and many (perhaps "most") indoor locations forbid the use of them. Their reasons range from "We don't allow them because somebody might trip over one of the legs," to "We don't allow commercial photos," and since they see the tripod as the "maker of pro shots," they don't allow them. You'll see "no tripods allowed" signs in so many places these days, and now I'm more surprised (more like shocked) when there's an indoor location that actually allows you to use a tripod. So, the way I get around this is by using a Platypod Ultra (seen here on the right), which is a small, flat plate made of lightweight aircraft aluminum that sits on the floor (or a table, or wherever you put it) and acts like a tripod (you screw your ballhead right onto it). I guess since it doesn't have three legs, the normally very motivated security guards just shrug and move on, because I guess there's no rule regarding flat plates. It really doesn't take up any room, and I've been able to shoot in all sorts of places that forbid tripods—like this shot inside St. Peter's Basilica at the Vatican. The security guards never hassled me. I used it all over the place and nobody cared. However, if at any time I pulled out a tripod, their snipers (located in platforms up high near the ceiling) would have taken me out in a split second. This is essentially my sharpness secret weapon because now I can shoot indoors in low light without worrying about security forbidding it.

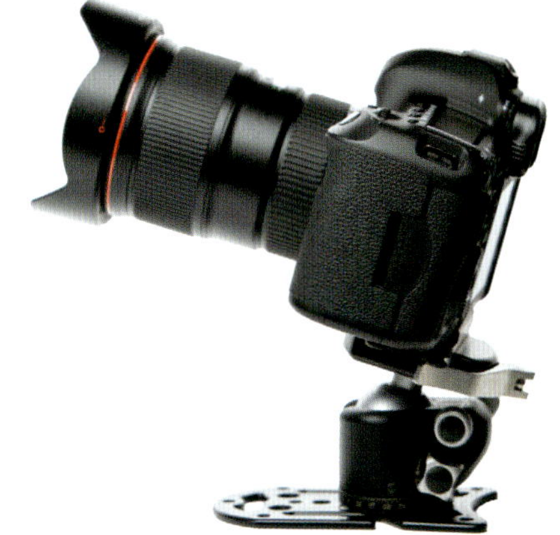

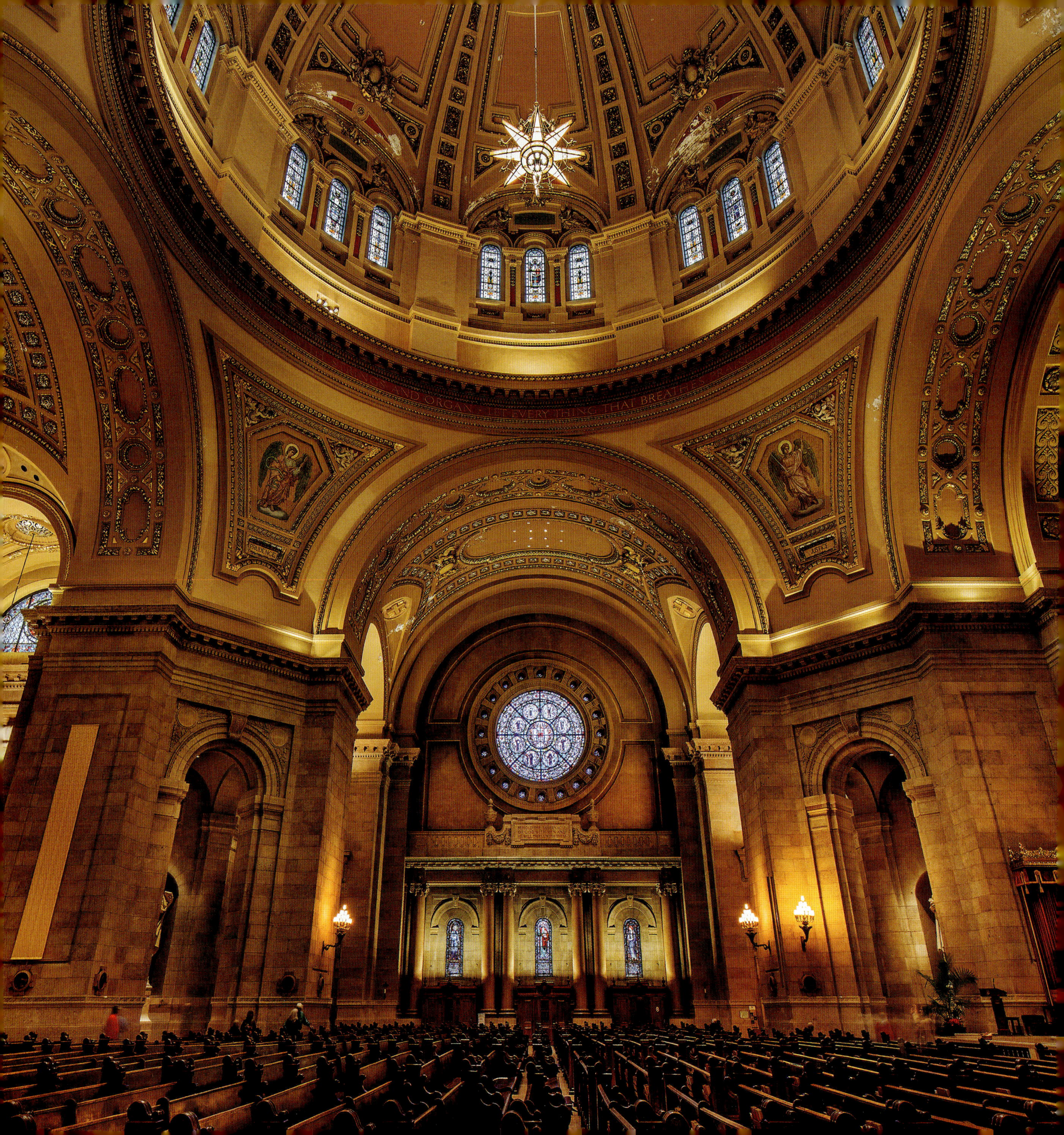

LEAN INTO IT

Okay, so what do you do if you're in a situation where there's no place to put your tripod (if it's allowed) or your Platypod, but there's a shot you want to make in a lower-light situation (like in this cathedral in Minneapolis, Minnesota)? In that case, we move on to Plan B, which is to look around and find something you can lean against (a column, a wall, a pew, whatever) that will help steady your body in these "hand-holding in low light" situations. You'd be surprised what a difference this makes in getting sharper shots because leaning against something helps stabilize your body, and if your body isn't moving, that's one more thing that isn't moving your camera when you take the shot. You'd be amazed at how slow a shutter speed you can get away with when you're leaning on something for that extra stabilization.

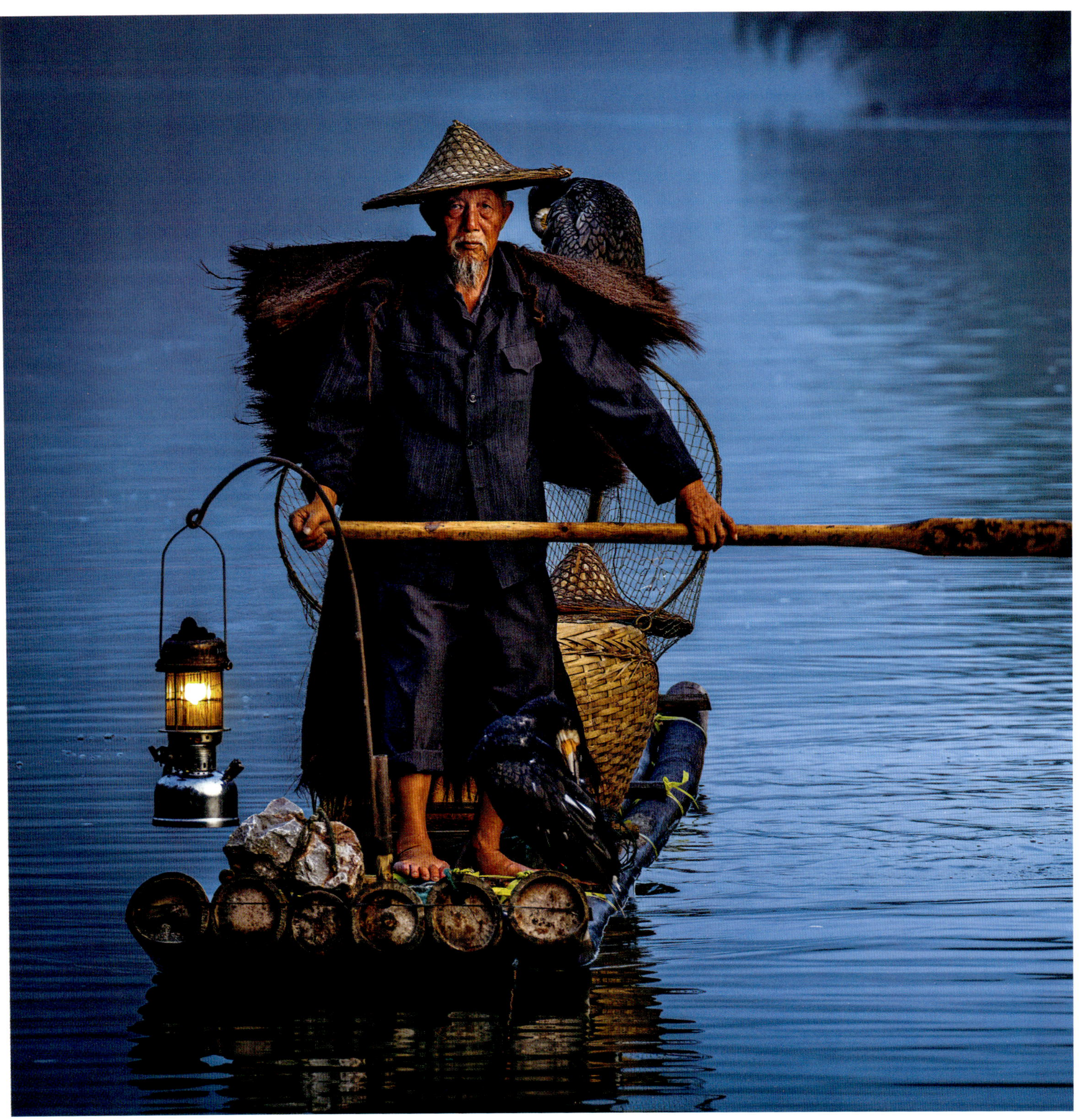

HOW TO GET AWAY WITH HAND-HOLDING IN LOW LIGHT

I'll never forget meeting a woman at one of my seminars who brought her camera just to ask me to look at it to see if something was wrong with it because she went on this wonderful trip and a bunch of her shots were blurry. I took a look at the LCD on the back of her camera, and sure enough, almost all of her shots were blurry. Then I looked at the camera data, in particular, her shutter speed, and I saw exactly what the problem was. Her shutter speed was dropping so low on so many occasions that it was just about impossible for her to have many shots in focus. The only ones that were in focus were taken in bright daylight, but inside all the temples, and on overcast days, and in the charming side streets, it was a blurry mess. Now, this is not just her—this happens more often than you'd imagine. But, have you noticed that this doesn't happen when you shoot with your phone's camera? That's right—even in low light your shots aren't blurry. Heck, even in candlelight they're in focus. What's the secret your phone's camera is doing that your DSLR or mirrorless isn't doing? It has auto ISO turned on, so when the shutter speed drops too low, it automatically raises the ISO to bring your shutter speed back up to a high enough number that you can easily hand-hold your phone and get sharp shots in low light. Luckily, this feature is on your DSLR and mirrorless, too, and

I highly recommend photographers turn this on (with one extra all-important setting), so when you're shooting travel photography (like the hand-held shot I took here), or street photography, or anything where you're walking around without a tripod, you don't wind up with a bunch of blurry shots. It's a two-step process to get the best results: (1) In your camera's menus, turn on Auto ISO (if you're not sure where this is on your particular make and model of camera, do a quick web search to find your camera's free downloadable PDF camera manual, which makes it easy to search for "Auto ISO"). Once you turn that on, then (2) set the minimum shutter speed to 1/125 of a second (again, check your manual for where this setting is, but it should be close to where the Auto ISO menu is), which is a shutter speed where most folks can hand-hold their camera comfortably and still get nice, sharp shots. Now if your camera senses your shutter speed dropping below 1/125 of a second, it will automatically raise your ISO just enough so it doesn't fall below that and your shots are sharp. This raising of the ISO is going to introduce a little or (in some cases) a lot of noise to your image, but if you had a choice between a shot that's a little noisy but is nice and sharp, or a shot without much noise but is blurry and unusable, which would you take? Of course, the sharp shot every time.

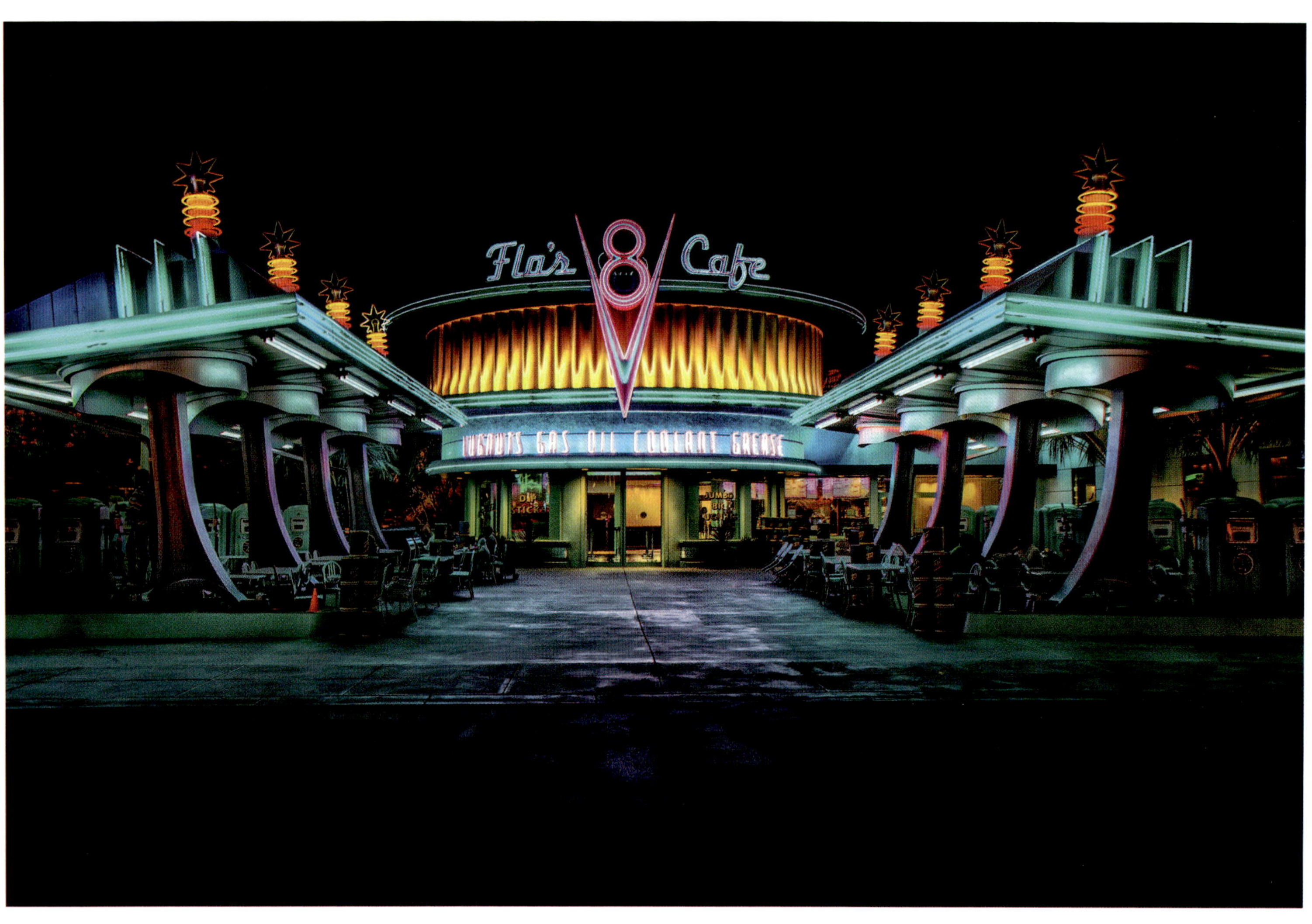

Flo's V8 Cafe
GAS OIL COOLANT GREASE

USE WHAT'S AVAILABLE

If you don't have a tripod (or aren't allowed to use one), and you don't have a Platypod (or some other portable tripod alternative) to work your sharpness, it's time to see where you can set your camera down so it will be still. This is especially important when you're shooting at night. Yes, you can get away with Auto ISO and leaning against stuff in low-light situations, but it's harder to get away with those at night. In the image you see here, taken at Disneyland in California, I didn't have my tripod or Platypod with me. I tried a few hand-held shots and I could see on my LCD that they were not going to be sharp. So, in those situations I look for something I can rest my camera on to keep it still for me. In the case of this image, I rested my camera on top of a trash can across the street from Flo's Cafe (a re-creation of Flo's Cafe from the awesome Disney movie *Cars*), and I was then able to tilt my lens up a bit by putting my wallet under the front of the lens barrel. I used the camera's self-timer to take a shot, and son-of-a-gun, it worked out perfectly. Now, was I super-lucky to have a trash can located directly across from Flo's? Absolutely. But sometimes we get lucky. I also tried positioning it on top of the end posts of a bench, but I couldn't get the angle right, so I had to try a couple of different things to set it on before I came up with the trash can solution. But, hey—that's part of "using what's available" to work the sharpness. So, add this one to your bag of sharpness tricks.

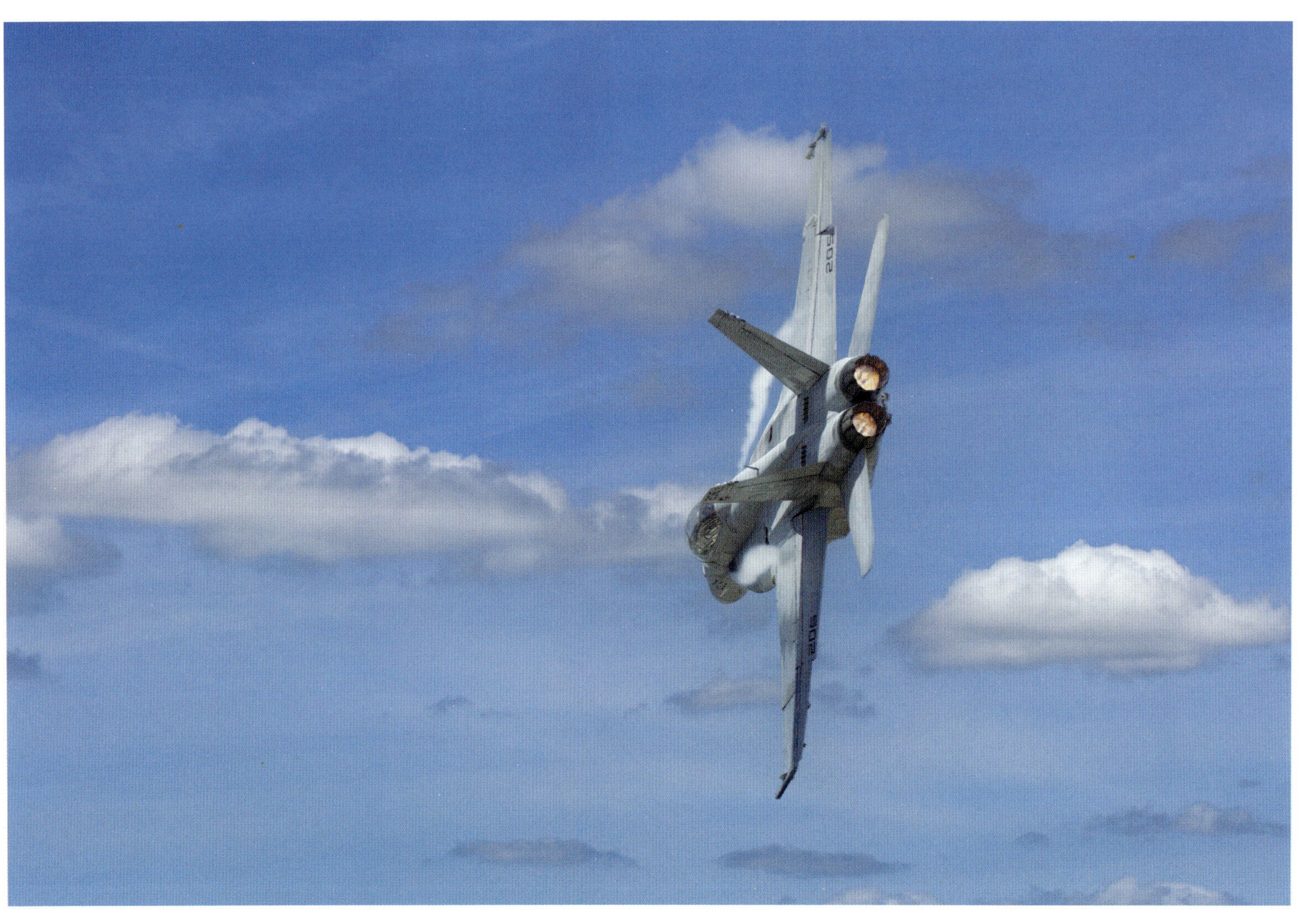

USE THE RIGHT FOCUS MODES

When you buy a camera, the camera manufacturer sets your focus mode so it will work best for things that are still. I guess they assume everybody is either shooting still life photos or landscapes because as soon as things start moving, your focus mode is going to fail you, and you're going to wind up with blurry shots. I remember a guy coming up to me at one of my seminars telling me something must be wrong with his camera because whenever he's shooting his son's Little League baseball games, the only shots that are in focus are the ones where his son is either standing on base or getting ready to bat. All the rest, where he's running, are all blurry and out of focus. That's because of that "shooting still life photos or landscapes" default focus mode. He needed to change to continuous autofocus mode (depending on your camera brand, it could be something like Continuous AF or AI Servo). This focus mode is made for moving objects and once it locks onto your subject, it automatically tracks along with them while they're moving, so you get sharp, in-focus shots. It really works amazingly well, and now many of today's cameras have special modes using AI to automatically track along with things like birds, or wildlife, or pets running in the yard, or cars driving (or racing). Of course, it depends on your make and model of camera as to how many of these specialized focus modes your camera has, but they all have either Continuous AF mode or AI Servo. So, if you want sharp shots of moving objects (like your kid trying to steal second base), then turn a continuous focus mode on.

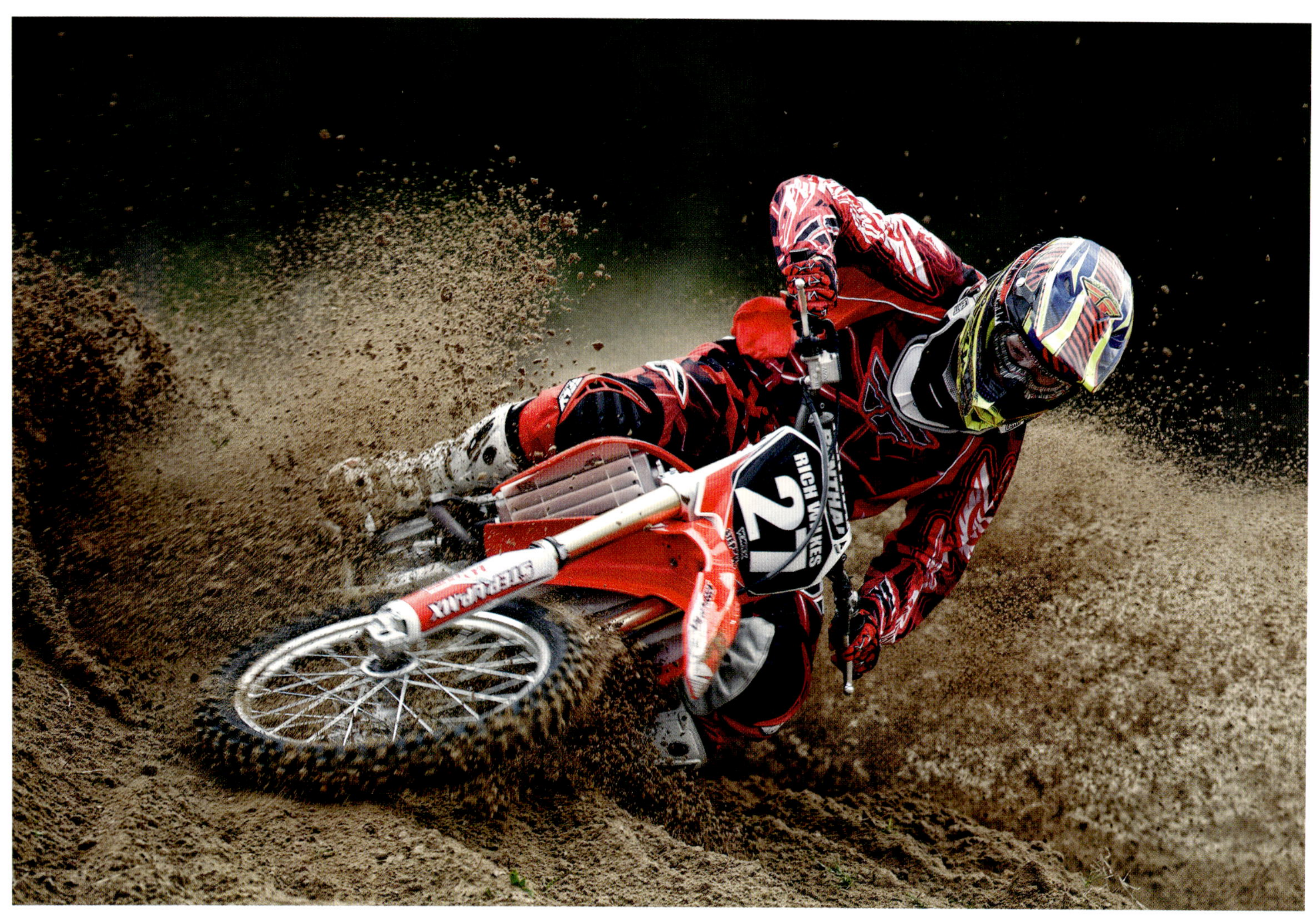
RICH VAJKES
21
RENTHAL
STEER JMAX

SHARPEN IN POST

I remember a few years ago getting a call from a very frustrated photographer who had bought a top-of-the-line DSLR body (something in the $6,000 range), and then bought a lens that he had read online was "deadly sharp!" He's using a tripod, doing everything right, but the images he's getting aren't anywhere near as sharp as the images from other photographers he's seeing online. The first question I asked him was: "Are you sharpening your shots after the fact, either in Photoshop or Lightroom or something else?" He told me he was not, and that he thought he didn't need to because he bought such a great camera body and a super-sharp lens. I asked him if he thought those photos from the other photographers he'd been seeing online had been sharpened. He thought about it for a second, and then said, "Yeah, probably." So, he was comparing his RAW, out-of-the-camera photos against everybody else's images, probably shot with great cameras and sharp lenses, but then also sharpened in "post" (short for "post-production"—meaning edited in something like Lightroom or Photoshop). In short, here's what he was missing: every photo gets sharpened. Every single one. I don't care how sharp my "glass" is or what

camera body I'm using, every single photo gets sharpened in post. You'll never get that level of sharpness without sharpening in post, and you'll be comparing your shots against everybody else's who are sharpening in post. Now, you can learn to sharpen in Photoshop or Lightroom, but I stopped doing that. Instead, I now use one of two plug-ins that use AI to do my sharpening for me, and they do a better job than I ever could. These plug-ins are flat-out amazing and I just let them do their thing (I don't have to mess with any settings). They analyze the image, determine where the sharpness problem is (and what caused it), and then they fix it—just like that. The two I use are Topaz Labs Sharpen AI and ON1 NoNoise AI (which include great AI sharpening features). These are real game-changers as far as sharpness goes, and in fact, they are the great equalizer if you don't own particularly sharp lenses—nobody will know after you run either of these plug-ins. (*Note:* ON1 is one of the sponsors of my weekly photography podcast *The Grid*, but I don't get any kickback or royalty or affiliate commission if you buy their plug-in. I'm just telling you what I use in my own workflow, but also that they are one of my sponsors.)

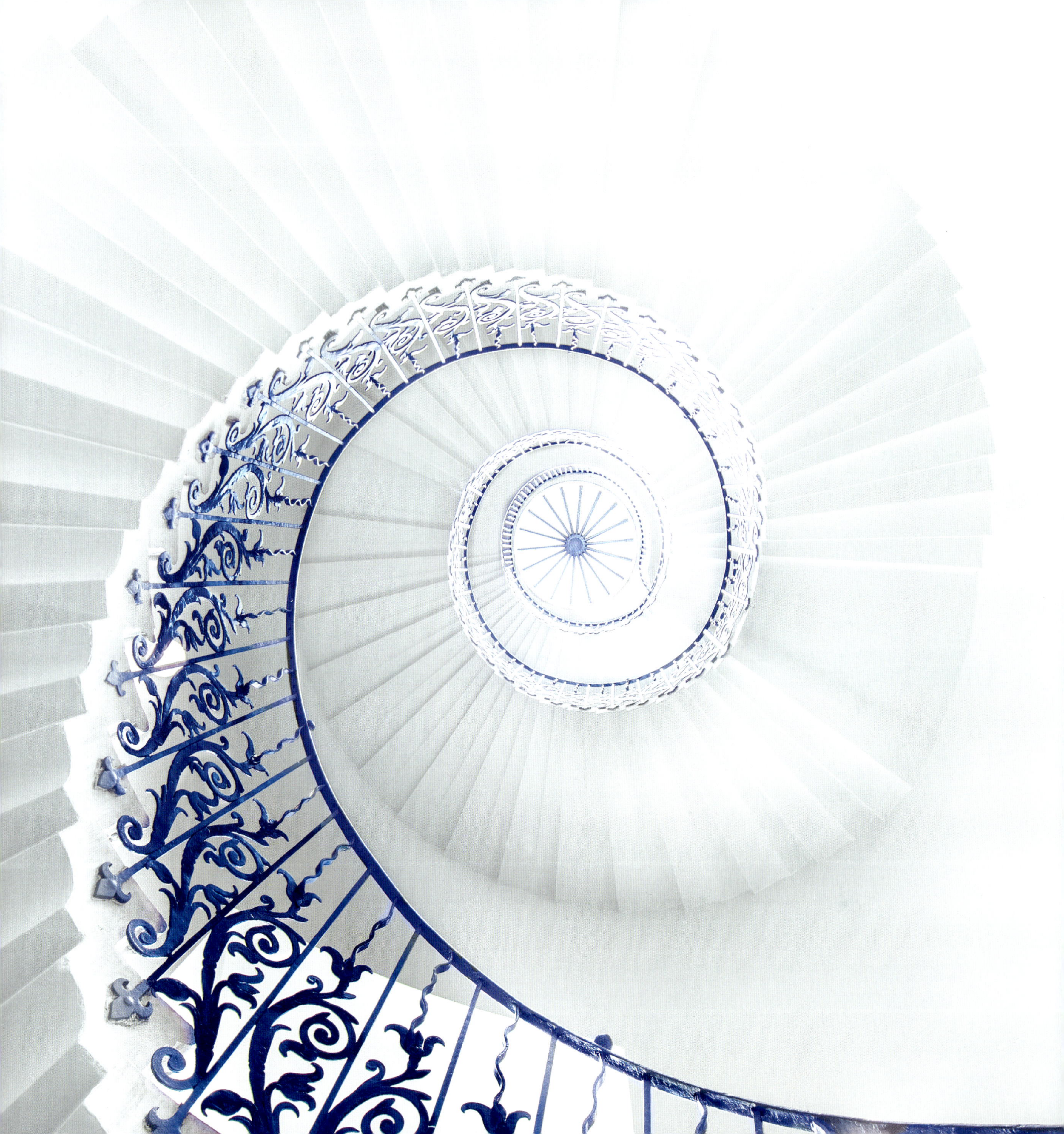

NOT TOUCHING THE SHUTTER

After you've gone through all the trouble of lugging (maybe I should say "toting" instead since it sounds way more low-impact than "lugging") a tripod around with you, or at the very least a Platypod and ballhead, and you've gone to all these lengths to keep your camera from moving even just a little bit, you're going to move your camera as you press the shutter button with your finger. Yes—pressing the shutter button absolutely moves your camera. Depending on your touch, it moves it anywhere from a little to just enough so you don't get as super-sharp a shot as you'd like. How do you get around this? The old-school method is to buy a cable release, which attaches to a port on your camera, allowing you to fire off a shot without actually touching the camera itself. It's a time-tested solution that works, but you have to carry it around with you, and connect it, and sometimes attaching it is a little bit...well, more trouble than it should be thanks to its location on your camera body.

Or, you could go with something even better: trigger your shutter wirelessly by buying a wireless cable release (most cameras offer this as an accessory—check B&H Photo). They're either really inexpensive or more expensive than they should be, totally based on the make and model of your camera. Or, you actually already have a way to trigger your shutter wirelessly—if you bought your camera within the last few years—because you have built-in wireless capabilities. You can simply download a free app on your phone, which each camera manufacturer makes, that allows you to connect wirelessly to your camera. You can then focus, change settings, see a preview of what your camera is seeing, and of course, trigger your shutter and take the shot, all without you touching the camera—or having to buy either a wireless controller or a cable release. The whole thing works better than it sounds. The most important thing isn't which method you choose as long as you choose one of them.

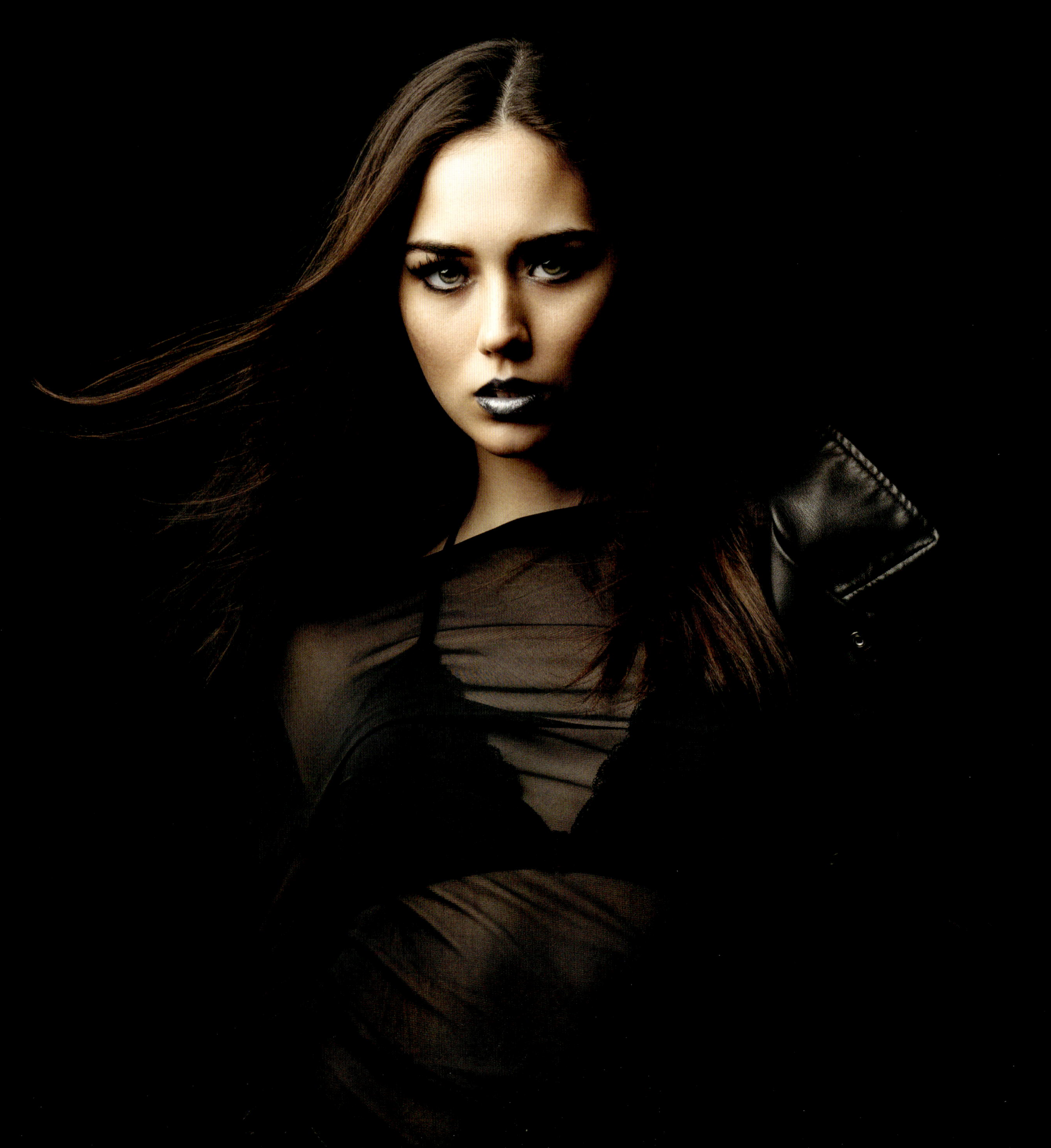

USE YOUR CAMERA'S BUILT-IN AI

I mentioned earlier that many of today's cameras have a bunch of focus modes for moving objects, especially for things like sports, or birds and wildlife, cars, aviation, and so on. But, there's a special focus mode that pretty much ensures your portraits or fashion shots will be super-sharp. When it comes to portraits the rule is: "If their eye isn't sharp, nothing's sharp." So, we always focus on the eye that's closest to the camera. For as long as I can remember, we've been using a focus technique called "focus and recompose." You put that center focus dot right over your subject's eye (whichever eye is closest to the camera, if they are turned a bit to the side), then you hold the shutter button down halfway to lock in that focus right on their eye, then you recompose the photo however you'd like (all while holding down the shutter button halfway), and then you fire the shot knowing the sharpness is going to be right on the money. Thankfully, we don't have to do all that anymore because we can now just turn on auto eye focus (or eye focus AI), which uses facial recognition to find their eye and lock focus on it automatically. So, no more holding the shutter button halfway down or having to focus and recompose. Just turn this on, and you'll see in the viewfinder that it automatically (nearly instantly) finds the eye and locks focus. Then, just take your shot knowing that your image's sharpness will be right on the money.

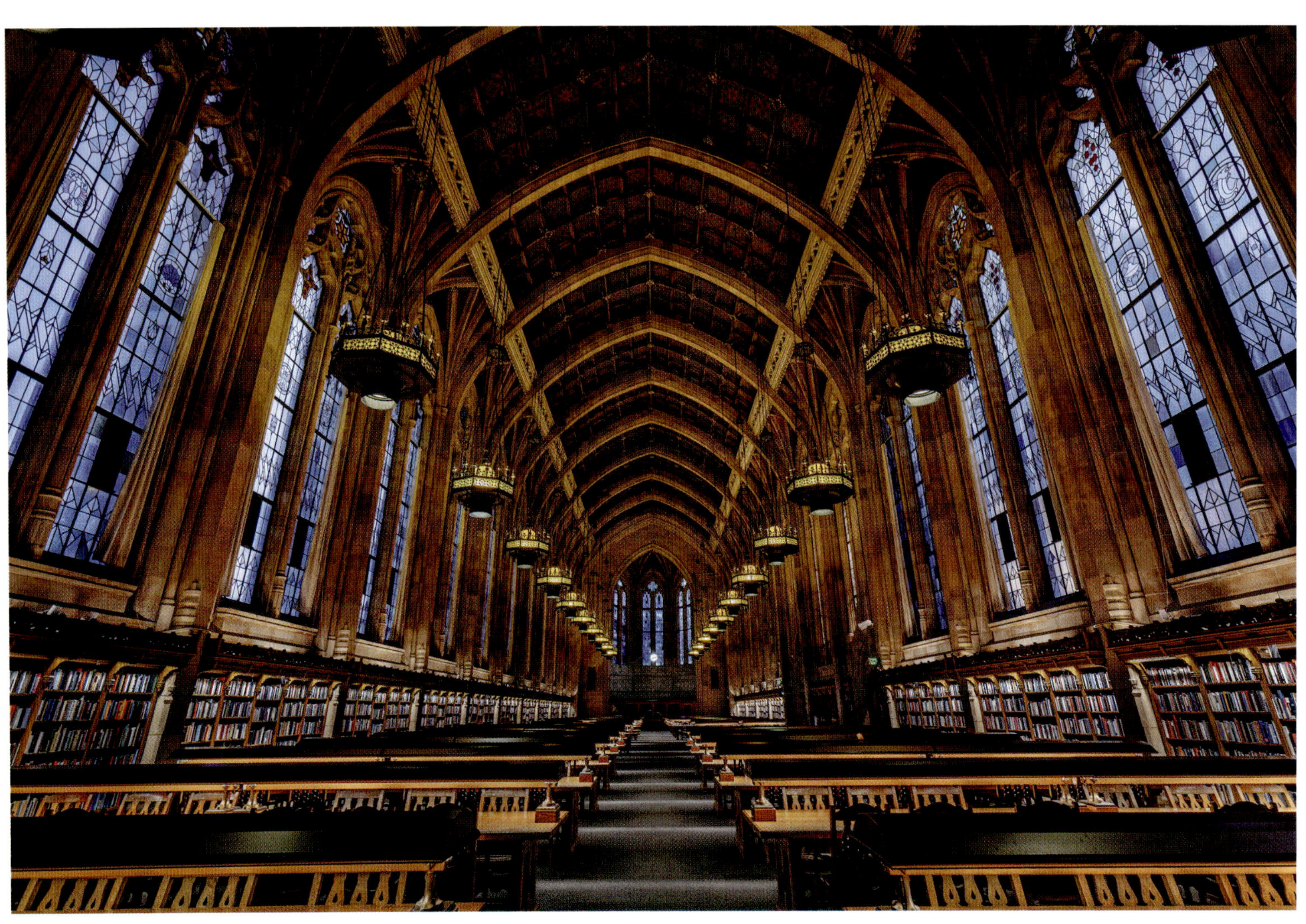

WORKING THE SHARPNESS ISN'T JUST ONE OF THESE THINGS

Once you get to that point in working the scene and it's time to start working the sharpness, chances are you're going to use a combination of these techniques to get the kind of sharpness we're all looking for. You just learned that the techniques are different depending on whether you're on a tripod or Platypod (those will be your hands-down, sharpest methods), or hand-holding (not quite as sharp as shooting on a tripod, in general, but in-studio using flash or strobes, or out shooting in bright daylight, your shots can still be super-sharp). But what you need to get that legendary sharpness is to have all of these techniques in your sharpness toolbox, and just know from the start these two things: (1) You are the one that's responsible for keeping your camera still while you're shooting—the more still your camera is, the sharper the shot. And, (2) every photo gets sharpened in post. Every. Single. One.

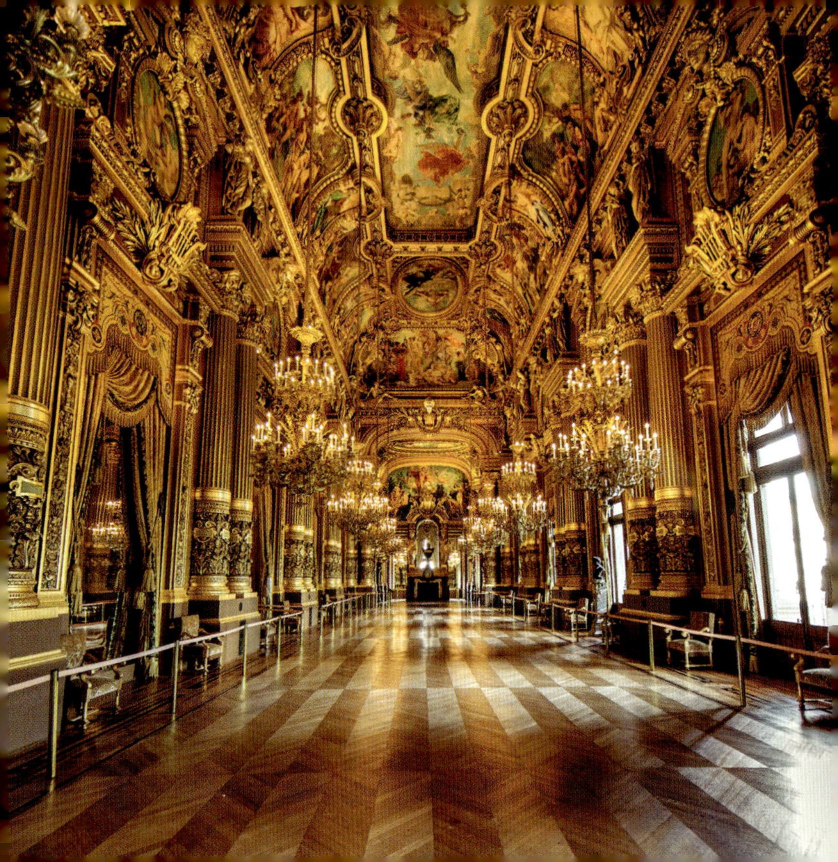

Chapter 05

WORK THE SETTINGS

Another part of "working the scene" is trying different settings to see if there's a setting that would help you build this composition. What if there were a setting that would take this scene you're working up a notch? That's what this chapter is about. We're going to look at which settings would make the biggest difference, when to try them, and why.

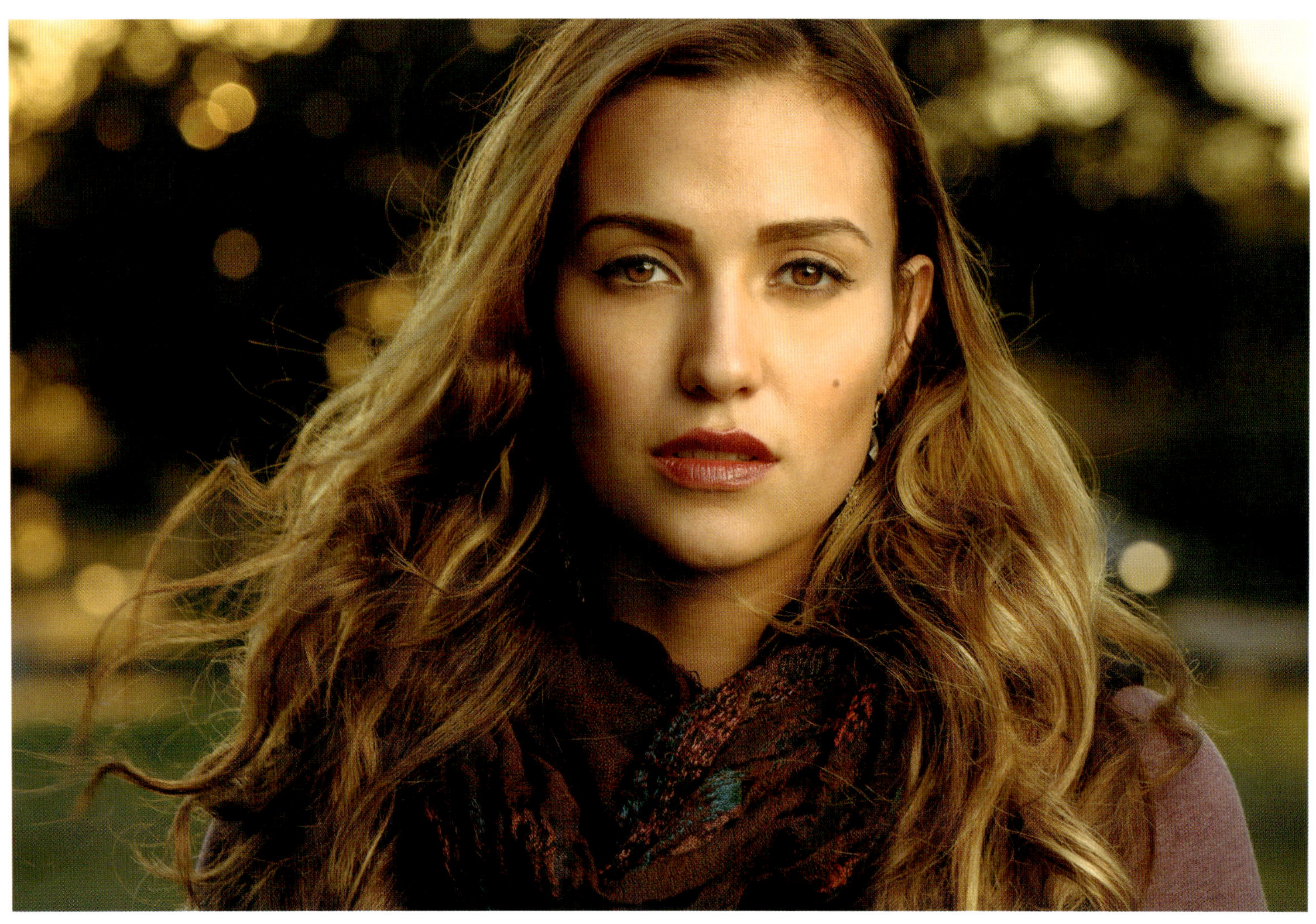

PUT THE BACKGROUND OUT OF FOCUS

One of the great advantages of this, composition-wise, is that by blurring the background, you're simplifying it, giving your subject separation from the background, which helps your subject stand out in the image (like with a flower, where a garden is behind it and it's out of focus, but you still get the overall sense of where it was taken). So, with that being said, would the image you're about to make look better if you put the background out of focus? Do you want to see the garden, just suggest it, or a little of both? If you decide you want to try it to see, there are three things you can do to really get that background nice and soft: (1) The first is a setting that helps, which is to use the lowest numbered f-stop your lens will allow.

That might be f/1.8, f/2.8, f/4, f/5.6—doesn't matter, just choose the lowest numbered f-stop you can. Then, (2) zoom in tight on your subject. You need a telephoto or zoom lens to do this (it won't work with a wide-angle, like a 24mm). You need a longer lens, but I feel this will be the biggest determining factor in how out of focus the background will be, so really get in there tight. The shot you see here was shot with a 70–200mm lens all the way in to 200mm. Lastly, (3) the farther the background is behind your subject, the blurrier it will be. If the background is too close, it won't be blurry enough, even with the right settings and a long lens. But, it's worth putting the background out of focus for a test shot to see if it helps your composition.

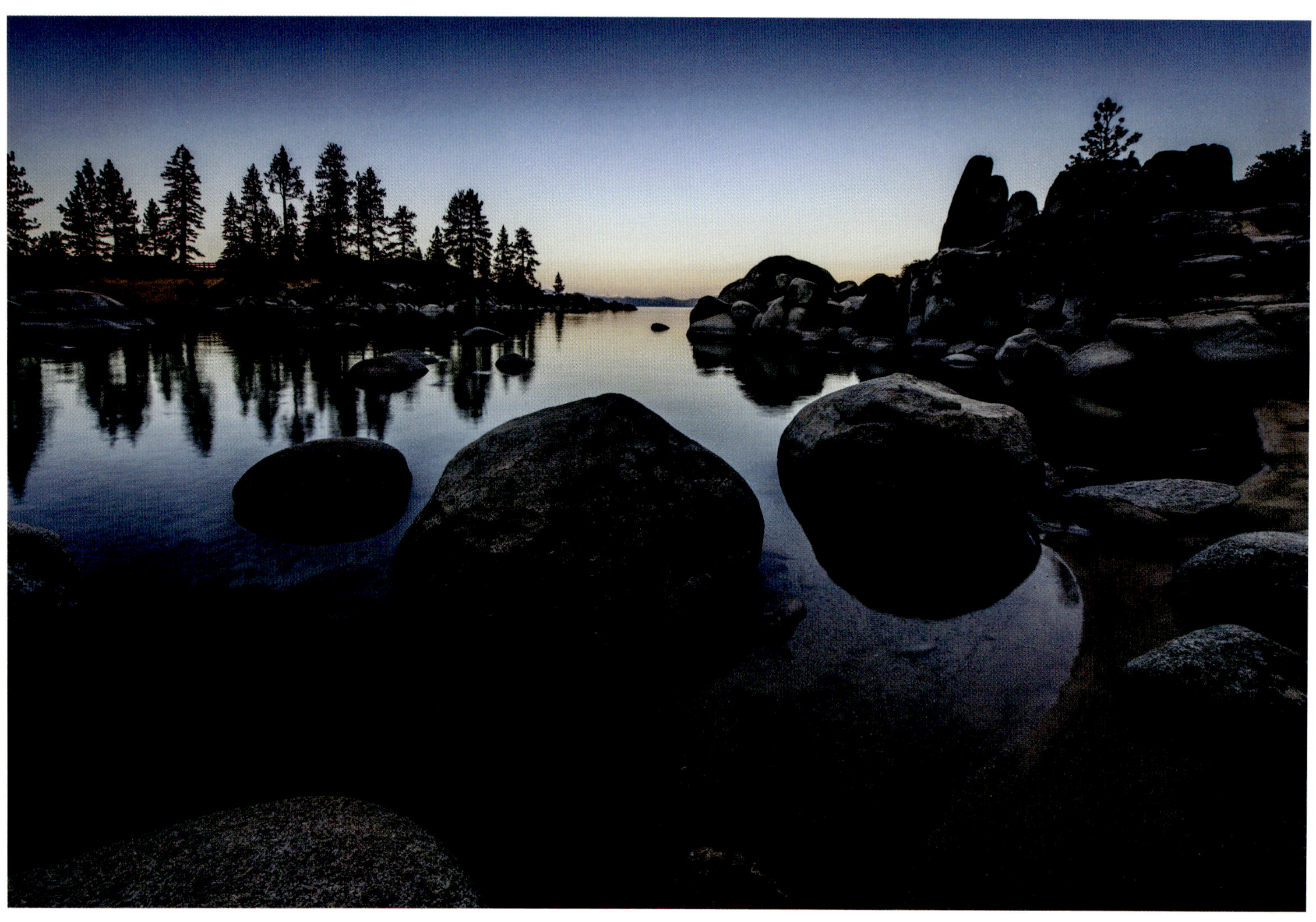

HOW ABOUT PUTTING EVERYTHING IN FOCUS?

There are times when putting the background out of focus makes sense, especially when you're shooting portraits or you have something important in your foreground that you want the viewer's full attention on (like that flower I mentioned earlier). But what if there are things in the distance that are important to the shot? Take the photo shown here of Lake Tahoe, Nevada. What if I put that large rock in the bottom center as the focal point for the image, and then I put the background out of focus? Now, granted that rock isn't a particularly appealing rock (it pretty much looks like the other rocks around it), and putting everything else out of focus might be awesome but it also might look weird (I would guess weird; I'm not certain). Put a dandelion right up front and that might work nicely, but in this case, without anything remarkable about that rock, I think it works better with everything in focus. If you don't try both, you won't know for sure. How much does it cost to try? Nuthin' That's a pretty good price.

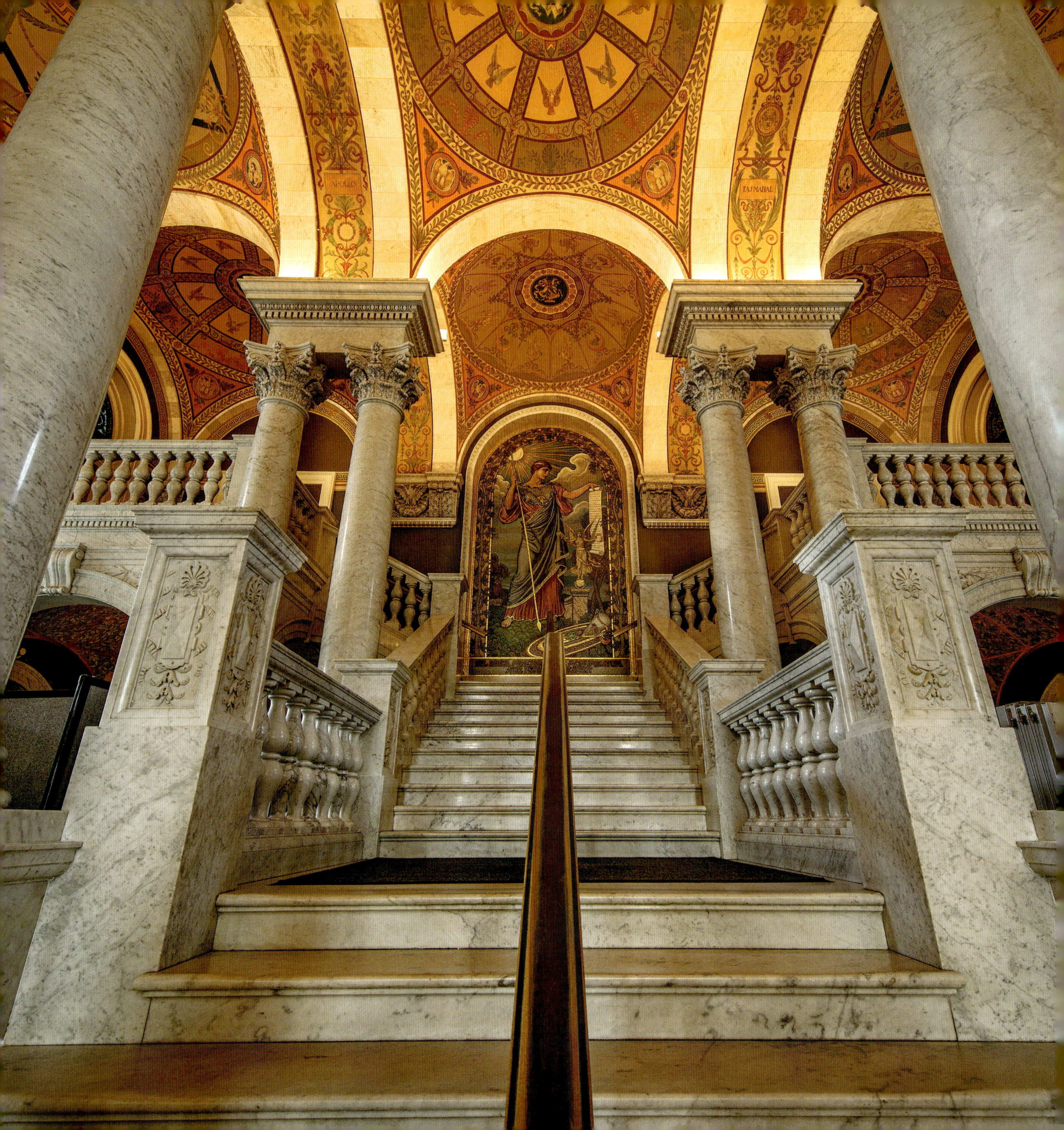

SHOULD IT BE
AN HDR IMAGE?

If the light varies a lot within the scene you're shooting—
maybe parts are a bit in the shadows and other parts are
bright (like in a cathedral, or palace, or like in this shot taken
in the lobby of the Library of Congress in Washington, DC)—
it might make sense to shoot the image as an HDR, knowing
that capturing multiple exposures of the same shot and having
Lightroom or Photoshop combine them into a single image
for you might really make sense. Plus, there's the hidden bonus
that when shooting HDR images like this, it pretty dramatically
lowers the noise once you combine them into that single HDR
image. To create an HDR image, all you have to do is turn on
Exposure Bracketing in your camera so that it shoots one shot
with a normal exposure, one shot that's two stops brighter,
and one shot that's two stops darker—so three shots in all.
(*Note:* Depending on your camera's make and model, when
you turn on Exposure Bracketing, it might take five shots with
one that's one stop brighter and one that's one stop darker,
but you'll only combine the shots that are two stops brighter,
two stops darker, and the normal exposure into one photo.
Well, heck you could use all five, but it'll just take longer and
won't look any different, so it's up to you. But, I will tell you this:
you can't make a real HDR image if you don't shoot it that way
from the start, so it might be worth "working this setting.")
There's another bracketing advantage on the next page.

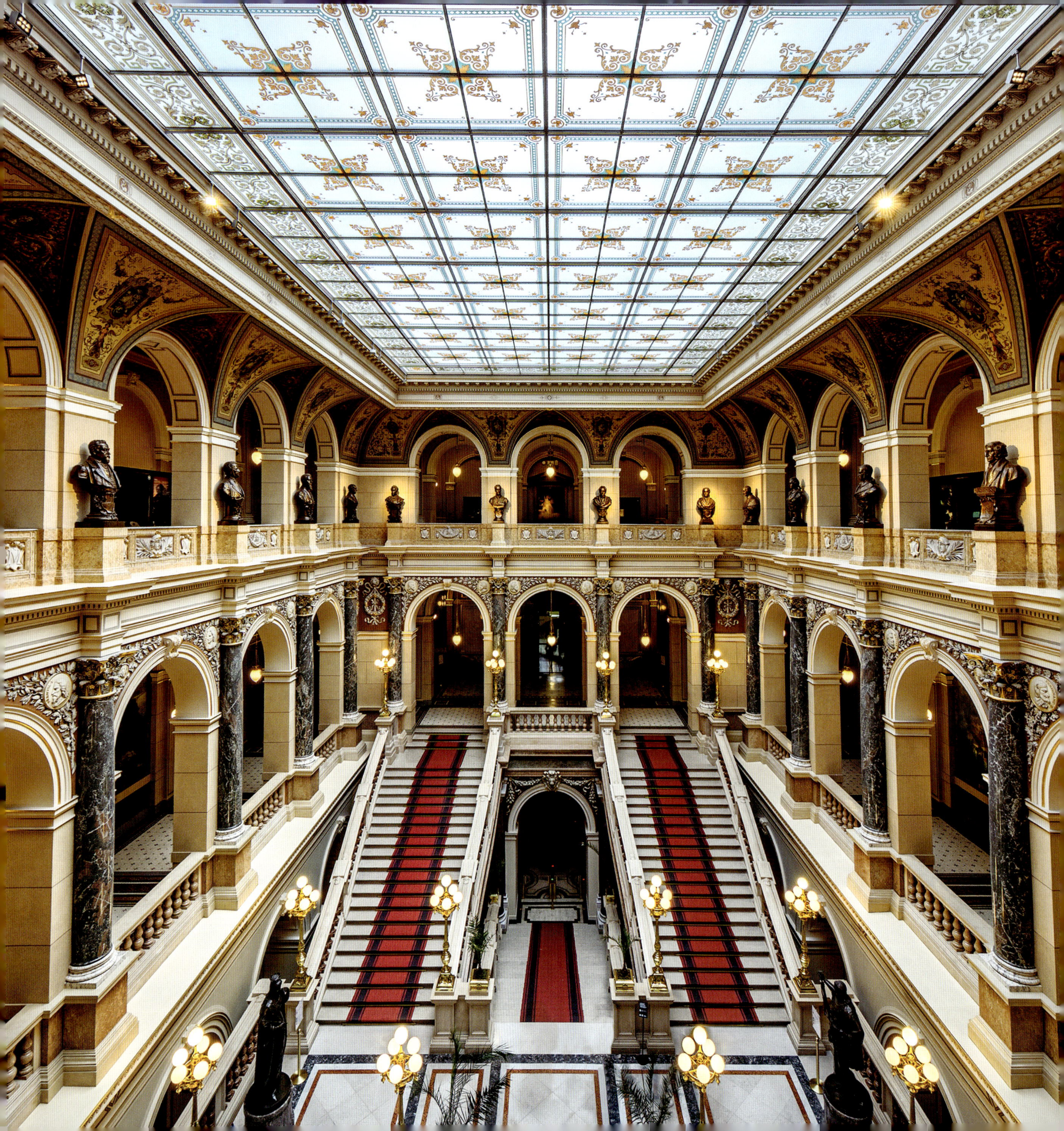

WHY YOU MIGHT WANT TO SHOOT BRACKETED

This is another thing I learned from living legend of photography Jay Maisel. He shoots bracketed a lot, but not so he can make HDR images. He shoots bracketed so that when he brings his images into Lightroom to look at them, and he sees the thumbnails of those three images side by side, he can immediately see if the image he took looks better darker, brighter, or at the exposure he took it at. He's using this strictly as a creative tool, which is pretty cool when you think about it. Now, couldn't he just select an image, make a virtual copy and darken it by two stops, and then make another virtual copy and brighten it by two stops? Yup. Or he could just turn on Exposure Bracketing in his camera and have it all already done as soon as the images come into Lightroom. Just another great case for Exposure Bracketing. By the way, the image you see here (taken at Prague's National Museum) was shot with Exposure Bracketing (two stops apart), and then it was combined into one HDR image in Lightroom. I knew I needed to shoot bracketed here when I saw the bright light coming in from the ceiling and the darker areas throughout the rest of the image. With an HDR image, which has a greater overall tonal range than a single image, I can bring all that detail out in post and open up the shadows without worrying about adding a bunch of noise. Just a little side note there.

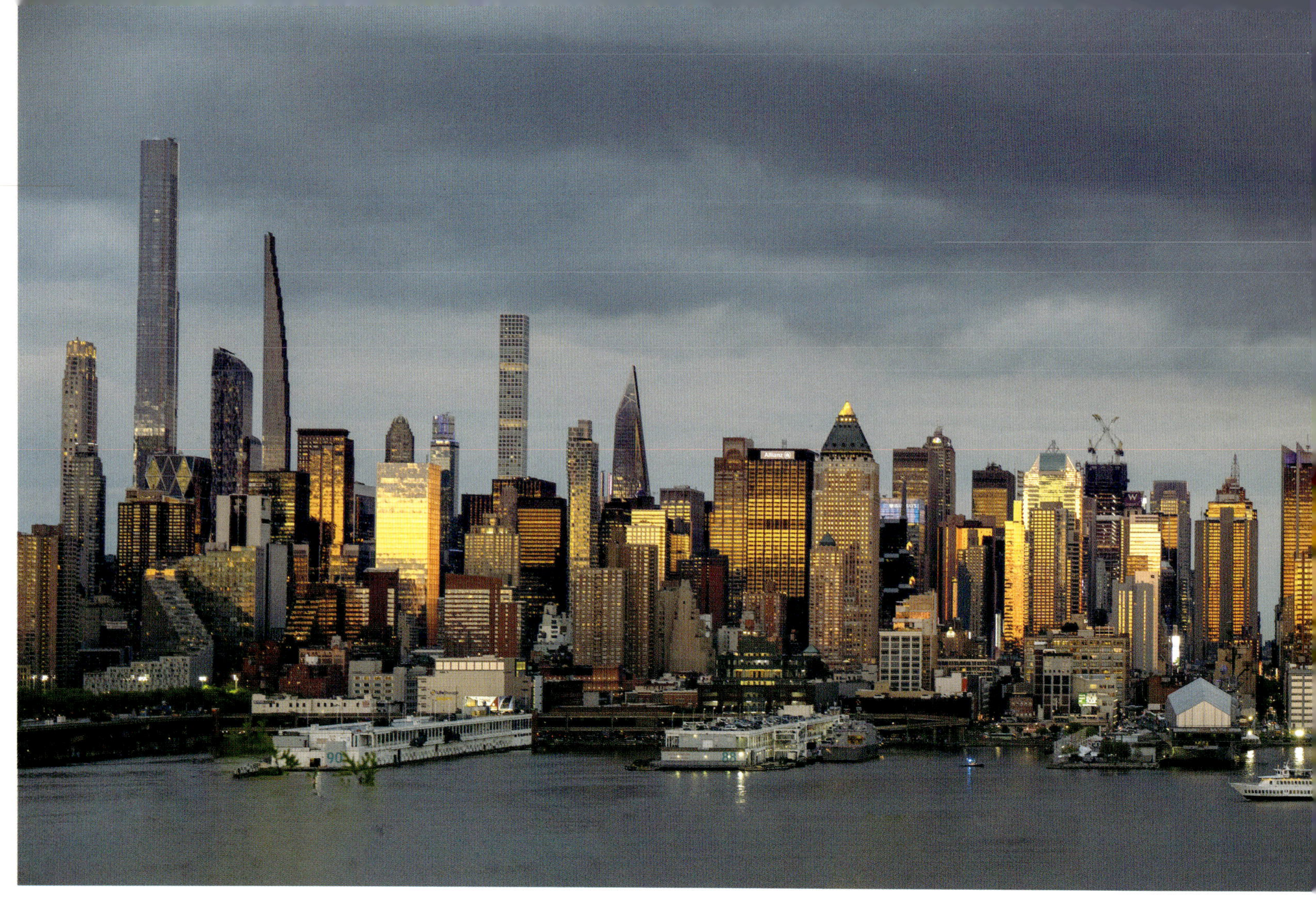

WOULD IT WORK AS A PANO?

When you're working your settings, ask yourself if the scene you're standing in front of might make a great panoramic image. Panos have impact and they've never been easier to make (just shoot going from left to right and overlap each frame by about 30%. That way, Lightroom or Photoshop will easily be able to stitch the images together for you). One tip on making panos: Don't make too wide a pano. The trick is to just use three or four frames (even two-frame panos can look great) because very long, thin panos look really small when you share them online. So, in this case, less is more. Also, if you're uncomfortable with shooting and stitching panos, don't worry—your phone isn't (you can easily shoot a pano with your phone's camera and it will stitch it together automatically). Add this to your mental checklist of options when you're composing your shot, and it's one more thing that will set your images apart.

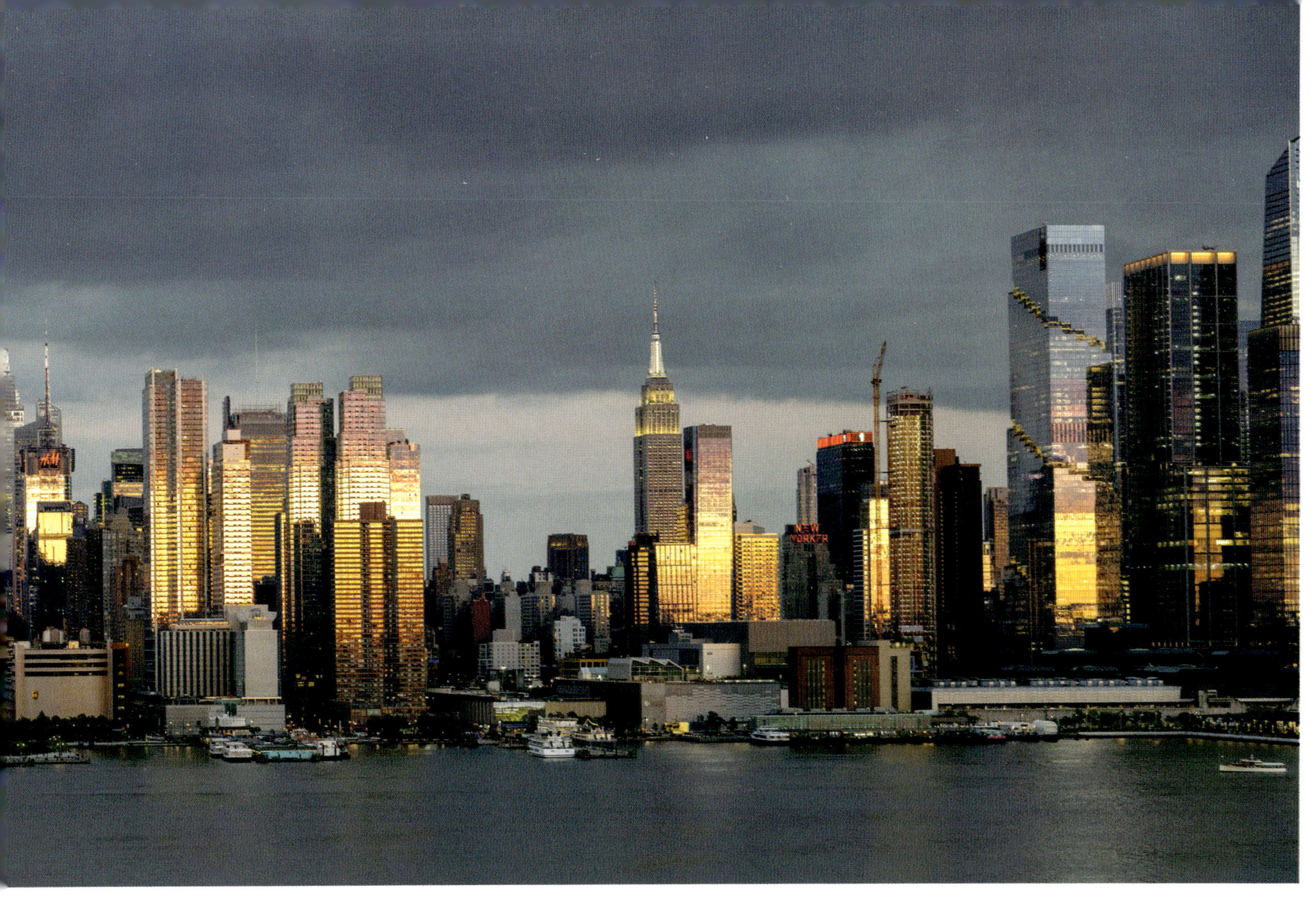

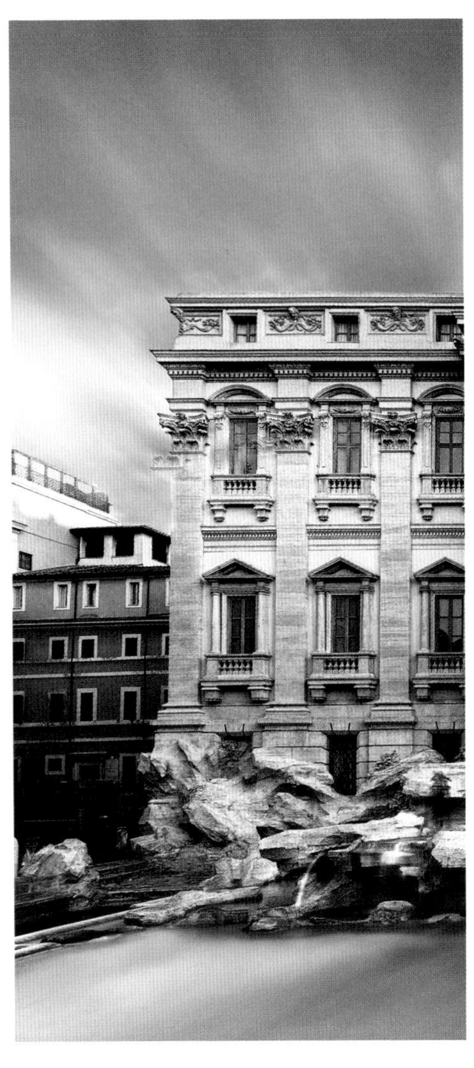
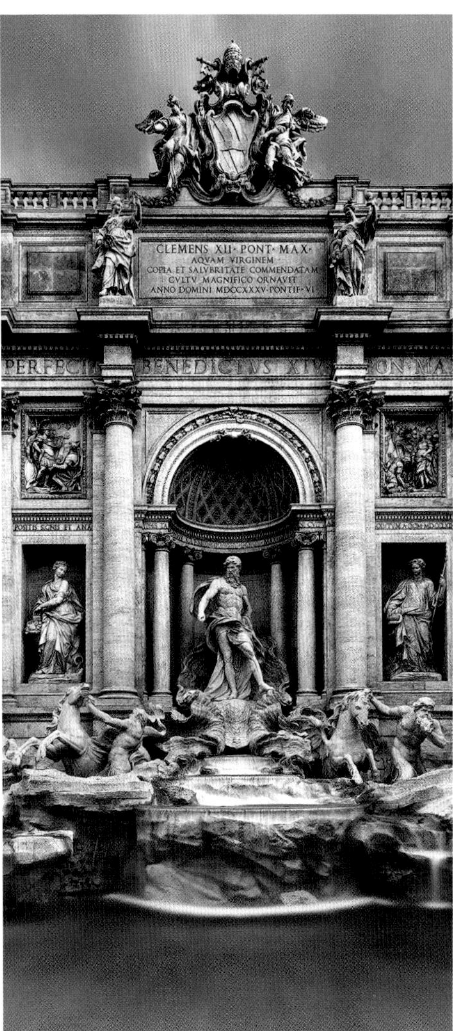

CLEMENS XII · PONT · MAX ·
AQVAM VIRGINEM
COPIA ET SALVBRITATE COMMENDATAM
CVLTV MAGNIFICO ORNAVIT
ANNO DOMINI MDCCXXXV · PONTIF · VI
PERFECIT BENEDICTVS XIV PON MA

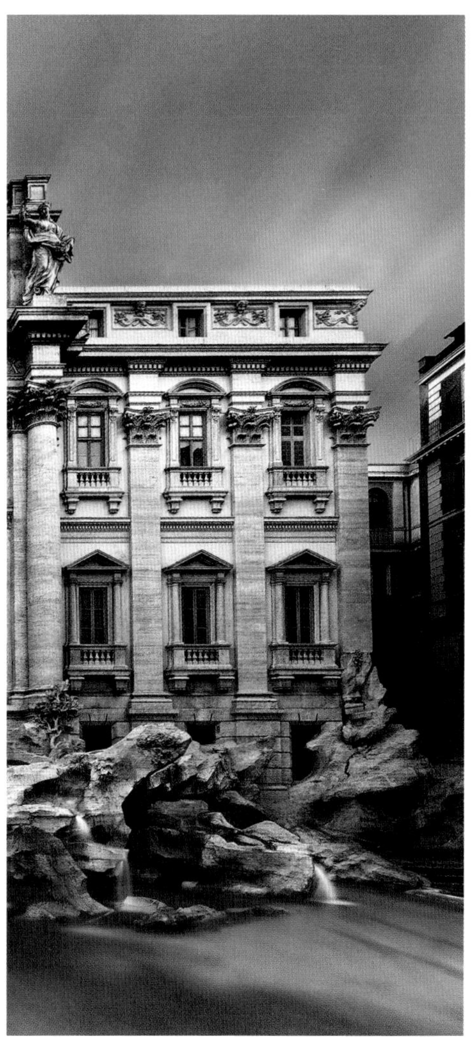

A TRIPTYCH MIGHT WORK EVEN BETTER

A triptych is when you shoot one wide shot (or three tall shots) and divide it into tall thirds (like you see here with this shot of Rome's famous Trevi Fountain), and is something you can add to your compositional (and presentation) toolkit. These look fantastic on the wall (triptychs look great printed on canvas), and you'll be surprised at the reaction you'll get from people seeing them in person (they react much differently than they do to a single image). You can also just create one and share it any way you like (like I did here on a printed page, and it's just as easy to share it on social media). It's really easy to take one image and divide it into thirds in Photoshop (go under the View menu, under Guides, and choose New Guide Layout. In the dialog that appears, type in "3" in the Columns Number field and it puts guides in place with your image divided into thirds, with a small space between them. You can then select each third and copy-and-paste each one into its own separate document). Also, some photo labs will create a triptych for you if you send them the single image. Either way, it's something else to consider, and to compose for if you see a scene in front of you that you think might look good as a triptych.

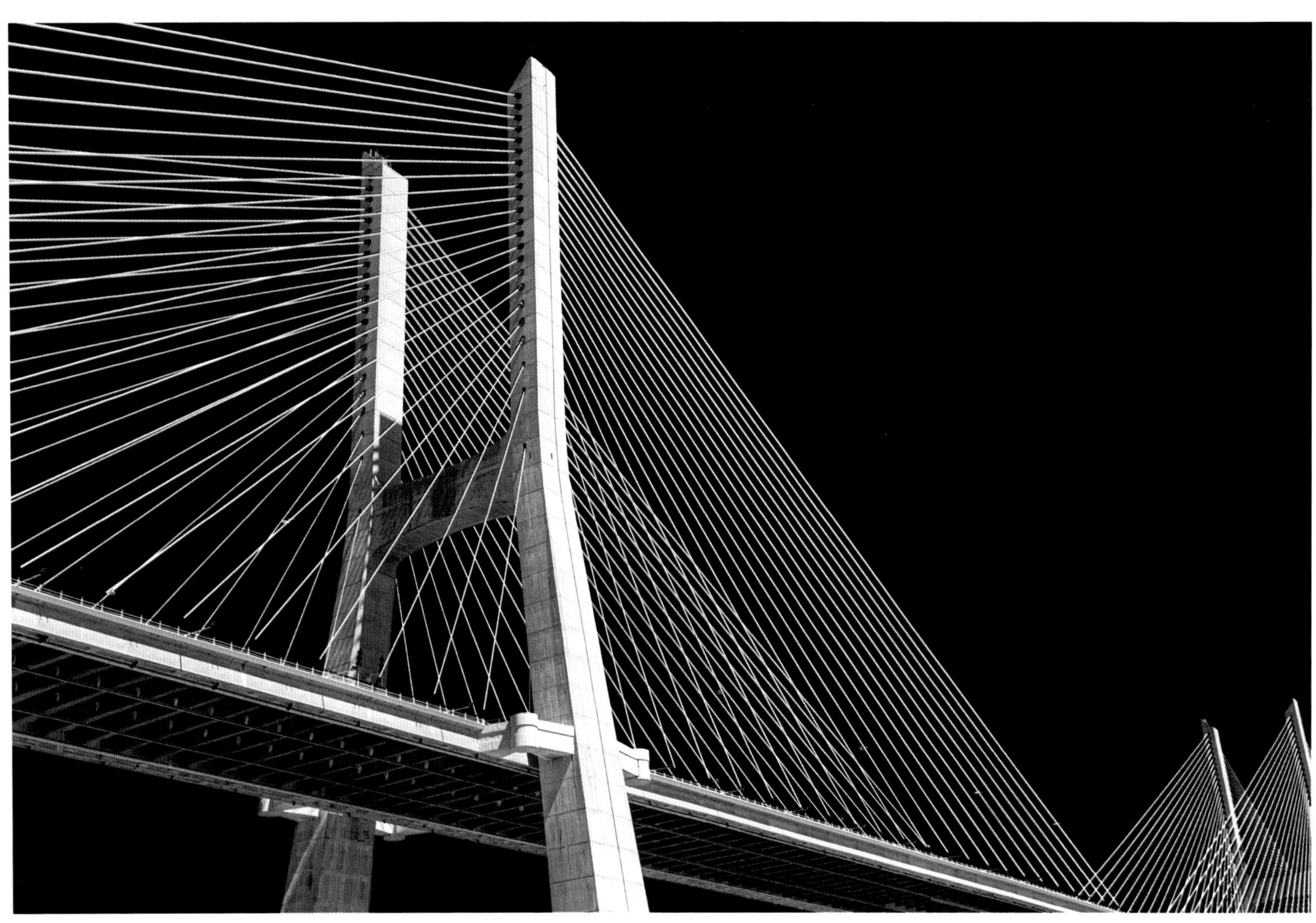

HOW TO VISUALIZE BLACK & WHITE

There are images that when you're shooting them you just know—I'm going to convert this to black and white. But then there are times where you're just not sure, which is why you might want to try changing this one setting: most mirrorless and DSLR cameras have a black-and-white shooting mode, and once you turn it on, all your shots will appear in black and white on the LCD on the back of your camera. This is a fantastic tool to help you visualize how the scene in front of you would look in black and white. I use this as a tool when I'm about to shoot, for visualization only, but once I start to shoot, I switch back to shooting in full color. Why? Because when you shoot in color, you have a lot more flexibility in Lightroom or Photoshop when it comes to how your black-and-white conversion will look. If it's already black and white from the start, well…it's already black and white. The conversion is done. So, I prefer to shoot in color, and then have the option to convert to black and white. But, it's nice to know that I can change one setting and take some test shots to get a decent idea of what they're going to look like when they're converted.

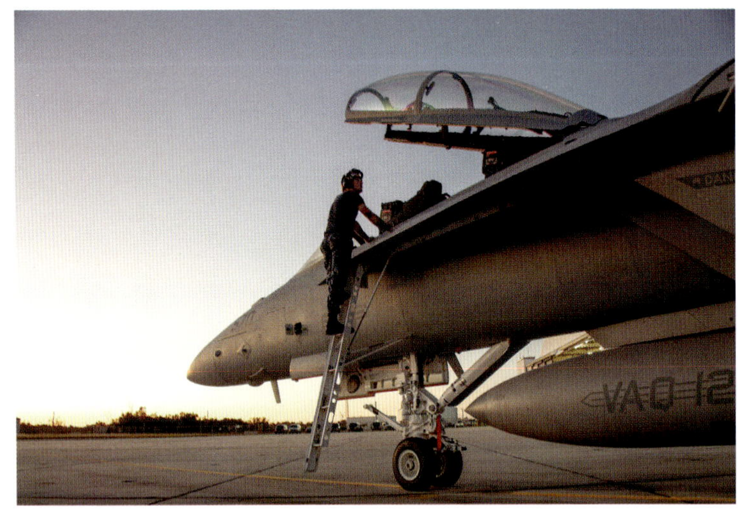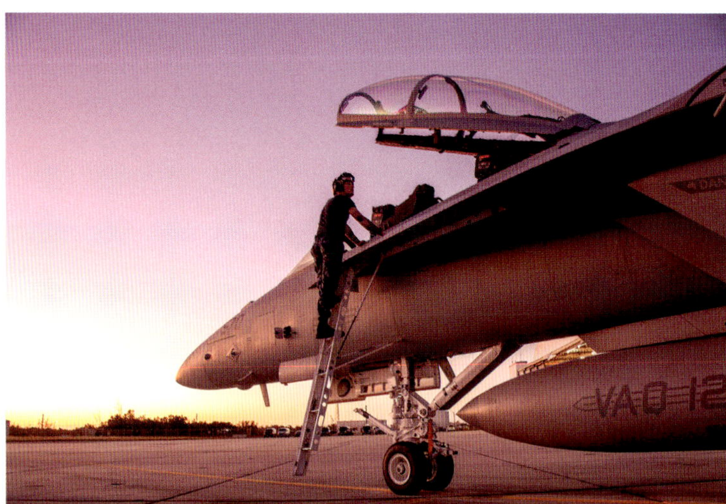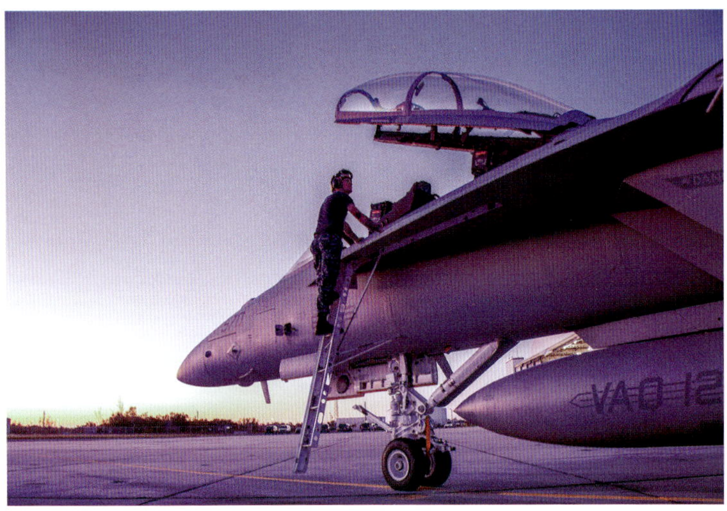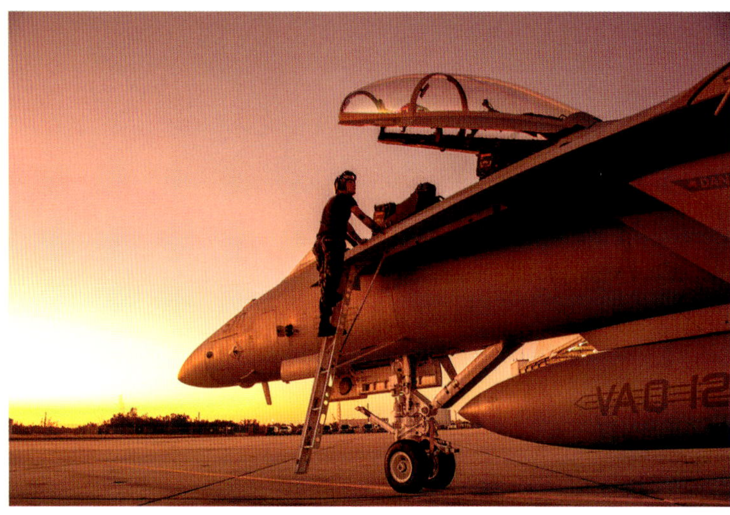

TRY DIFFERENT
WHITE BALANCE SETTINGS

I feel there are two types of white balance: (1) An accurate white balance, where what you're seeing in the image is accurate to what it looked like when you were standing at the scene. There are times where this is really important, like when you're doing portraits (although most people look better with a slightly warmer white balance, which is why if you go to an online camera store, you'll see white balance gray cards, and you'll also see what are called "warm cards," which are for wedding and portrait shoots). Or, when you're shooting for news (journalism), where capturing what the scene really looked like color-wise is important to the news story you're covering. Then, there's (2) artistic white balance, which is

what I do. Artistic white balance is where you're going to choose the white balance that looks good to you even if it's nowhere near what the actual color of the scene was. I'm showing an example of that here with a US Navy jet parked on the ramp down at Naval Air Station Key West. The top-left shot is the actual white balance as it appeared at the time; the rest are my artistic white balance choices. You can try different white balance settings right in your camera, using the presets in the white balance menu, or by adjusting the Kelvin setting (the amount of color from warm to cool), or of course, you can change the white balance afterward in post. But, if you're not a journalist, this opens up a world of new possibilities.

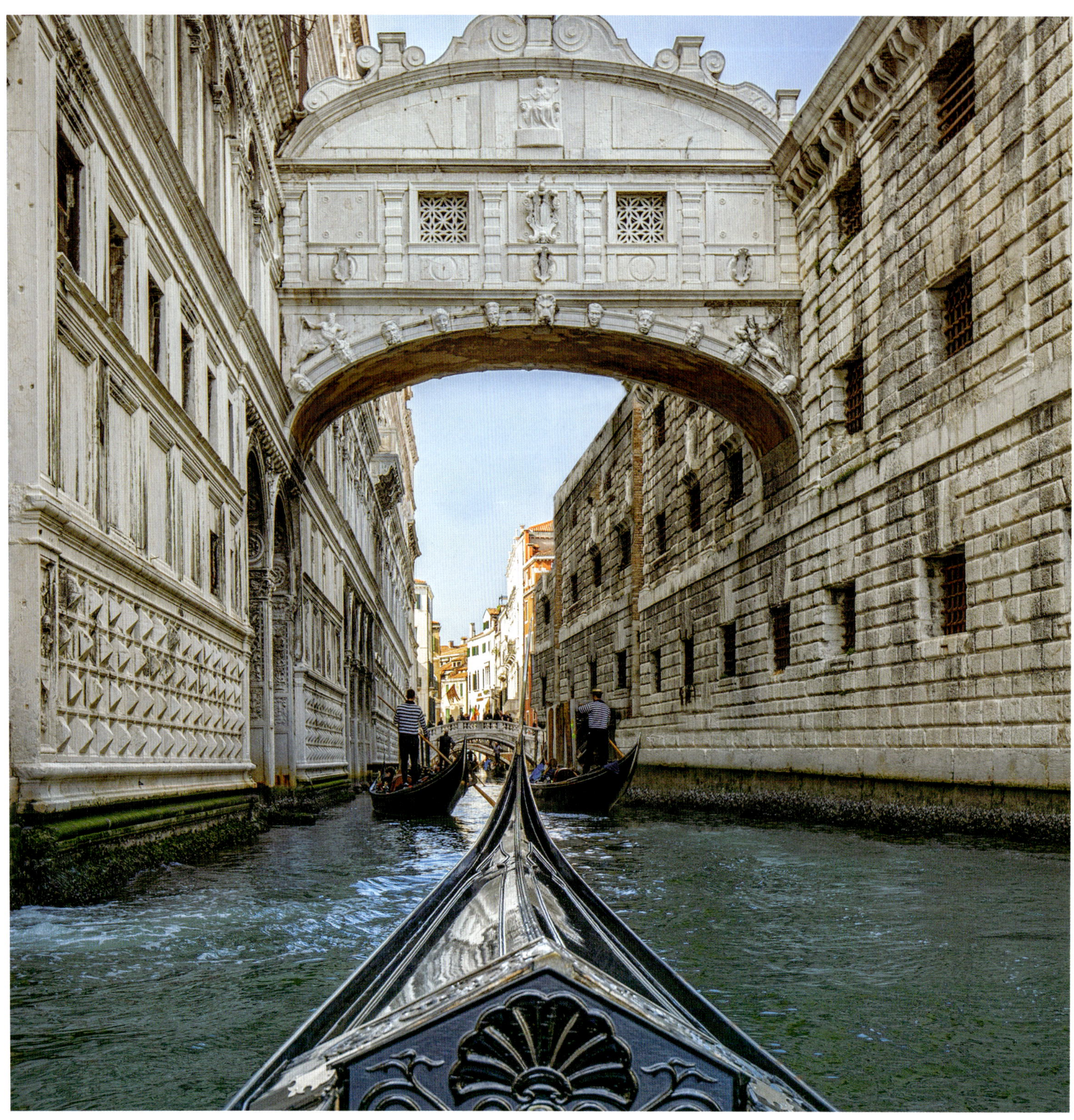

DOES GETTING IT RIGHT IN-CAMERA MATTER?

You hear a lot of people talking (okay, bragging) about how they always get everything right "in the camera." I get asked this question a lot, and by getting it right "in the camera," they mean the shot that comes out of their camera has the proper exposure, proper white balance, etc. So, the image they show you as their final image is pretty much what they took in the camera from the start. They might add some sharpening in post, but essentially, they "got it right in-camera." I like to get as much as possible right in-camera as I can because (a) it makes my life easier when I get to Lightroom or Photoshop. Since I'm not fixing problems as much, now I have time to experiment and be creative. But, I think it's really helpful to get your color and exposure right (or visualize it in black and white, like I mentioned earlier) for an even more important reason: (b) If I really like what I'm seeing on the back of my camera, I get excited and I get inspired, and it pushes me to keep working the scene because I can see I'm getting something. If I look at the back of my camera and the color is way off, I know that while, yes, I can fix it later in post, that doesn't inspire me. It doesn't push me. It doesn't excite me. So, I go to the white balance menu, I choose the white balance preset that best matches the lighting conditions I'm shooting in, and now I'm seeing something that makes me want to keep shooting. So, yes, I do think for those reasons it's worth the few extra seconds of getting the right settings to get the image looking good on the back of my camera. If I see images looking good back there now, it probably means they're going to look better and better as I keep working the scene. That's why working the right settings now can pay off later.

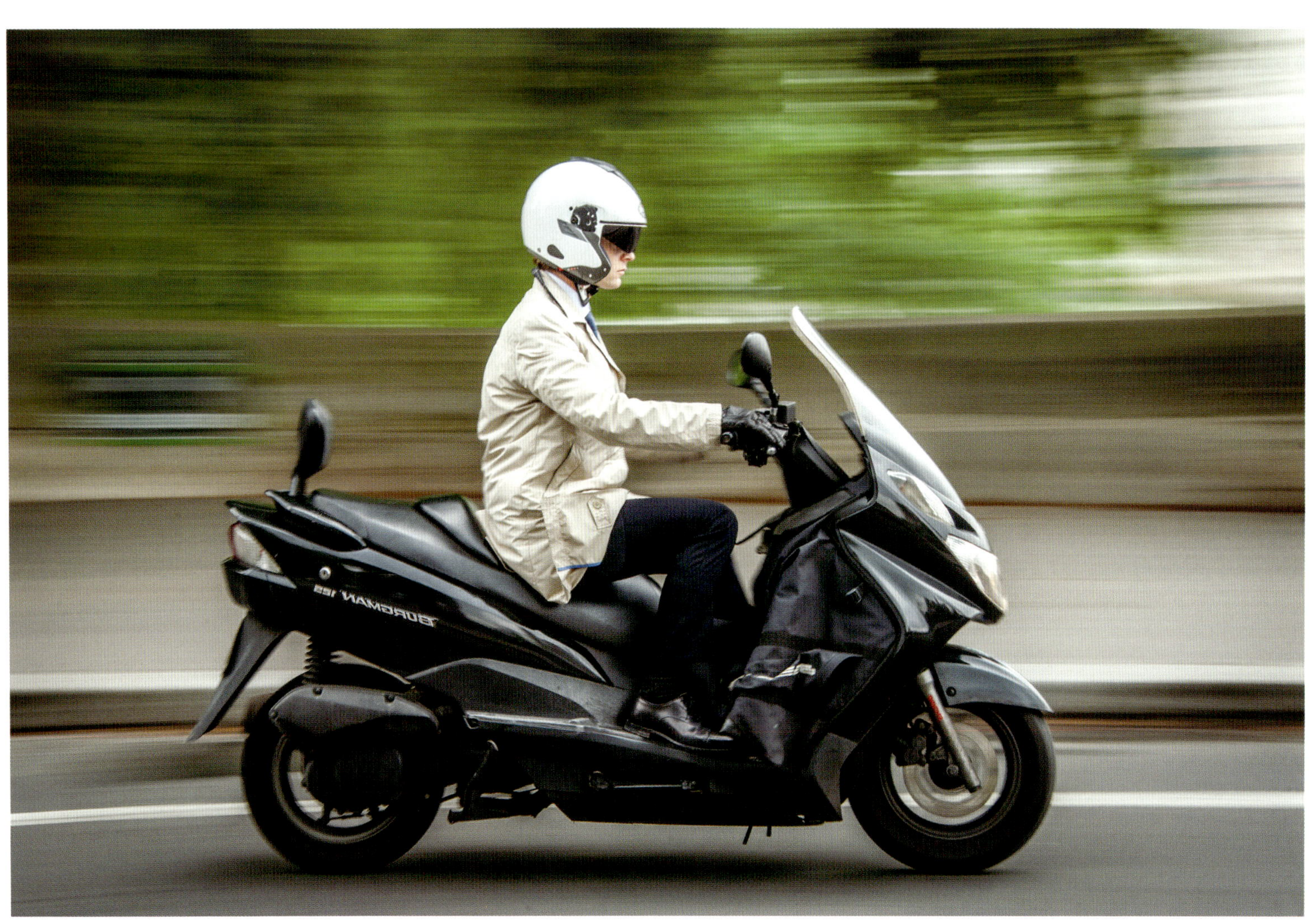

ADD MOTION

This is one of the most effective ways to bring life to a photo because adding a sense of motion to your image (by slowing your shutter speed) adds an energy that's hard to get any other way. Showing motion like this ranges from being absolutely simple (if you have the right accessory) to a method that takes a little bit of practice, and trial and error, which is why so few people do it and why your images will stand out more when you do. The first method (the super-easy one) just requires one accessory: a tripod. Your camera has to be absolutely still for the first part of this method, so once you put your camera on a tripod, the other part is simple. Just switch your camera to shoot in Shutter Priority mode (usually, the letter "S" on your camera's mode dial), then choose a slow shutter speed like 1 second or even longer, and anyone that walks by the scene (great in train stations or busy streets) will have a blurry motion to them. The slower you make the shutter, the more blur and movement, so experiment (with 3 seconds, and 1/15 of a second, for example) to see which one you like best. The second method is harder: it's where you pan with the subject (you move your camera to follow along with the subject like you're tracking them). But while you're doing this, you're trying to keep your camera as still and level as possible. It takes some practice, and even then, you'll wind up with a lot of blurry shots. If you shoot a burst of 30 shots while you're panning, expect that around 28 of them will be unusable. But, one or two will probably be right on the money, with your subject in focus. Like the guy and scooter here—the wheels are spinning and there's background motion and the image has that energy. Now, did I have a bunch of shots in this series of the scooter guy that were out of focus? Yes. A ton! It was pretty brutal. But, I got that one, and that's all I needed—just one sharp, in-focus shot. As you practice panning, you'll get more and more shots in focus, but since you're using a slow shutter speed, don't expect a whole bunch. That's okay. It's all part of the process, and now you have yet another setting you can use to work your settings.

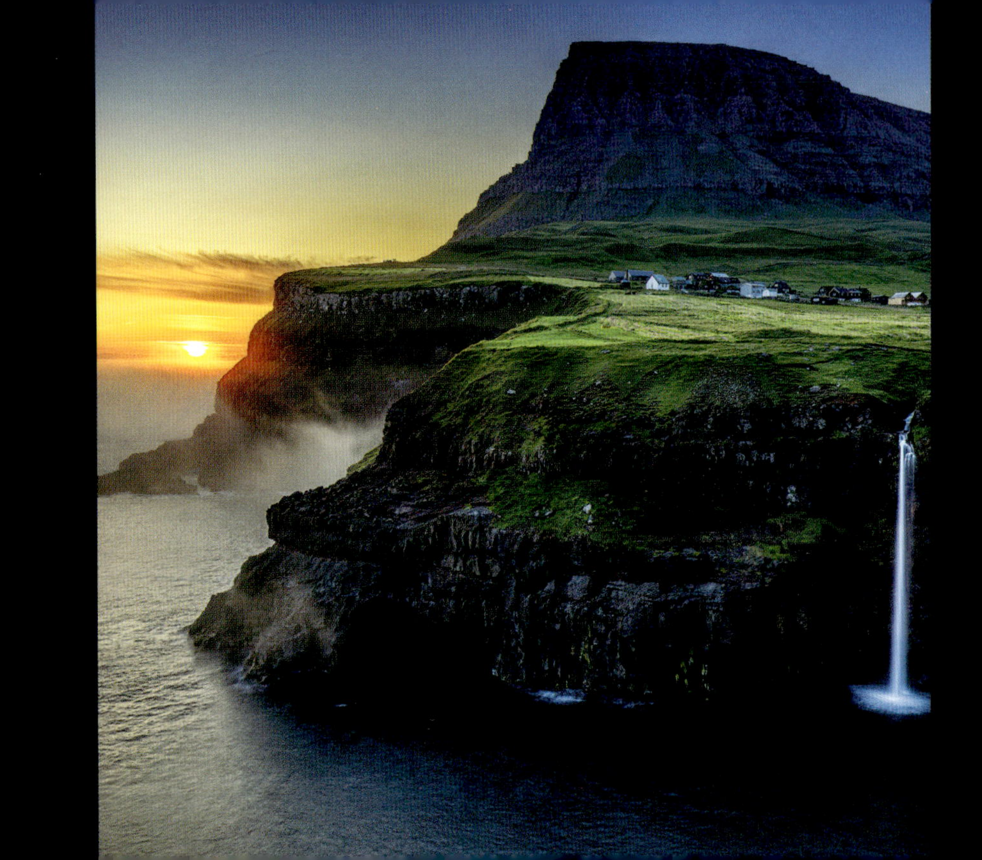

Chapter 06

ADD DEPTH TO YOUR COMPOSITION

This question gets asked a lot: "How do I add more depth to my images?" We want images that draw our viewer into the scene or portrait and really captivate them. We want them to do more than give our image a quick glance. We want them to engage with the image and one of the best ways I know how to do this is to add depth to the image. A lot of images can look "flat," but when you compose the image to have lots of depth, it can give it that soaring, epic, expansive feel that almost makes a 2D image feel like it's 3D—like the viewer can walk right into the image. That's what this chapter is about—how to add that depth through composition techniques. Once you start using these techniques, you'll see an immediate difference, and so will those viewing your images and getting drawn into them.

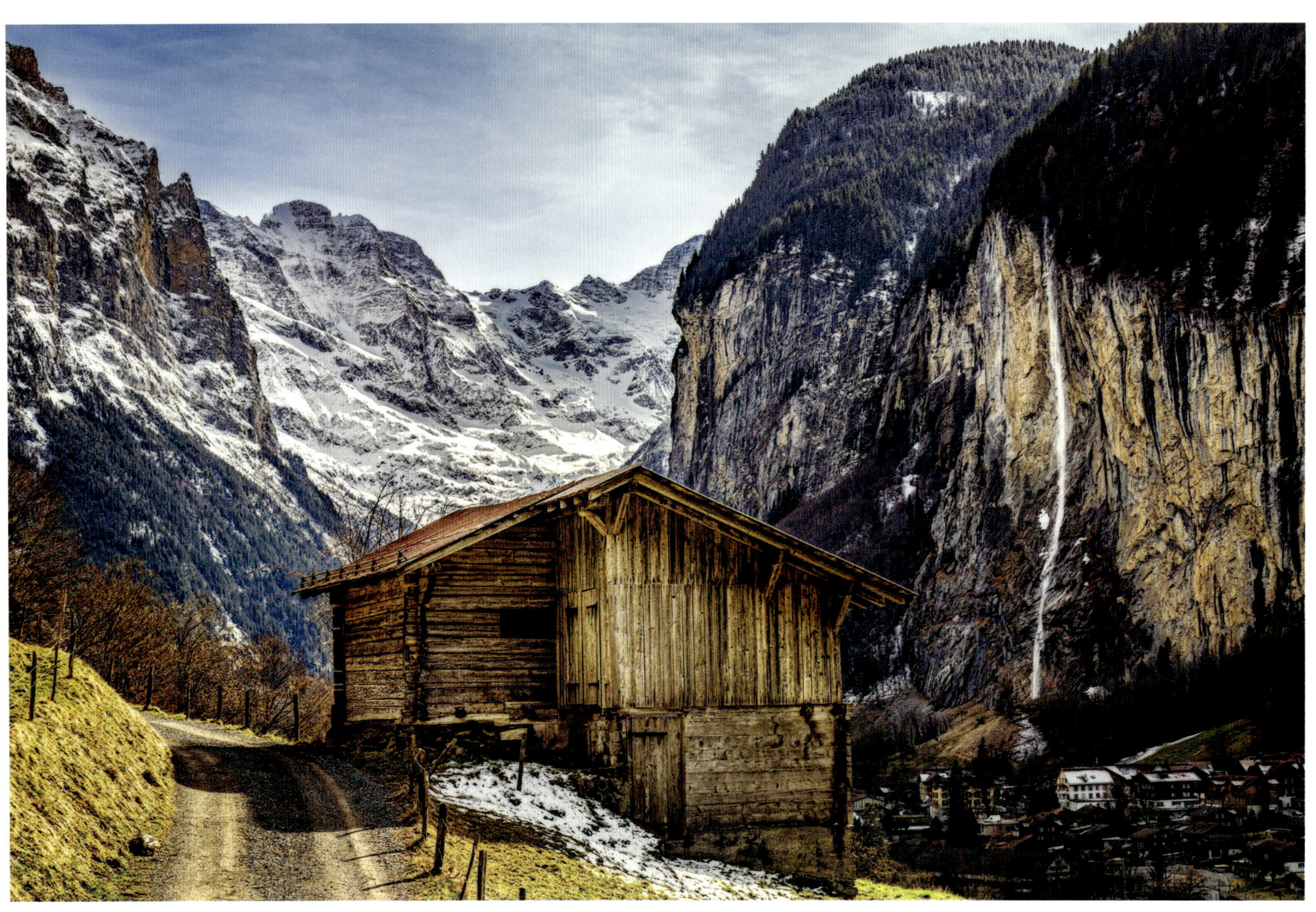

ADD LAYERS TO YOUR COMPOSITION

This is one of the most powerful techniques for adding depth and dimension to your image because you're going to create layers within your image with some things right in front, some things in the middle, some things in the background, and the sky behind it all. This stacking of elements in your image is a can't-miss way to create depth. Take a look at the image here. It has a foreground element: the little cabin (I'm guessing it's a cabin. Could be a storage shed. Doesn't matter, it's our foreground element). Behind it, in the middle ground of the image is the small village of Lauterbrunnen, Switzerland, and the waterfall coming off the closest mountain. Now, go further into the image into the background and you have the snow-covered mountains, and behind that you have a sky. This is an example of an image with layers: foreground, middle ground, background, sky behind them. That's why it feels big and expansive—it has one layer stacked in front of another. Take the cabin in front out and it loses some of its depth. You could almost count the village as another layer, so then it goes cabin and road in front, village, then waterfall and mountain behind it, other mountains, and then the sky. That's a lot of depth, and this is the type of thing we're looking for when we're composing to create depth. Look to create layers from the very start.

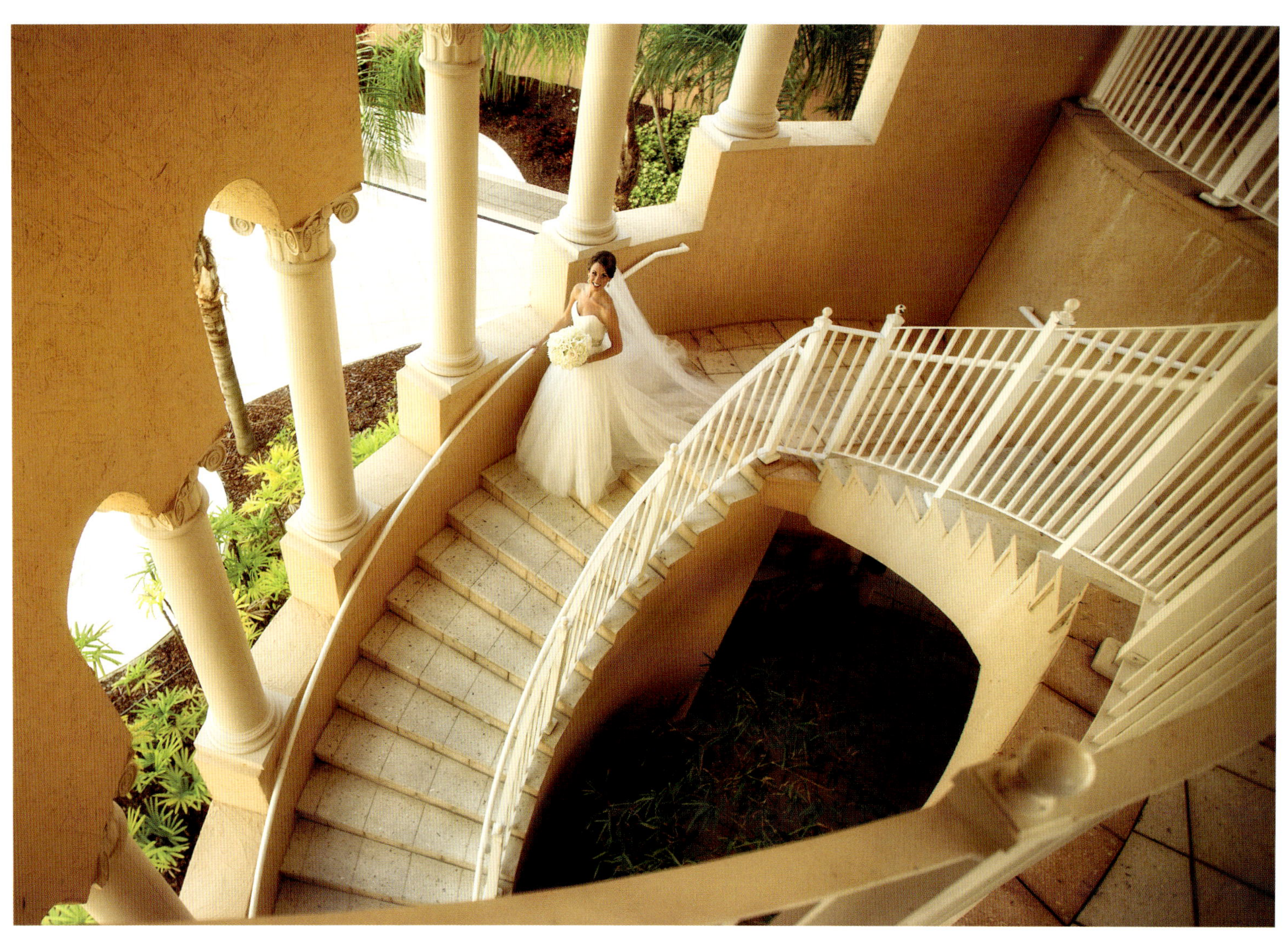

USE A WIDE-ANGLE LENS

This one is almost cheating because the very nature of a wide-angle lens is that it takes in more, making the scene look bigger, wider, and more epic. So, when we're trying to create depth, this is the lens to reach for. Take a look at the image of the bride here. She is only like a dozen steps down from where I'm shooting—just a short way away—but I'm using a super-wide-angle 16mm lens on a full-frame camera, and it makes the scene look much bigger and much more epic than it really is. It looks like she's much farther away, and like I'm up really high, but I'm just standing there at the railing looking down, just steps away. The scene looks so much bigger than it did when I was standing there, and that's the magic of a super-wide-angle lens. I mentioned earlier in the book that wide-angles push the scene away from you, and when you're trying to create depth, that's a big advantage. Also, notice the layers. I included the railing in the foreground to help create them within the image. The bride on the stairs is in the middle ground, and behind her are columns that help create more depth, and behind them is the background area. So, now you're combining two compositional techniques for creating depth: a wide-angle lens to make the scene bigger and the layers technique you learned on the previous page.

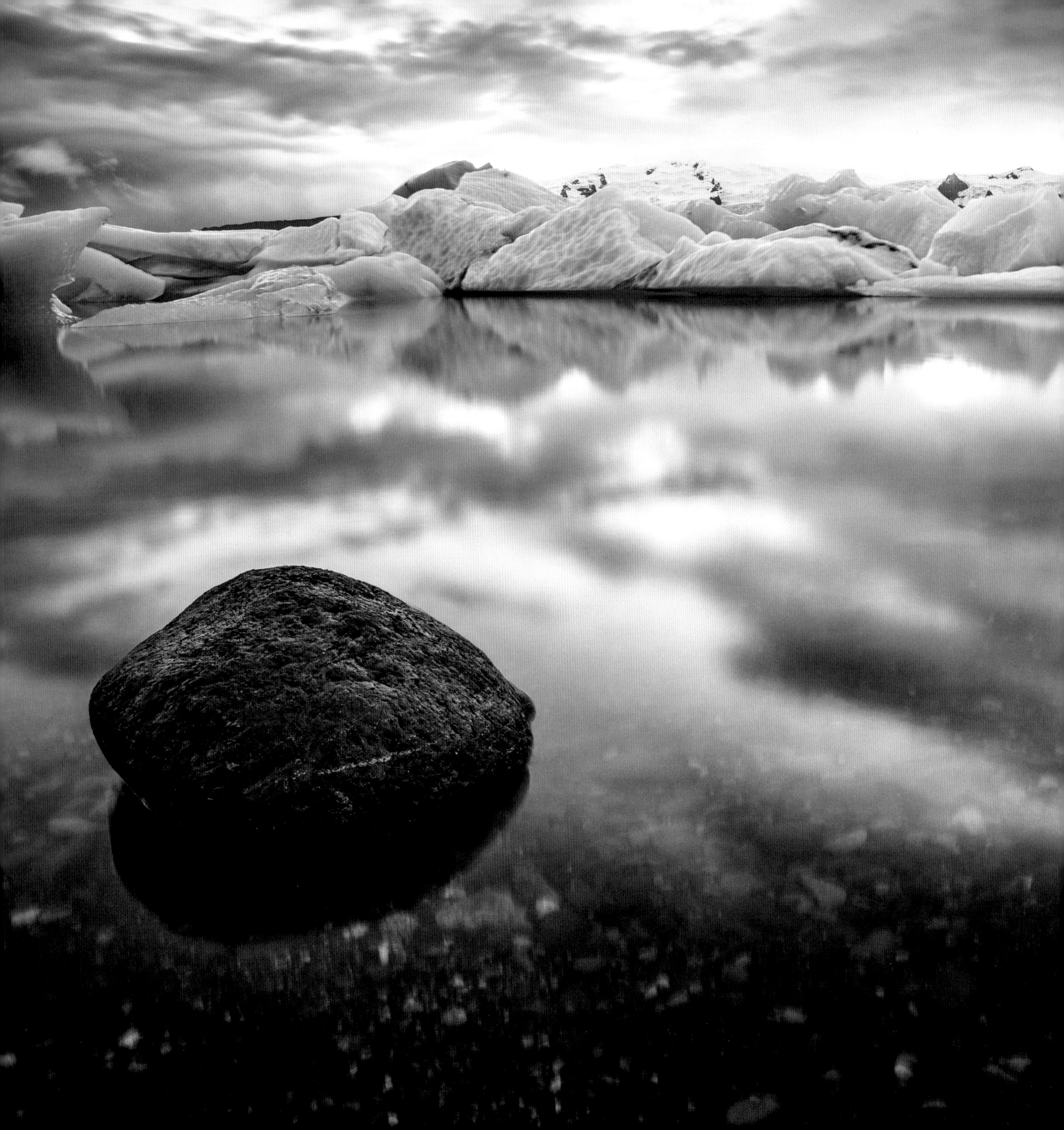

THE IMPORTANCE OF FOREGROUND OBJECTS

If you want to create layers within your image, I feel the best place to start is with a foreground object of some kind. Back on page 113 it was a cabin that was right in the front of the shot, and that starts the viewer's eye on a visual journey into the image. In this image, taken in an ice lagoon in Iceland, I positioned myself so this rock would be my foreground object. I wanted something right up front to create the first layer. To the left or right of the frame you're just seeing still water. If I started there, I would be starting in the middle ground, so I wouldn't have that depth and added interest that having that rock brings to the layers in the image. I see so many shots where the photographer was standing at the edge of a lake and they started their composition in the lake—in the middle ground—when all they had to do was step back a few feet or tilt the camera down at the water's edge to add something in the foreground. It could be some driftwood, some rocks, a dock—something to add that all-important foreground element that starts the layering of depth. Now, there are not always rocks, or a dock, etc., and sometimes you can't get the layering you'd like, but if you're aware of the power of layering, and you keep an eye out for it while you're composing your frame, including a foreground element can be the difference between having a flat image or one with lots of layers and real depth.

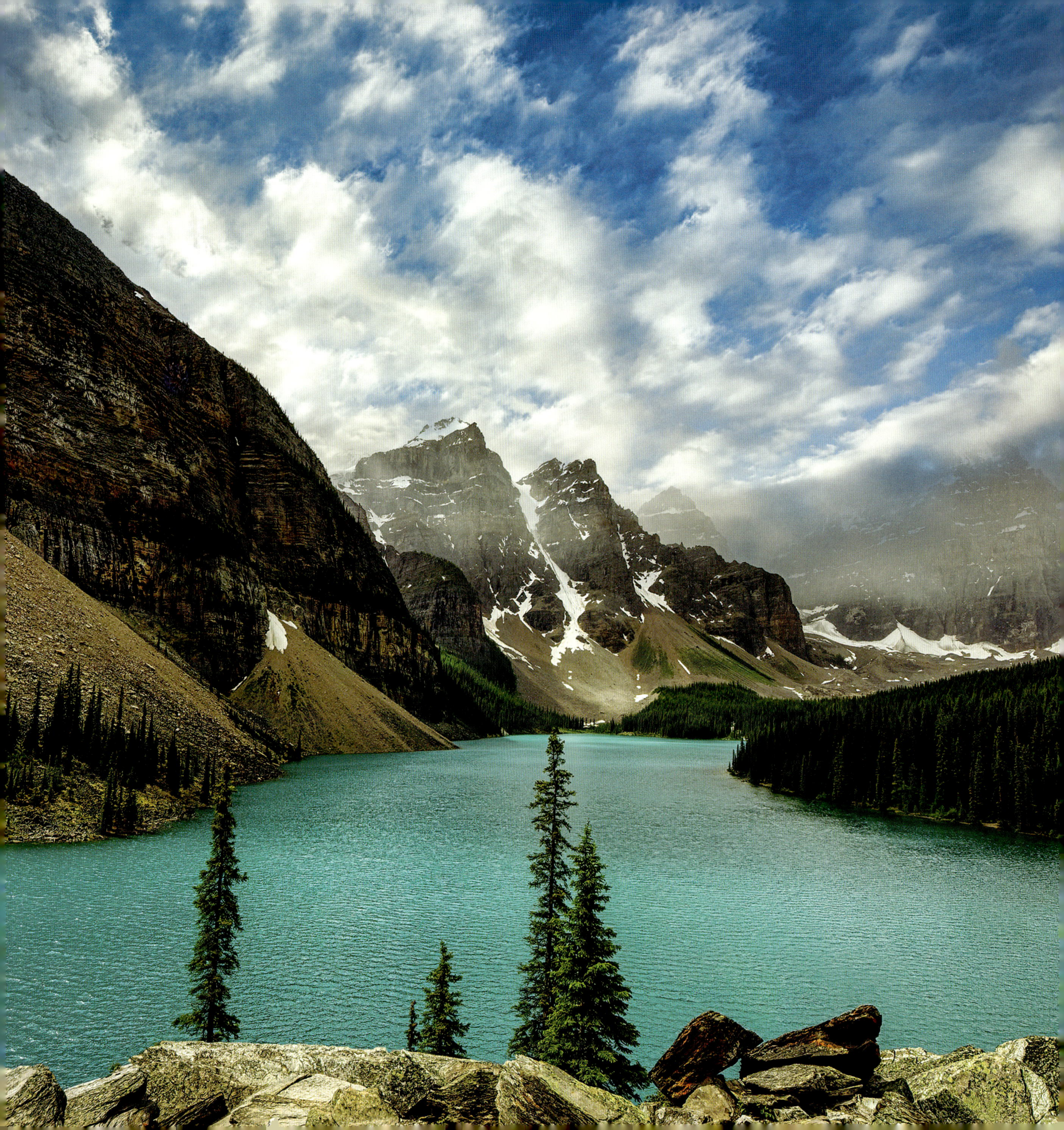

ANOTHER FOREGROUND EXAMPLE

Once I started talking about composing for a lake shot back on the previous page, I went and dug up one of my images from years ago, taken at Lake Louise in Canada's Banff National Park. The reason I wanted to show this additional example is so that you can see the rocks in the bottom (foreground) of the image. Those are used as the first layer in this shot. I could have walked up a few feet and composed the shot so you didn't see the rocks at all, and at the bottom of my image would just be lake, but then you'd lose that layer altogether. You'd be starting in the middle ground, so the image would seem more flat and have less depth and dimension (granted, this is no killer shot, but it does help to illustrate the point). This image has the rocks as the foreground, then the lake as the middle ground, then a layer of trees on the right with mountains on the left, and then as you go farther into the image, you can see those snow-capped mountains in the background, and then finally the sky (though, in this image, the sky doesn't seem as far back, so I would say it's just part of the snow-capped mountain background layer). But, most importantly, the image has depth and it all started with intentionally having a foreground, instead of starting the frame in the middle ground, and that gives it that added depth.

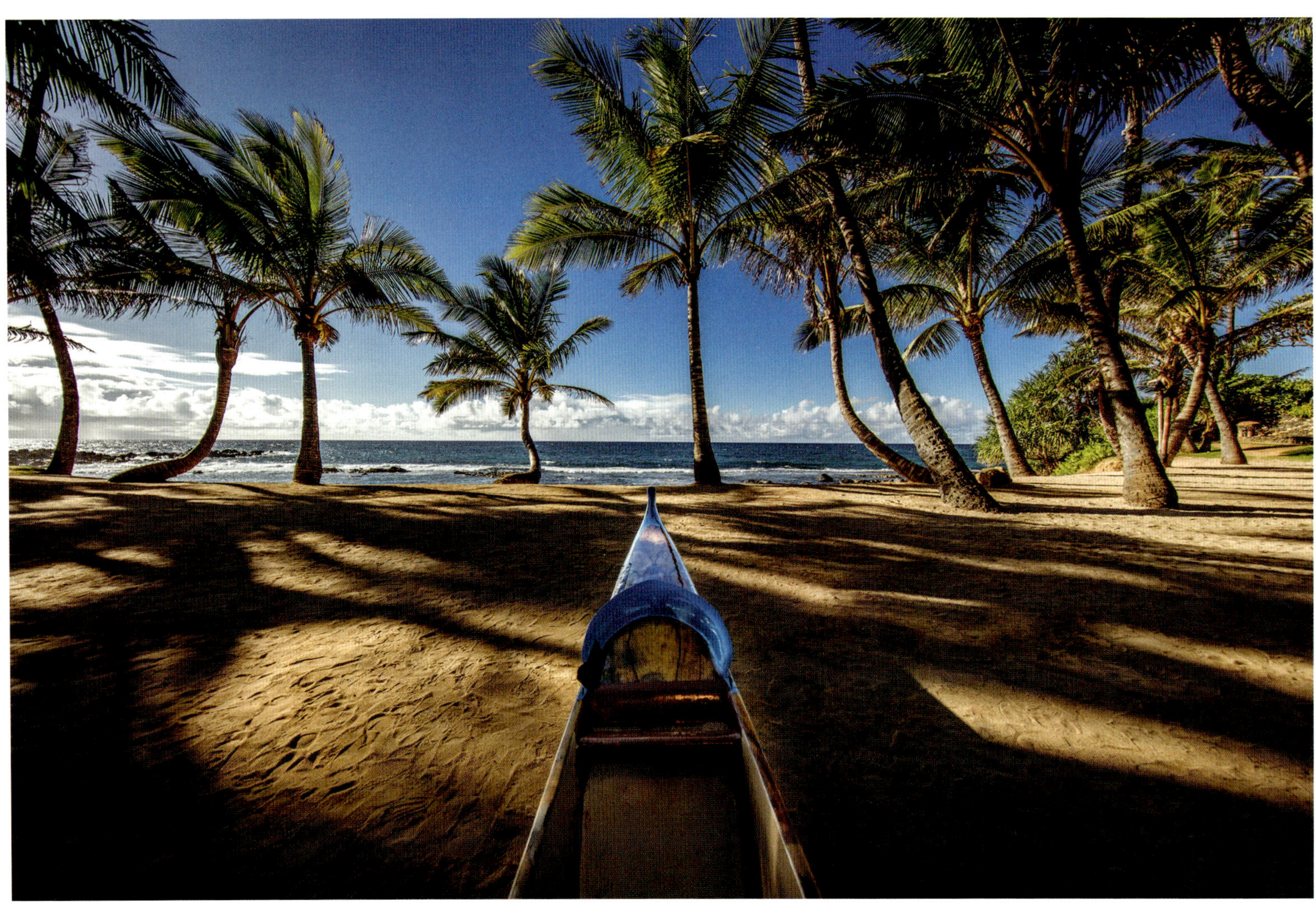

FOREGROUND WITH AN ULTRA-WIDE-ANGLE LENS

One of my favorite techniques for adding more visual interest and depth when I'm using an ultra-wide-angle lens, like a 16mm or 14mm on a full-frame camera, is to get close and down low to whatever I choose to be my foreground element. For example, in this case, I'm sitting at the other end of the outrigger, so I'm not standing up and shooting from eye level. This makes the front of the outrigger the clear subject of the shot, and it makes it bigger in the frame than it otherwise would be. This getting close and down low with an ultra-wide is a magical combination, and now you're taking multiple depth techniques and using them together, which is ideal. First, we're using a wide-angle lens, which already helps with creating depth. Then, we have a strong foreground element, and by getting down low we're making it bigger and more prominent in the shot. Beyond the outrigger is the row of palm trees. Beyond that, the waves crash up on the beach (okay, "crash" might be too strong a word), then the ocean behind that, and then the sky beyond that. Three techniques all used together creates an image with a great sense of depth.

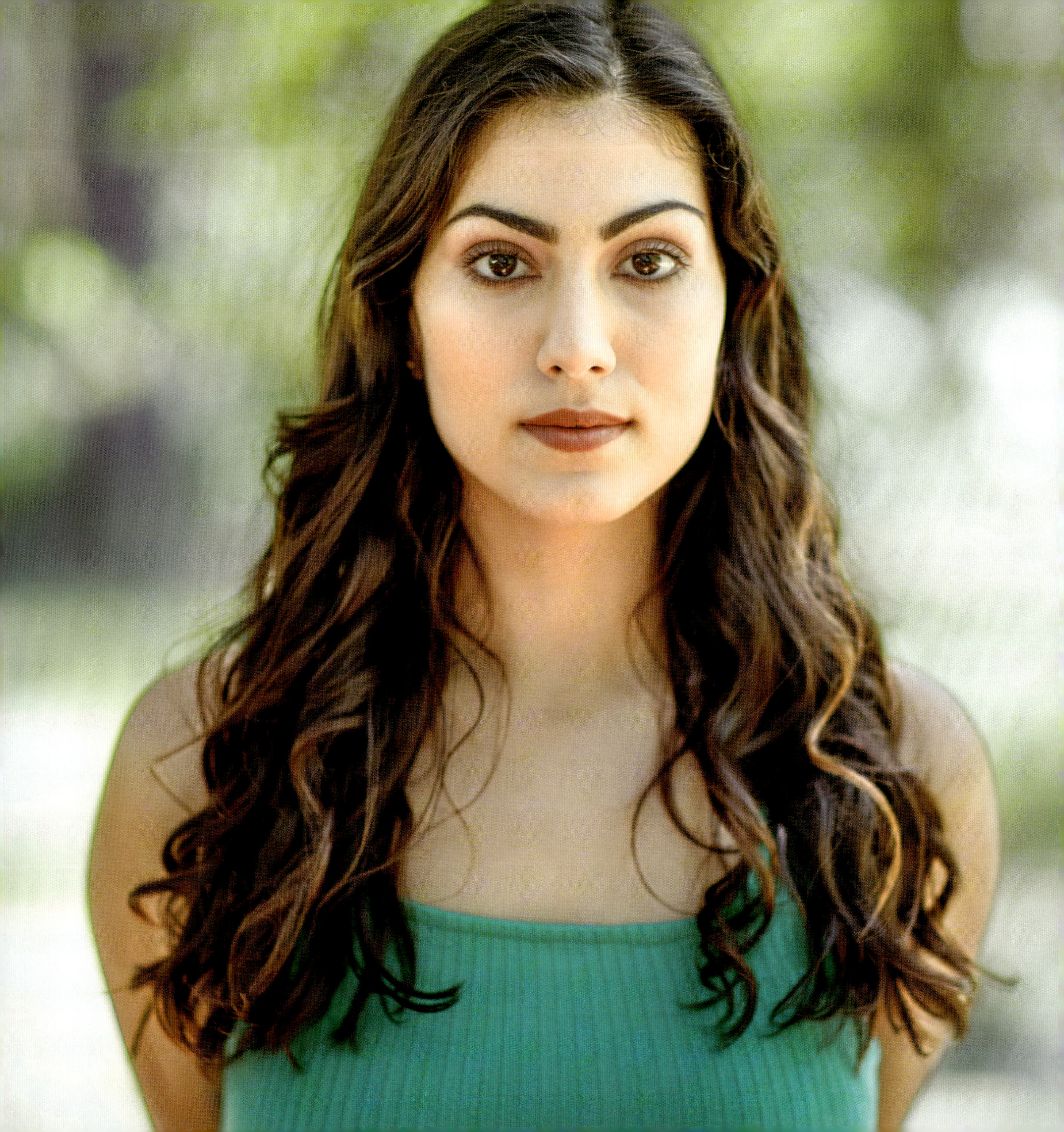

SHOW CONTRAST
WITHIN THE IMAGE

There are actually two things going on here to create depth, and the first is really obvious. By putting the background out of focus behind my subject (using a long lens, like a 200mm, and shooting wide open with the lowest numbered f-stop my lens will allow—in this case, f/2.8), it separates her from the background. Beyond the benefits we've already talked about (simplifying the scene and removing distractions), just that blurring of the background alone adds depth to the image. The second thing that is helping to add depth is the contrast between our subject and the background. If you look at the background, it's much lighter tone-wise and contrast-wise than she is—there's a big difference in contrast (though, when I did the post-processing on this image, I tried not to add too much contrast because you don't want it to look like a composite, like she was copied-and-pasted onto the background in Photoshop. So, I went with a light touch in post, but her dark hair really helps create the contrast and depth against that light background). Yes, this is a little thing, but a lot of little things added together can create a lot of depth. In this case, we used two: blurring the background and contrasting our subject from the background.

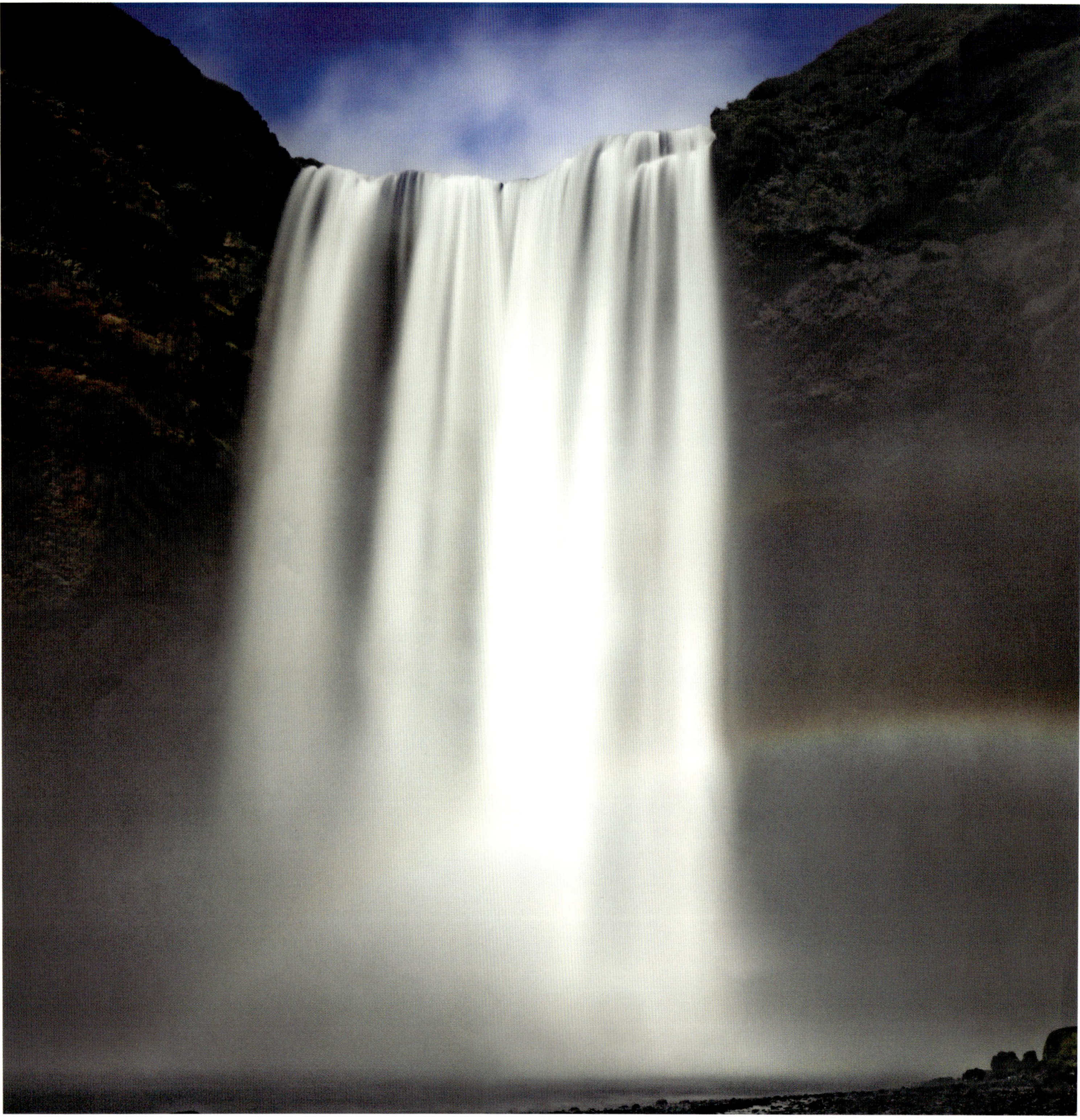

OUR IMAGE NEEDS A CLEAR SUBJECT

Every Wednesday at 1:00 pm ET for about the past 10 years or so, I've hosted a live photography show called *The Grid*. Once a month, we do an episode called "Blind Photo Critiques," where we ask our viewers to send in three of their best images and we give them a seriously honest critique of them. These are "blind" in that we don't display or mention the photographer's name, so we don't publicly embarrass the person we're critiquing. One of the most common compositional mistakes we see is that when we look at their image we have to ask, "What is the subject?" "What's the focal point we're supposed to be looking at?" If the person looking at your photo doesn't know what they should be looking at, or even what it is, your image has failed. When I do in-person portfolio reviews at conferences and workshops, I'll sometimes run into a photo like this and I'll ask the photographer, "Okay, what's the subject of this image?" and after a few moments of silence (as they're probably asking themselves the same question in their head, and for the first time), they usually answer, "Well, it's the whole scene?" Nope. That's a failed image. Anyone should be able to look at your image and say, "It's the waterfall," or "The bird," or "The cabin," or "That big tree on the left," etc. If you want your image to work, depth alone won't pull the whole wagon. You need a clear, definable subject. By the way, note how I included some ground as my foreground in this shot.

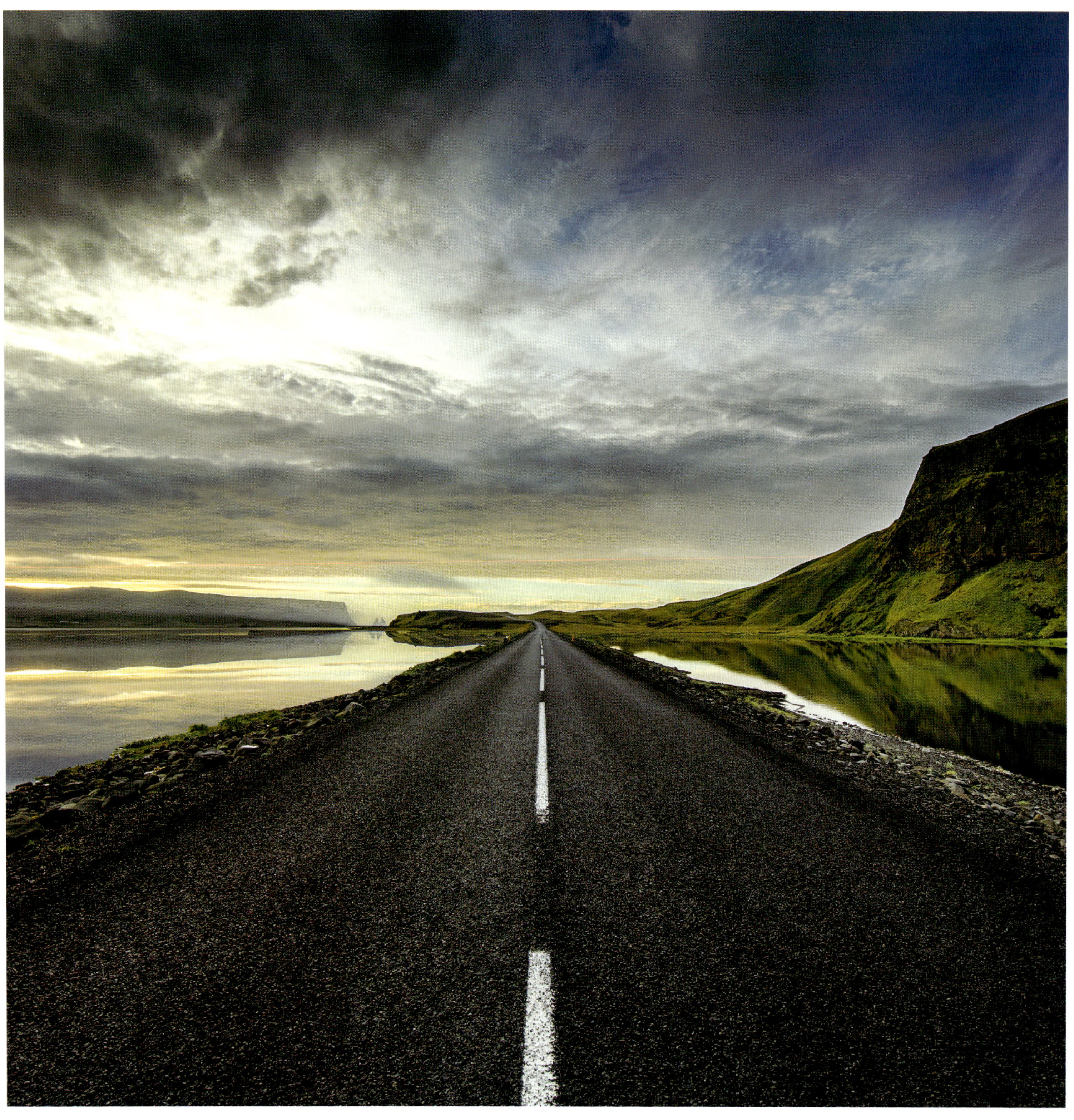

INCLUDE A VANISHING POINT

Another technique for adding depth is one you won't always have the opportunity to add to your frame, but when it's there, it really helps. It's to have what's called a "vanishing point" in your image that leads your viewer off into...well...the rest is up to their imagination. For example, in the image here, look how the highway, with its converging lines, leads you farther and farther down the road until the road simply vanishes. You draw the viewer deeper and deeper into the image as their eyes follow along that road (which is a perfect leading line by the way) until it vanishes at the horizon line. Vanishing points have been a very popular technique in traditional painting, and if you get the chance to add one to your image, it will add another level of depth to the other techniques you're already using.

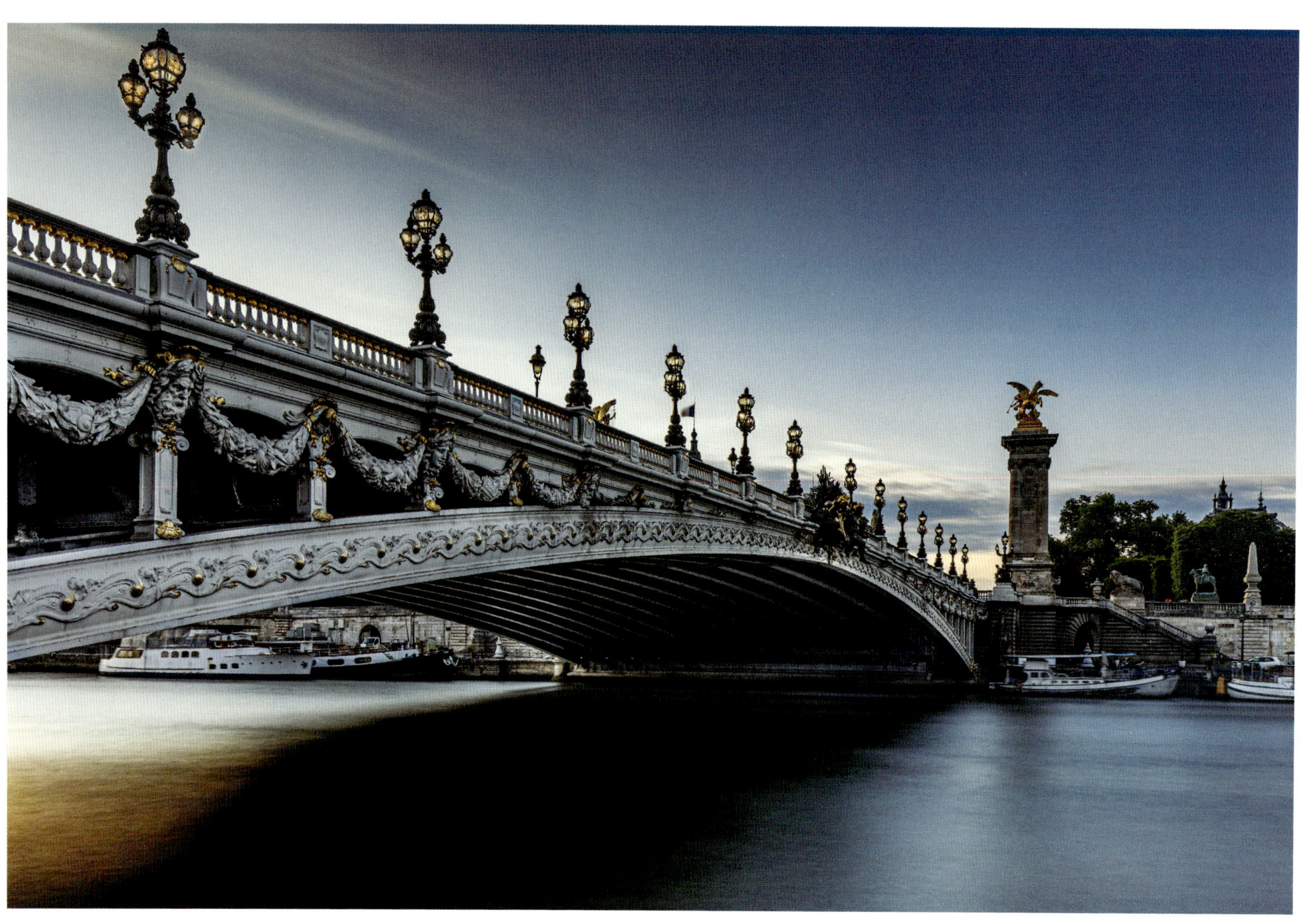

USE SCALE AND REPETITION

This is another technique used to draw the viewer into your image, and if you've got the right scene for it, it's really effective. For example, take a look at the image we have here. By shooting at an angle from the shore of the Seine River in Paris, you get a descending scale of the bridge, which goes from larger on this side of it, leading the viewer into the image, and across the river and the bridge, with its repeating pattern of lamp posts, getting smaller and smaller as it goes. The added bonus here is that the bridge acts as its own foreground and middle ground as it crosses the river. Then, of course, you've got the opposite side of the river and the sky behind it to add more layers and depth. This technique of shooting at an angle, using the shrinking scale of the bridge to add depth, really helps to lead the viewer into the image (like a leading line), and it works to add depth and dimension at the same time.

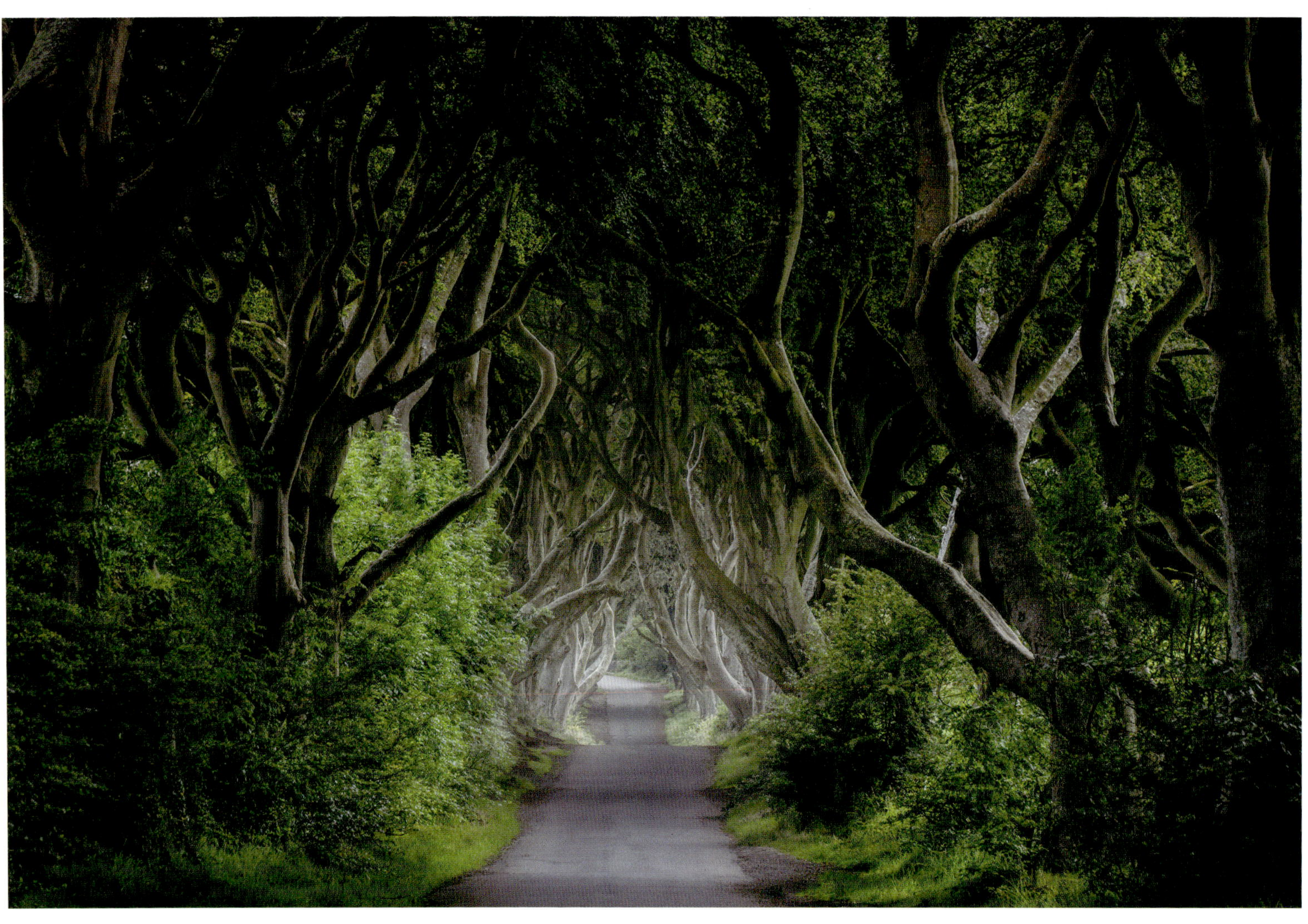

NATURAL ATMOSPHERE

I know that you already know this, but in a landscape scene, things that are closest to you will appear the sharpest, and as we move deeper and deeper into the image, we often see that objects that are farther away are hazier. You see this a lot at dawn in distant mountains, where each row of mountains gets hazier and hazier as it goes, and while you might not be thrilled that you're shooting on a hazy morning, you have to love the sense of depth that natural haziness brings. This can be used to your advantage because natural atmospheric effects can add a lot of depth to your image. You might be tempted to grab a polarizing filter to cut through some of that haze, but if your goal is to add depth, you might want to put it back in your camera bag. Take a look at the image here, taken in the Dark Hedges in Northern Ireland, not too far from Belfast (they are now fairly famous thanks to their cameo appearance in *Game of Thrones*, so if you go, expect a lot of Instagrammers out there shooting selfies—some with rolling suitcases so they can change outfits). As we move farther and farther down the road, you can see the morning fog lighting the area toward the back, and that separation adds depth to your image because it's telling the viewer, "This is farther away." Keep an eye out for using this natural atmospheric effect to add depth to your shots.

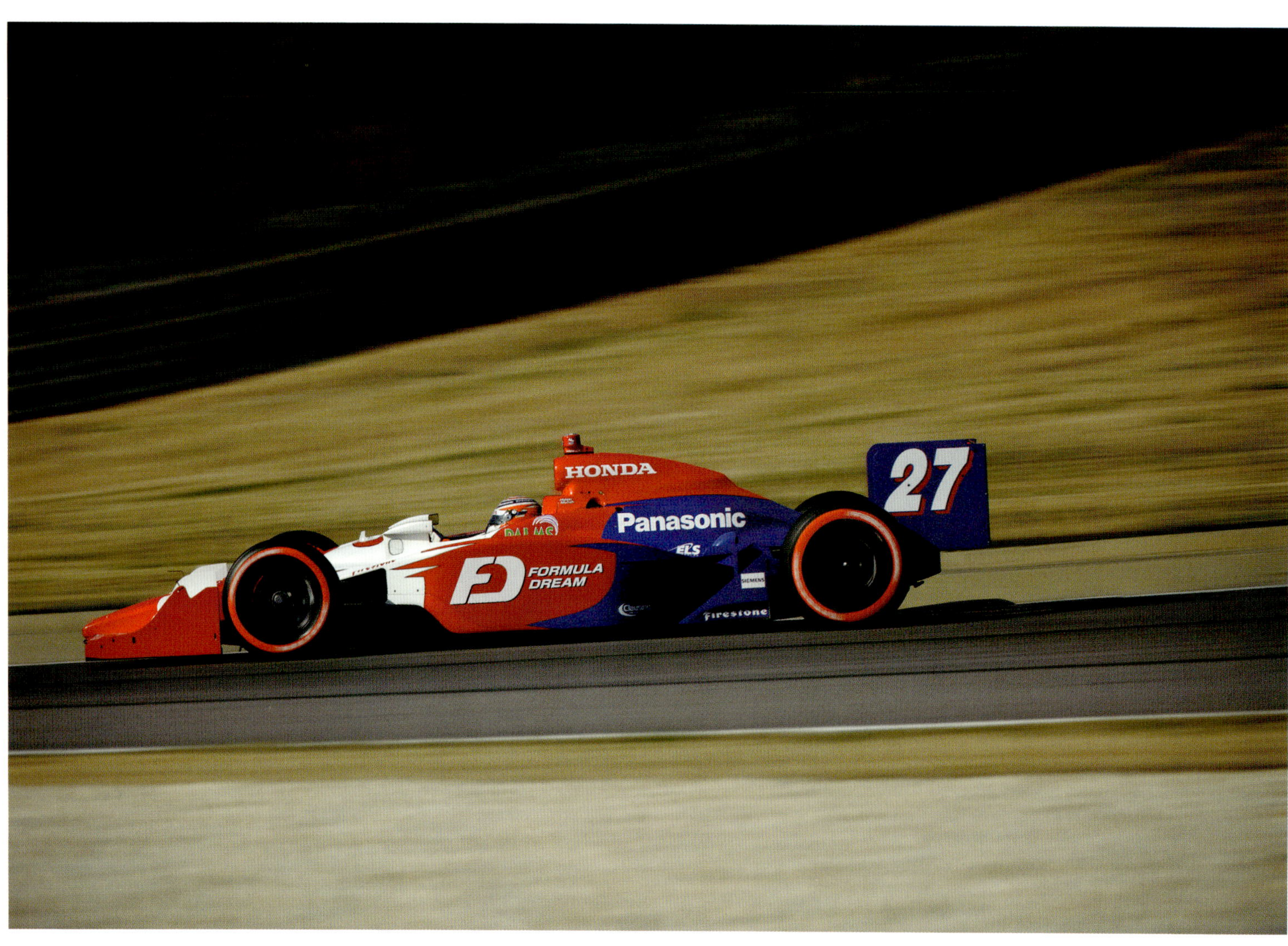

DON'T BOX IN YOUR SUBJECT

This is one for photographers who shoot things like wildlife or sports, but compositionally, we need to avoid creating a "boxed in" feeling in our image. That means that we avoid composing the image so that the bird or animal (or in this case, the Indy car) doesn't have room to move—they are so close to the edge of the image that it psychologically creates an uncomfortable situation for the viewer. They won't be able to tell you exactly what's wrong with the image, but there will be something about it that they don't like. Sometimes that'll make them uneasy about it, but they won't be able to articulate it. It's an easy thing to fix compositionally—you just need to make sure that some nice room is left in the direction the animal (or the race car, in this case) is traveling. Take a look at this image and how close the front of the car is to the edge of the frame. That's way too close. See how much room is behind the car? That's how much room you'd like to see in front of the car, giving it room to move into. Something to keep in mind if you're shooting things that move: compositionally, leave room for your subject to move into, and your viewer will like the image better.

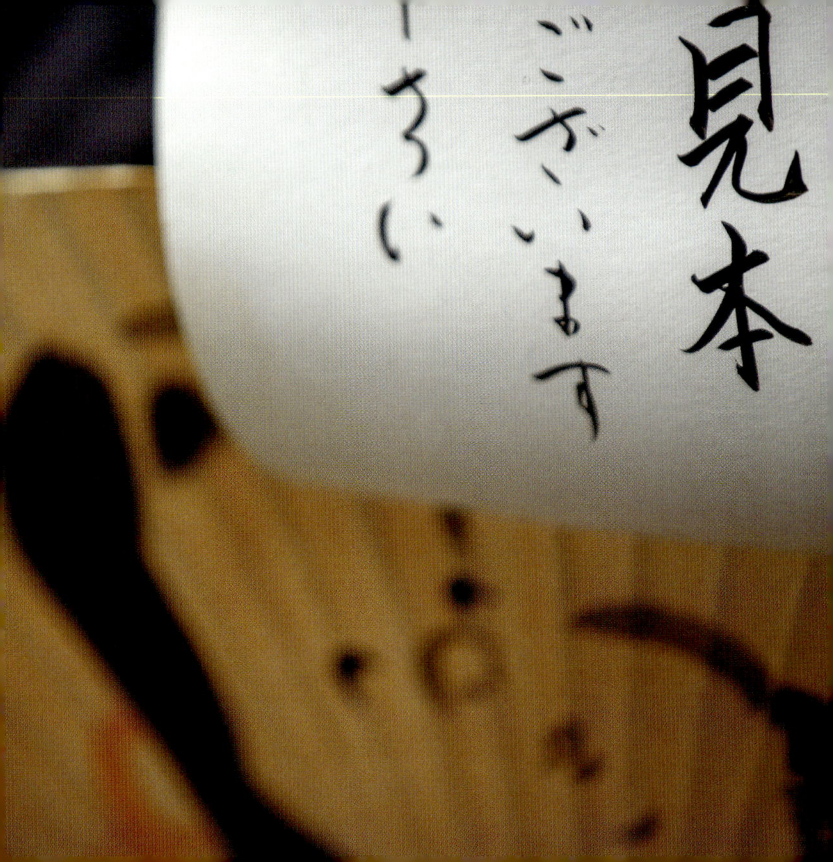
見本
ございます
ちい

Chapter 07

THE POWER
OF SIMPLICITY

I wasted so much time looking through my viewfinder and not liking what I was seeing and thinking to myself, "This doesn't look great. What do I need to add to this to make this look good?" when all along I was asking myself the wrong question. What I wish I had known earlier was the problem wasn't usually what I needed to add; it was what I needed to take away. I didn't learn this until a photographer buddy of mine was telling me about when he had this same revelation. He told me, "Go look at the photographers you look up to. Look at their images that you love and ask yourself why you love them. Are they complex images with a lot going on, or are they very clean, simple images?" Well, I did just that, and it hit me like a ton of bricks. I went straight to the images I loved from these photographers and I was blown away by their simplicity. In my mind, I imagined them to be these intricate compositions with lots of items and facets, when in reality, they were so simple, but that's what made them so strong, and that's what this chapter is all about. It's about looking at the scene and nailing it down to the things that are really important. This can be an awakening, where you look at scenes in a very different way and you get stingier about what you'll let in your frame, and your compositions can get so much stronger for it.

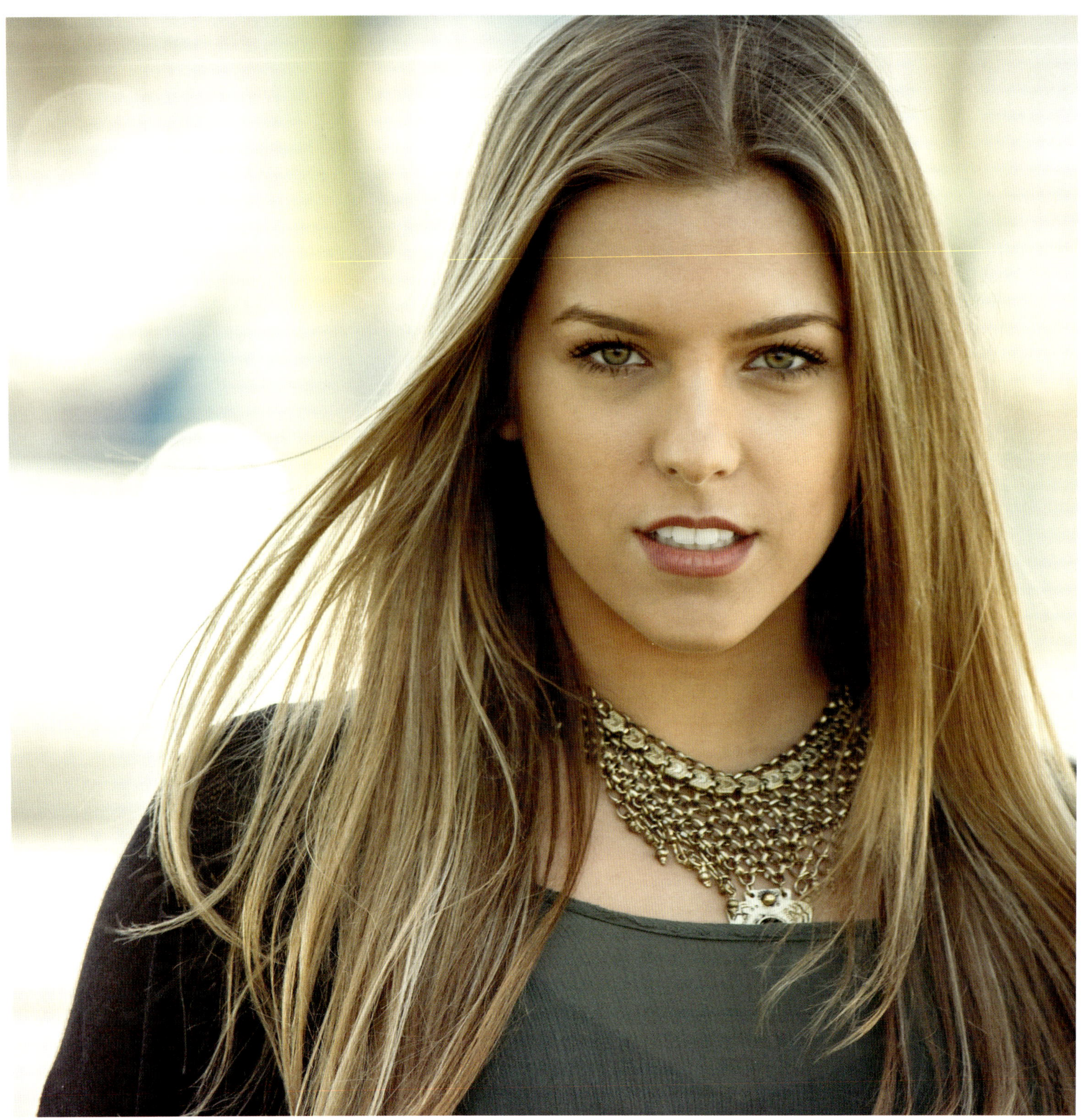

ISOLATE YOUR SUBJECT

In the image here, can you tell what's behind her? Was it taken in a park, in a stadium, at the beach? It's impossible to tell, and that's the point. By choosing a long lens (this was shot at 200mm), zooming in tight, and using a low-numbered f-stop (in this case, f/2.8), you put the background out of focus. Spoiler alert: she's standing in a marina. You're hiding all the businesses and boats and masts and trees behind her by choosing a shallow depth of field. As you learned earlier, it not only separates her from the background, but because you don't see all that distracting stuff back there, it simplifies the scene big time, and that's one reason we often shoot portraits with a shallow depth of field. Without the background, this image is all about her, our subject. If this was for a magazine article about our subject's love of sailing, then we'd probably want the background to be at least somewhat in focus because it's visually important to her story. But, in this case, where it's not about sailing at all, blurring that background greatly simplifies the shot.

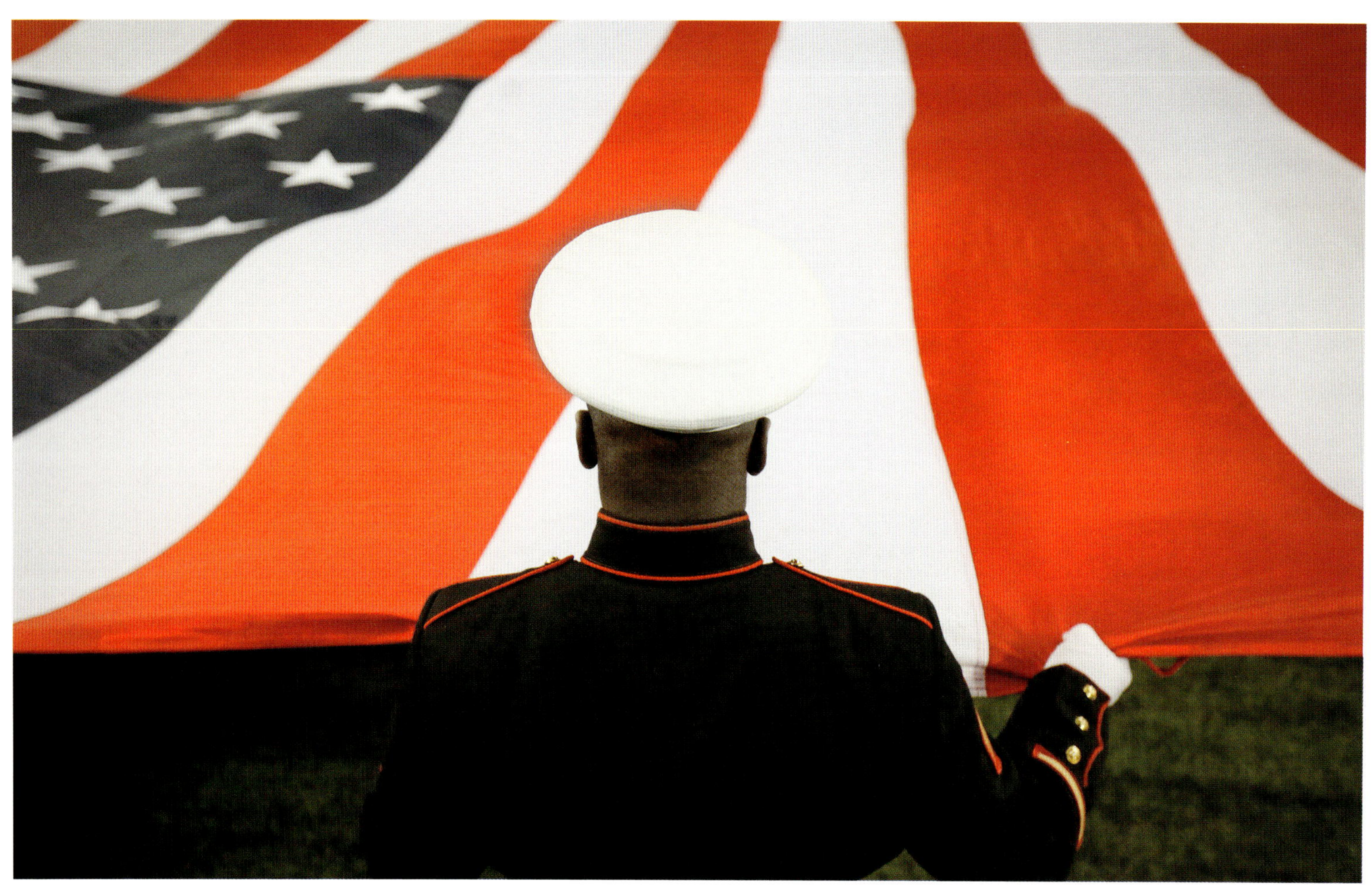

FRAMING

You can't tell from the picture shown here, but there were approximately 150 people holding this 1,100+ pound flag, covering almost an entire football field as part of the pregame festivities at an NFL game. Yet, you're only seeing one soldier. What gives this photo its strength is the simplicity. Since you're only seeing the one soldier, it feels like the entire image is about him, his country, and his flag. You're telling the story without saying a word, and around 149 volunteers who are all around him were cut out. Just a foot or two to the left and to the right are other people, who might be wearing t-shirts and shorts (they most likely were because this shot was taken on a hot, sunny day in Florida), and while including them would have given a more accurate accounting of what was really happening in the scene, the image would have lost that strength. It changes the story from a symbol of a soldier and his patriotism, defending his country, to: "Oh, that's the flag they roll out before the game when they sing the national anthem." There's nothing that says you can't shoot both—the shot of everyone holding the flag, along with just the soldier isolated like I did here. But, if you want an image that goes beyond just recording what happened that day, that's when the composition—what you choose to include in your frame or intentionally leave out that can add strength and emotion, and in this case, a storytelling aspect—can make the difference.

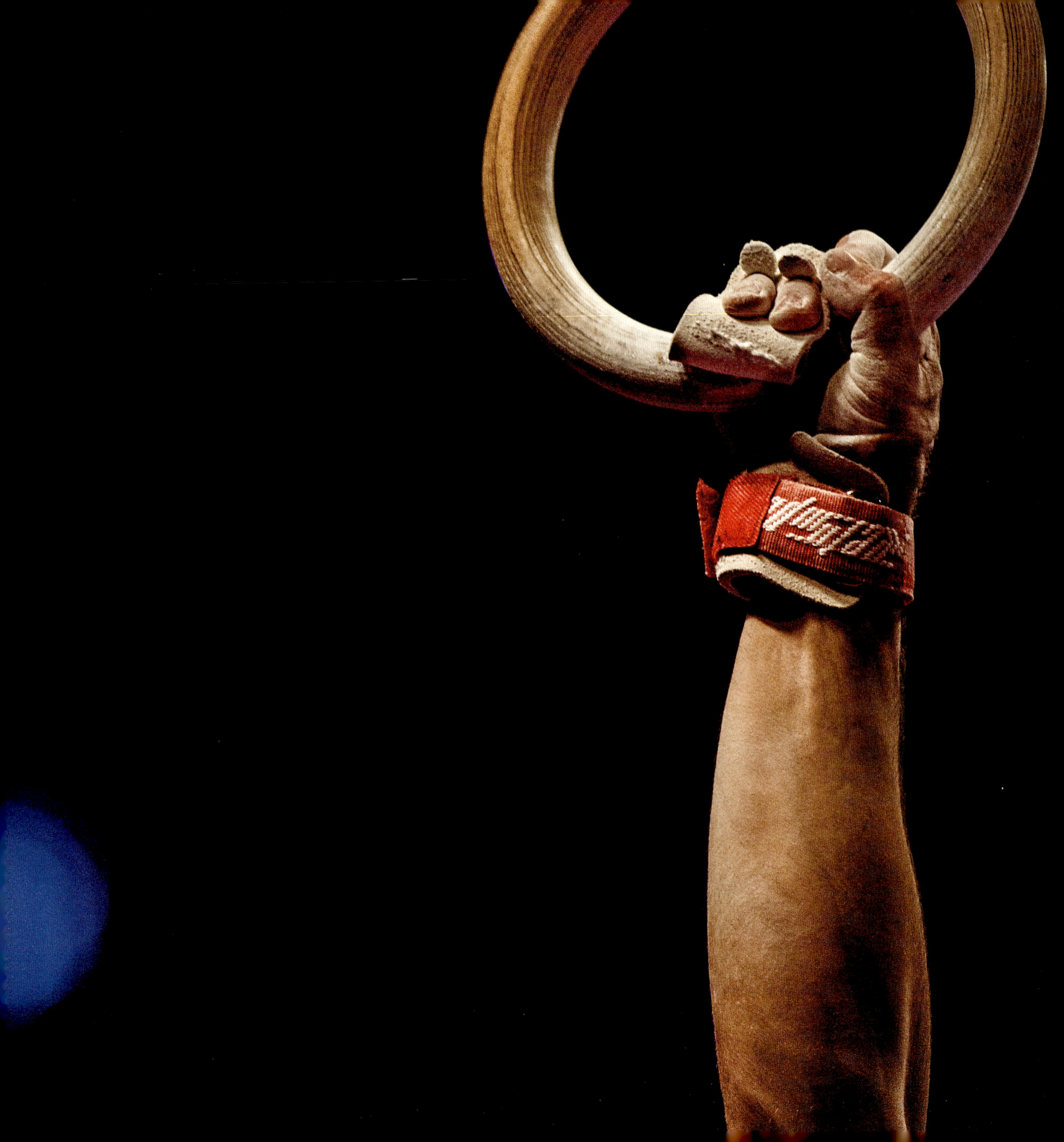

SHOW STRENGTH

Here's another example from the sports world, but of course, this invokes a very different type of feeling— it's one where the photo itself is showing strength (the strength of the athlete). Again, we've taken this down to its most simplistic view by just focusing on the ring, the grip, and the arm. It couldn't be a simpler shot, or easier to take—you're just zooming in on one part of the athlete—but it still tells a story. It draws its energy from the fact that by zooming in tight like this, you're bringing the person viewing the shot a vantage point they can't see from up in the stands or often even on TV, and that alone—showing something up close and interesting—can make for a very compelling image. Notice that while we're not showing the full scene, or even the full athlete, it doesn't feel like we're looking at a disembodied arm—our minds fill in the rest of the scene for us without even thinking about it. Also, why leave the blue light on the far edge of the image (well, there are actually three blue lights over there, but the image had to be cropped to fit the page here in the book)? The blue light(s) is to add balance to the shot.

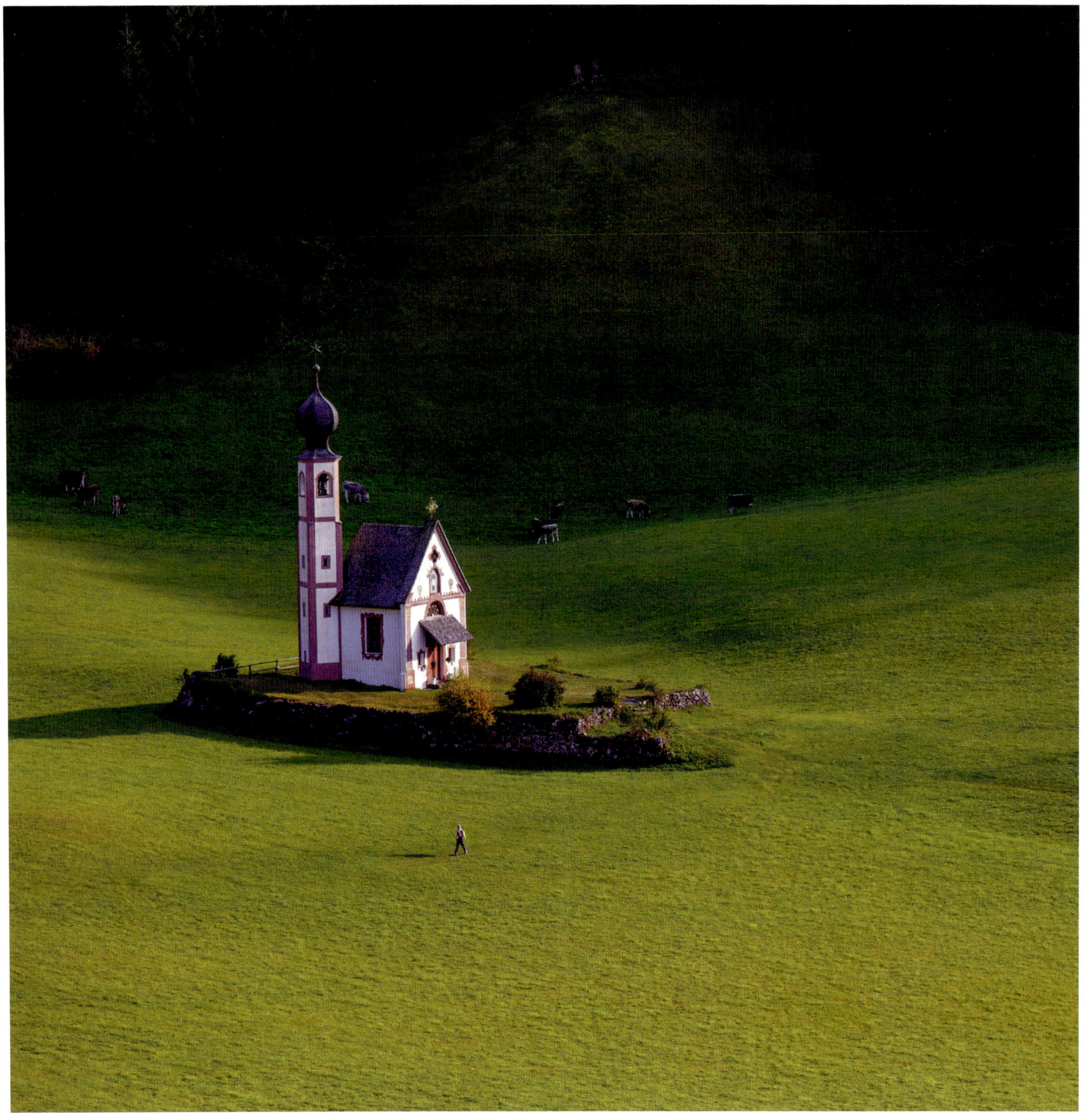

BE PICKY

The famous artist Henri Matisse once said (and I'm paraphrasing here) that if something in your image isn't helping the image, it's probably hurting the image. When you're framing up your image, ask yourself if the things you're seeing in your frame are making the image stronger or weaker, better or worse. I tried to do that in the shot you see here, and if the chapel looks familiar it's because you've probably seen it dozens of times before (well, you would have if you're on Instagram), but you normally see it as part of a much bigger scene. This chapel sits down in a valley surrounded by one of the most recognizable groups of mountains in Northern Italy's Dolomites region rising up from behind the chapel. Usually the chapel is very small in the frame because that mountain formation is the "star of the show." But, in this case, I zoomed in tight to simplify the scene and make the shot about the chapel, and the old man walking away from it (and the cows in the background), which are all things you rarely see when you see photos of this chapel. I left a lot out in this photo, but what I left in is what I think makes it most interesting.

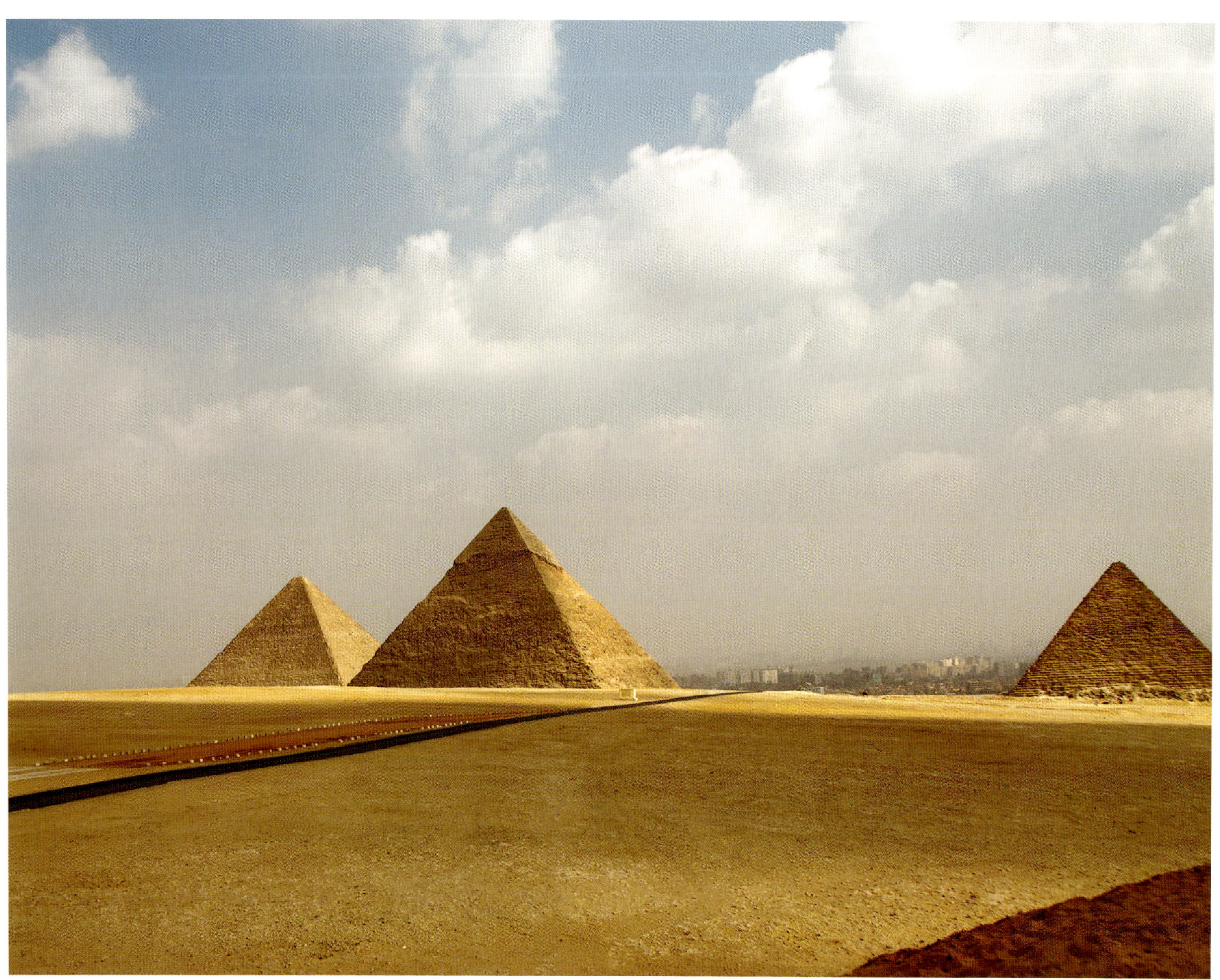

EXCLUSION

It was an amazing day. It was just me and the Great Pyramids of Giza. Just the four of us, all alone. Well, my wife was there. And, everybody from our tour bus who you can't see just to the immediate left of the frame. Well, not just everybody from our tour bus, but from a number of tour buses and, of course, where there are tour buses there are vendors and porta-potties and tourists wandering everywhere and…well, it was quite the scene. Except you don't see any of that here, or have any sense whatsoever that's even happening just feet from where I'm standing, because I intentionally framed up the shot so the viewer doesn't see that circus going on, distracting them and taking their eye off the subject. Another thing you would see if you were standing there would be people posing, where it looks like they're leaning with one elbow on the point of a pyramid or pinching the point on top of it with their fingers or one of a dozen other things that people post on Instagram. But, again, like my buddy Matisse asked me over drinks at the hotel bar one night: "Does including the tourist pinching the top of the pyramid add to your shot or take away from it?" I guessed: "It takes away from it." I was right and he bought me a frosty mug of Kronenbourg Lager 1664.

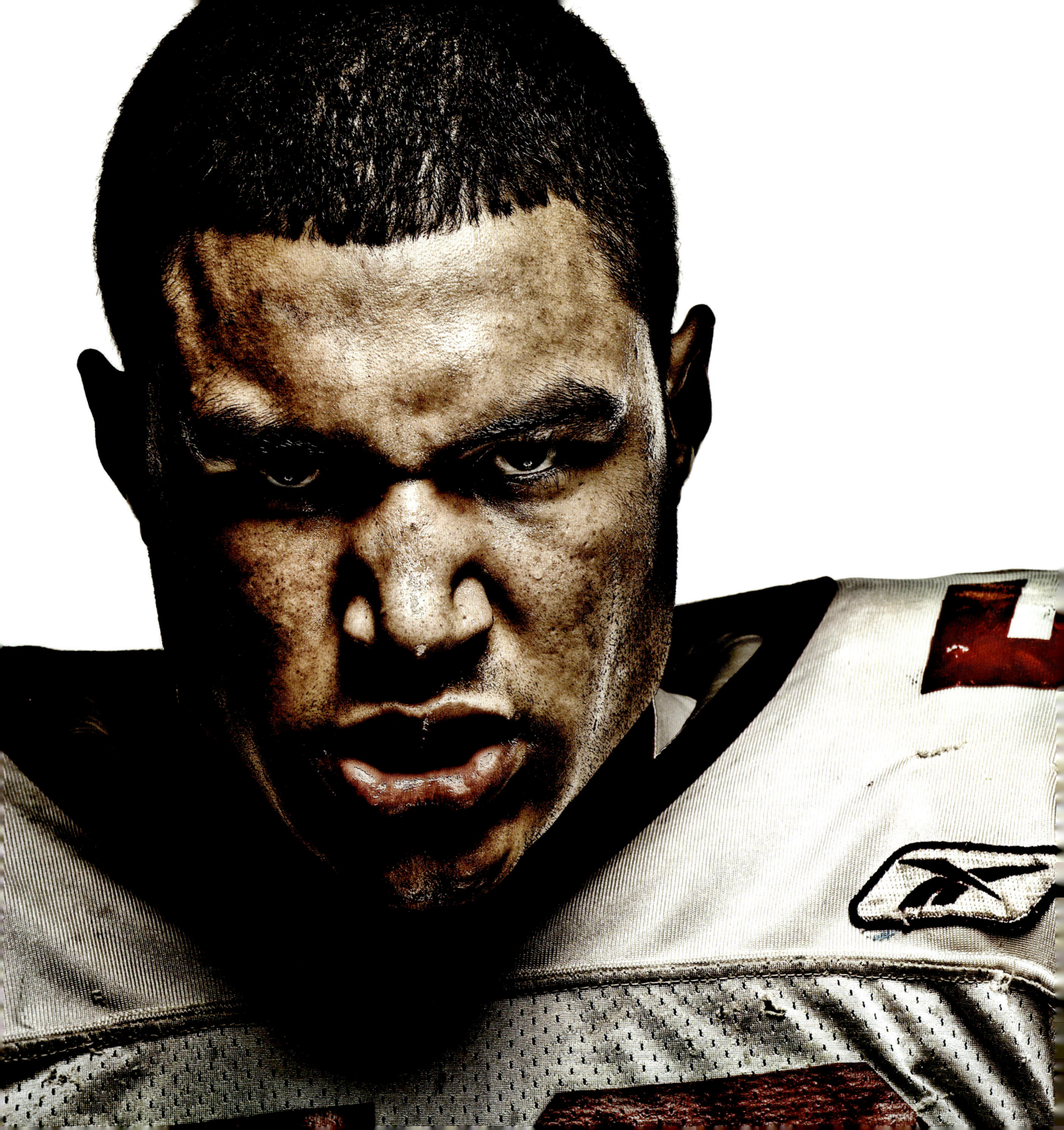

ROLL OUT

———————

Next time you're at a bookstore, take a quick look at the magazine rack. I know, I know…there are a lot less racks than there used to be, but there's enough there to help with this experiment. Take a look at the covers that feature people, and you'll find that by far the most common background used for cover portraits on the big magazines, like *Time*, *Cosmopolitan*, *Elle*, *Vogue*, *Maxim*, *Details*, *W*, and so many more is seamless paper. Sometimes it's solid white, like I used here, but often it's gray or a pastel color. These seamless paper backgrounds aren't so ubiquitous because they're cheap (you can get a roll that's 9 feet wide by 36 yards long for around $72); it's because they offer such a clean, simple background, which makes the image all about the subject. It focuses the viewer's attention on the portrait and they don't really take notice of the background. It might match the color of what the subject is wearing or be a contrasting color, so it has a small supporting role there, but its job is to simplify the portrait.

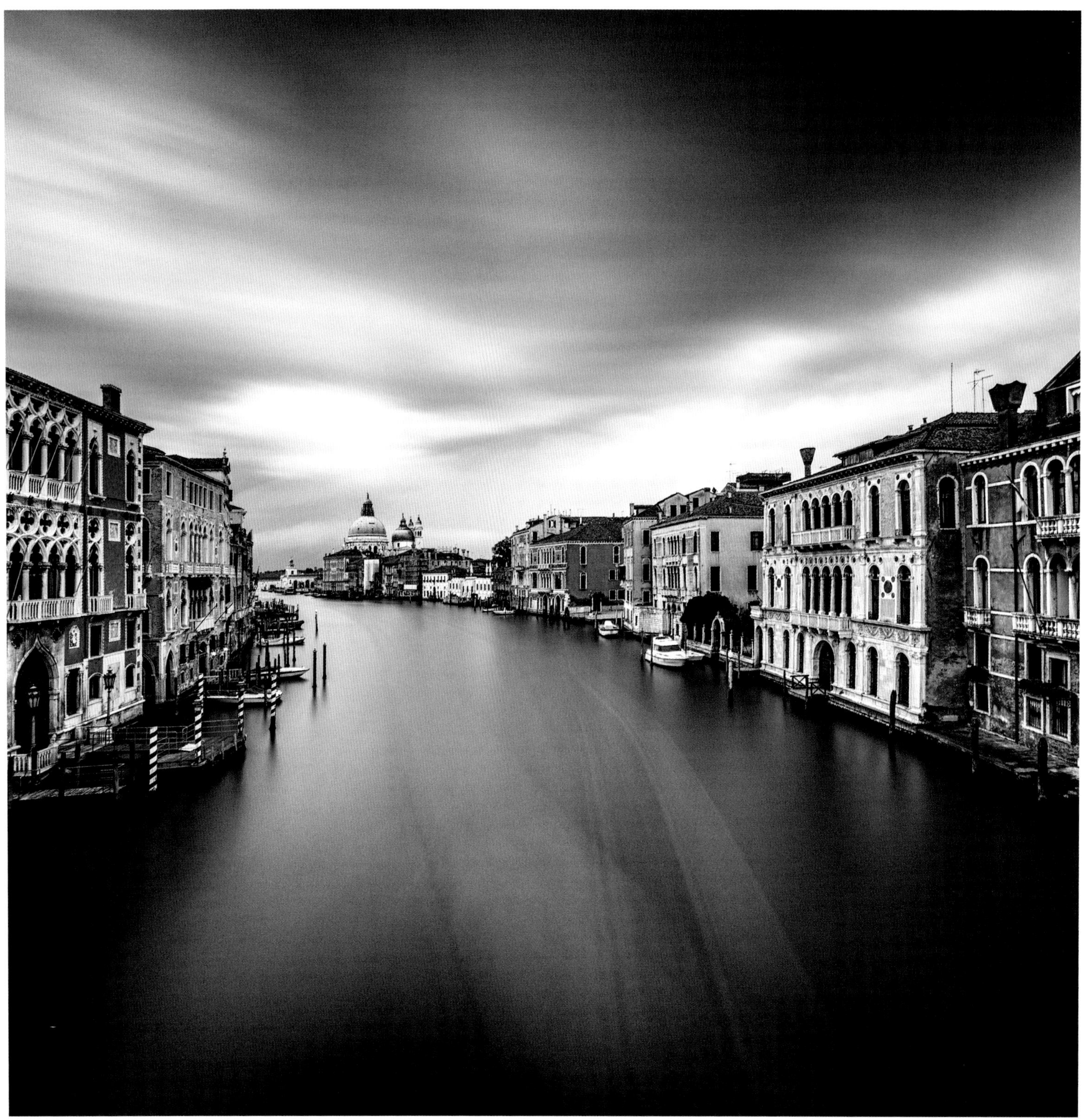

GO LONG

Another tool you can use to simplify your scene is a neutral density (ND) filter. This filter makes your camera see the scene as much darker than it is, so it forces your shutter to stay open longer, which works wonders for things like making choppy water smooth as glass. Just that alone helps simplify the scene big time (as you can see here, where the water is smooth and the boats coming down the canal are erased from the scene). Things that move during the time your shutter is open won't appear in the shot, in most cases. Choppy water in the canal is busy. Smooth, glassy water is less distracting, and it's one reason we use ND filters— to simplify the image.

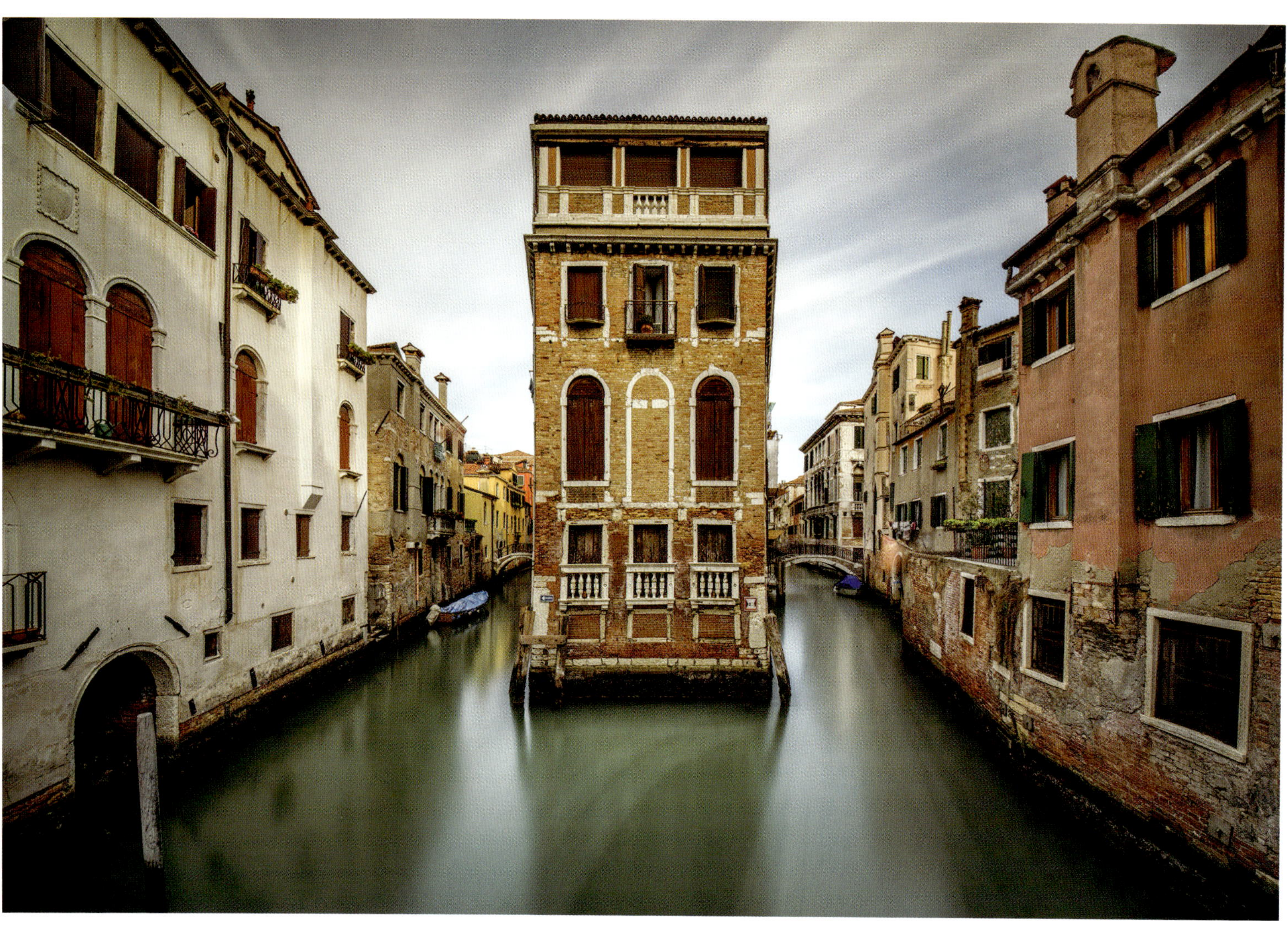

GET UP EARLY

For travel photography, one of the keys to simplicity is to limit the number of tourists in the scene. There are several ways to do this, starting with getting up at sunrise and shooting while all the tourists are still asleep (tourists do not like getting up early). You can set up in front of some of the world's most popular monuments or palaces or attractions and, literally, be the only one there. Plus, you get the benefit of great light, which makes it all worthwhile. Another method for removing tourists is to do a long exposure using a neutral density (ND) filter. That way, tourists that are moving during your exposure will be removed from the scene (though any that stand still during your long exposure will still be there). However, the easiest way to get rid of tourists is to avoid having them in your frame, which often means how you frame up your shot (and how much of the scene in front of you you're going to show) and patience. Remember, you don't need a particular doorway to be tourist-free for 5 minutes; you only need it to be clear for 1/125 of a second. So, stand there, with the viewfinder to your eye, and wait for your moment to catch a tourist-free image. I've done it during the middle of the day at the castle entrance at Disneyland. It took around 20 minutes, but I got it.

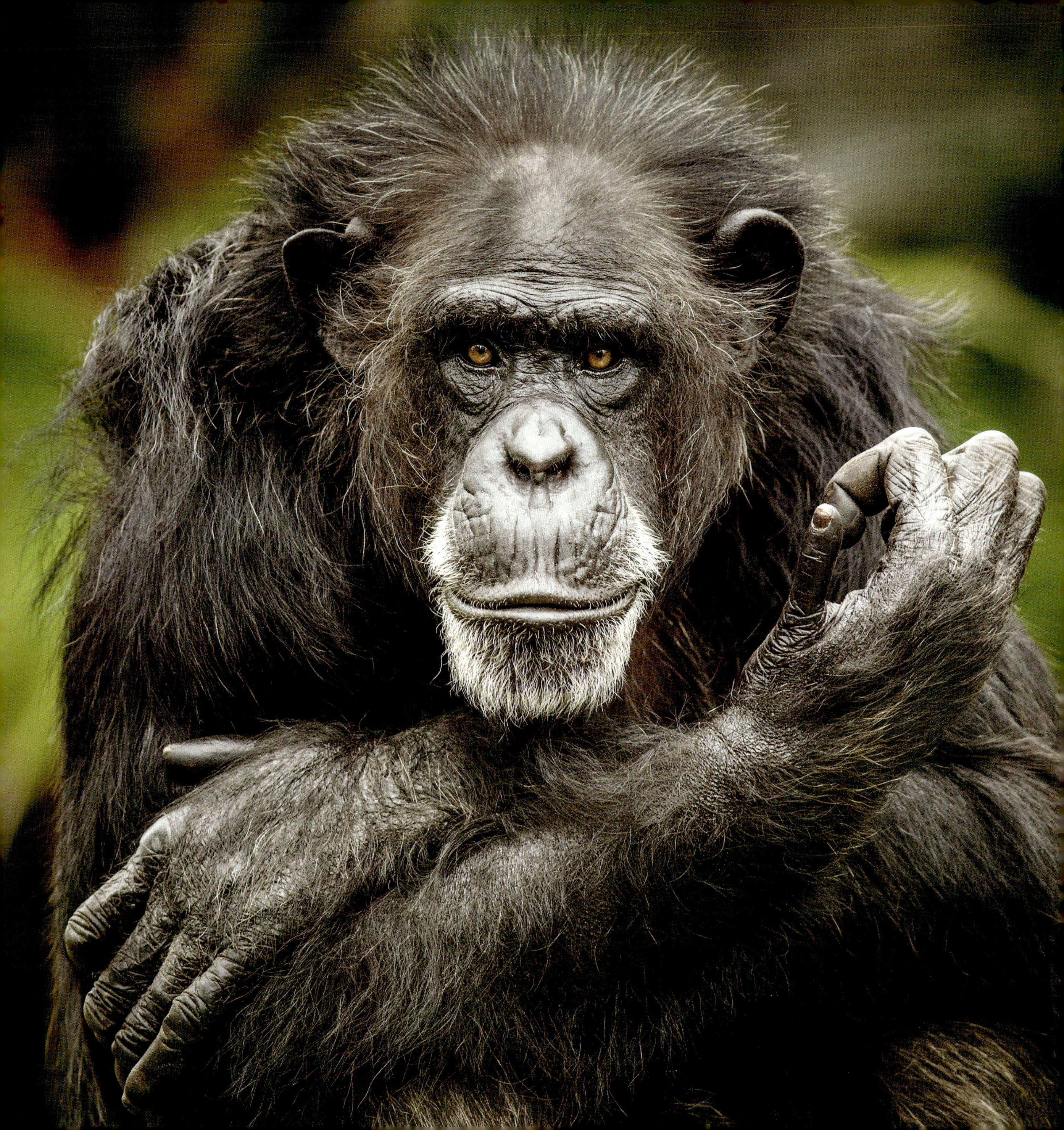

COMBINE TECHNIQUES

The genre or category changes, but the fundamentals of simplicity are still the same. This photo was actually taken in a zoo, but by combining two things we've already talked about, I was able to make the type of image I was hoping for. The first was zooming in tight to avoid showing the chain-link fence that keeps the primates from finding the nearest exit, and secondly, by blurring the background we're able to limit the visual distractions of the palm fronds directly behind him. I'm combining those two techniques to simplify the scene and take the monkey out of the zoo.

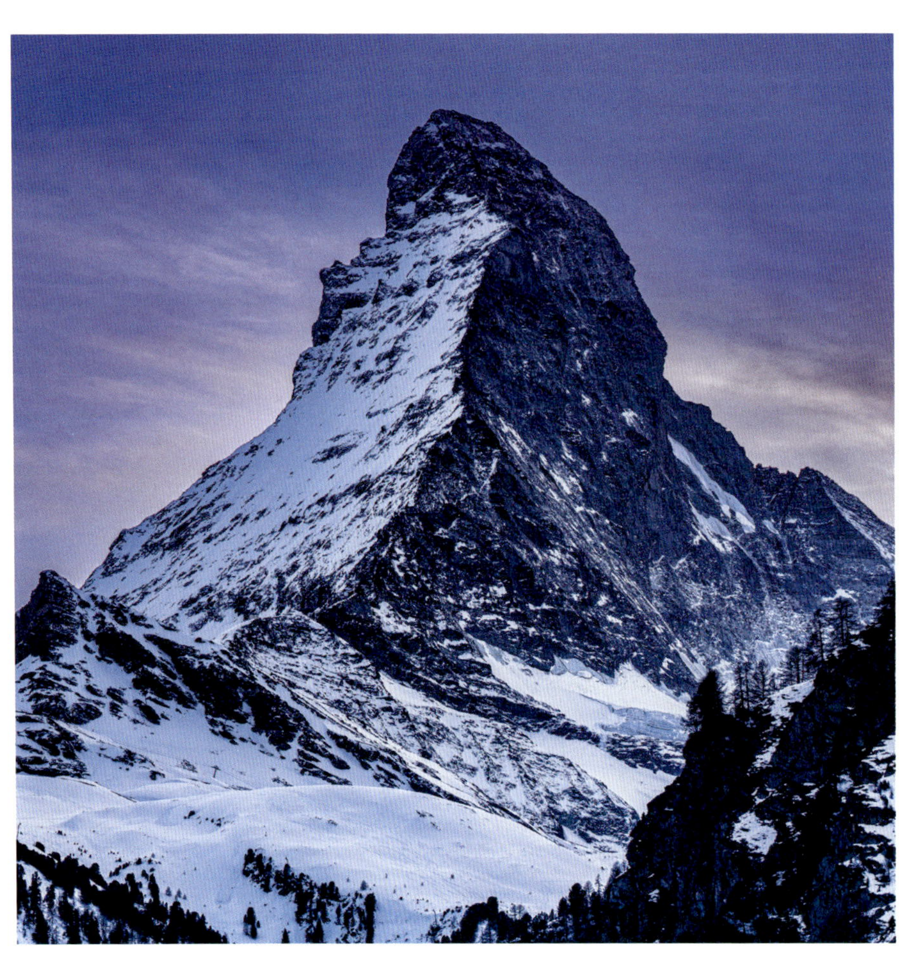

GO BIG

Another technique you can use to help simplify your scene by removing distractions is to make your subject large and dominant in your frame. This helps to minimize distractions as it focuses the viewer onto your subject and away from other objects in the scene, so you're already starting off in a strong position compositionally. Also, when your subject is big in the frame, it makes its details more visible and that draws your viewer's interest.

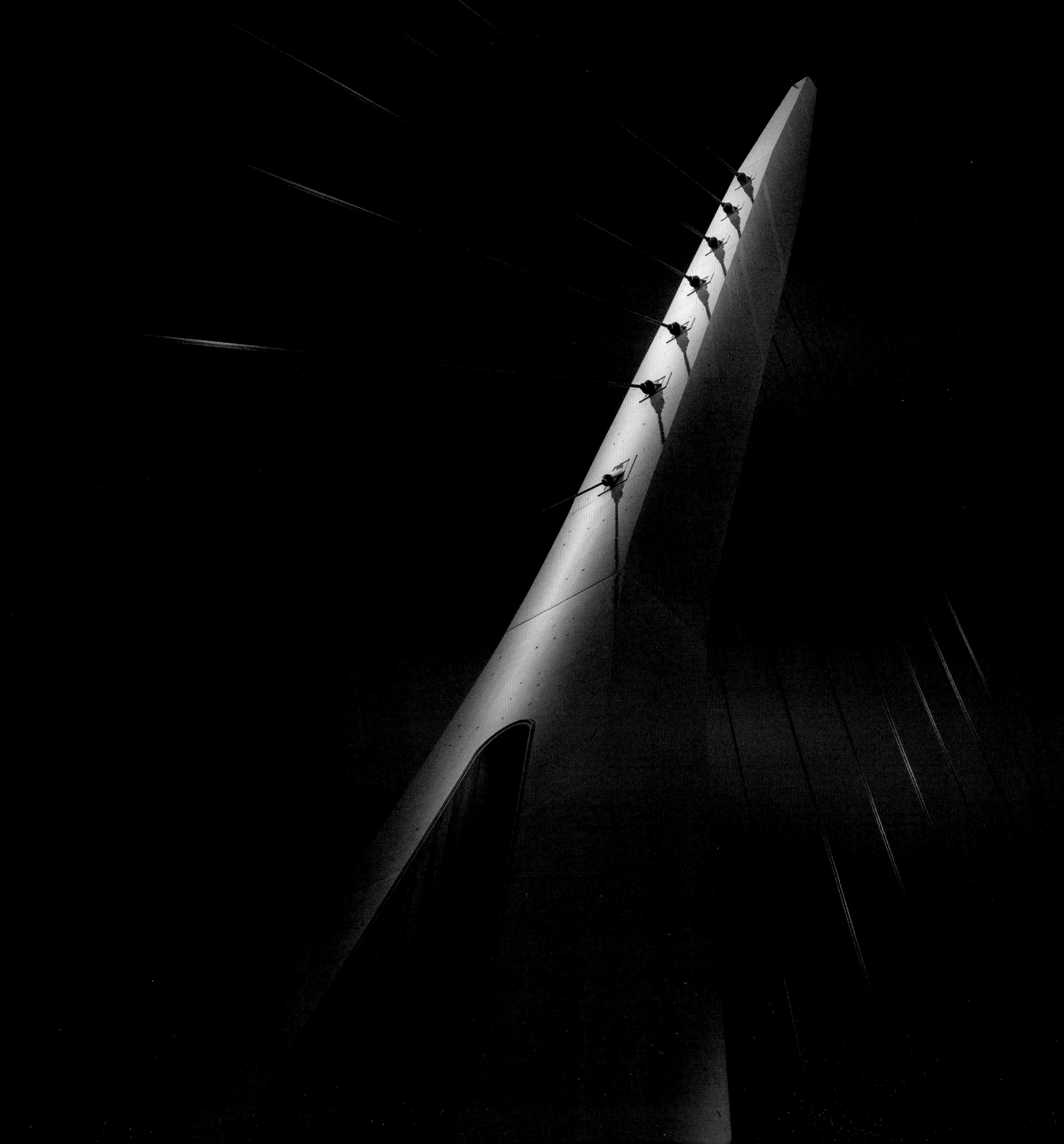

WHEN COLOR DISTRACTS

You'll find images where the color is what makes the image, and you'll also run across images where the color is a distraction. That's when converting to black and white can help simplify the image. One quick way to see if an image works better in black and white is by using Lightroom: When you're in the Develop module (in Classic) or Edit mode (in the cloud version), press the V key on your keyboard, which converts your image to black and white, and you'll probably know right away whether taking away the color simplifies the composition or not. If you like the conversion, you can move on with editing your black-and-white image. If you don't think it strengthens the simplicity of the scene, then just press the V key again and it returns your image to the color version.

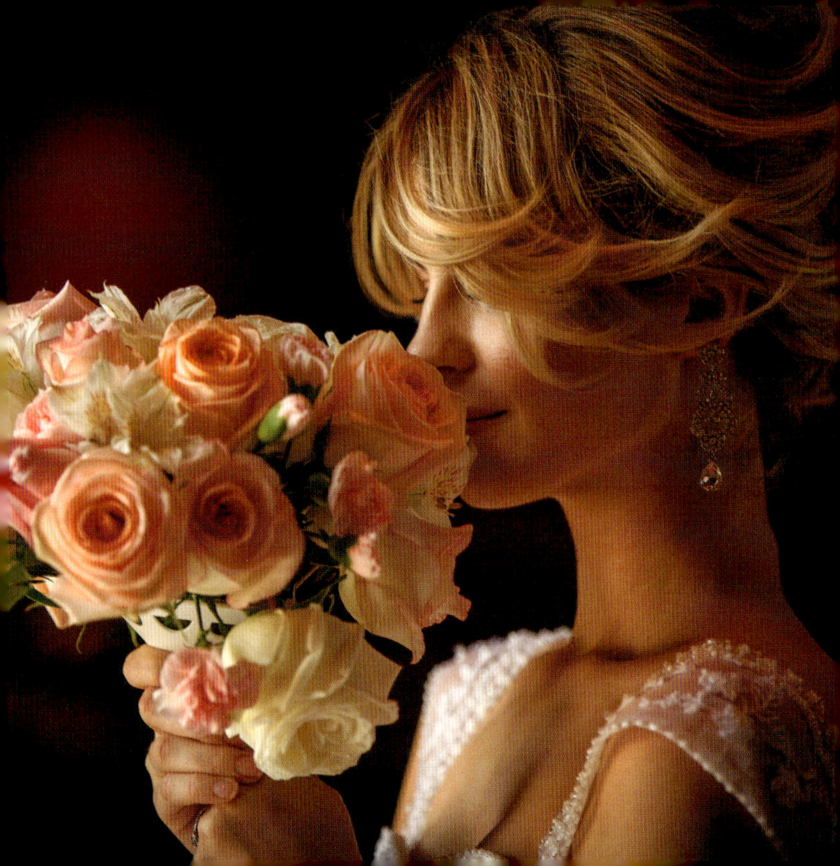

Chapter 08

COMPOSITION
FOR PORTRAITS

When it comes to portraits of people, we still use many of the tried-and-true composition rules (like the rules of thirds, which is widely used by positioning your subject in the left or right third of the frame, and positioning their eyes where the lines cross—more on this later in the chapter). But, there are also some very specific composition techniques that only apply when you're doing portraits, so that's why these are in their own separate chapter. What I've always found interesting about the rules of composition we use for portraits is how certain rules are real deal breakers when it comes to things like having your portraits judged for competitions or photo contests—those folks get really sticky about what is and isn't acceptable, composition-wise, in a photo. We'll cover that stuff in this chapter so you don't run afoul of the portrait police (who are somewhat like the grammar police, but a bit stuffier).

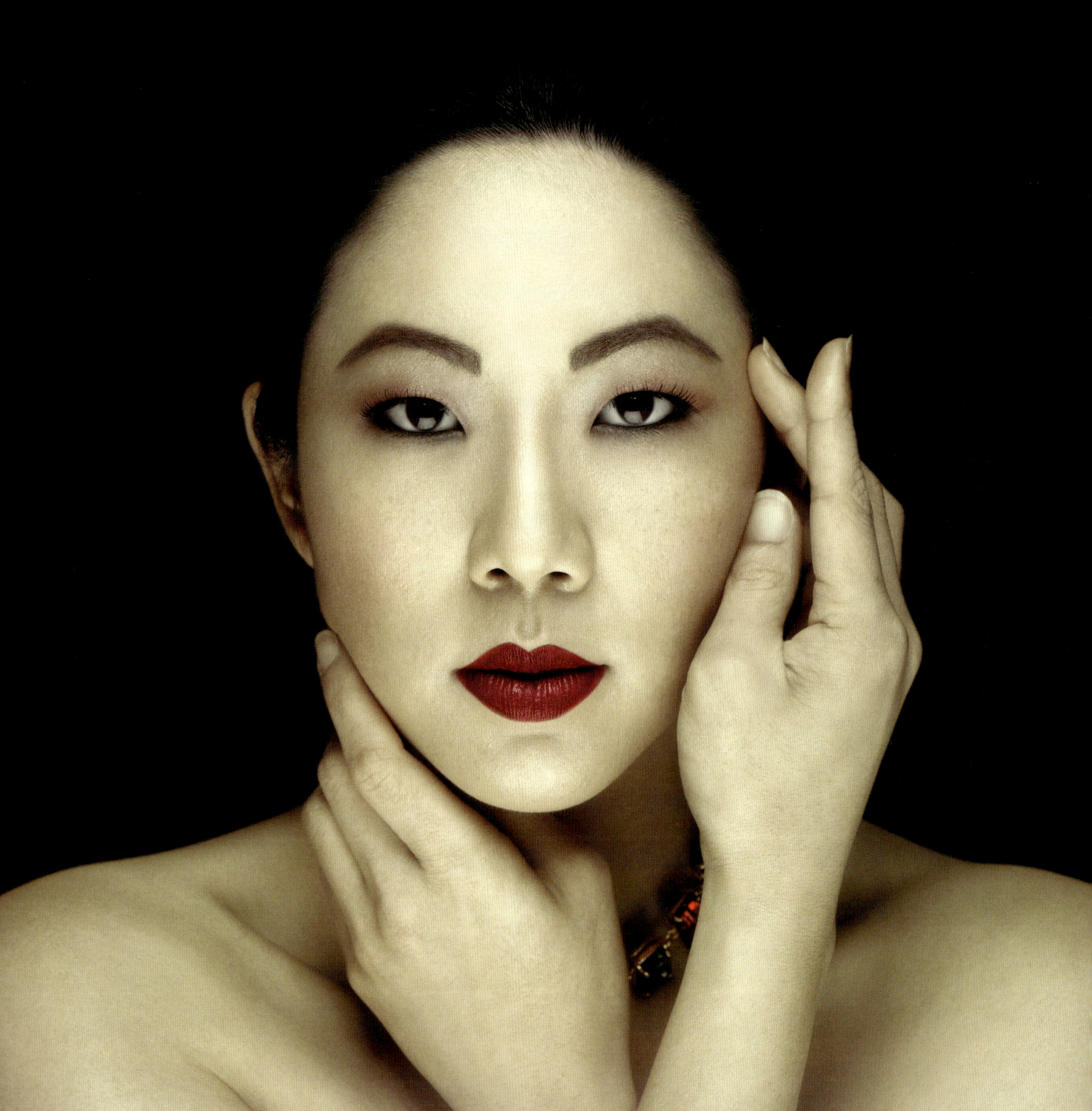

SHOOT FROM
A HIGHER ANGLE

If you ever see someone who is really good at taking selfies with their phone's camera (so, basically, any teen), you'll notice one technique they all seem to share. When they take a selfie, where do they hold their camera? Up high, slightly above their head, with it tilted a bit down toward them, so they're looking up at the camera. Why do they all do this? Because when they take a shot from that slightly higher angle, they look better. It's a more flattering look overall, but it's not just for selfies. If you can shoot from a little higher than your subject's eye, it strengthens their jawline, makes their face look slimmer and longer, makes their eyes look bigger and better, and generally, is just a more flattering look all the way around. That's why pro selfie takers are consistently using this technique— because it works. I know a top portrait and fashion photographer who built a small platform in her studio so that when she was shooting portraits, and her subject was standing, she could walk up on her platform to make her shooting position a little higher than her subject's eyes. I know photographers who shoot portraits standing on an apple box (yes, they sell these at B&H Photo) to get that higher angle or on the first step of a step ladder. Or, if your subject is seated (like my subject was here), you're shooting from a standing position, or maybe sitting on a bar-stool-height chair, so your camera is slightly above their eyes, tilted down toward them to get that more flattering look.

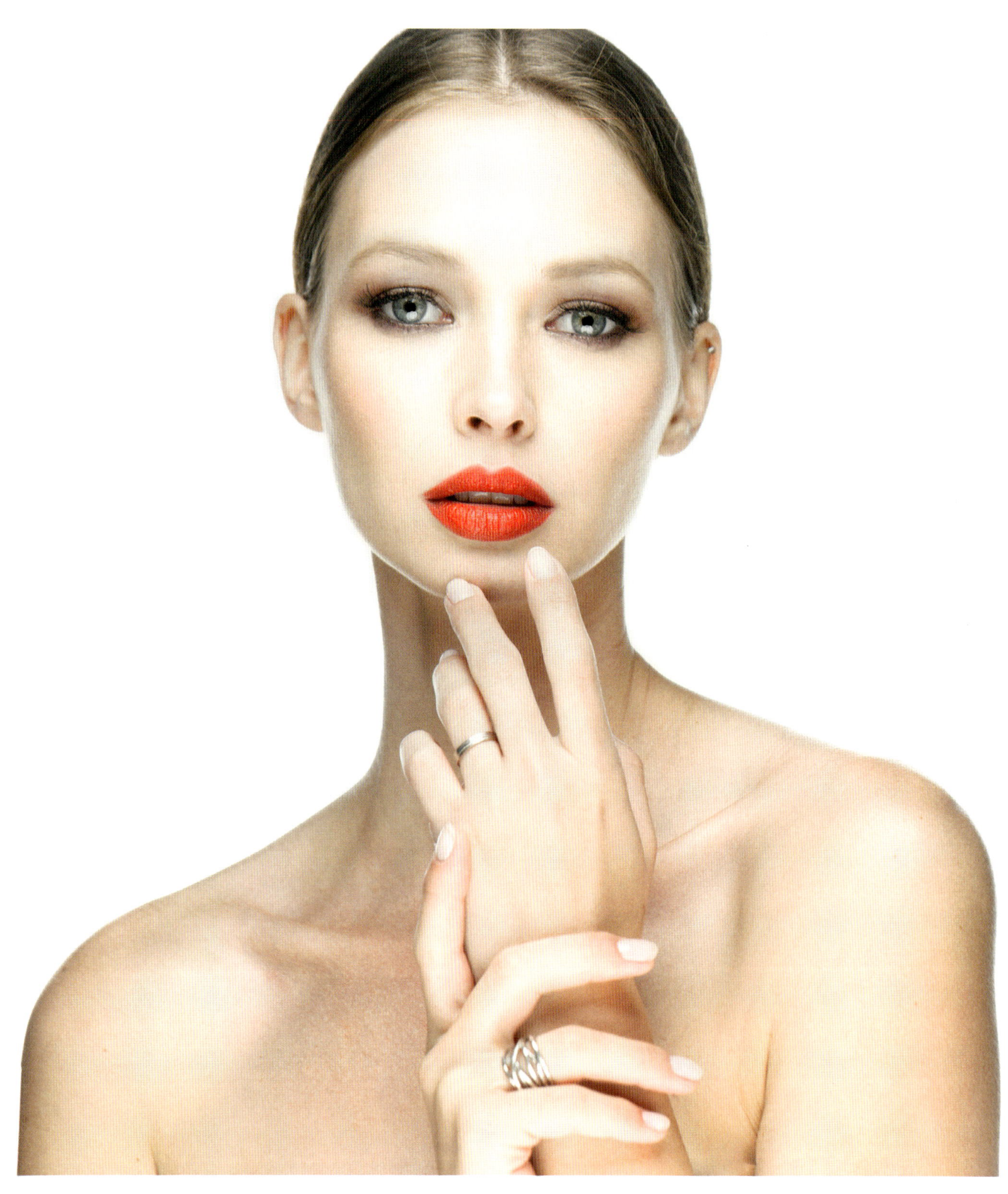

CUT OFF THE TOP OF THE HEAD

Cutting off the top of your subject's head is a very popular and very modern way to compose a shot, and the simple rule is this: take around a third off the top or at least enough to where it appears to be intentional. If you only take off the very tip, you'll hear someone say, "Aw, that's such a nice portrait. Too bad you clipped off the top of his head." If that happens, it simply means you didn't take enough off the top. Don't take the tip. Take a full third and it'll look so intentional that your viewers won't notice it. They see shots like this every day online and in magazines and ads. It brings the subject in closer, filling more of the frame, and creating a more intimate portrait to get a greater connection with the subject. When you turned to this page and saw this image, you didn't think, "Oh my gosh, he messed up! He cut off the top of her head!" You probably didn't even think about it at all. We're so used to seeing this style of portrait composition that there's really no thought about it on the viewer's part. But the closeness and intimacy of the photo is enhanced by bringing the subject that much closer. You don't have to do this all the time, but knowing this is an option, and a popular one at that, you can at least add it to your portrait composition toolbox. One more thing: while it can look great to cut off the top of the head compositionally, cutting off the bottom of the chin is a no-go, so stay away from that one.

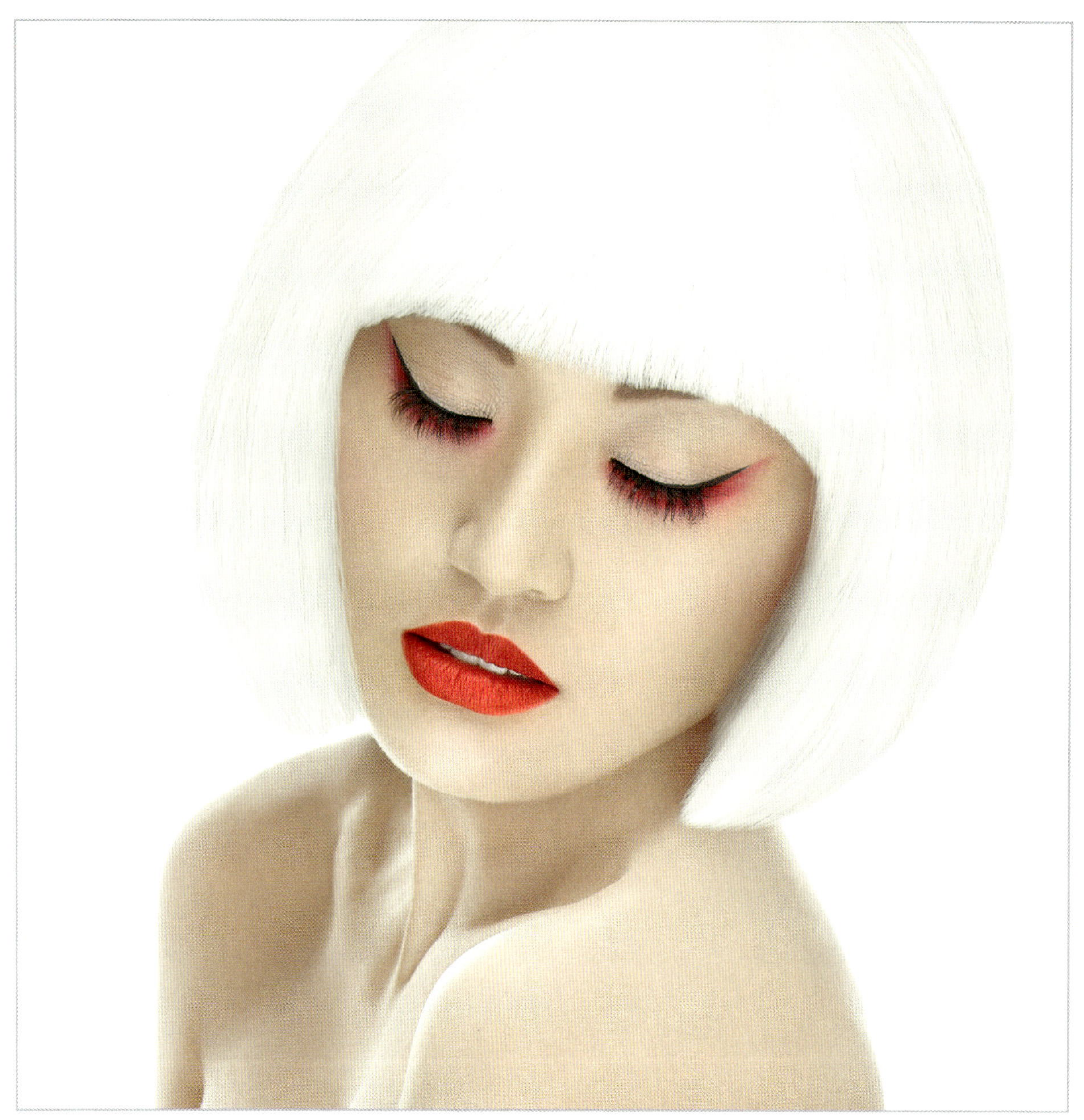

WHAT NOT TO CUT OFF

This is a pretty easy rule to follow, but I see it broken every day, so it's just one of those things to keep an eye out for. The general rule is: we don't chop off fingers or feet. It seems pretty simple (and probably pretty obvious), but again, I see this daily in portraits. It's one of those things that someone looking at a portrait with this problem might not be able to tell you exactly, like "Oh, you cut off her fingers on her right hand." But, there would be something uncomfortable about the portrait, and they wouldn't know what it was. That's the last thing we want to create in our portraits—a photo where some little compositional thing is making the whole portrait a little uncomfortable for the viewer. Now, in the portrait we have here, I'm cutting off a lot of stuff—the top of her head, a lot of her chest, etc.—and those are all fine. It's those little things, like fingers, and the ends of shoes, and things like that, that we have to watch out for. An easy thing to take note of is this: If you see their shoes in the frame, make sure you see all of the shoes. If either hand is near the edge of the frame, make sure all their fingers are accounted for.

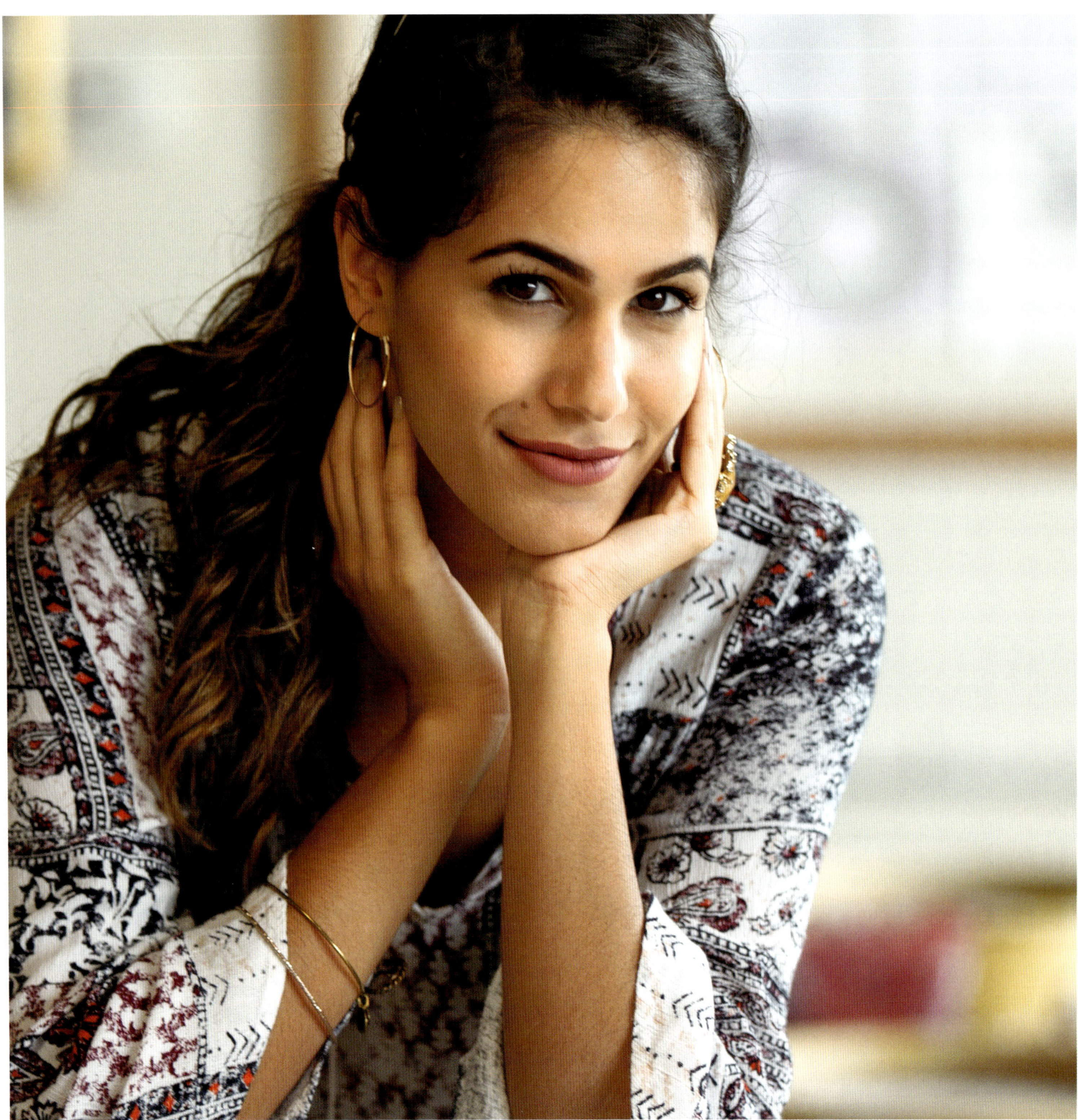

WHERE TO POSITION EYES IN THE FRAME

This is a pretty simple one to follow because you can use the rule of thirds to help. The idea is that you generally want to position your subject's eyes in the top third of the frame (like you see in this example). Now, depending on how close your subject is in the frame (or to the camera), this might also cause the top of their head to be cut off (like hers is here, but again, it's enough that it's obviously intentional and not cut off by mistake). You can easily keep their entire head in the frame by either zooming out or backing up, but positioning their eyes somewhere in that top third is the general rule.

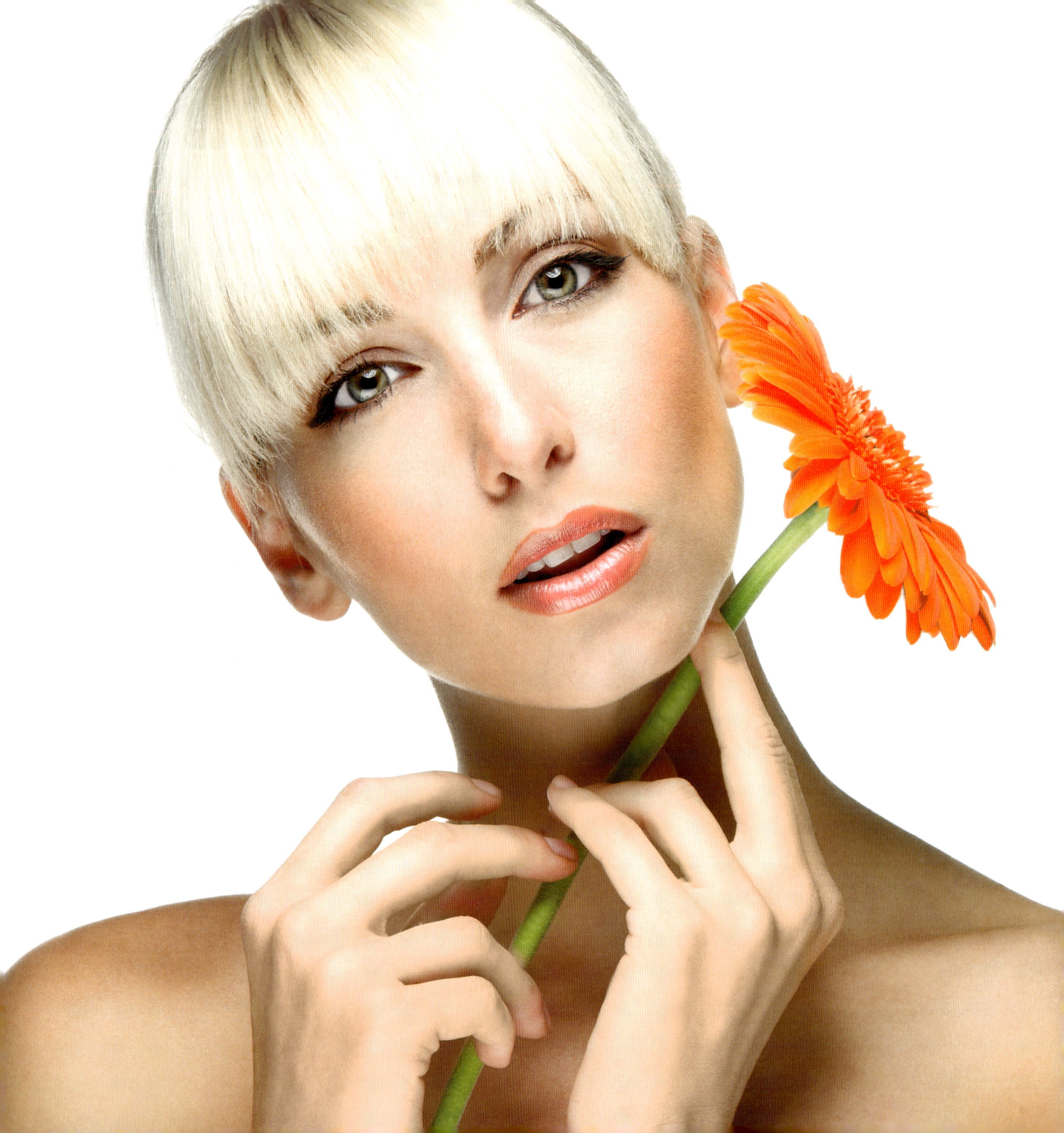

WHAT NEEDS TO BE SHARP

Generally, the most important part of a portrait is the eyes, so it stands to reason that the one thing in your portrait that absolutely needs to be sharp is your subject's eyes. In fact, it is literally the part of the face where we lock our focus, especially if you're using the "focus and compose" method of shooting sharp portraits (where you position the center point of your camera to where it's directly on your subject's eye that is closest to the camera, hold the shutter button halfway down, then recompose the shot, and then press the shutter button down the rest of the way to actually take the shot). If you bought your camera in the last year or two, chances are it has a special AI-powered facial recognition feature called "Auto Eye Focus" (or something close to that, depending on your particular brand of camera) that automatically locks focus on your subject's eye. That's how important it is that the eyes are in focus. It's not only in portraits; it's the same for photos of your pets, or even wildlife shots—if the eyes aren't in focus, the shot goes in the trash (well, that's the general rule anyway). When we're shooting team sports, like football or baseball, etc., we focus right on the number on the center of a jersey, since it's mostly on the same plane as someone's eyes. So, if their jersey is sharp, we know their eyes will be sharp, too. One more thing: If you're shooting group shots, like the formals for a wedding, or a business group where there are a few rows of people, where do you focus? You focus on the eyes of someone in the center of the front row. As long as their eyes are in sharp focus, the rest will look okay, too.

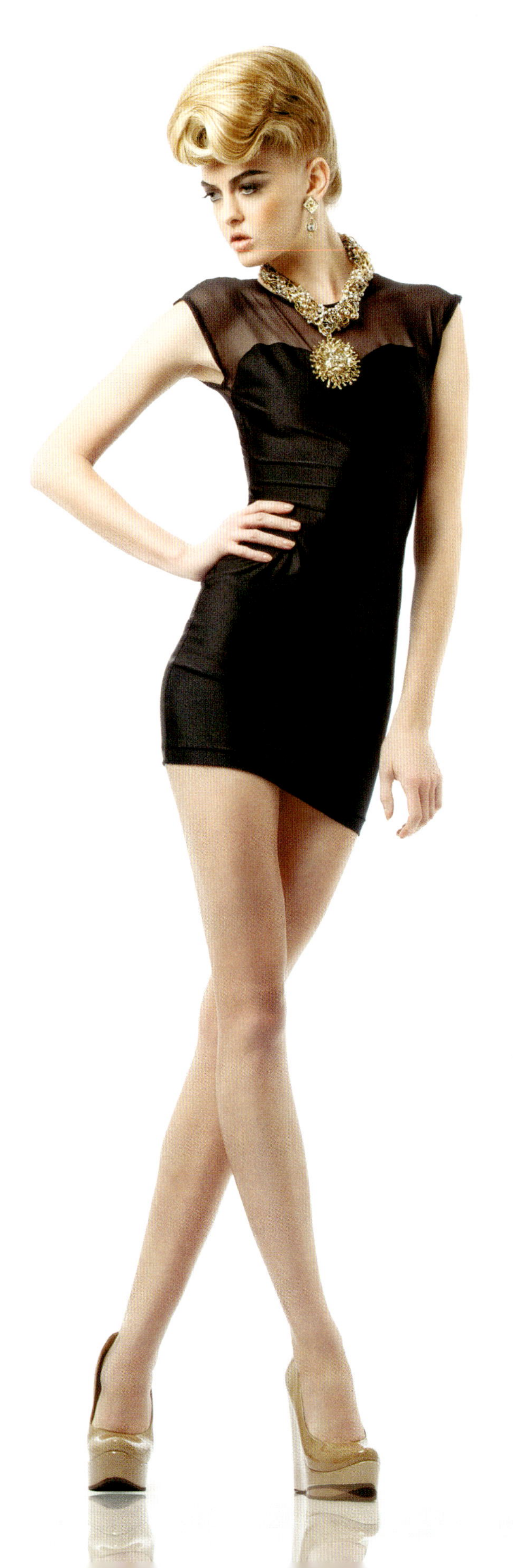

COMPOSITION FOR FULL LENGTH

This is one where your composition helps keep your subject from suffering an unflattering distortion issue, especially if you're trying to use a wide-angle lens so you fit your subject's entire body (full length) into the frame. Also, shooting full length when you're in a standing position can make your subject's legs look shorter and a bit "squatty" in comparison to what I recommend for shooting full-length shots. As we learned earlier, when it comes to full-length shots, we shoot from down low, at least at waist level. Not only does it avoid some distortion, it is also, generally, a very flattering position, making your subject's legs look longer, which makes them look thinner and taller as well. I will often shoot either sitting on a chair, or sitting on the floor cross-legged (that's what I did for this shot), or sitting on an apple box turned tall on its side (those wooden boxes you buy from camera stores are incredibly sturdy). Also, to avoid distortion, I recommend not using a wide-angle lens if you can help it and instead, use a longer lens, like a 50mm or 70mm, and just shoot from farther back. I know that's not always possible based on space, but it's what will get you the best, most flattering, and least distorted results.

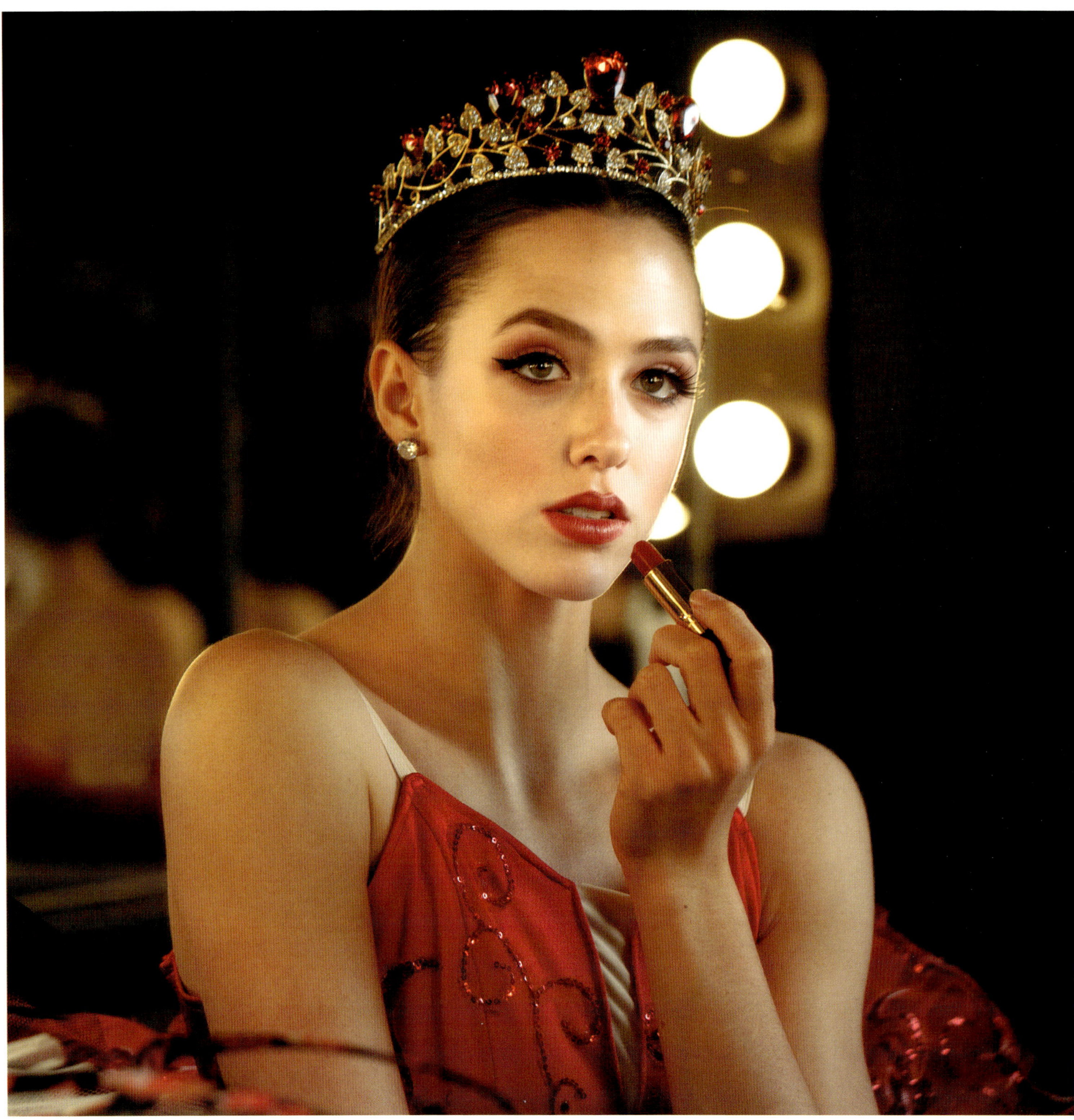

AVOID CROPPING JOINTS

This is another one of those things that make people uncomfortable when they look at a portrait, and the general rule is when we're framing up our shot, don't split through any of our subject's joints. So, don't cut them off right at the elbows or the knees (remember that saying, "Don't cut 'em off at the knees"?), or at the wrists or ankles, giving them the double amputee effect. Those spots are the big no-nos (and will draw boos from the judges of photo contests). So, if we don't cut those out of our frame by going right through the joints, where can we cut those parts off where it looks natural? Right above or below the elbows, knees, or ankles. Take at look at this image of a ballerina here, backstage in her dressing room. I've cropped off her entire elbow on the right, but I did it well above the joint, so it doesn't feel uncomfortable for the viewer. Same with her arm on the left side of the frame—I'm high enough from the crook of her arm so it all looks perfectly natural.

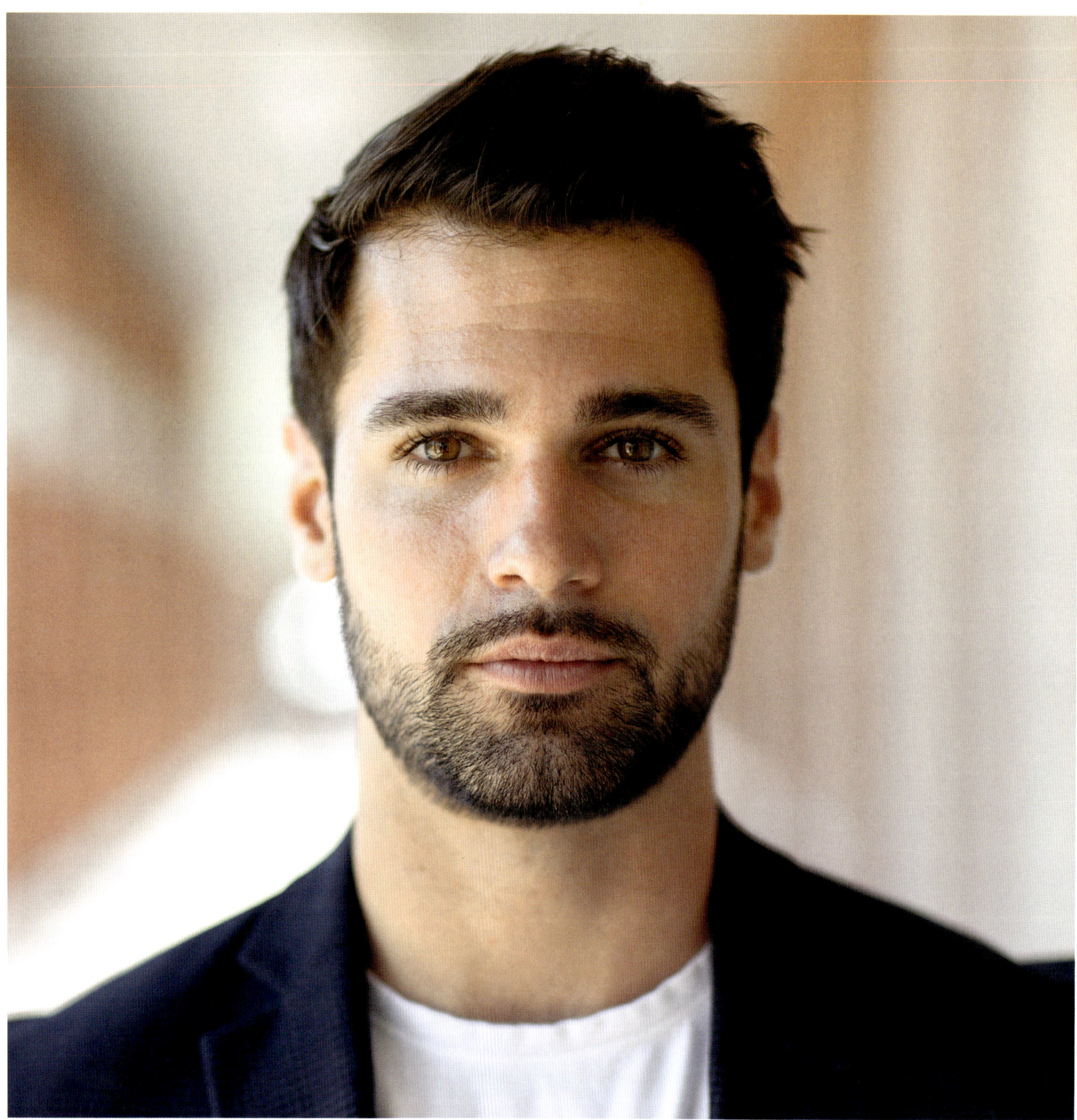

DON'T ALLOW TOO MUCH HEADROOM

If I had to pick what the most common composition mistake I see photographers who are new to shooting portraits make, it's that they leave way too much space above their subject's head. That's fine if the image you're shooting is supposed to be for the cover of a magazine and you're intentionally leaving that space for the magazine's nameplate (name of the magazine) to fit above their head. But, if you're not shooting a cover shot, you need to tighten up that space. In the example here, you can see his head is fully in the frame, but there's not a bunch of empty space above it. I think the reason this happens so often is that people who are new to portraiture will position the subject's eyes in the center of the frame, and if you do that, it's generally going to leave way too much space above their head. Moving their eyes above center, or ideally into the top third of the frame, will help make sure you don't have too much space up there.

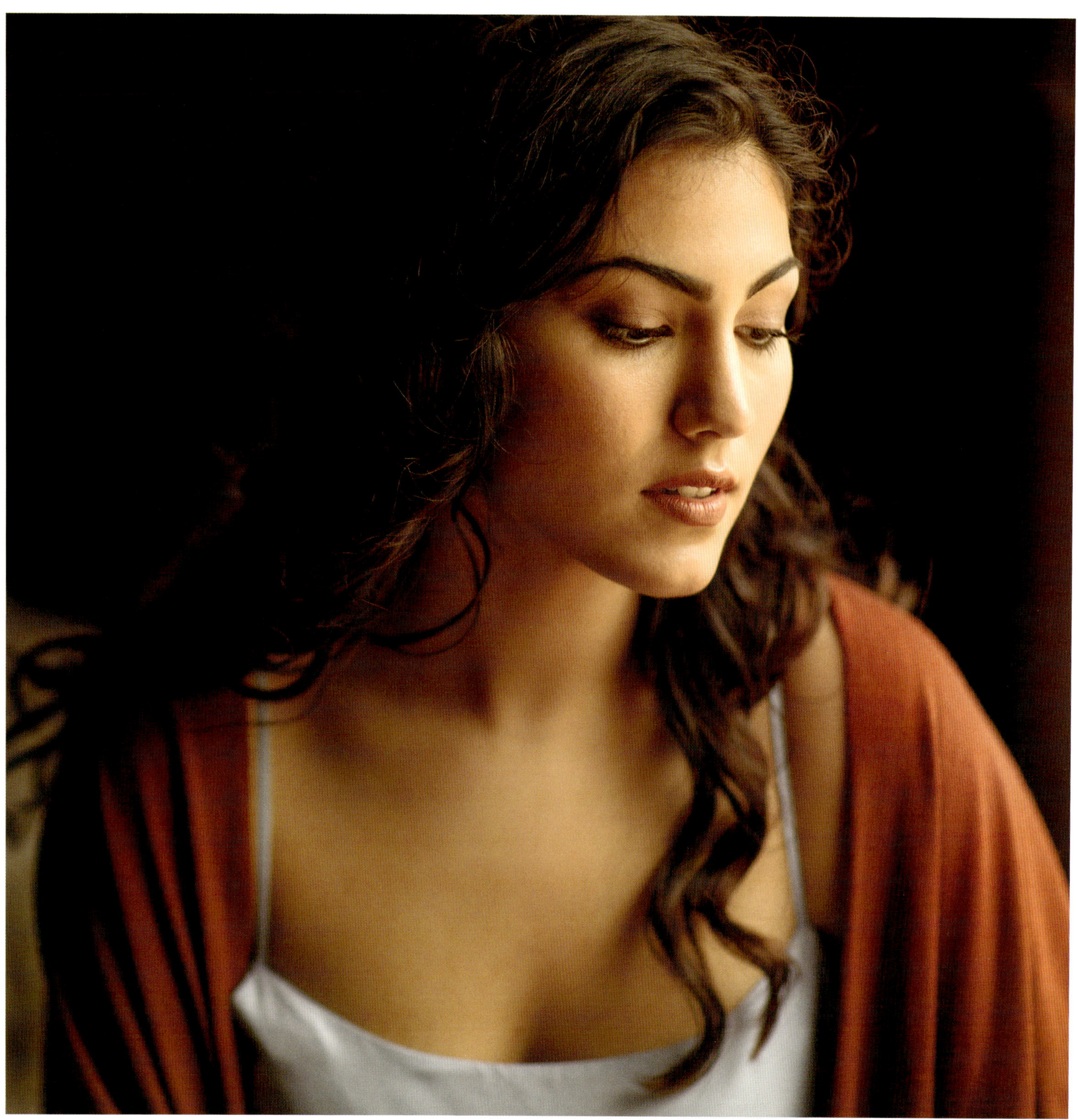

WINDOW LIGHT PORTRAITS

Window light portraits are among my favorites just for the sheer quality of the light, and making a successful window light portrait is about where you position your subject and where you position your camera to make the most of that light. Now, ideally, when making a window light portrait, we would choose a north-facing window so we don't get harsh, direct light, but you can still make a great window light portrait at other windows that do get direct light. You just need to position your subject a little farther away from the window—ideally, a foot or two behind the window, so they are getting the edge of the light (which is softer) rather than direct light. Next, you want to have them stand (or sit, as in the example here) so they are parallel to the window (you want them beside the window, not facing it like they're looking out it). Now, they are back a few feet from the window, but you're going to position yourself at the window aiming a bit back toward them. Position your camera up a little higher than their eye level (which I did here, standing up, but crouching down a bit to lower my camera height, so it's just above her eye level), and then you take the shot. I had my subject turn her face a little bit toward the window, so the light would wrap around her face, but not too far because you still want those shadows on the opposite side of the face.

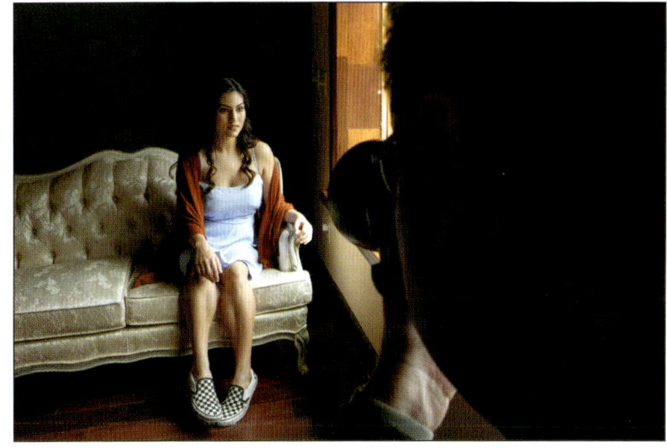

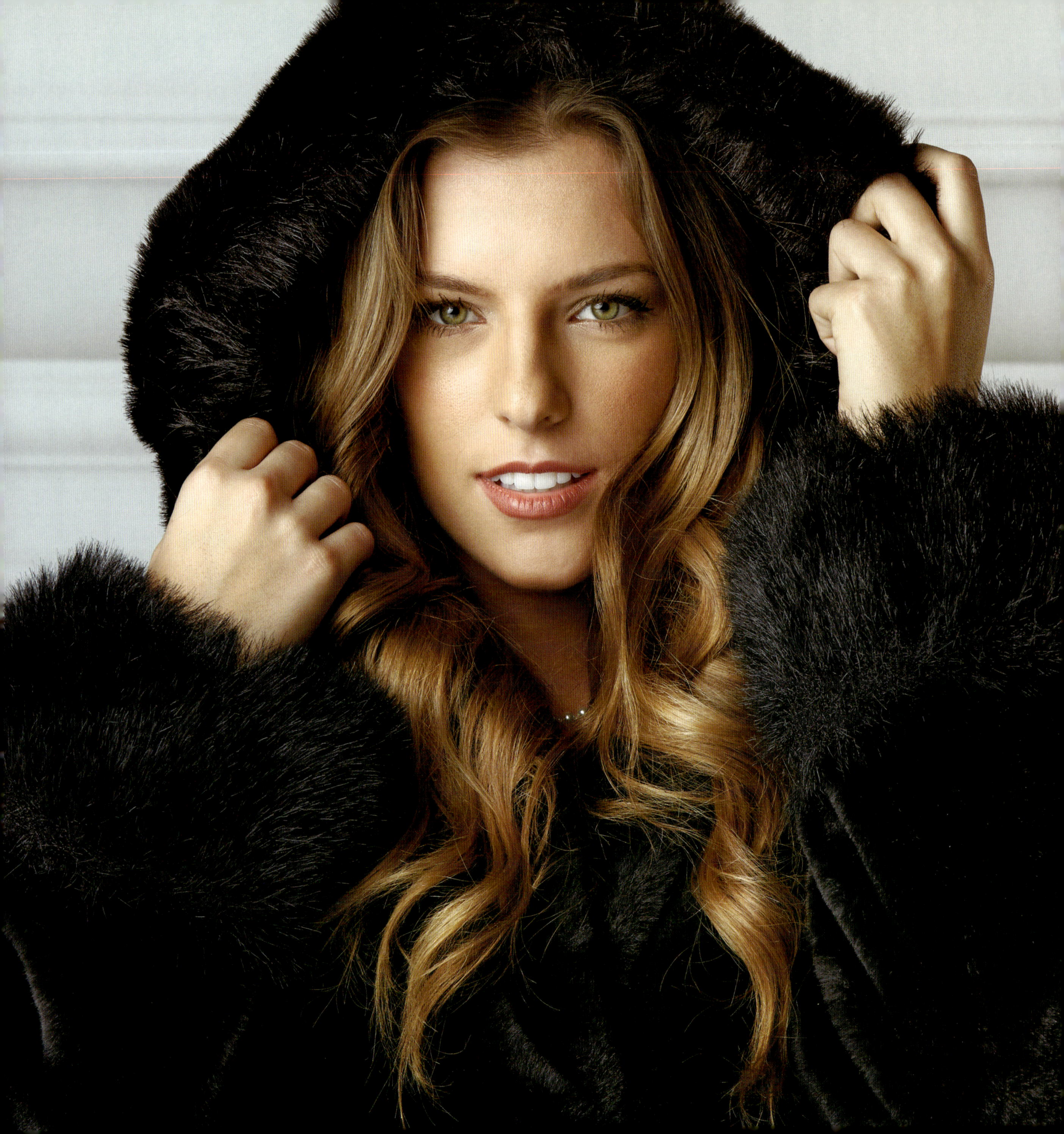

USE A LENS THAT FLATTERS

We've talked about how the lens you choose has a lot to do with the composition of your photo, as it has a lot to do with things like your background being out of focus or all in focus, and the compression of the lens determining if your background looks far away (wide-angle) or right up close to your subject (telephoto). But when it comes to portraits, it also has a lot to do with how your subject looks in general, and there are lenses you can choose that literally flatter your subject and help make them look their best. These are called "portrait" lenses and it really has a lot to do with the length of the lens, with longer lenses generally being more flattering for portraits. Today, there are two lenses I use that are super-popular for portraits. The first is an 85mm prime lens (prime just means it doesn't zoom—it's just one focal length, 85mm, all the time). Because it's used as a wedding and portrait lens, it comes in a bunch of different f-stops, ranging from f/1.2 to f/1.4 and f/1.8. At f/1.2, you can really make that background go out of focus and super-soft. But, the depth of field is so shallow (meaning, the range of

what's in focus on your subject's face) and so thin that if you're not deadly accurate with your focus, the overall image will be a bit out of focus. It's a big lens, too, and heavy, and expensive as all get out, so I recommend the way lighter, way cheaper, and way smaller f/1.8 version. You'll still get that background nice and blurry, but without breaking the bank or your back, and it's easier to shoot in focus at f/1.8 than it is at f/1.2. My other go-to lens is my 70–200mm f/2.8 (yes, you can get away with the way lighter, cheaper f/4 version), and I'm usually shooting between 150mm and 200mm, so I'm standing a bit back from my subject and zooming in, which puts the background out of focus. There are other long lenses that are flattering for portraits (and, yes, you can use a 50mm f/1.8, but it has its own learning curve and isn't flattering for every type of portrait). You can make a portrait with any lens you have, including wide-angle lenses, but to take a flattering portrait with one has its own learning curve, too. My advice: buy a lens that flatters people right out of the box (why make it hard on yourself?).

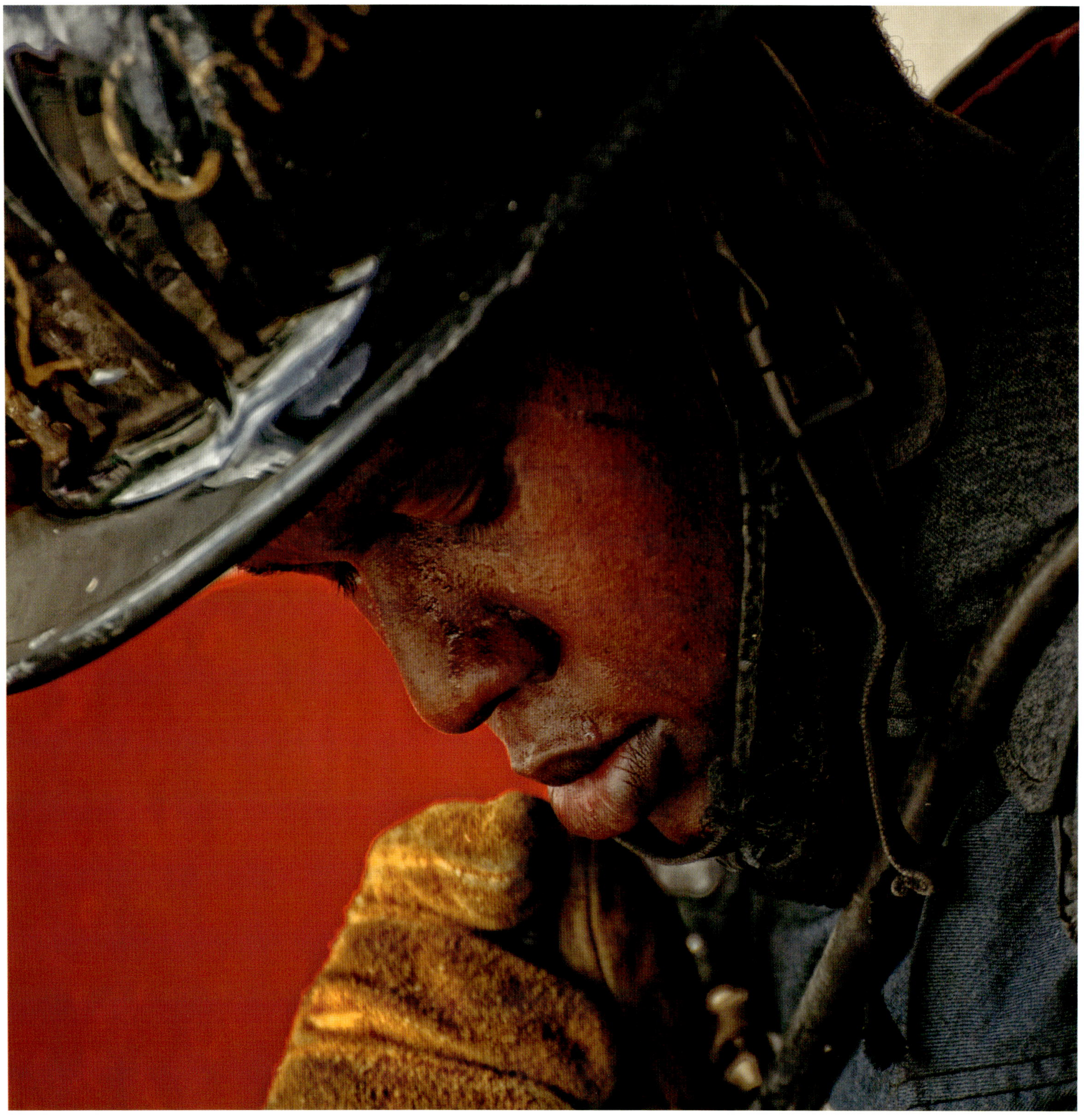

POSED OR NATURAL?

I've never had a client or subject say, "What I'm looking for is a shot where I look like I'm posed." Not once. What I hear again and again is that they're looking for a natural, genuine-looking portrait, and even though it might be posed, they don't want it to look posed. They want it to look like they look. Well, at least like they look after a really good night's sleep. One of the best ways I've found to do this is by connecting with your subject to the point that they stop thinking about the fact that they're being photographed, and they are engaged in a conversation with you. When they're engaged and chatting, especially about things they love or are passionate about, they lose the worry and uncomfortableness they feel about being in front of the camera—their real, genuine smiles and expressions come out. This starts when they walk in the door. Don't have your camera in your hand when you're first talking to them because they know you could, at any moment, bring it to your eye and snap off a shot. Put the camera down and just talk. Find out as much as possible about them and their

interests, but don't explore those interests until you start shooting. I let them start with a regular old stiff pose (for guys, that's standing there with their arms crossed in front of them, like they're posing for the cover of *Forbes* or a wrestling magazine), and then I start digging deeper into their interests. If they have pets, I start asking them questions about their dogs or cats, and you'll see their eyes light up. When they tell stories about the funny thing their dog or cat did last night, you'll start to get those genuine laughs and expressions, and you'd better have your finger on the shutter button, so you can capture those all-important moments between the poses. Get them talking about their hobby, about their favorite music, the best concert they've seen, their kids, their last vacation, or their dream vacation, and once they start really getting into it, the rest takes care of itself. Just keep them talking, laughing, and engaged, and you'll make the best, most-natural portraits they've ever had taken. The ones where their friends look at the portrait and say, "Oh, that is so you!" That's a home run right there.

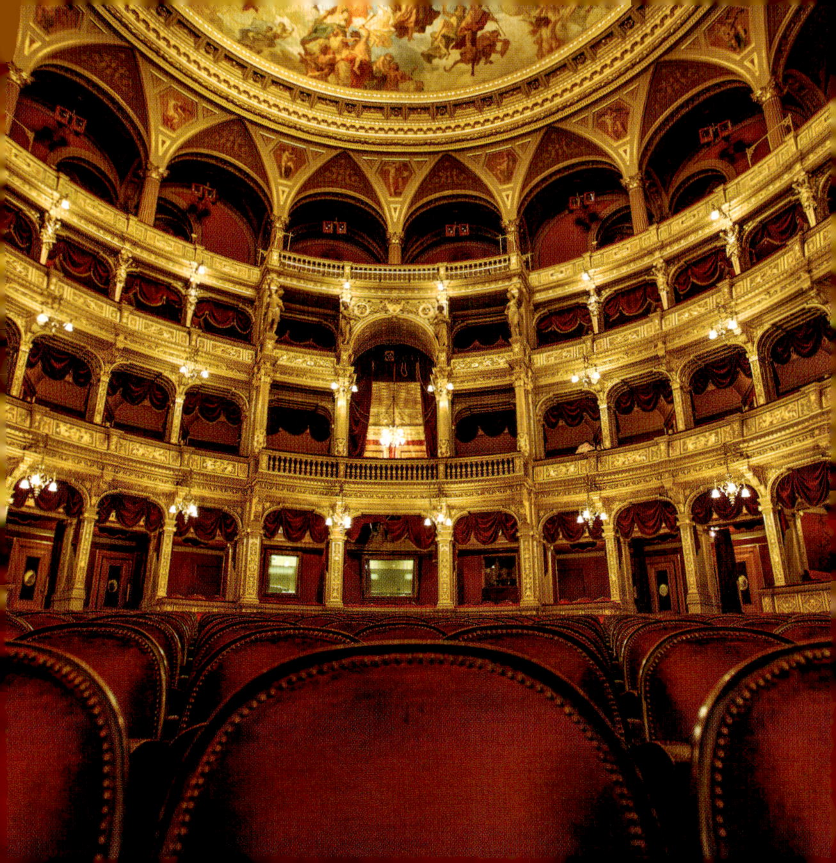

Chapter 09

HOW TO CRITIQUE YOUR OWN WORK

It's often really hard to look at our own work objectively, especially because we don't see our images the way other people do, but being able to critique our own work is an important part of our job as a photographer (more on this shortly). There are all sorts of reasons why it's so hard: For example, let's say you took a shot of a stream, and it was warm and sunny that day, but not too hot, and your spouse was there with you, and you both just came from a picnic you shared right up the road, with a yummy lunch packed by the bed and breakfast where you stayed the night before, and then you met a kindly old farmer who told you about this stream when you were buying some homemade preserves from him while giving his dog Ruby a belly rub, and well, it was just about the perfect day. When you look at that picture, those wonderful memories are baked into that picture. But when someone else looks at that same image, they just think: "Yup, that's a stream." Another thing that makes it tough is that we'll focus on the part of the shot that was a challenge for us, or even a success, like when you shoot a waterfall. When you look at the photo, you're focused on the waterfall, and how you used an ND filter to get that smooth, silky water, but when someone else views the image, they see all of it—including the ugly dead branch sticking in from the side, and that crumpled up beer can on the far left. Another thing that makes critiquing our images tough is when we take a shot that falls under the "I always wanted to take a shot like that" category, and though it checks a box for us, when other people look at it, it doesn't move them or cause any emotion—it's just another photo. All of these, both technical and emotional reasons, make it hard to objectively critique our own work. In this chapter, we're going to look at some of the technical things we can consider when looking at our own images so at least, if we do have a great shot, it won't be marred by a technical flaw or error.

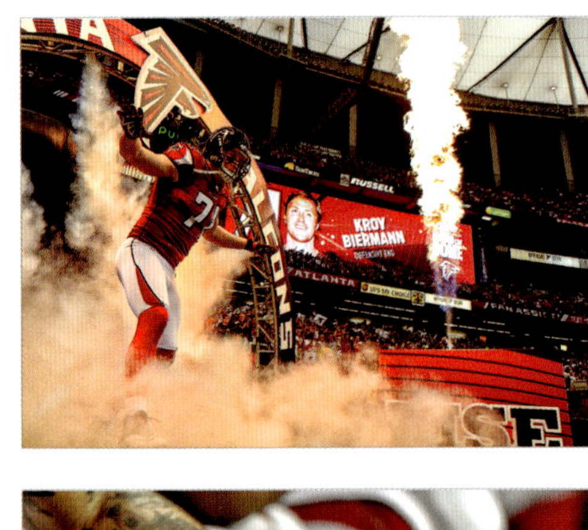
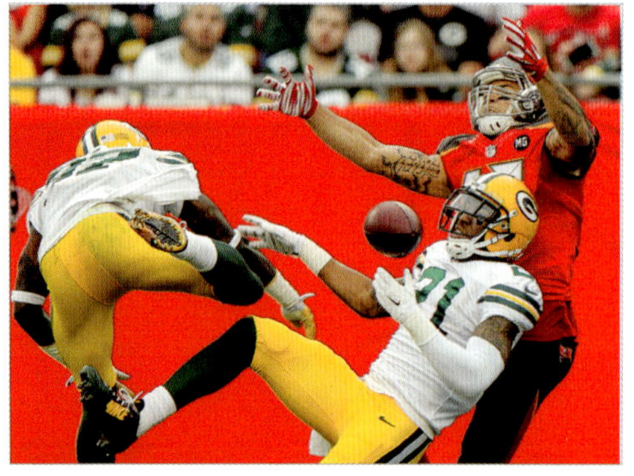
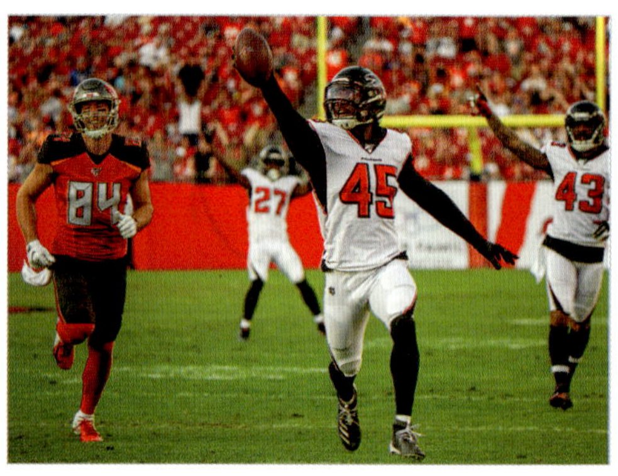
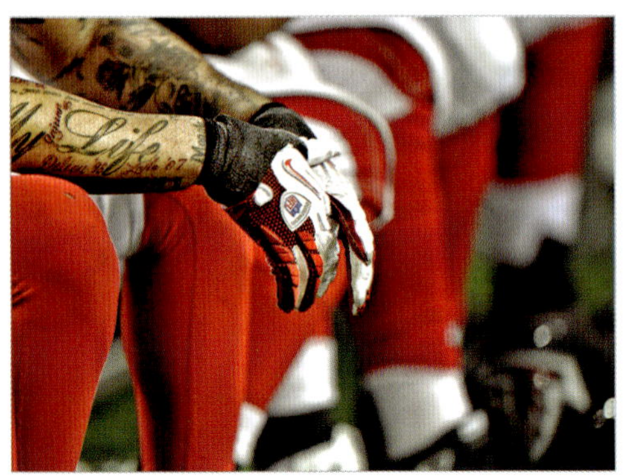
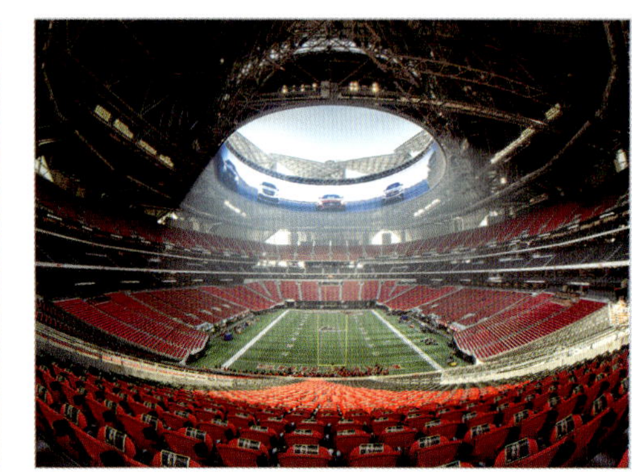
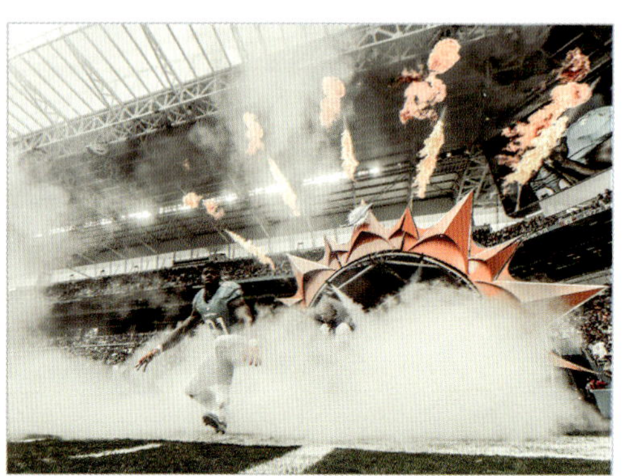
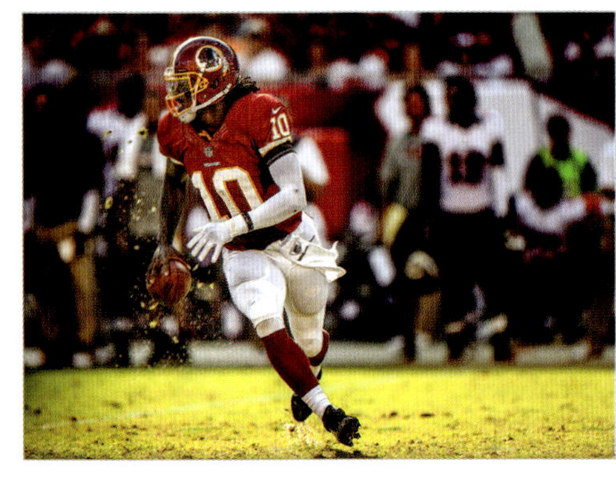
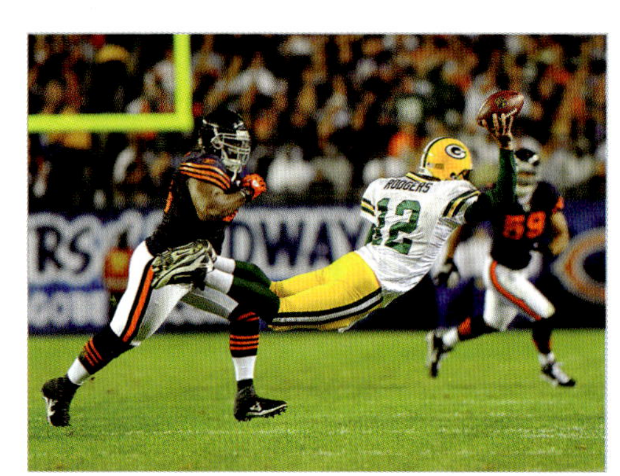
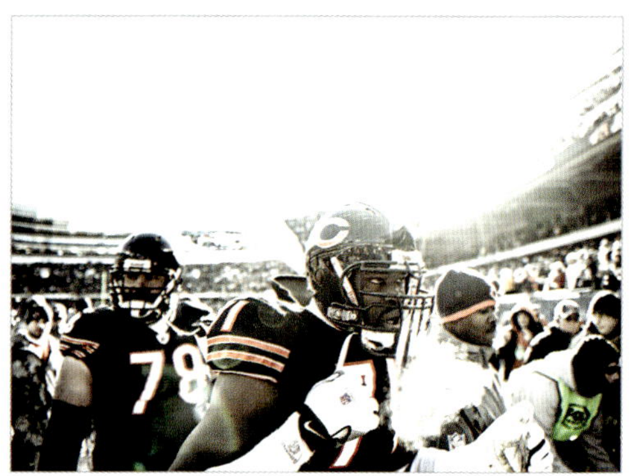
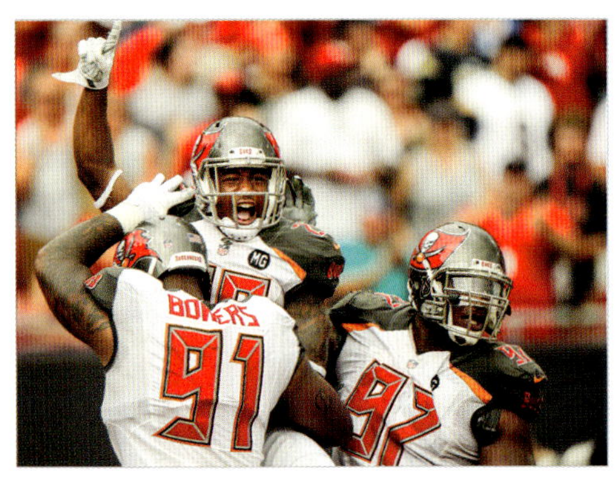
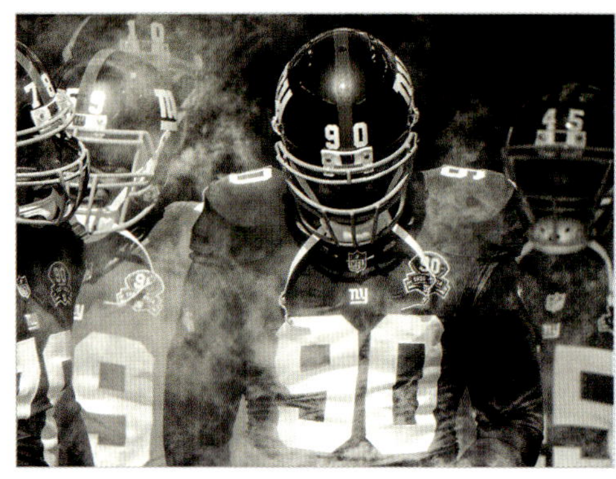
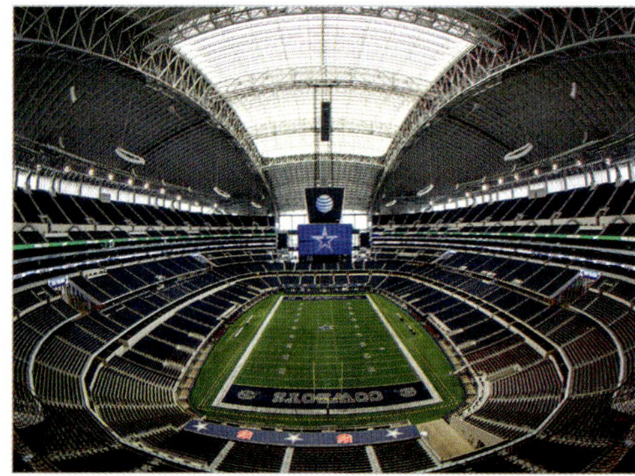

WHY YOU NEED A PORTFOLIO

If you want to really start critiquing your own work, there's an important exercise you can do that will help you on so many levels, and that's putting together a portfolio of your best work. One of the most important reasons for this is that, perhaps for the first time ever, you're forced to look at your entire photo library and pick just your very best images. This is harder to do than you might think, and more valuable to your progress as a photographer than you can imagine. I would start by choosing a maximum of 24 images—only your very best shots—and then put them all in a collection or a folder (even a folder on your hard drive—doesn't matter—but you need to separate them from the rest). This alone will stretch your self-critiquing muscle as you'll have to make some important decisions about which of your images are your best, so it's great practice, but there's more to it than that. Once you have these 20 or 24 images together, at that moment, you'll finally know where you stand as a photographer. My guess is, you'll look at them and think, "Hey, I'm doing pretty good." But you also may look at them and think, "I've got some work to do." Either way, at least you'll know. Also, you'll only add a photo to this portfolio of your best work if you take an image that's better than one of the current images in there, and then you'll remove that weakest one, so you don't go over 24 images total. This way, during the year, your portfolio continues to grow and evolve, and you're growing and evolving as a photographer right along with it.

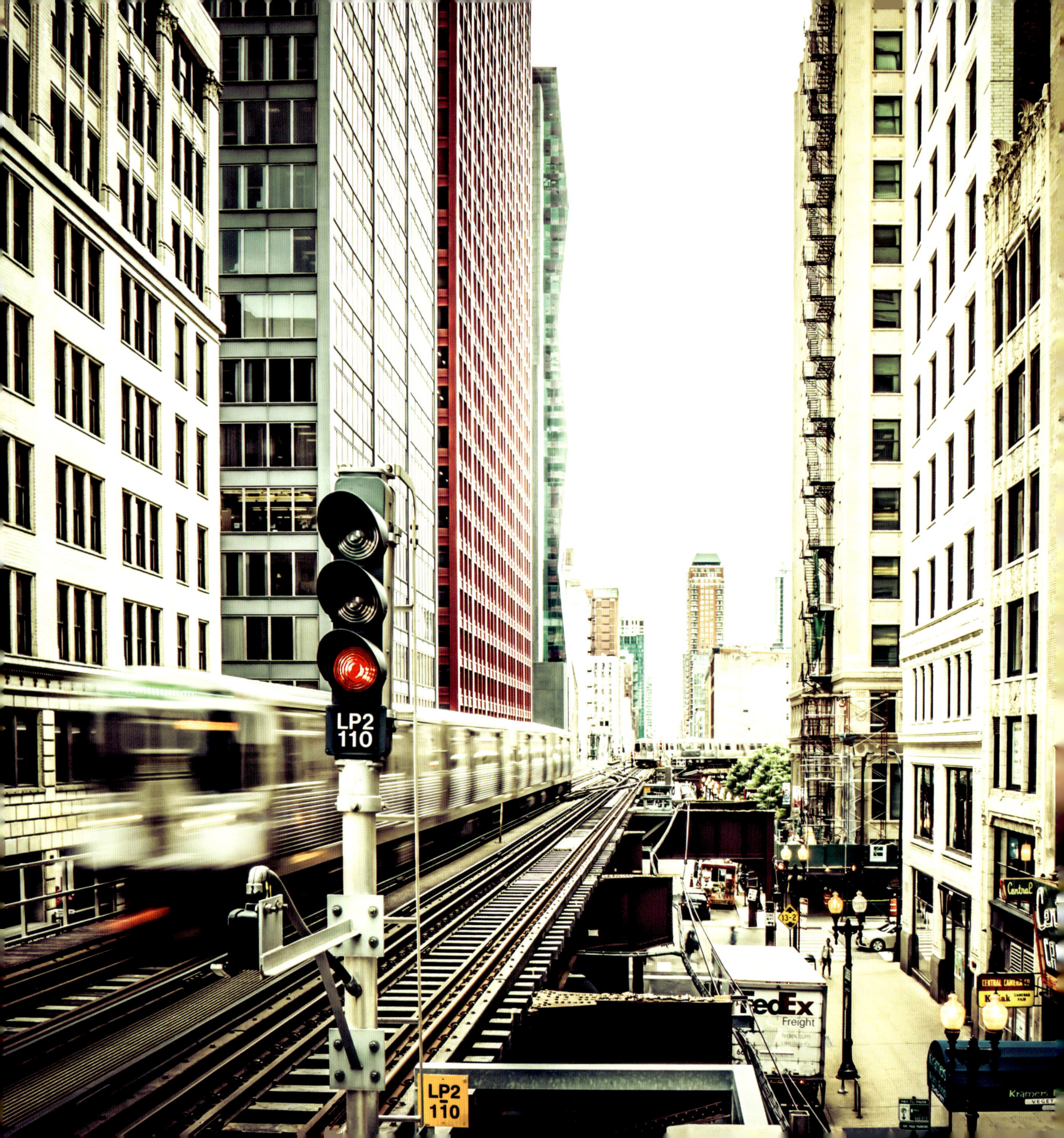

LP2
110
LP2
110
FedEx
Freight
fedex.com
Central
Central
CENTRAL CAMERA CO.
Kodak

THE IMPORTANCE OF BECOMING A PHOTO EDITOR

Outside of actually taking the photo itself, there are two things that happen after the fact that are just as important: one is, of course, getting really good at post-processing our images in Lightroom, Photoshop, or whatever application you wind up using, and the other is becoming a really good photo editor. By that, I mean the ability to look at a group of similar images and be able to figure out which one of those is "the one." I had a friend who was a decent enough photographer, but if he took 80 shots during a portrait session, you could bank on him picking one of the very worst shots as the one he would share online. I'd say to him, "Why did you pick this one? You had so many great shots from that shoot?!" And he'd say, "I dunno. I thought there was something about it." There was. It was the worst one. Always. He had a knack for picking and sharing the worst shot from a shoot. It was uncanny. You need to develop just the opposite. You need to be able to objectively look at a bunch of similar shots and pick the very best one. It might come down to two or three that are so close it's hard to go wrong with whichever one you pick, but you've got to work on your skills at becoming a good photo editor. That starts with looking at your images as thumbnails and seeing which ones jump out at you. Great photos stand out, even at small sizes. If it looks good at a small size, as long as there aren't technical issues, it should look even better larger.

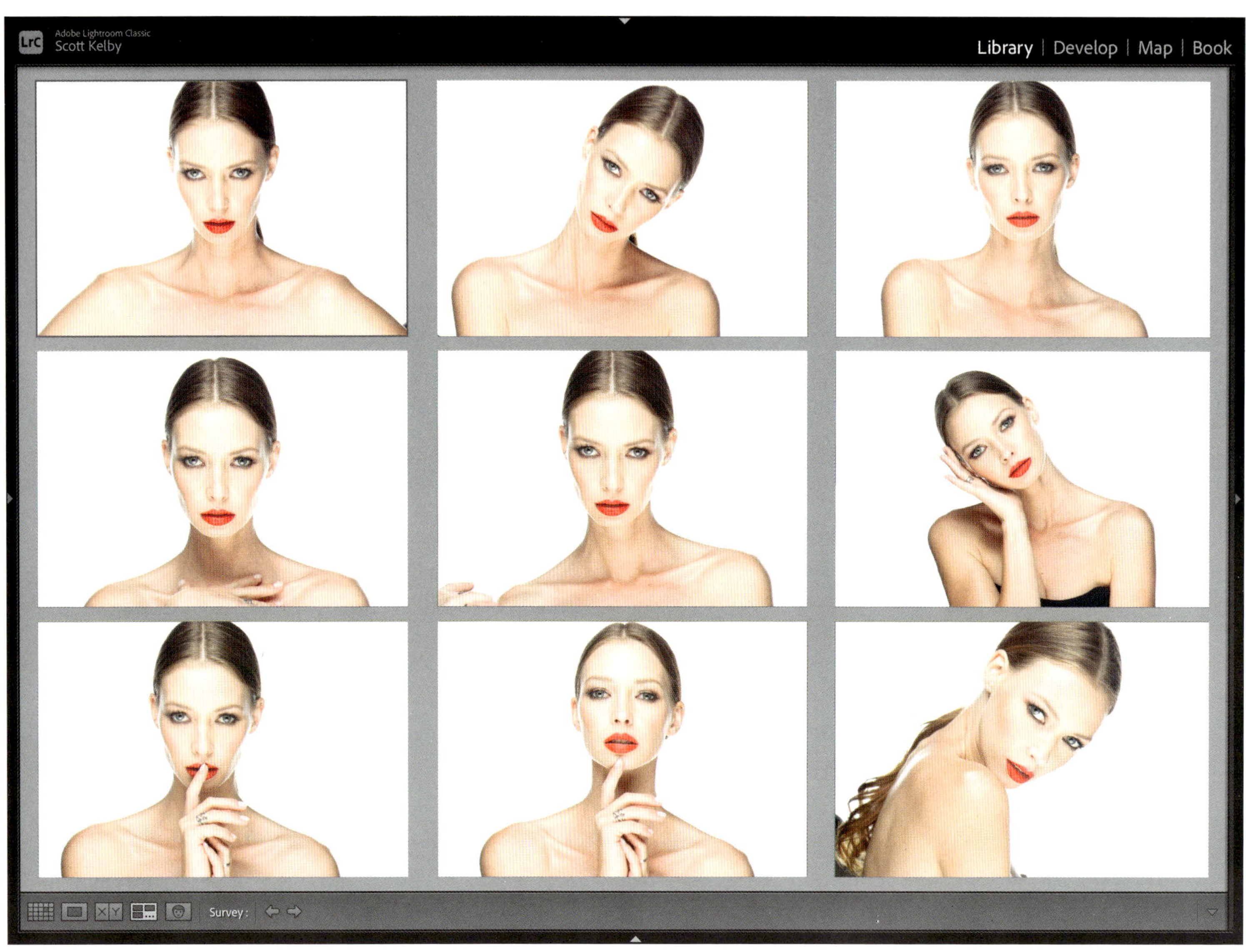

Adobe Lightroom Classic
Scott Kelby
Library | Develop | Map | Book
Survey :

HELP NARROW THINGS DOWN

Lightroom Classic has a great feature for helping you narrow things down when you have a bunch of images that look fairly similar, but I'm going to recommend a method for doing this that will make the process much faster and easier, because honestly, looking at a bunch of similar images and just picking the very best one is often really hard. But, it's our job (and a very important one at that). So, the feature that's going to help us is called "Survey mode." You start in the Library module by selecting a number of similar images (in this case, I chose nine images from a beauty headshot shoot), then you press the letter N on your keyboard to enter this mode, and it displays all your selected images onscreen (as seen here). Now, here's the method I recommend: Don't try to pick the best image. Instead, ask yourself, "Which image do I like the least?" Then, move your cursor over that photo and a small "X" will appear in the lower-right corner of the image thumbnail. Click that "X" and it removes that image from contention. It doesn't delete it or do anything bad—it just removes it from this group of images. So, that's the process. Just keep asking yourself, of the images left onscreen, which one do you like the least? When you get down to, ideally, the last one, that's the best shot from that batch of nine (or 12 or whatever you chose). If you get down to the last two or three and you can't make a call on which one is best, that's okay—these are all great shots. So, mark them with a 5-star rating, and now you know which ones from that shoot are the best shots.

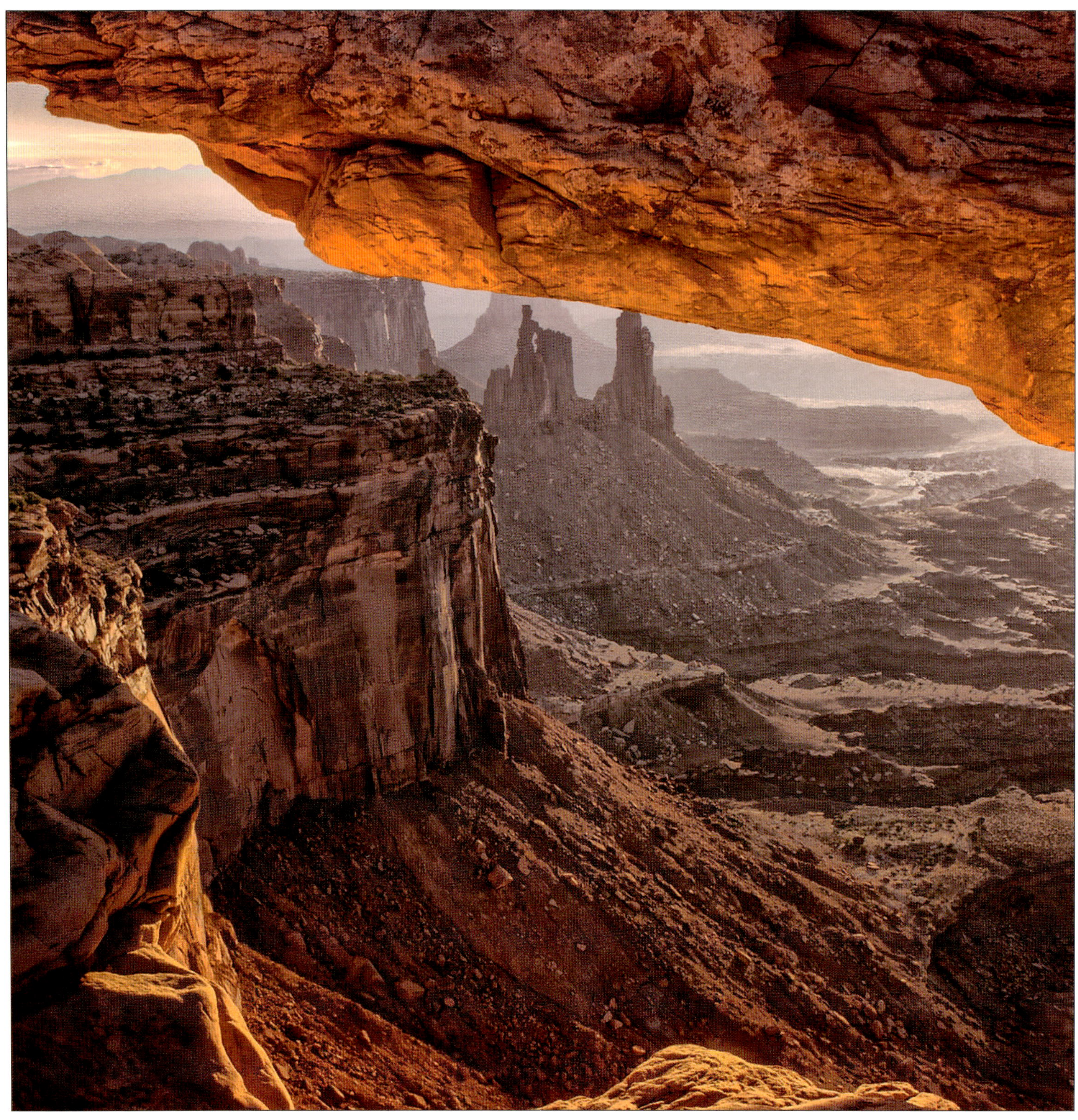

CRITIQUING YOUR LANDSCAPE PHOTOGRAPHY

When you're looking at one of your landscape images, wondering if it should be in your portfolio, start by looking to see if there are any technical problems with the image. That way, with those out of the way, it can then just be down to looking at the artistic value of the image, but at least you'll have reviewed all the technical stuff already. For example: Is your landscape image shot in beautiful light? (Basically, did you shoot it at the right time of day?) Is the horizon line straight? Is there a clear subject in the shot? Are there any distracting things creeping into the sides, top, or bottom of the image? Is the sky interesting? Did you have great clouds that day or was it a boring sky? How's the overall focus for the image? Is it really sharp and crisp? Does the image have depth? Is there anything in the foreground—does it draw you into the image? How is the overall composition? Did you employ some compositional techniques that will draw the viewer into the image—leading lines, rule of thirds, etc.? Does it have an interesting perspective? Is the shot simple enough? Would the image look better in black and white? These are all just technical issues, but they all do make a difference. Now, with all that being said, you could check off every single one of those, and the image could still be a boring, soulless, snooze of an image. But at least it wouldn't be shot down because you chose one with a bunch of technical errors.

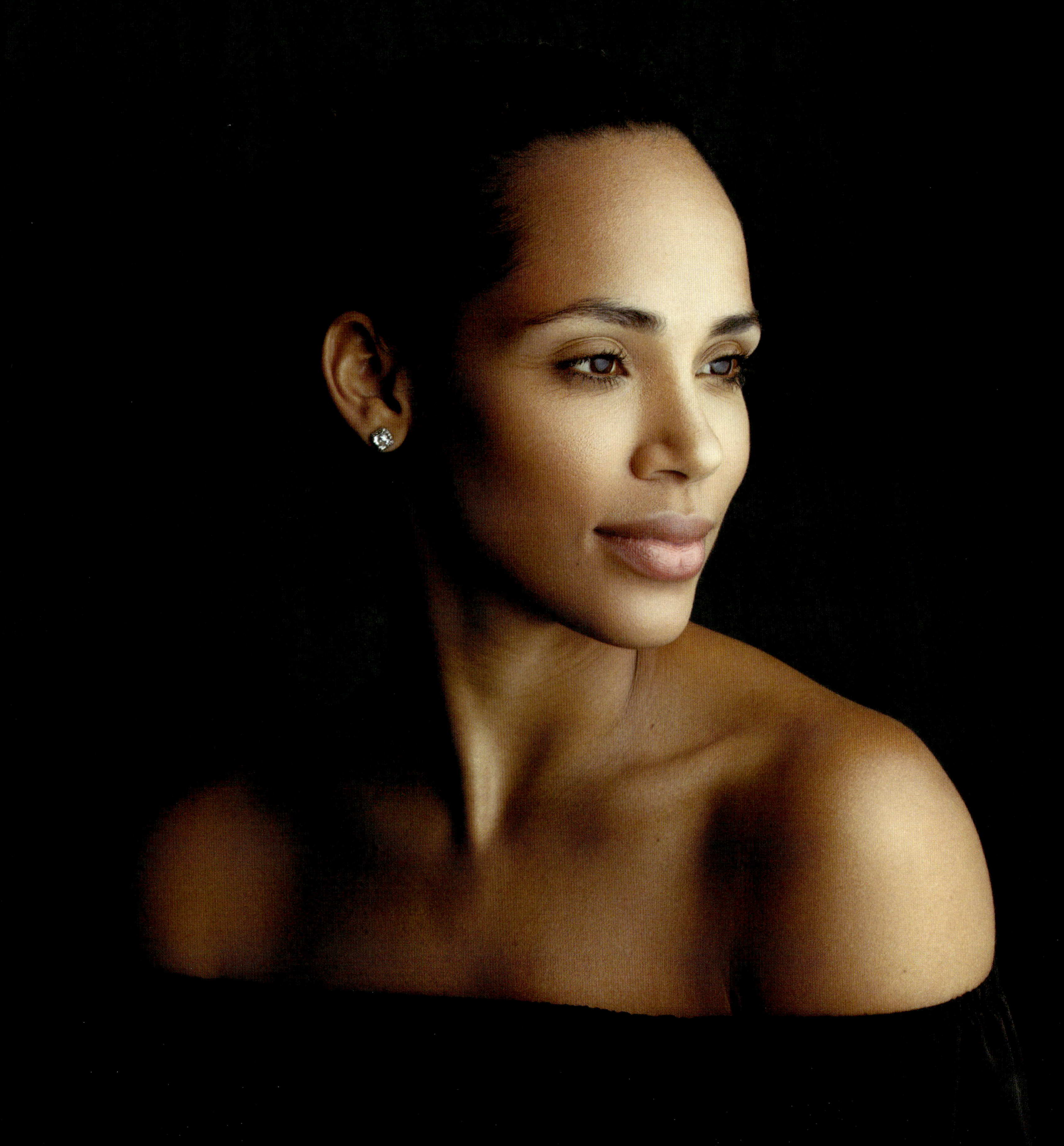

CRITIQUING YOUR FLASH PORTRAIT PHOTOGRAPHY

There are two different categories for portraits in this chapter because using a flash creates its own set of technical things to look out for when critiquing an image. Some of these technical things will also be included when we look at critiquing our natural light images in a bit (just a heads up). First up, is the light flattering for your subject? You pretty much have total control over the lighting, so does it make your subject look their very best? Did you use a softbox in front of your flash to spread the light to make it soft and wrapping? Are there shadows where there should be shadows (in other words, does their face look flat lighting-wise or are there shadows on one side of their face that add depth and dimension)? Is your subject overlit (is the light from the flash or studio strobe too bright)? Are there any hot spots (areas that looks shiny or sweaty) on your subject's face? Are your subject's eyes in sharp focus? If you're shooting in a studio, is everything in sharp focus? Or if you're shooting on location, is the background out of focus enough to create some separation from it? When you look at the portrait, is your subject's face the brightest thing in the image or are their arms or upper chest so bright lighting-wise that they're drawing attention away from the face? If you shot full length, did you shoot from a lower angle so there's no body distortion? Did you leave too much space above their head? Are their eyes in the right position in the frame? If you shot with flash on location, did you add an orange gel to the flash so the light from it doesn't look white? Once these technical aspects are checked off, now we can look at the artistic aspects, like does their pose look natural? Does the shot look stiff and posed or does it look genuine and real? Is their facial expression blank or are they engaged with the camera (or engaged with some far off spot they're looking into)? Is the subject connecting with the viewer? Does the photo tell a story or give you insights into the subject? When it comes to the art and creativity part of a portrait, it's totally subjective, right? But at least if we get the technical stuff out of the way, it won't stand in the way of the photo being considered for its artistic merit.

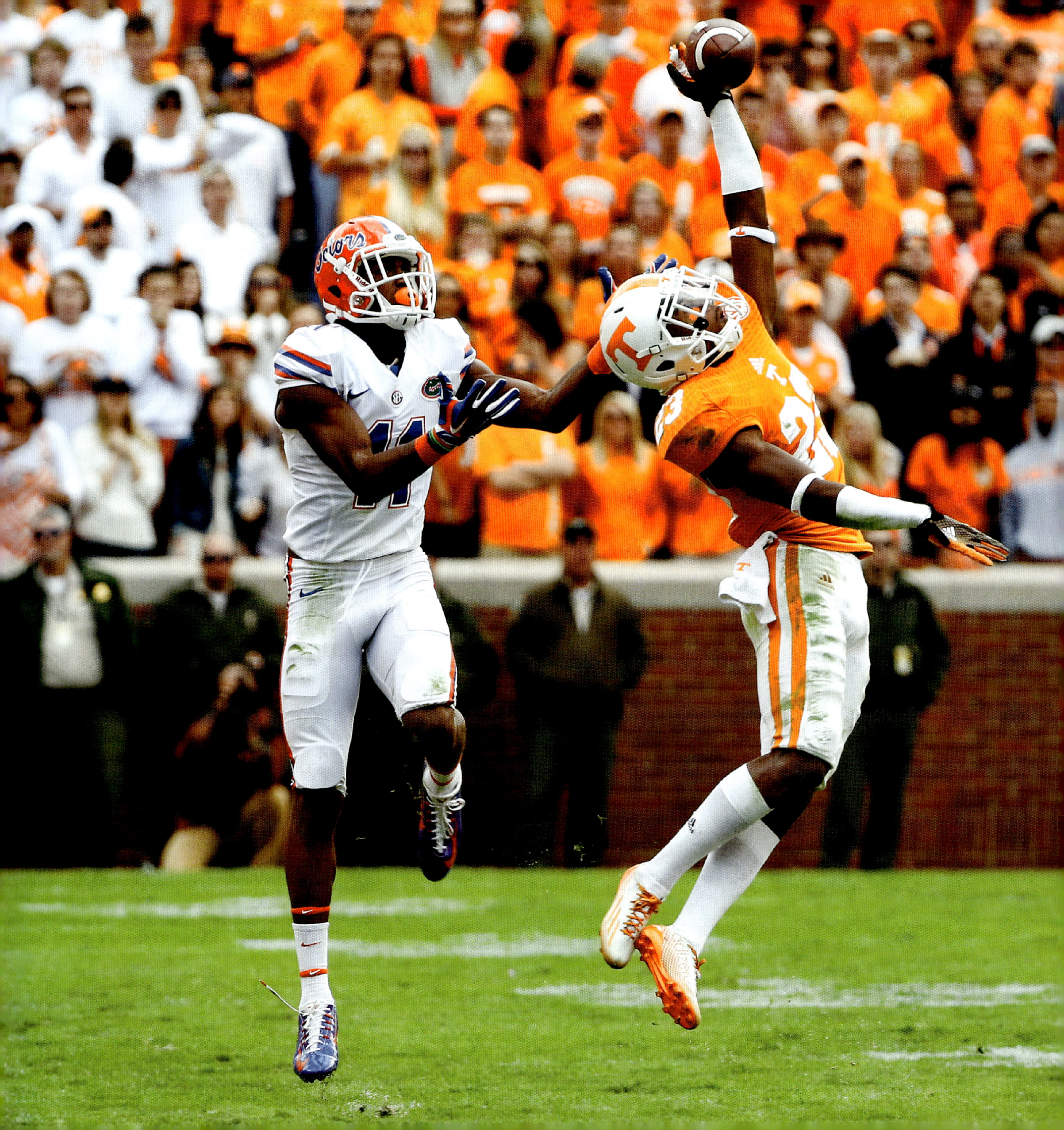

CRITIQUING YOUR SPORTS PHOTOGRAPHY

You might be shooting sports for fun (you're covering your daughter's softball game), or you might be shooting for reportage (you're covering the game for a news outlet or wire service), but either way, being able to remove the shots that have technical issues will get you to the great shots that much quicker. Here are a few things to consider, and for me, #1 is to ask yourself if the shot is tack sharp. Did you use a fast enough shutter speed to freeze the action and did you nail the focus, so the player-who-is-the-focus-of-the-play's sharpness is on the money? Is the shot cropped tight enough? Are you showing players in the shot that don't really have anything to do with the action that's taking place? Is the background behind the main subjects out of focus, so there's nice separation from the background? Did you shoot from a location where the background behind the players isn't busy and distracting? If it's a game with a ball (or puck), can you see the ball (or puck) in the frame, and do you also see the player's eyes (the old adage of "I need to see two eyes and a ball" comes to mind)? If you're shooting motor sports, are the wheels spinning and does the shot show motion, or does it look like the race car or motorcycle is parked on the track? In a team sport, are there multiple players in the shot? And, of course, the all-important: does this shot show a peak moment of action? Did you compose the shot so the athlete has room to move in the frame (is there space in the direction they're moving or driving for them to move into to keep the frame from feeling uncomfortable)? Did you shoot from a lower perspective, so the shot looks dynamic? Did you avoid empty seats in the stands, so it doesn't look like nobody showed up to watch the game? Does the white balance look right (or do the players' jerseys have a blue tint because the field is in shade)? Are the colors crisp and vibrant and did you add additional sharpening in post? These are some of the technical starting points for a great sports shot, but like most shots with people, after the technical stuff is checked off, it comes down to capturing the emotion, the spirit, and the action of play. But at least you won't get burned by missing some of the technical errors that might have sneaked past the goalie.

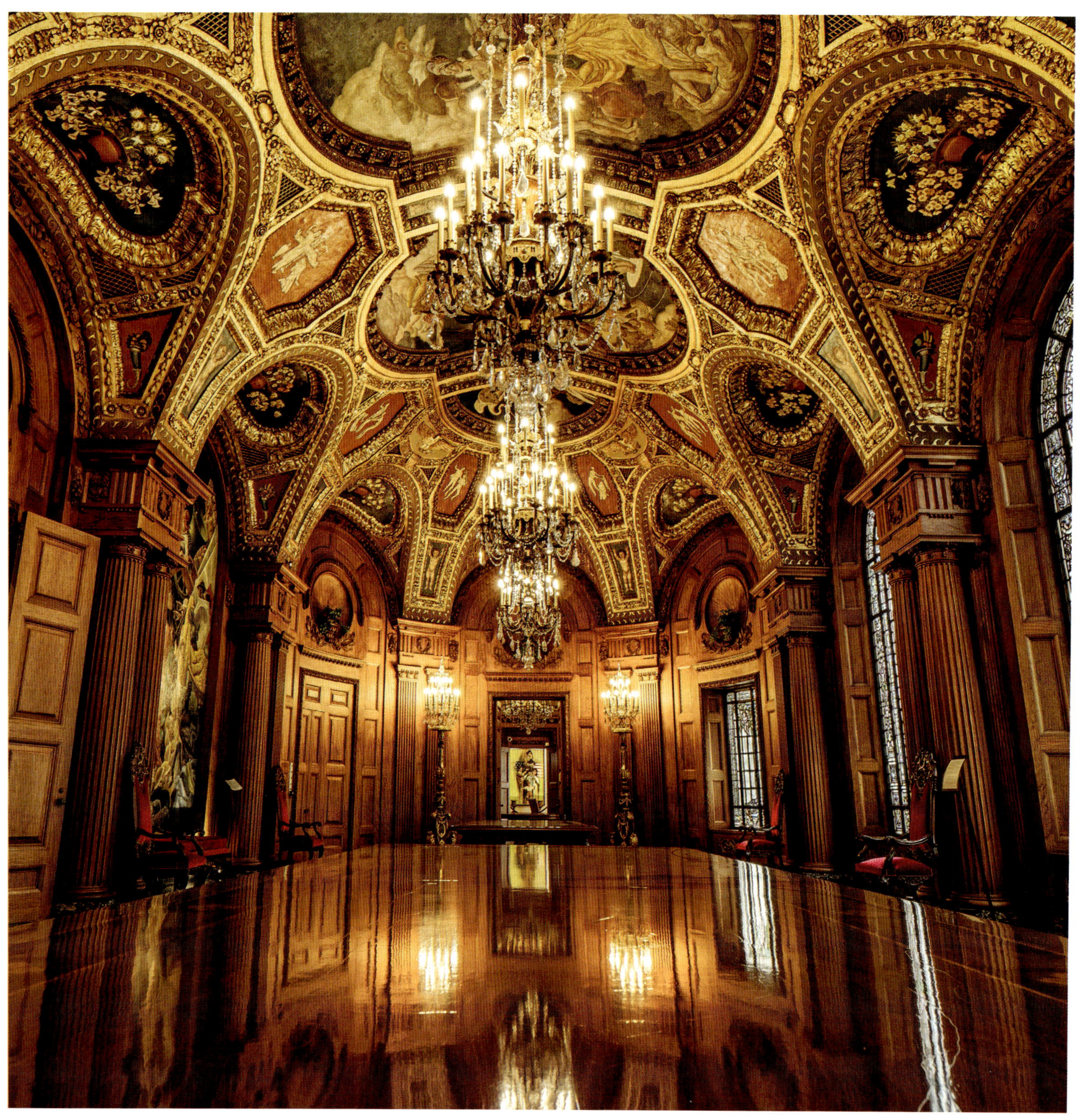

CRITIQUING YOUR TRAVEL PHOTOGRAPHY

If you're like me, most of your travel photography will be done on vacation with your family (which is my favorite way to shoot travel), so while that does limit the time we get to spend at certain locations, we don't have to let technical issues get in the way. Let's start with: Is the lighting good? Did you get up before dawn and shoot when the streets are empty and the light is great, or is it a bright, sunny afternoon where all the colors are washed out and boring? If you didn't shoot in good light, did you shoot in interesting light? For example, is it just a thin beam of light coming from a small window up high in a monastery? Or a trickle of light between two buildings? Interesting light can be wonderful for travel. Did you avoid having a bunch of tourists in your shot? If you shot the food on your trip (and I hope you did), did you sit where the light was nice (outside under an umbrella or by a window)? Does the white balance on the food look right (or does the white plate look blueish)? Is the scene messy with lots of distractions or did you keep it as simple as possible? Are there distracting signs and poles and other things that take away from the romance of travel? Does your image have a clear subject? Does your shot tell a story or make people want to visit that city or village? Did you include photos of the locals, so you're not just showing an abandoned town? Is the shot sharp? Is the composition interesting? All things to consider when you're picking which shots to share.

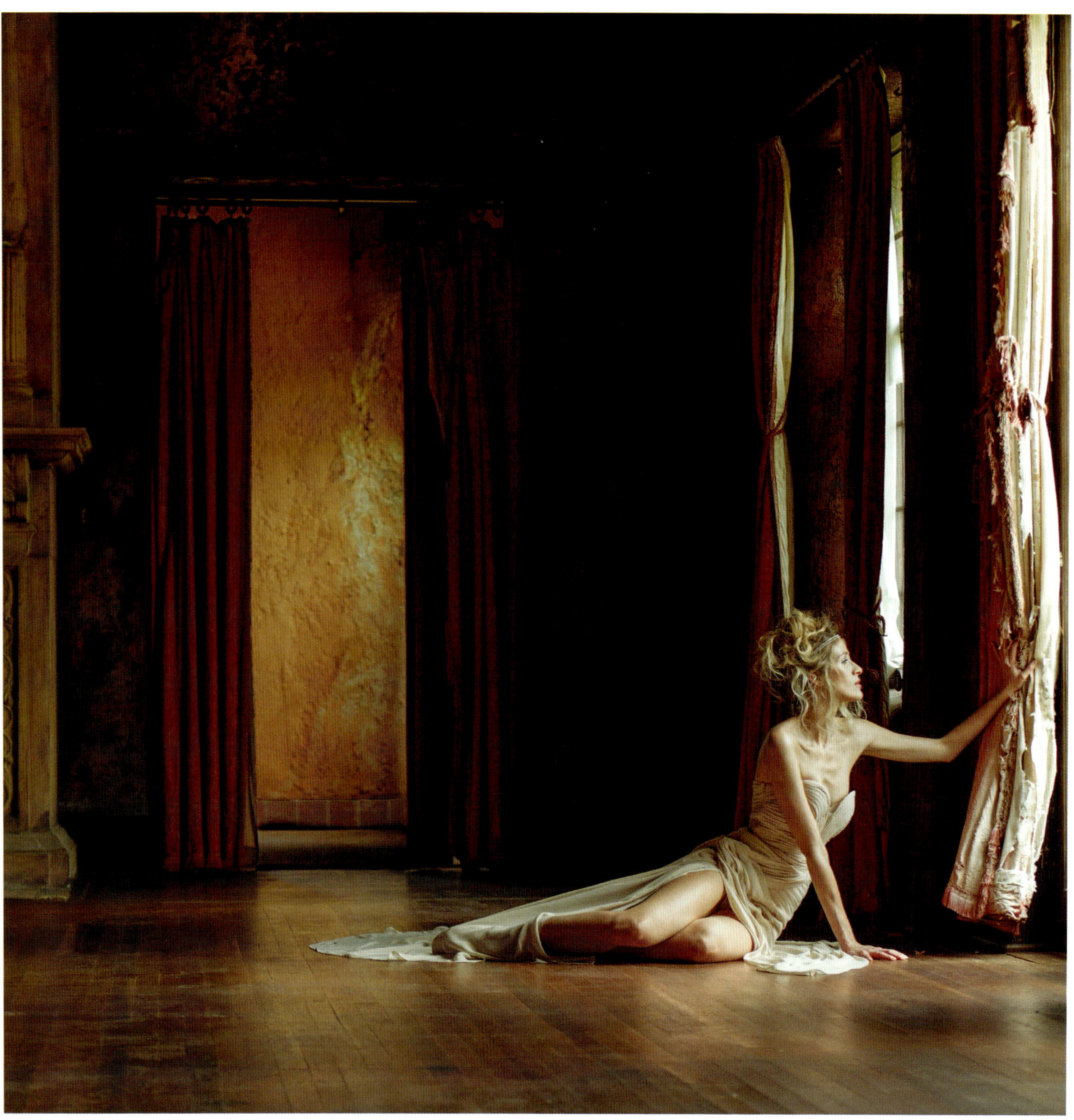

CRITIQUING YOUR NATURAL LIGHT PORTRAITS

Like I mentioned earlier, some of these will have a lot in common with some of the flash/strobe portrait critique ideas, so we'll start with the things that are unique to natural light portraits, like does the white balance look right (did you change the setting in camera or in post, so their skin tone looks natural)? Did you use a lens that flatters the subject? Did you shoot from the proper height (a little higher than their eyes unless you were shooting a full-length shot)? Did you use a long enough lens and a low-numbered f-stop to put the background out of focus and get separation for your subject from the background? When you framed the shot, did you crop off the ends of any fingers or the ends of their shoes or feet? Did you frame the shot to where there are no uncomfortable cropping areas, like cropping across an elbow, or cropping at a wrist, knee, or ankle? Did you shoot in tight enough to fill the frame? Did you expose properly for the shot (in other words, are the highlights clipping on their skin or their clothes)? If you shot outdoors, did you move your subject to where they're not out in the harsh, direct sun? Are the shadows on their face soft and flattering? Did you place the sun behind the subject, so they're not squinting, and then did you overexpose so their face isn't too dark? Did you compose the shot so that your subject isn't right in the middle (unless that's the exact right place in this particular image for them to be)?

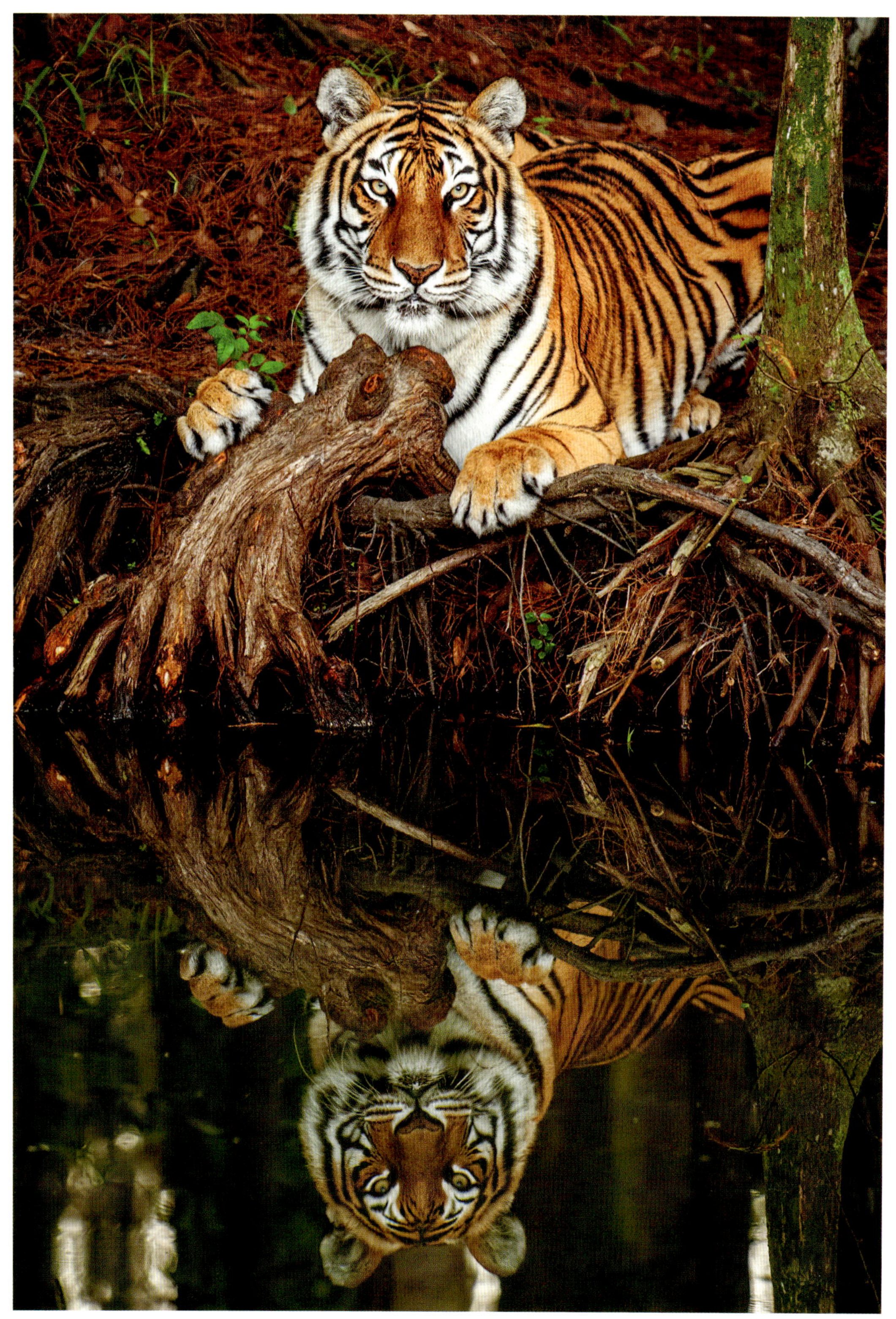

CRITIQUING YOUR WILDLIFE PHOTOGRAPHY

Wildlife photos are a lot like natural light portraits in that many of the same principles that apply there also apply when you're critiquing your own pet or wildlife images. One of the first things I always check for is are the eyes sharp and in focus? For many wildlife photographers, this is the barrier to entry—if the eyes aren't sharp, it's not a good shot. Next, is the animal engaged with the viewer (like in the shot here), or engaged with another animal (is the animal doing anything interesting)? Like with regular portrait photography, is the lighting good? Does it flatter the animal or is it bright, harsh light (morning and late afternoon side lighting are flattering to animals, just like they are to people and landscapes)? What about the background behind the animal? Did you put it out of focus to minimize distractions, or is it in focus, but has distracting things that draw the viewer's interest away from the animal? If the animal was moving, did you freeze the action so the shot is sharp, or did you intentionally use a slow shutter speed to show motion, but the head and eyes are still sharp? Of course, none of this accounts for the beauty, emotion, intrigue, and intimacy of capturing stunning wildlife photos. But again, these are just technical tools you can use to help you remove the technical things that might be ruining otherwise wonderful images.

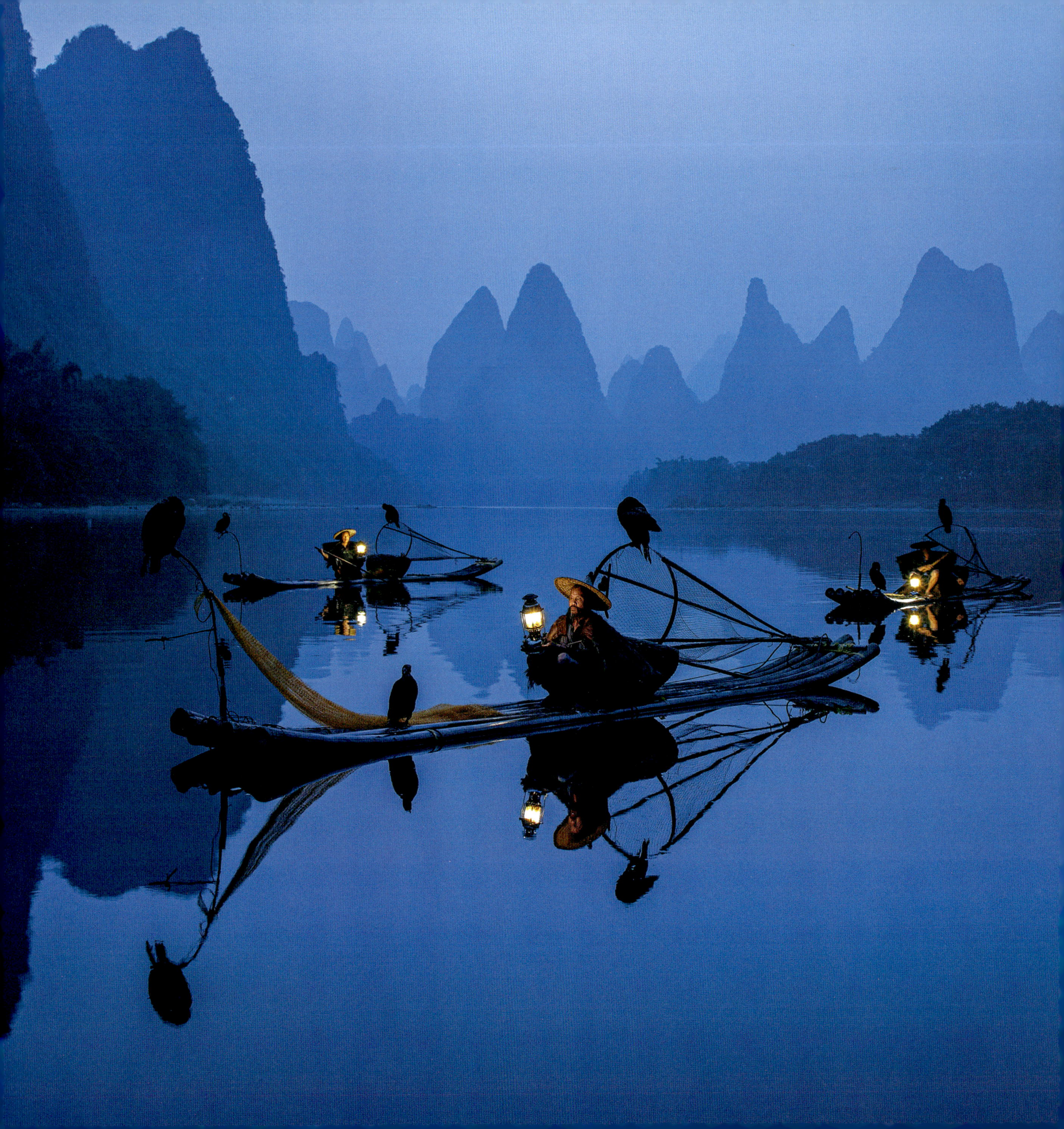

SHOW ONLY
YOUR BEST WORK

A few years ago I was teaching at a popular photography school and one night during the week, each instructor would do a presentation of their own work. On this night, one of the other photography instructors shared his work. His first image was amazing. His second image was amazing. His third image was okay. The fourth one just wasn't very good—it was like a different photographer took it. Then another great image. Then another blah image. Then kind of a bad photo. Then an amazing one. It went on like that for around 25 minutes. The next morning, when we got to class, I asked my students what they thought about the instructor's presentation the night before. Dead silence. Finally somebody said, "He had some really nice images." And then, immediately, somebody else yelled out, "Yeah, and he had a bunch of bad ones, too," and everybody seemed to agree. So, I asked the class, "Okay, what if he took out all the bad ones—every one—and just showed the really great ones, so his presentation was only

15 minutes. What would you think then?" One of the students said, "We would have thought he was a great photographer." Exactly. The problem was he didn't just show his best work. He showed his best work, his second best work, his third best work, and some work he just shouldn't have shown at all. What you share, how much you share, and the quality of what you share is what people use to form an opinion of you as a photographer. The top pros only show their very best work. They may take thousands of bad shots—shots where they are experimenting, or having a bad day, or just aren't coming up with anything good—but you'll never see those images. Ever. A top pro doesn't post a "meh" image with the comment: "This is something I was experimenting with, but I'm not happy with how it came out." If they took a bad shot, it stays safely out of the public's eye. They may have hard drives packed with mediocre images, but top pros have learned that you only share your best work.

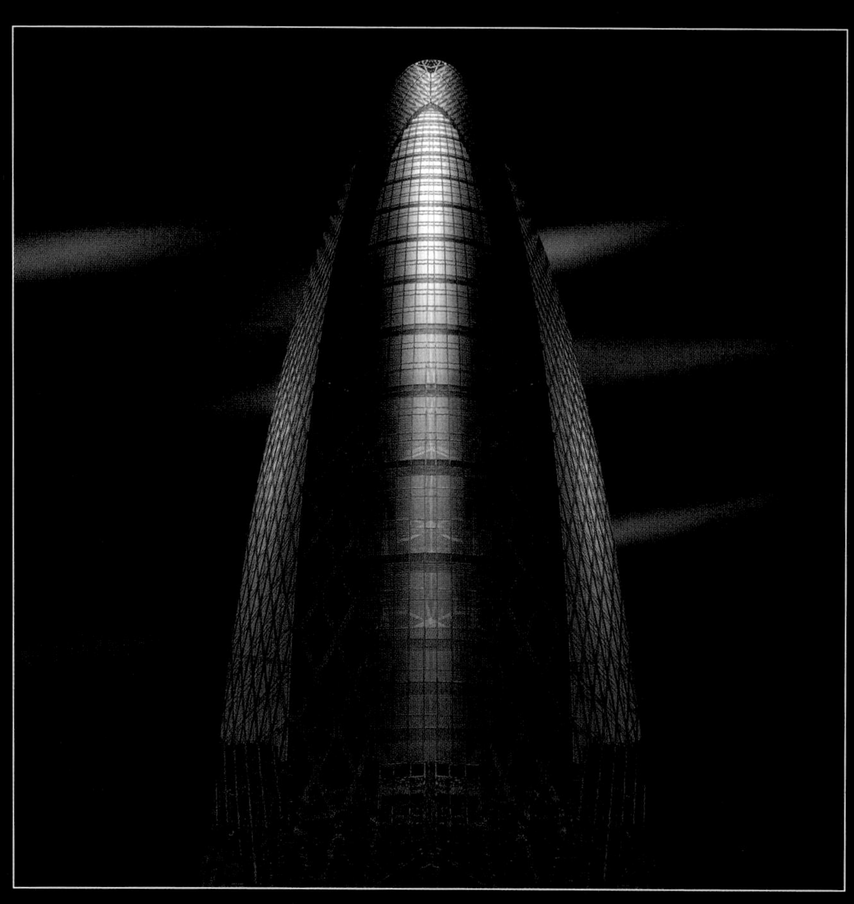

Chapter 10

COMPOSITION TIPS

I figured we needed to have a chapter where composition stuff that didn't fit neatly into any of the other chapters could have a home, and this is the place. Now, technically, I could have put composition tips for "shooting food" into a travel chapter because I always try to shoot the food when I travel (studies show trying the food in different countries is one of the main things we love about foreign travel). But, there are people who shoot food at their favorite local lunch spot, or even at home, so...well...it's winding up here.

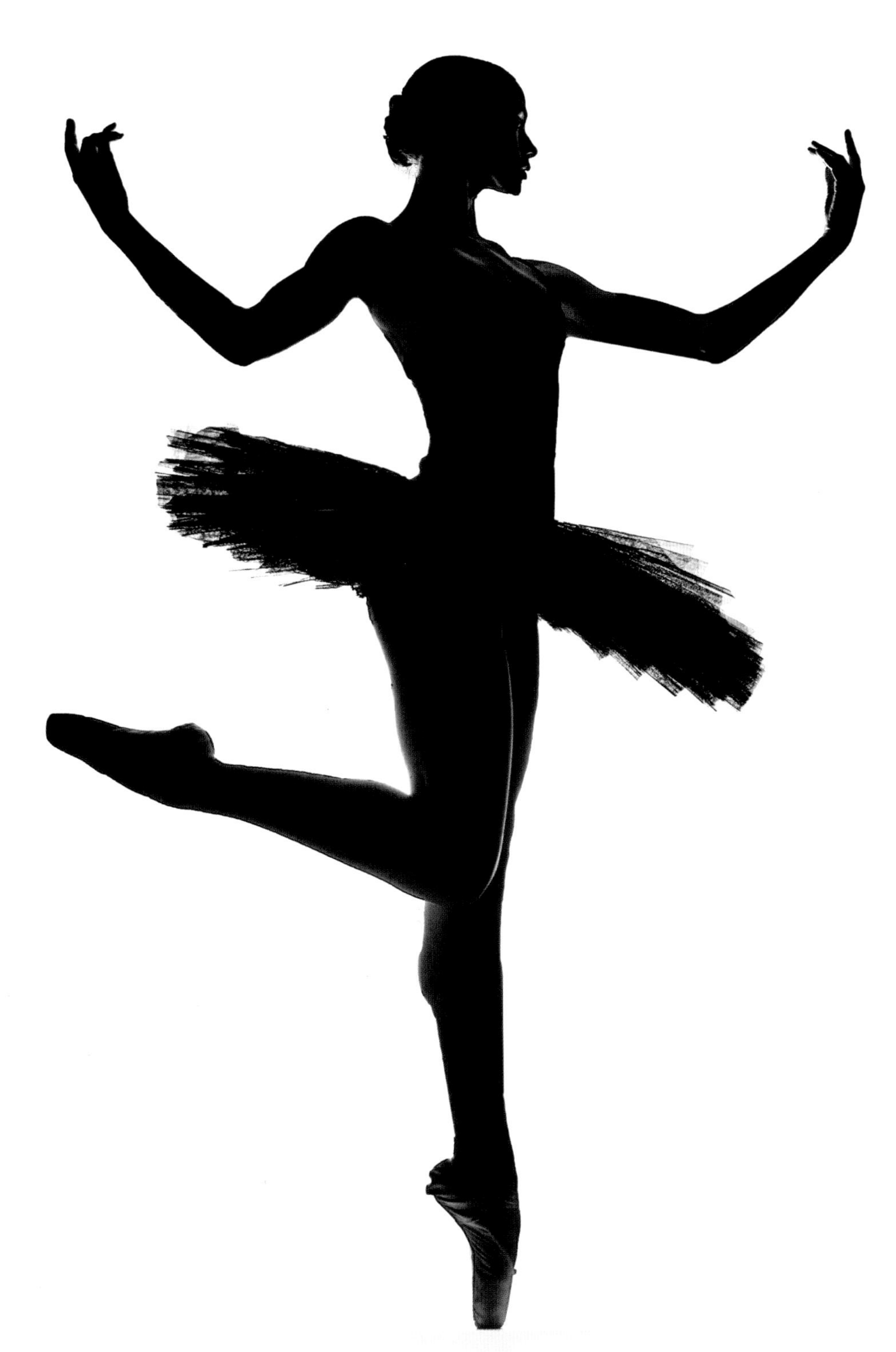

THE TRICK TO SILHOUETTES

For a silhouette shot to work, there's one pretty overriding thing you need to have, and that is the viewer can immediately recognize the subject you've silhouetted. Your subject's outline has to be clean, and unobstructed, and most often, to create a silhouette, your subject has to be backlit with the light behind them. Otherwise, if the light is in front, it will light them, instead of creating a silhouette (more on the lighting in a moment). For example, in the shot you see here, you immediately know, "That's a ballerina." You're not thinking, "What is that?" If people look at your shot and the subject isn't immediately recognizable (that's a cowboy, that's the Leaning Tower of Pisa, that's a tree), then it failed as a silhouette. In the shot here, I put a large scrim behind her (a scrim is a large sheet of translucent material attached to a lightweight aluminum frame, and it's made of pretty much the same stuff you'd put in front of a softbox to soften and spread the light), and then I put a flash behind the scrim, turned the power all the way up, and fired it through that material to create the silhouette. That's why you see some highlights on her face, upper arms, décolletage (five points for using a French word), her leg closest the camera, and her slipper (the one en pointe). If I had shot her on a solid white background, you wouldn't have those nice high-lights. Also, without her being backlit, she wouldn't be a silhouette. The light has to be behind your subject, and you in front of them, shooting into the light.

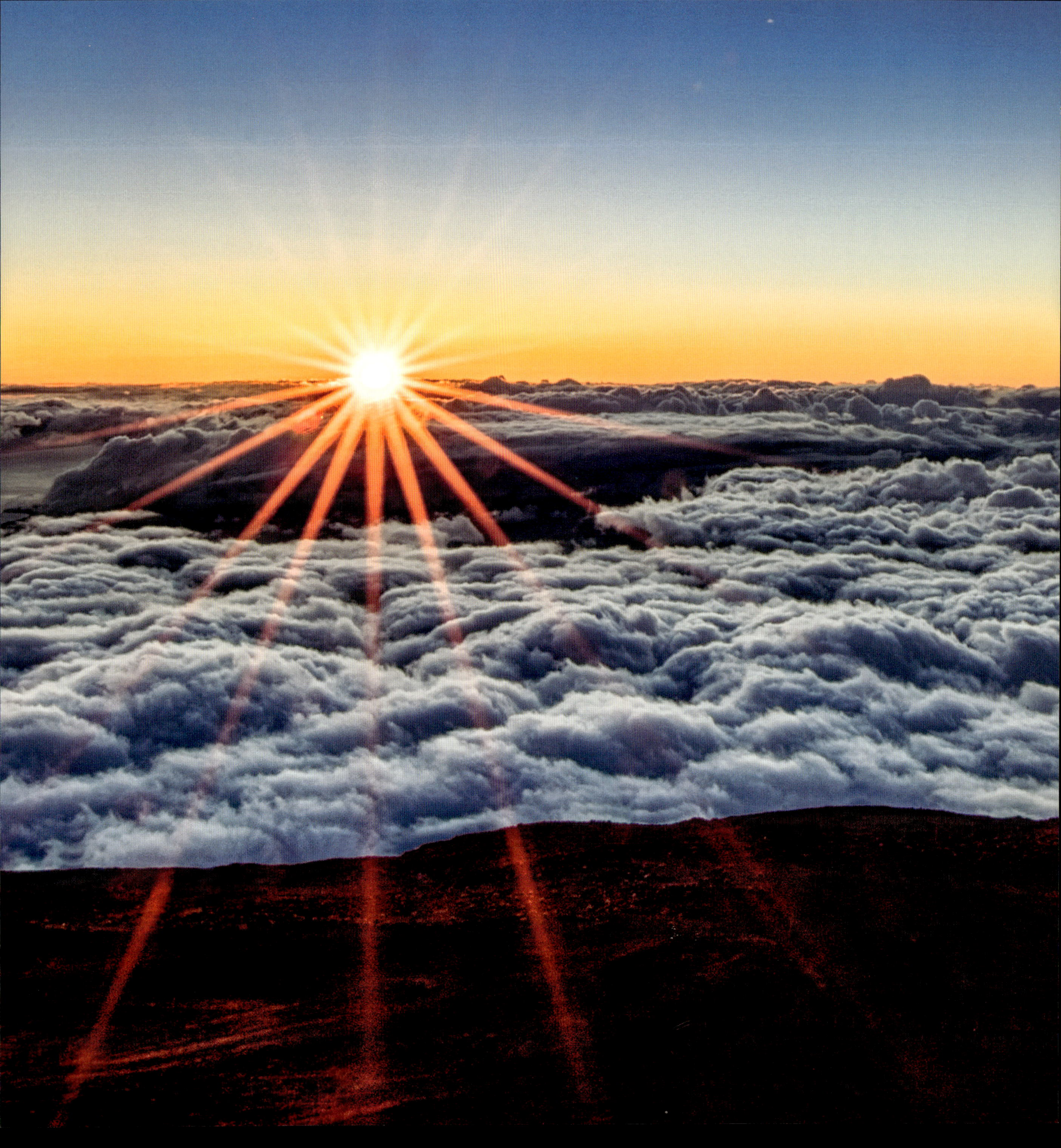

IS SOMETHING DISTRACTING SNEAKING IN?

When we've taken a shot and we're looking at the image afterward, we're usually focused on the subject. If we got it right (the exposure is good, the white balance, sharpness, etc.) because we're so focused on the subject (in this case, the sun peeking through the clouds—that's what made us want to take the shot), we often miss some technical issues that can ruin the image. That's why there's this old saying: "Don't forget to do your border patrol" (probably time to revisit that saying—just sayin'). This essentially reminds us to go around the entire image and visually check all four borders (edges) of it to see if there's anything sneaking in that shouldn't be there. It could be a tree branch sticking in from the side, part of another person that's just outside the frame (like the tip of a foot or a hand), a road sign—it could be anything that distracts the viewer from the subject of the image. It's so easy to miss these if you're not looking out for them. I see this problem so often when people submit images for critiques, and I know why—they're looking at the subject. But, like I said earlier in the book, when other people see your image, they see all of it (not just where you were looking). So it pays to take the time to see if something is sneaking into your frame and drawing the attention away from that all-important subject.

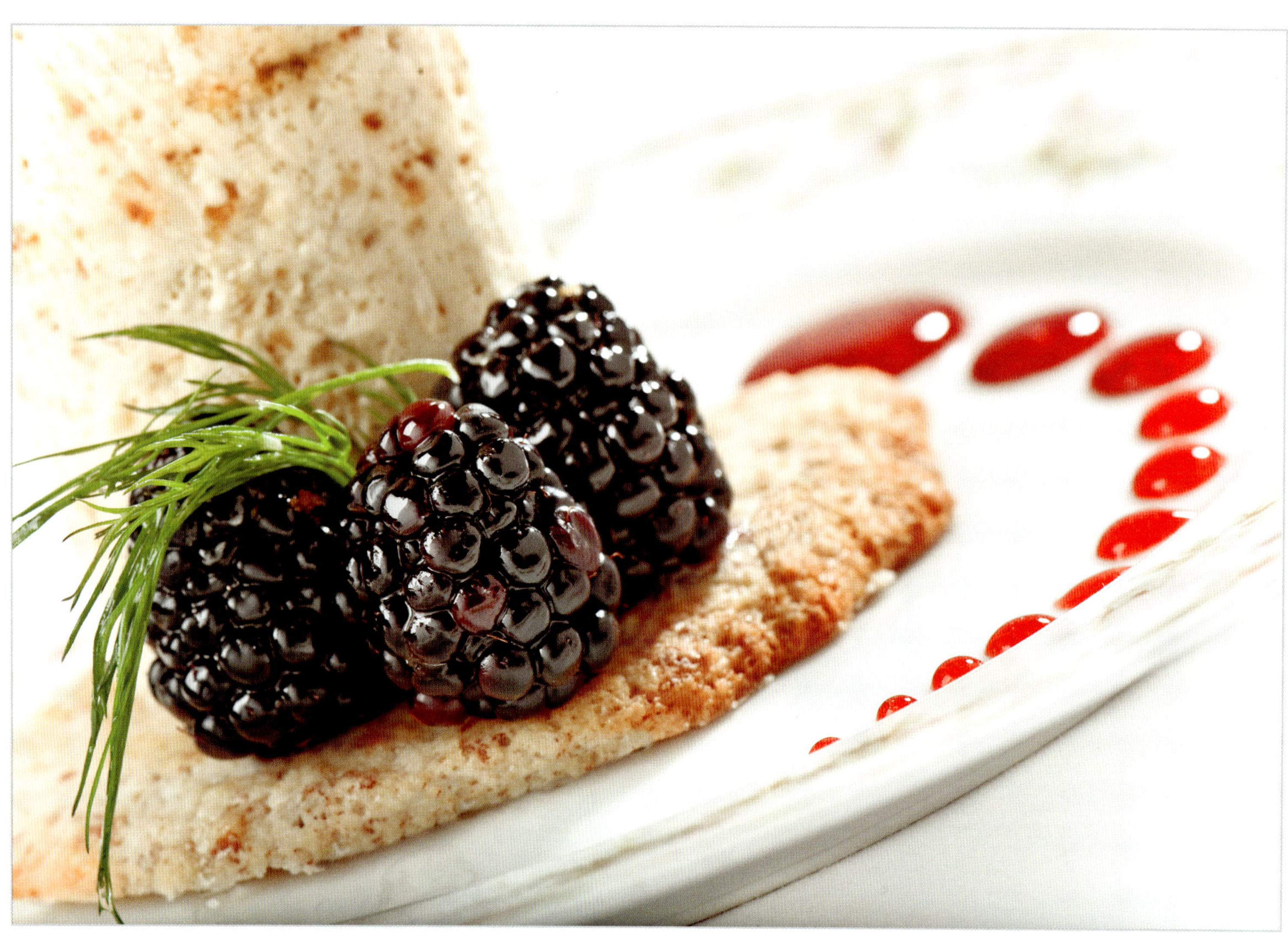

SHOOTING FOOD

Like I said in this chapter's introduction, I'm always shooting the food when I travel (though the image I'm showing here is a dessert shot I took for a client for their restaurant's menu), and there are some easy composition rules (more like tips) that can help make your shots look more dynamic. One of the first things I would tell a friend about shooting food is that, outside of the straight overhead shot that's so popular today (I use my iPhone for that because it has a feature using two crosshairs that ensures your shot is perfectly flat, so you don't have any weird perspective issues), my compositional tip is that I don't show the entire plate. You don't need to see the whole thing. Our minds know that the plate is round (or square) and they fill in the missing parts automatically. I try to fill the frame as much as possible—composing this tight brings the viewer closer to the image and makes the shot look more inviting (and yummier). My go-to lighting technique for shooting food is to shoot it with natural light (mostly backlit if at all possible, but then I use a little fill flash in front), or I use natural window light, but with most of the light coming from behind. I use a long lens (usually my 70–200mm) and I stand back and zoom in really tight, which helps create a very shallow depth of field where the front edge of the plate is in focus, and then I tilt the camera to one side or the other to give the shot more energy (after all, it's a still life, so this helps to add energy and interest, plus tilting the camera like this is now a "cool thing" again after an absence of about 10 years).

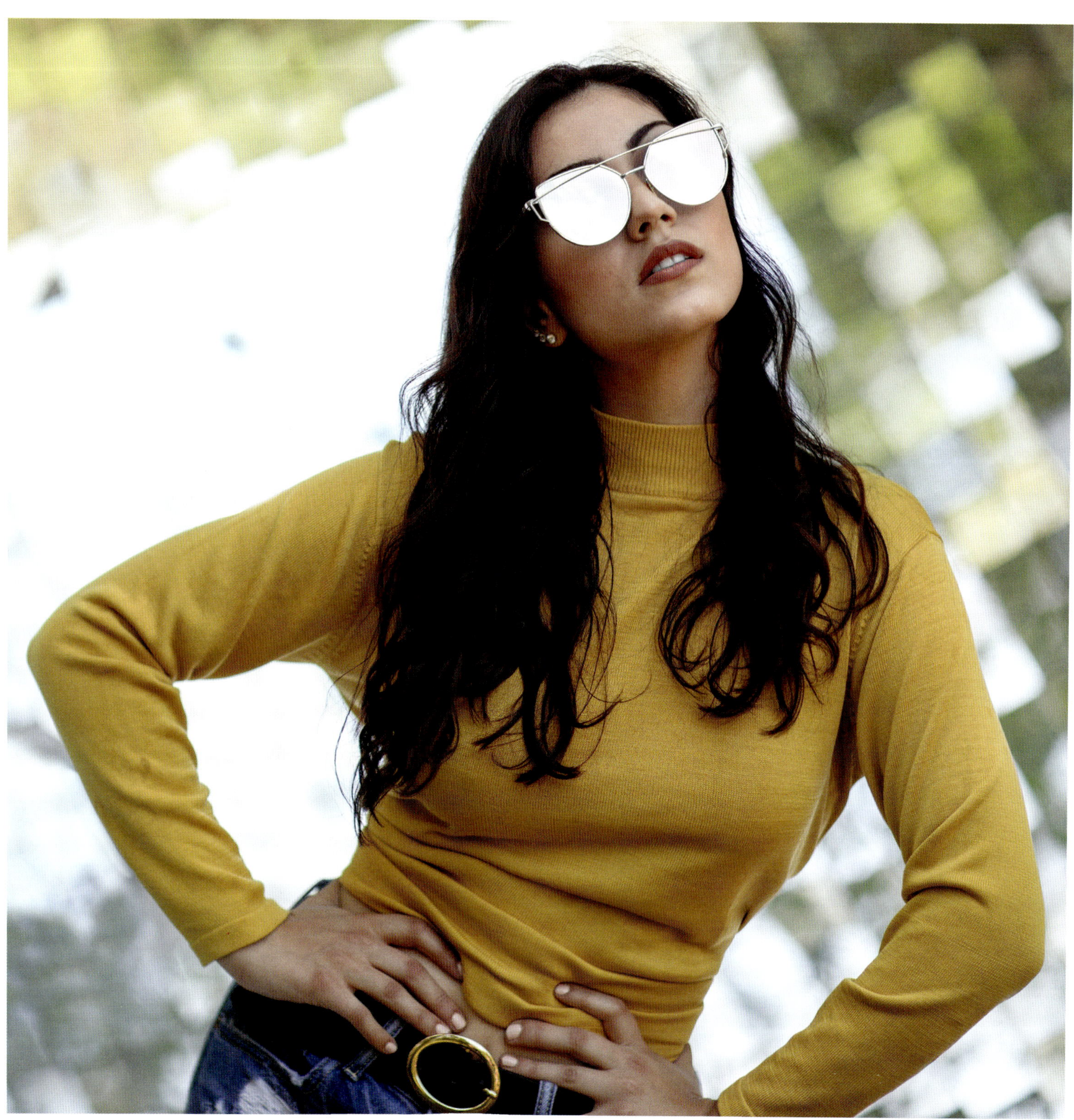

AVOID BRIGHT BACKGROUND AREAS

You've heard me talk a lot throughout this book about avoiding distracting things in our photos, and since we know that our eyes are drawn to the brightest thing in the image, we need to make sure the brightest thing isn't in the background behind our subject, or our eyes will go there first. If that happens (you see the bright background when you're framing your shot, like the one you see here), the goal is to either reposition your camera or your subject, so the bright areas aren't behind them. In the shot you see here, those white tiles behind her are drawing the eye, and I definitely should have repositioned her. I didn't, which is the reason why you won't see me sharing this image on social or anywhere else (other than here, as an example, of course). I wasn't paying attention to the background like I should have been, and now I have the background competing for attention with my subject. The only saving grace might be the solid white reflections in her sunglasses, but I don't think those two small ovals are enough to offset that sea of white tiles behind her. This is something to keep in mind while you're shooting because this is very hard to fix in post-production. When you back off the brightness of really white or bright areas in Lightroom or Photoshop, the result usually isn't that those areas are now less bright; the result is that those areas now look kind of gray, and though it might not be as distracting, it usually looks worse. That's why it's good to keep an eye out for this during the shoot while you still have a chance to recompose the scene, so you avoid those bright areas in the background altogether.

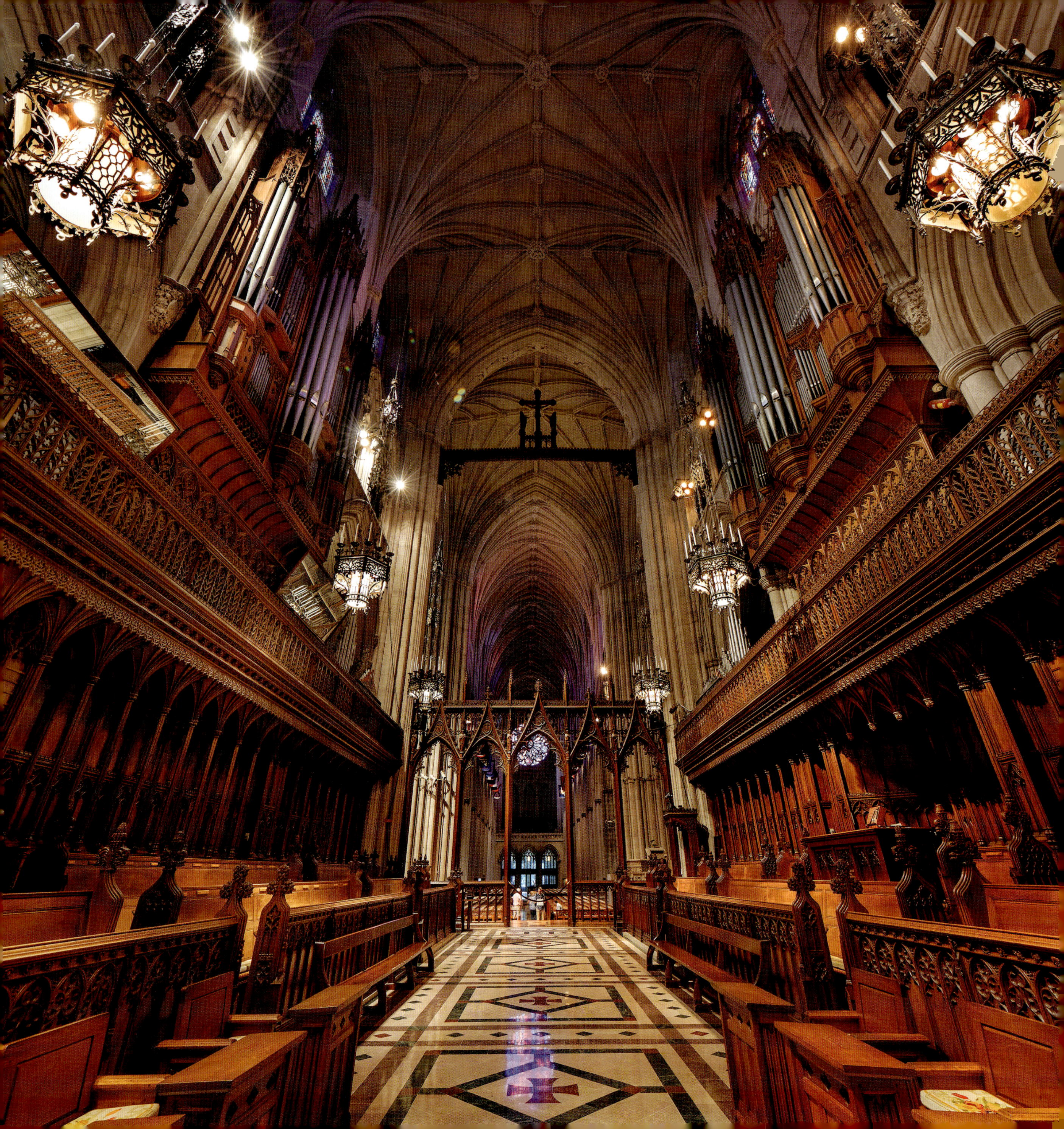

WHY CAREFUL CENTERING IS IMPORTANT

If you're shooting a building or a monument or an interior of a palace, museum, or cathedral (this is inside the National Cathedral in Washington, DC), or any other architectural wonder, one thing you can do to make your image look right (and not create post-production nightmares) is when you set up to take a straight-on shot, make absolutely certain you are lined up in the exact center or the whole image will be off perspective-wise, and you might not be able to easily fix it (or fix it at all) in post. Take a look at the image here, where you can tell I shot it just off center—to the right of center—and even though I've worked on straightening out the perspective, it's still just not quite right (by the way, if you're wondering how I feel about sharing shots like this, and a few other shots here in the book that have obvious problems—for example's sake—I can tell you, it's a pretty icky feeling). Anyway, to keep from having these perspective issues, all you have to do is take a few extra moments and really make sure you're lined up right at the center. There's often a line, or a crack, or some tile or something that you can use as a guide to make sure you're directly in front of the object you're shooting. It's worth the small, extra effort (it takes way, way longer to try to fix it in post than it does to move a foot or two over when you're shooting).

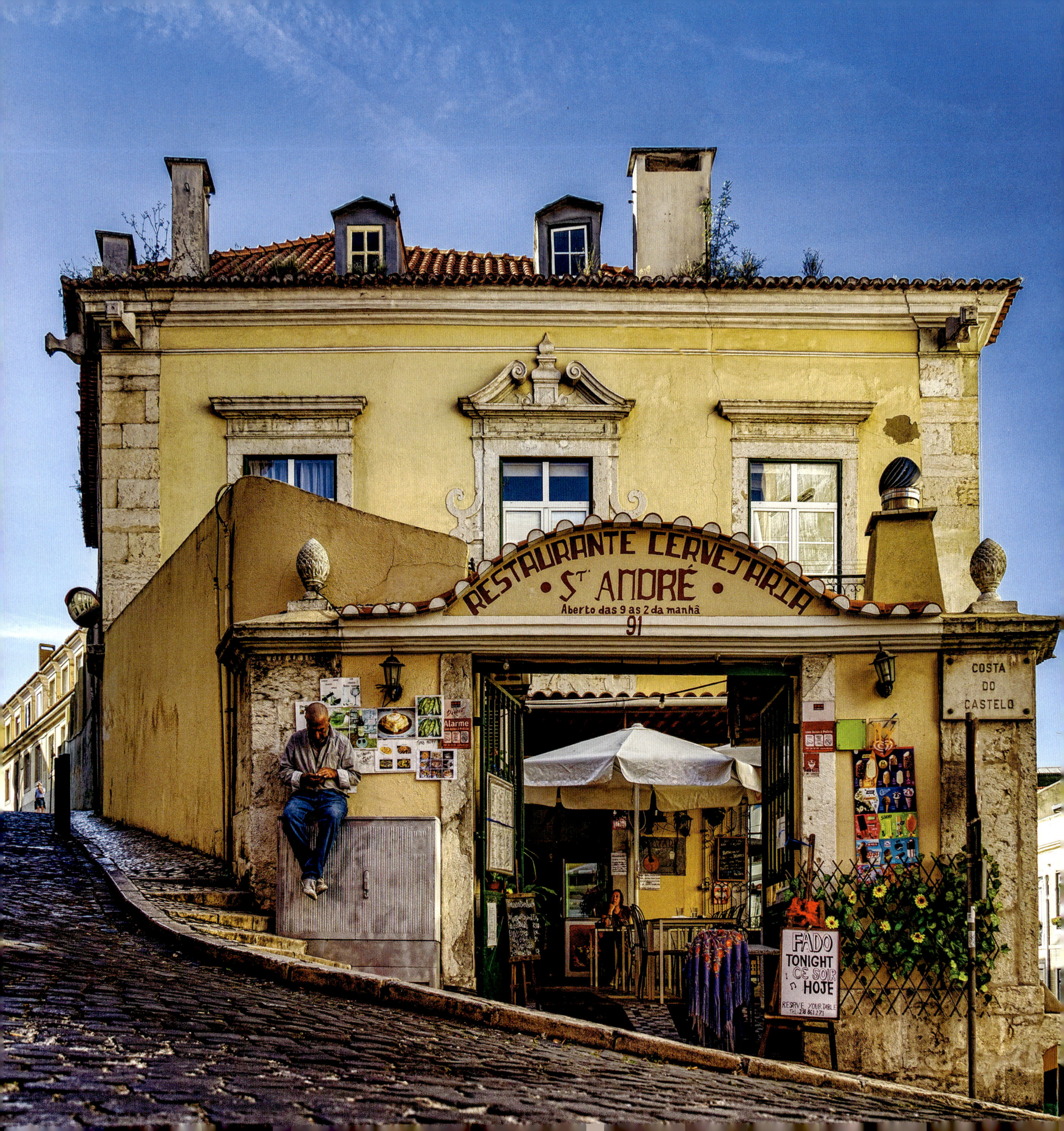

RESTAURANTE CERVEJARIA
• St ANDRÉ •
Aberto das 9 as 2 da manhã
91
COSTA
DO
CASTELO
FADO
TONIGHT
CE SOIR
HOJE

ADD ONE PERSON
TO ADD MORE INTEREST

Adding just one person to your frame can add a whole different level of interest to your image, and I think that's the case with this shot taken in Lisbon, Portugal. I have a bunch of shots of this charming restaurant, but this one with one person out front is by far my favorite. That human element brings something to the shot that it didn't have in the shots of just the building alone. The "just one person" concept is very popular right now, and while you will see shots of couples or a small group of friends, especially on Instagram, the single-person shot is by far the strongest. Once you get a few more people in the shot, it often starts to transform from an interesting, single-person shot into a shot of a group of tourists, and its value as a shot plummets.

Getting a shot with just one person can often take a lot of patience, as it did here, where I'm set up directly across the narrow cobblestone street on a tripod just waiting to see what happens. Sure enough, this gentleman comes by, walks inside, and then shortly afterward, comes out and sits right in front. It's almost like he knew he'd help make a nice shot even better, and, again, it's what made this my favorite of my many shots of this restaurant. It also plays into the compositional "Rule of Odds" (more on that on page 241 in the next chapter). Keep an eye out for an opportunity to add one person to your frame, or have your friend or spouse be the person that walks into the empty frame and makes the shot.

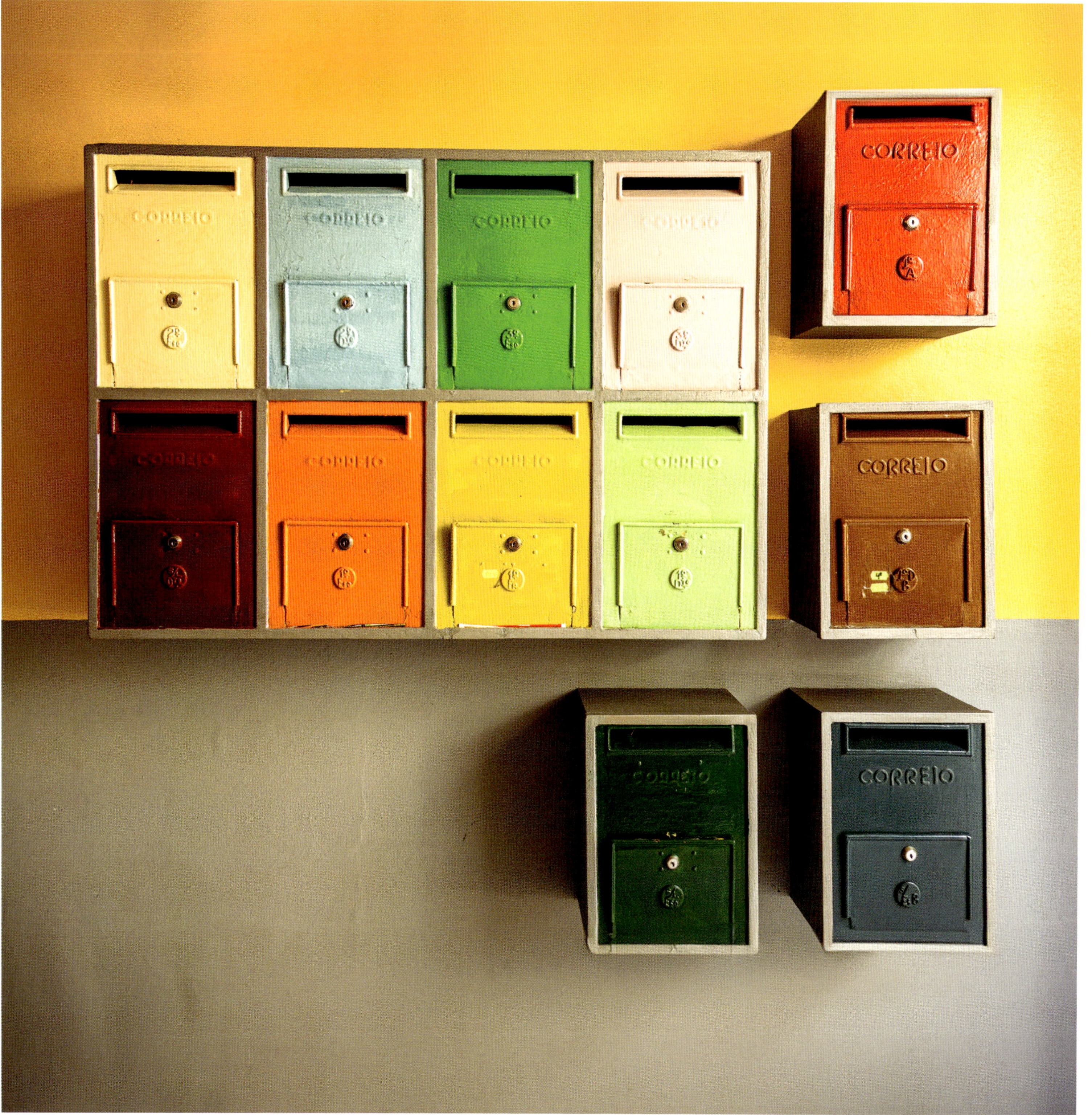

USE COLOR AS YOUR SUBJECT

People love color. There are all sorts of scientific studies attempting to explain why we love color so much, and our emotional attachment to certain colors, and how colors affect our moods and our choices—there are as many studies and theories as there are colors in a really big crayon box. But, one thing is certain: humans love color. I think that's exactly why so many images where the subject is "color" are so popular. Take a look at the image here, taken inside the doorway of an apartment building in Lisbon, Portugal. Now imagine this same image in black and white, without the color. It's a bunch of dumb mailboxes, right? (And the question, "What made you shoot that?" comes to mind.) But the multiple colors of the boxes, and the two-tone wall they're mounted upon, are what make the shot. Also, the person who painted these mailboxes knew what they were doing color-wise. These aren't a bunch of arbitrary colors slapped together; they all work too well together to not have been planned that way. It creates its own piece of art. It's a mini art installation and a way to make something otherwise fairly boring (apartment building mailboxes), bright and cheery. Even their arrangement on the wall is graphically pleasing. This was no accident. This is graphic art, and the subject is color. Contrasting colors, in particular, make great subjects, and when you shoot one of these types of images and share it, pay particular attention to how a shot where color is the subject is received. You'll be pleasantly surprised.

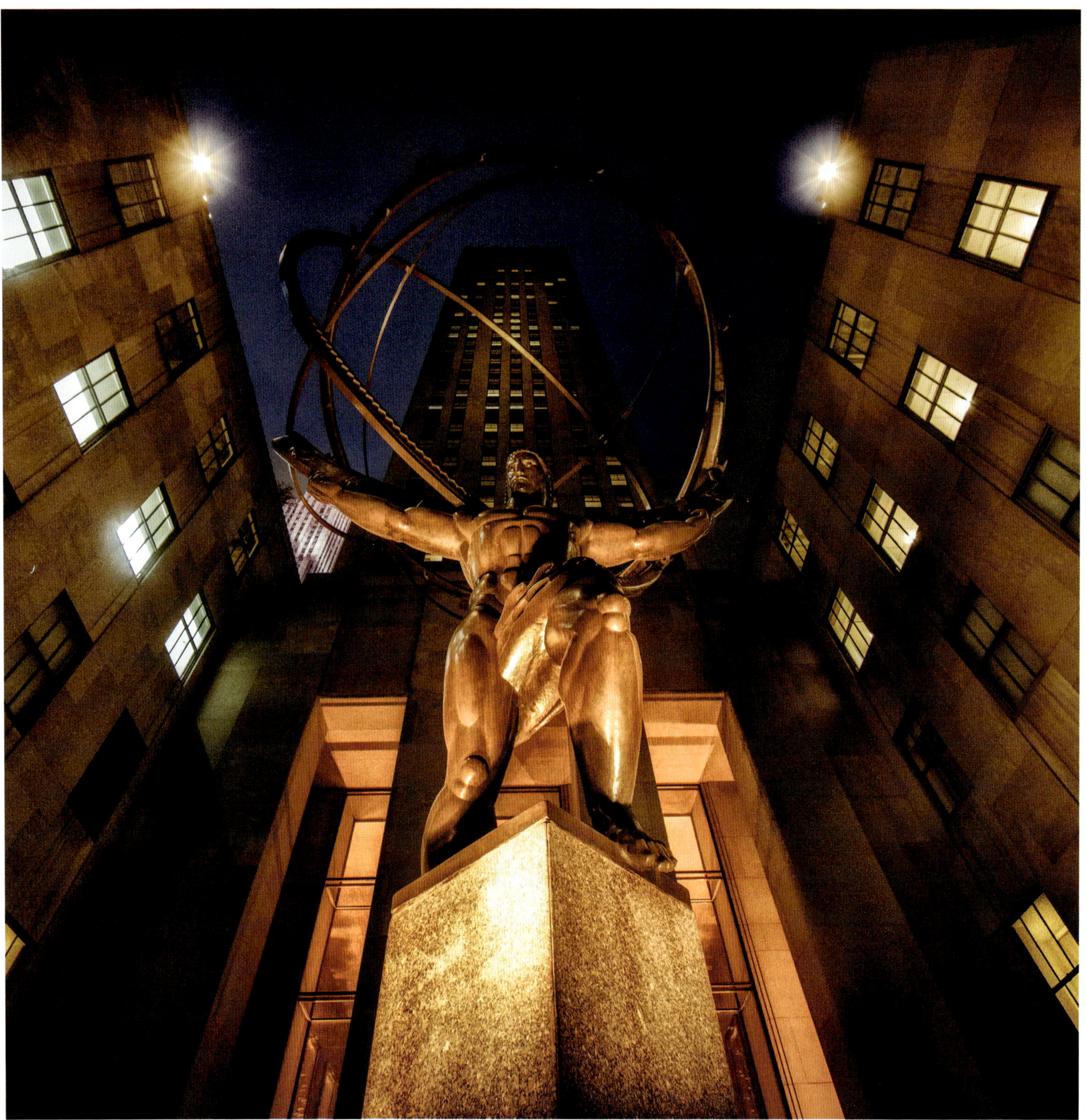

CREATE A TIMELESS LOOK

This is a compositional technique that can be a bit challenging, but it can also be a lot of fun, and that is framing up your shot so there's nothing in it that gives away when it was taken. Was it taken five years ago or 50 years ago? This is especially important when shooting travel photography to help you capture the mood and romance of a city, and not only do I talk about this in my books and talks on travel photography, I've even done an entire course on how to shoot (and post-process) to give a timeless look. Take a look at the image here of the famous statue of Atlas taken in New York City's Rockefeller Center (that's "30 Rock" behind it, which includes NBC's studios, the Rainbow Room, and the Top of the Rock Observatory). The statue was erected in 1937, so when was this photo taken? That's the thing—I framed it up so that you wouldn't see anything that would tip off when it was taken. Was it in the 1950s?, 60s?, 80s? Or 2019? There are no hints as to when, nothing modern to distract you (no signs, or satellite dishes, no modern architectural accents, etc.), so you're totally involved in the timeless scene that the photographer is presenting. You've removed modern distractions, and what's left is a glimpse into a different time, without using an old historical photo. It's not always easy to avoid including some of that stuff in your frame, but that's what makes it challenging, and a lot of fun.

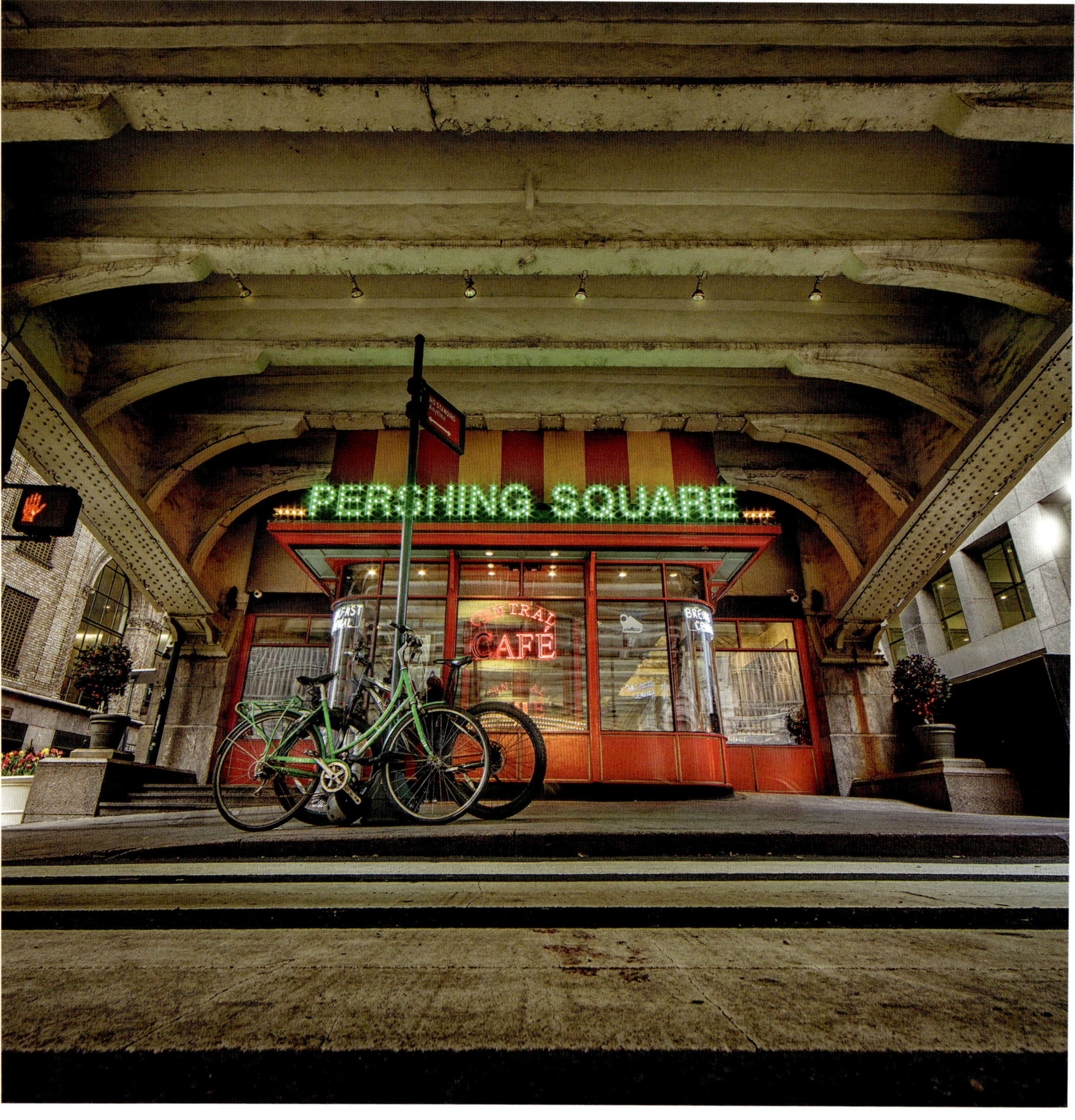

PERSHING SQUARE
CENTRAL CAFÉ

CREATE CLEAN IMAGES

It's hard to make a busy shot look good. But, it's not impossible. I've seen some incredibly great shots where so much was going on you didn't know where to look first (one of my favorites being Randy Olson's wonderful long exposure shot of the Churchgate Railway Station in Mumbai, India). But I can tell you this: they are a lot harder to make. The more things you have in your image, the more they all have to work together, and one thing you can do to help is to frame your shot to have as simple and clean an image as you can. Clean images communicate by removing distractions. Take a look at the image here, taken in the middle of New York City during the day from just outside the doors of Grand Central Terminal. There are not many places on earth busier than right there, but this is when framing up the shot to include just the essential things you want in the image, and then waiting until the pedestrians and tourists and taxis and buses and crazy amounts of traffic are all out of your frame pays off. For being taken where this was, it's a pretty clean frame. So, if you're thinking, "I want a clean, simple frame," and you compose just to let in the things you need to include to tell the story, you'll wind up with a winner.

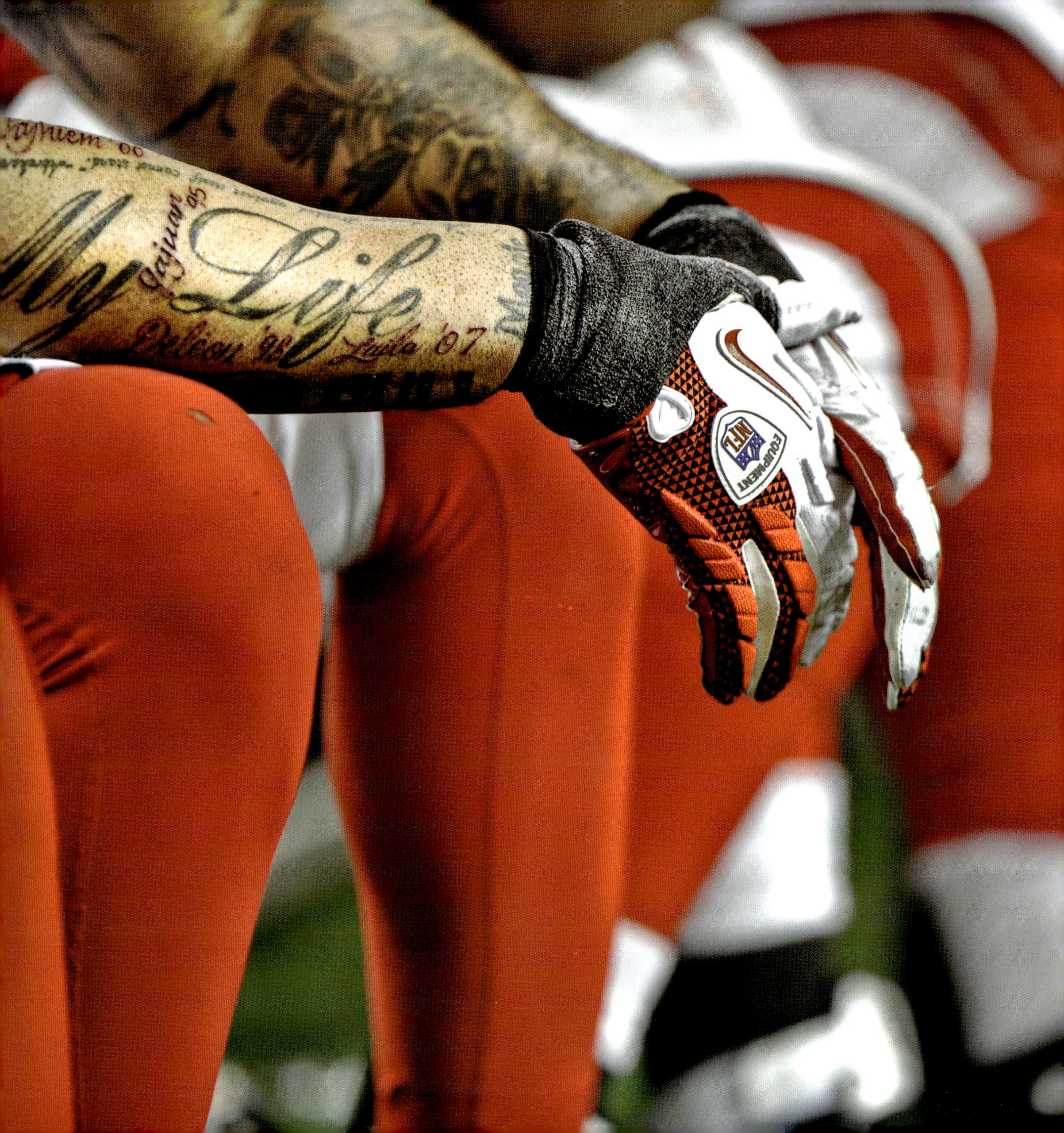

EVERY SHOT DOESN'T HAVE TO BE A HERO SHOT

You may have heard some photographers refer to a "hero shot" as a shot that is a showstopper. It's the shot you put on the cover of the photo book from your trip, or it's the first two-page spread in the book. Maybe it's the shot you add to your portfolio or Adobe Express webpage, or the big, full-screen shot on the welcome splash screen of your portfolio. They're big. They're "wow" shots. But every shot doesn't need to be a hero shot when you're telling the story of your trip, or your vacation, or an event you captured, like your kid's graduation or a concert you went to. You need those other shots that help tell the story, like the one you see here taken on the sideline while I was covering an NFL game. It's just the player's arms and gloves, and I love seeing the tattoos and the messages on his arms. It's not an action shot. There's no ball. There's no peak moment of action. It's a part of the story of the overall game day and of the athletes that make up the game. It's not a hero shot—you can't even see the athlete's face—but it tells a story and it works. Don't just go for the big hero shots—there's a story to be told.

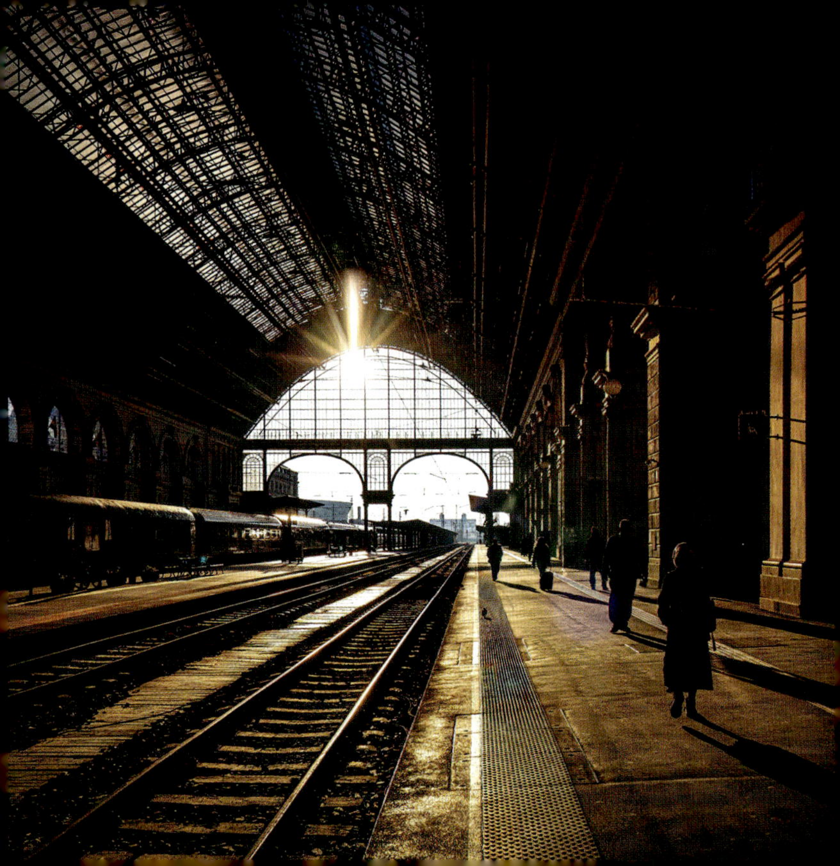

Chapter 11

———

THE CLASSIC RULES
OF COMPOSITION

I felt I needed to include at least one short chapter on the classic rules of composition, even though there have already been hundreds of books written on these, which have been around since the late 1700s (for example, the rule of thirds was first mentioned in print back in 1797—a full 12 years before I was born). Not only have hundreds of books been written about these classic rules, pretty much all of those books (well, at least all the ones I've seen) are only about those rules. So, why am I including them in this book? Because, well…darn it…they're actually really helpful. They are not actually "rules" per se. They are ideas or concepts we can use and learning them can be really helpful because once you learn the rules, then you can break the rules, and when you break them, you're not breaking them because you're some goober who doesn't know what they're doing, you're breaking them because you know the rules, and you're overriding them intentionally as a creative decision, which makes you awesome. Okay, now in this chapter, I've included 10 of my favorite of these rules. To their credit, these classic rules are time-tested and really do work, so I didn't want to ignore them or pretend they don't matter because they do. But rather than devoting another whole book to these, we're just going to devote this one chapter to them, so we have the whole rest of the book to uncover the things they haven't been writing about for a few hundred years, but can be an important part of your composition journey. Also, I get the luxury of being able to refer to the things in this chapter anywhere throughout the book, so there's that.

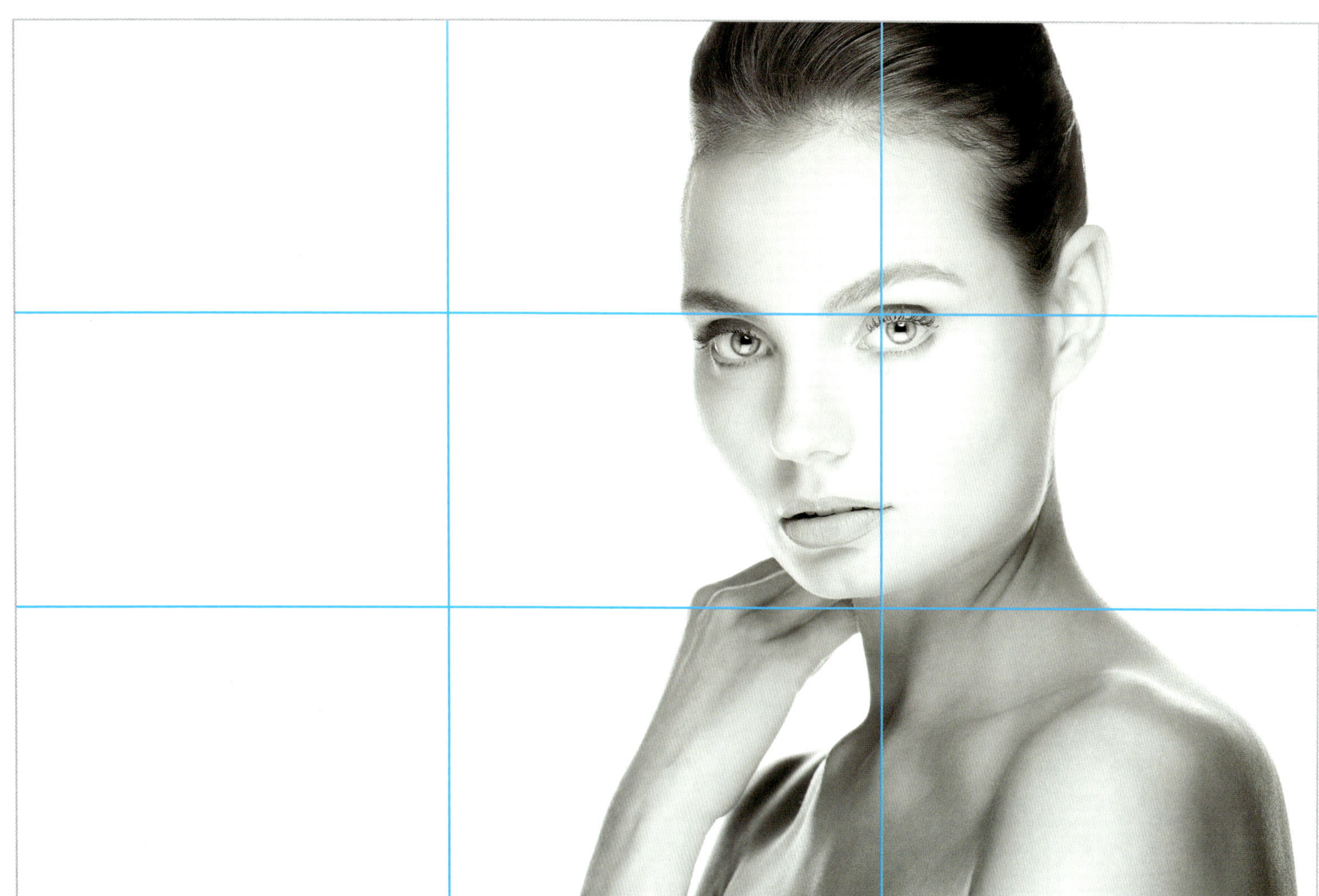

THE RULE OF THIRDS

I'm starting with this one, not only because it's one of the most-used of the classic old rules of composition, but mostly because it's one we still use a lot to this day. So much so that camera companies (and even your cellphone's camera) have added the ability to display a rule of thirds grid right within your viewfinder (or screen). The idea is really simple and it's based on the idea that, for the most part, your subject shouldn't appear in the dead center of your frame. Dead center is dead boring, and it's where photos go to die. Now, you will find times where the exact perfect place for your subject is in the dead center, and that's okay if you know the rule is "don't put your subject in the center," but you're choosing to break that rule because of artistic reasons and not because you didn't realize that was a rule. So, to make the image look more dynamic, we mentally divide it into thirds horizontally and vertically, and we place our subject (or the object we're focusing on) in the thirds where these horizontal and vertical lines intersect. In other words, we place our subject either in the left third or right third of the frame instead of in the center. This is really popular in portraits, and again, we still use this a lot today. When it comes to things like landscapes, that's when we use the horizontal thirds, and there's a pretty easy guide to follow here: If our sky is amazing, we show more of it by putting the horizon line in the bottom third of the image. That way, two thirds of the image is sky. If our sky is boring, then we deemphasize it by placing the horizon line in the top third of the image, so it shows less sky as two thirds of our image will be foreground. This is an easy rule, but it's really effective for making more dynamic looking images.

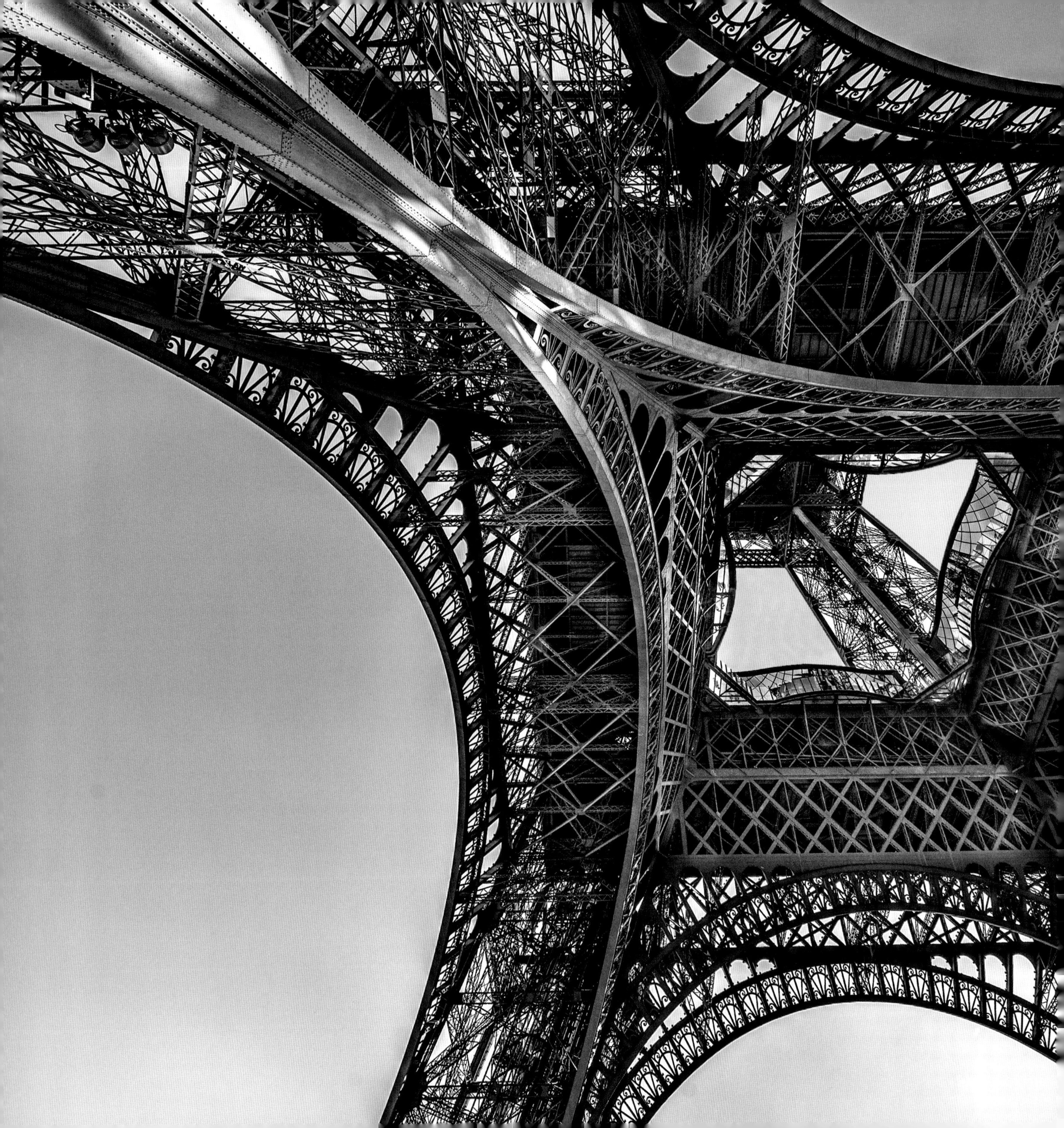

FILL THE FRAME

There's an old saying in photography (by Robert Capa) that goes:
"If your pictures aren't good enough, you're not close enough." It's one
of my favorites, and I think it's right on the money. Making your subject fill
the frame—simply bringing them closer to the person viewing the image by
filling the frame—makes the image more intimate. This doesn't just work with
portraits (though I think that's what Capa was referring to when he made that
famous quote); this works wonderfully well for other types of shots. For example,
you can show a photo of the Eiffel Tower. All of it. Like everybody else has done
for more than a century. Or, you can get in tight, show just one leg of the tower,
and we'll still get exactly what it is and we'll know where it is. You don't have to
show the whole tiger. You can fill the frame and show just the tiger's eyes.
You don't have to fill every inch of the frame, but either move in tighter or
zoom in tight and make them (or it) the star of the story you're telling.

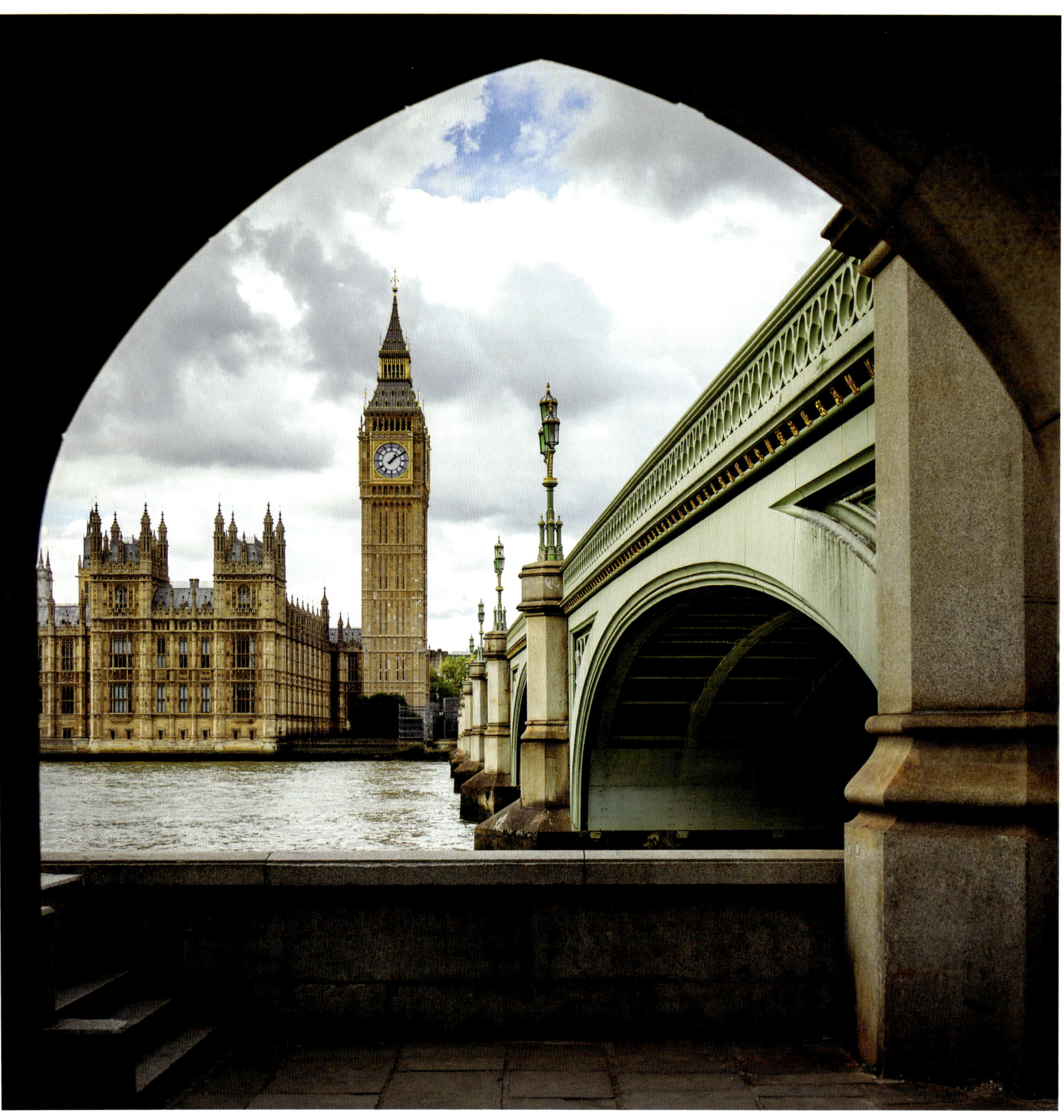

A FRAME WITHIN YOUR FRAME

What do most people do when they have a photo they really love? They frame it. We love frames. Love them! There's an entire multi-billion dollar industry built around framing because (say it with me) people love frames. So, it kind of stands to reason that people like when we take photos where our image appears inside a physical or literal frame within the scene. This can be anything from an archway, like we see here, or a window with shutters, or double-doors opening into a room, or using a tree to frame an image, or a hallway, or a small opening in a wall. It can be any number of things. What's nice is it's up to your creativity. You can find opportunities to frame your image in any number of ways, so it's something you might consider adding to your compositional bag of tricks. I've seen how people react to images that are "framed," and I think you'll be surprised at what a hit this can be with folks viewing your images. Now, imagine if you use a literal frame, and then you print your image and frame it at the framing place—it becomes a whole *Inception* thing, right?

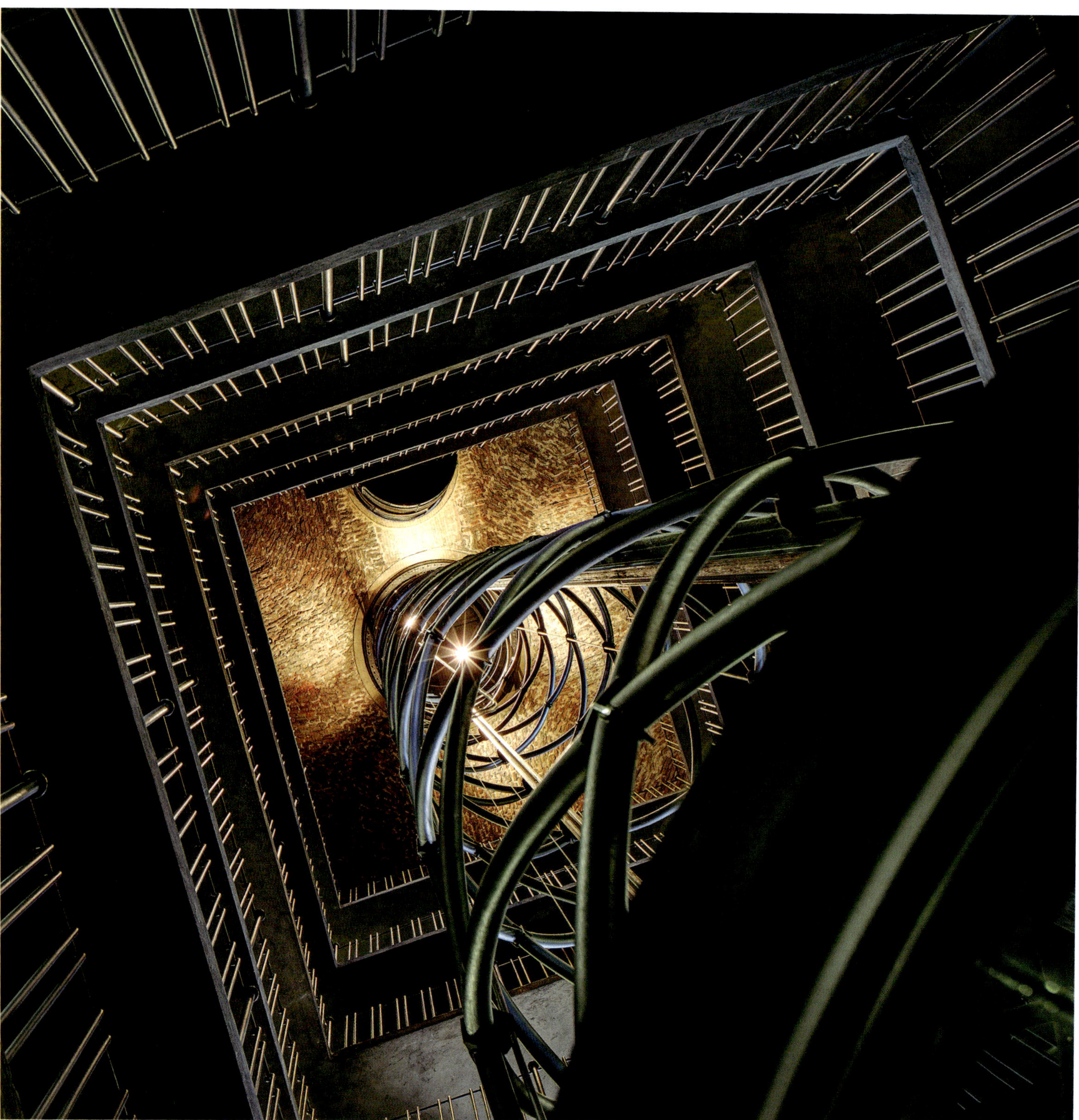

LEADING LINES

Leading lines are physical lines in your image that draw the viewer into the image and guide them to where you want them to look. The whole idea is to draw them in, and these lines (like the lines on a highway, or a fence leading down a trail, or in our case here, all the lines aiming upward, leading the viewer up into the shot—which is an elevator shaft in the Old Town Hall Tower in Prague) are created by how you frame the shot. Position yourself so the lines lead the viewer into the image. Unfortunately, this isn't always possible because there's not always something in the scene that's pointing directly to the main subject. I remember being up in Banff National Park, out on the ice of a frozen lake and trying to find one of the long cracks in the ice that might be aiming at the mountains I wanted to use as my subject. It took me wandering around the frozen lake for about 20 minutes until I finally found a crack aiming at the mountains, but it just as easily could have gone the other way, where I didn't find a leading line at all. This is one where you'll need a little luck, or help from Mother Nature, but when you do find a clear, obvious leading line, it really can help create a strong composition.

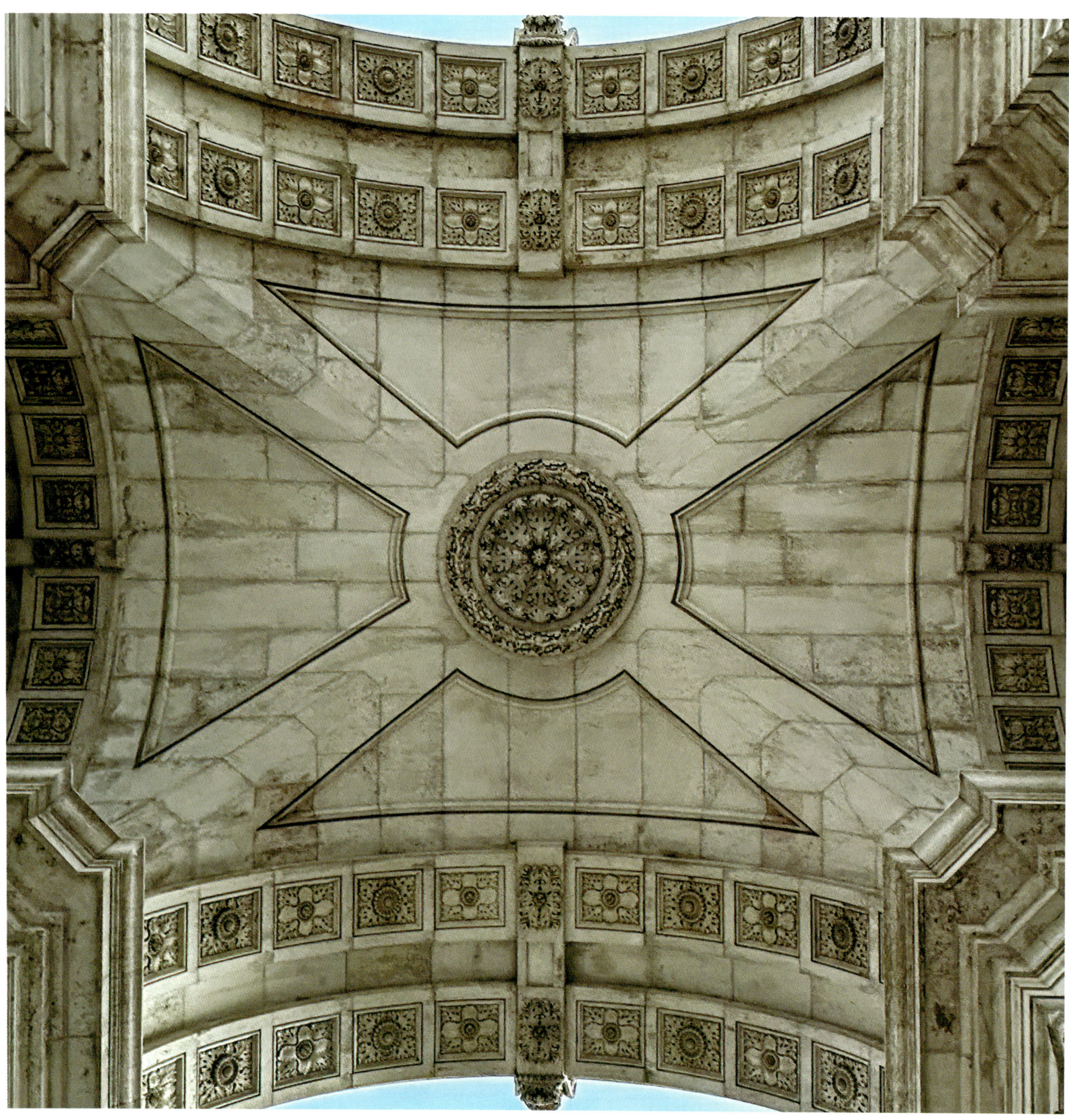

SYMMETRY

This is when the two sides of an object in your frame, like a building or a pattern, look the same on both sides. It's a really powerful compositional tool because people, whether they're cognizant of it or not, really like things that look similar. That's why we see symmetrical patterns in so many places and things in our lives. Take a look at the ceiling of this archway in Lisbon, Portugal. The architect could have easily made each side different, but by making them exactly the same, it creates a wonderful symmetry that people love to look at (well, if they think to look up). They've done studies that show our love for symmetry starts at a crazy early age—they've shown photos of people to babies and they react most positively to people with very symmetrical faces (their left side looks pretty identical to their right side). So, when you get an opportunity to show symmetry, or even a mirror-like reflection, with your images, you can pretty much bet people are going to like it.

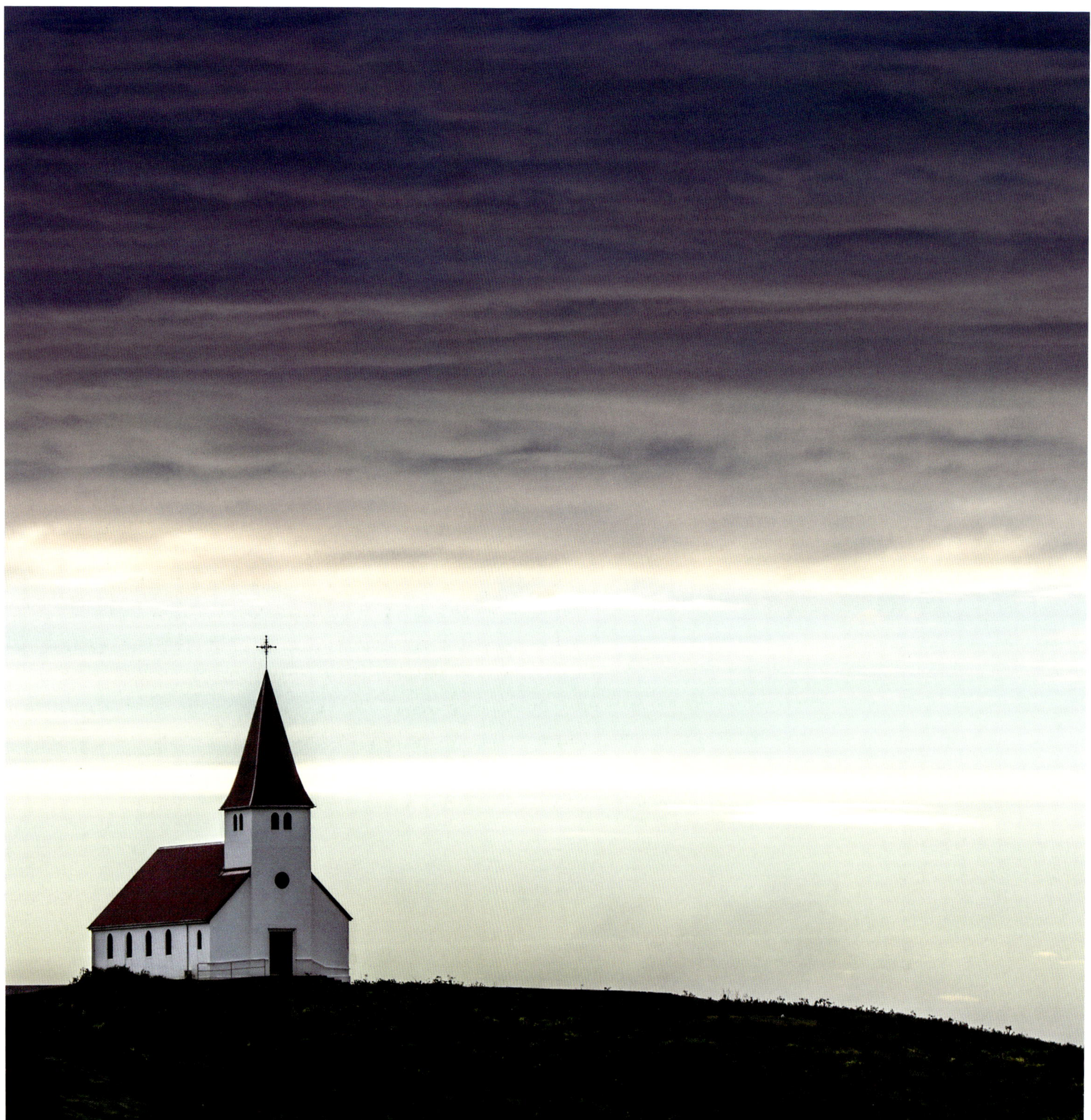

NEGATIVE SPACE

This is a really effective compositional technique (and one of my all-time favorites) where you intentionally leave a large area of your image empty, so the viewer's eye goes directly to your subject. This empty area can be sky (like it is in the image here), or a wall that's very simple (so, it wouldn't have windows, or shutters, or a lamp). Generally, I think of this as empty area, even if the area is a physical object, like a wall, or the sky. I usually combine this negative space concept with the rule of thirds, and you can see this with the image here where the chapel (in Vik, Iceland) is way off to the left—in the left, bottom third of the frame—and the rest of the image is negative (empty) space (even though the clouds are there, it's still considered negative space). This one is fairly easy to do because it really comes down to what you allow to appear in your frame. In this case, if I moved my camera a little to the right, you'd see a lot of man-made distracting stuff. Same thing on the left. So, I framed it up to simplify the image, used the negative space as a compositional tool, and put the subject off to the left (by the way, picture how this image would look if the chapel was centered).

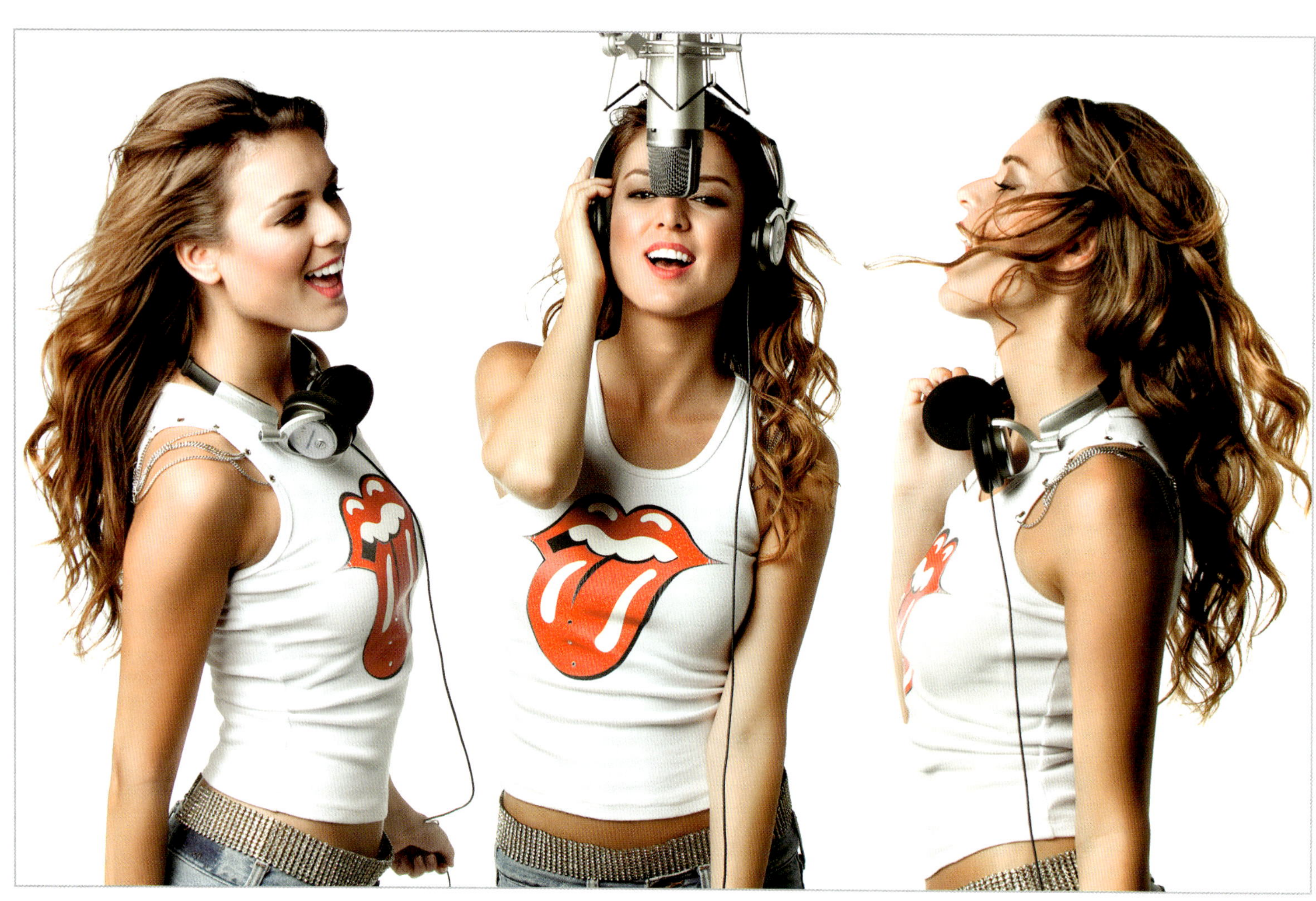

THE RULE OF ODDS

A number of these techniques are based on how people react to certain types of images, or elements within your image, and the rule of odds is a simple one, but I think it's really fascinating. The rule is that people tend to like images more, and find them more interesting, when there are an odd number of elements in the image. For example, if you're capturing some birds flying in formation, if you have a group of three or five, people will like that more than they would a group of four. Once you get a bunch of objects it doesn't matter as much (if it's high enough that you'd have to count them, that's the number), but like with three images of the same person (as shown here), three is way more effective (and more pleasing to the eye, or the mind) than two or four. The odd number rule really works when it's a small number of objects (or in this case, people, even though it's the same person), so this is something to keep in mind when you're framing up your shot. (Now that you know this rule, it's amazing how often you'll see it put into play in advertising or still photography.)

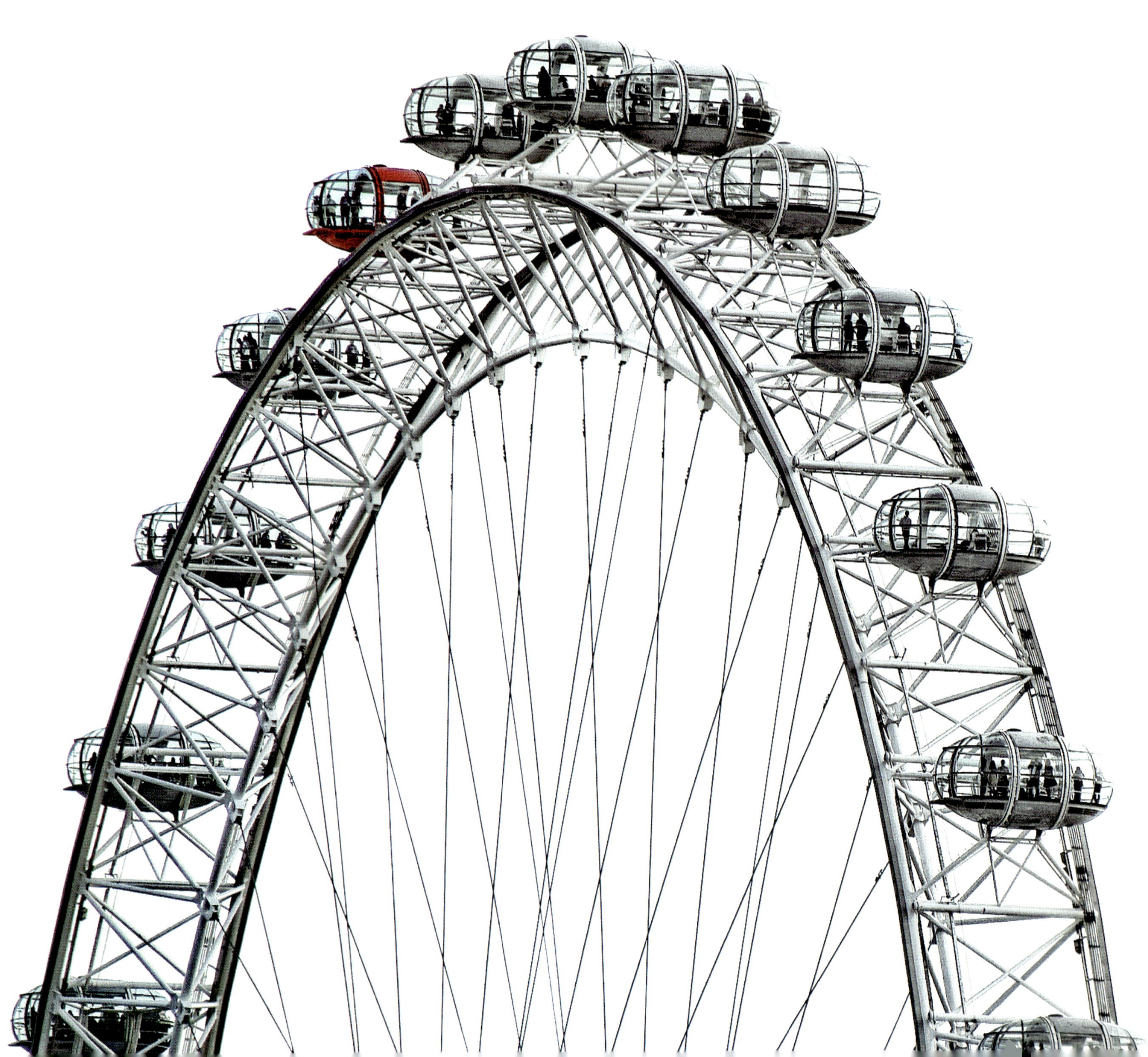

PATTERNS AND INTERRUPTION

This is another one of those psychological effects, and it's based on the fact that people like patterns. We see repeating patterns used so often in our everyday lives in things as simple as tile floors, or a pattern in a rug, or on a wall. Take a look at the lighting in your ceiling (or your ceiling at work), your kitchen cabinets, or things even as simple as leaves in nature. Patterns are everywhere, and we love them. We put things in perfect rows and line everything up so often because it's pleasing. But you know what's even more pleasing than a pattern? It's a pattern interrupted (something I learned from living legend of photography Jay Maisel). Patterns are interesting, but when you interrupt a pattern—like you see here in this image where one capsule is red—it creates an entirely different and much more fascinating image than if everything was the same (by the way, that capsule was actually red—I didn't change it in Photoshop, but I would have no reservations about doing so. In fact, I wish I had thought to do that, but since it was already there, I was happy with my "pattern interruptus." I have no idea if that is an actual Latin word, but it sure sounds good).

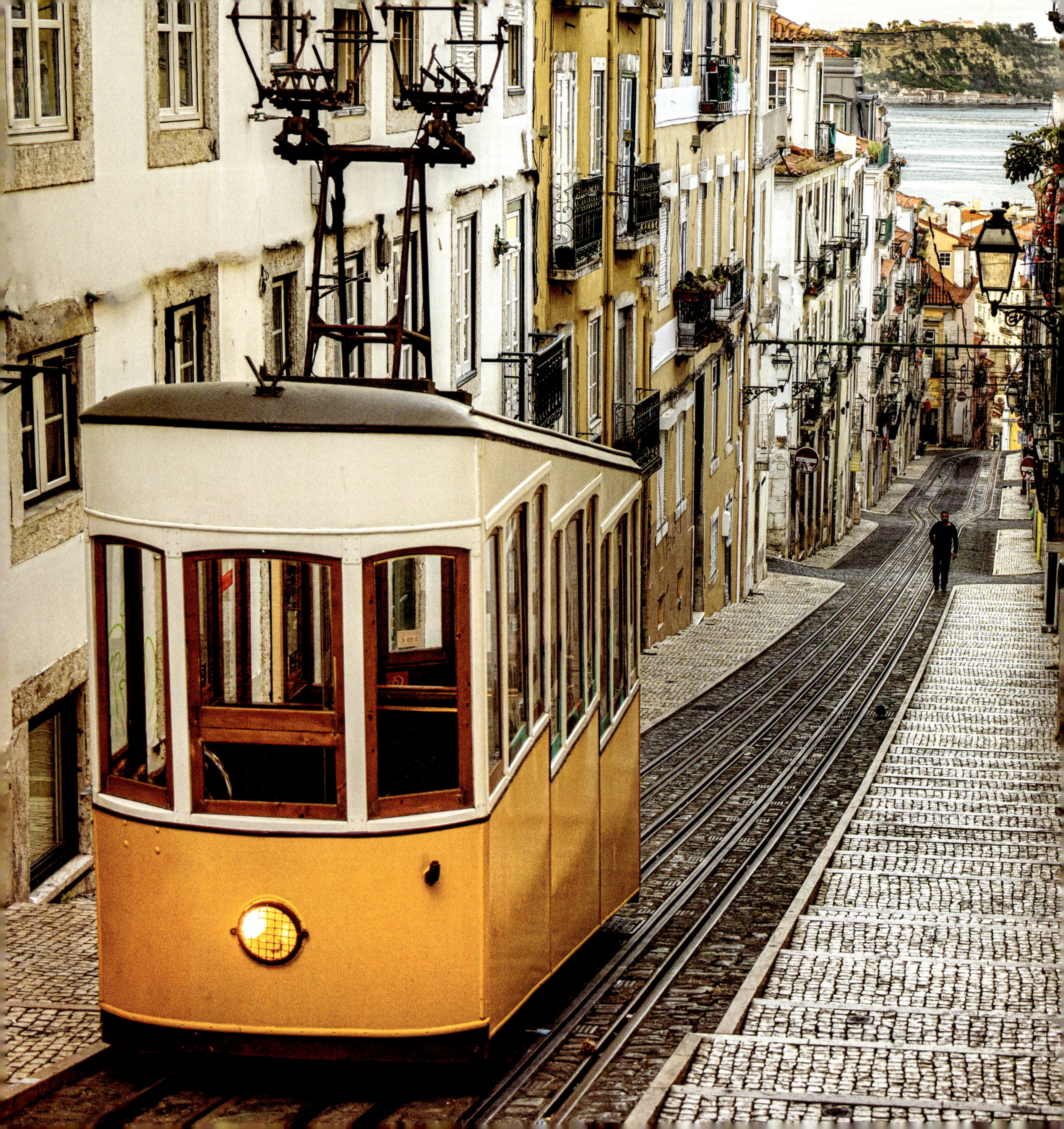

THE GOLDEN RATIO

This is another one of those techniques that is kind of similar to leading lines in the way that it's designed to lead the viewer's eye, or even to the rules of thirds, but it leads the eye by balancing objects in the image in a really pleasing way. The idea is you place the main subject of your image in the center of a spiral, which sounds like it would be challenging inside your viewfinder, but I don't use this inside my viewfinder. I use it afterward when I'm cropping the image in Lightroom. If you get the Crop Overlay tool, you'll see different cropping overlays (you do this by pressing the letter O on your keyboard to see the overlay, then pressing Shift-O to rotate the spiral 90° at a time, and now you can crop so your main subject appears inside the spiral). This concept has been around since the 12th century when Italian mathematician Leonardo Fibonacci came up with the Fibonacci sequence, which

is a more advanced spiral used very much like the Golden Ratio, which is kind of a simplified version of Fibonacci's sequence. It's essentially the same thing, creating a more balanced and overall more pleasing composition. Who doesn't want that?

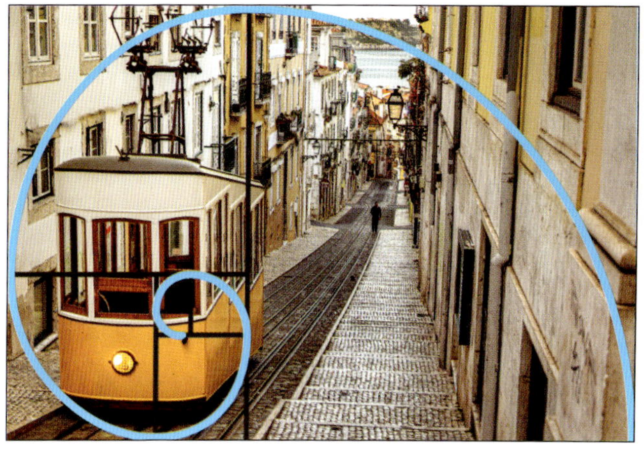

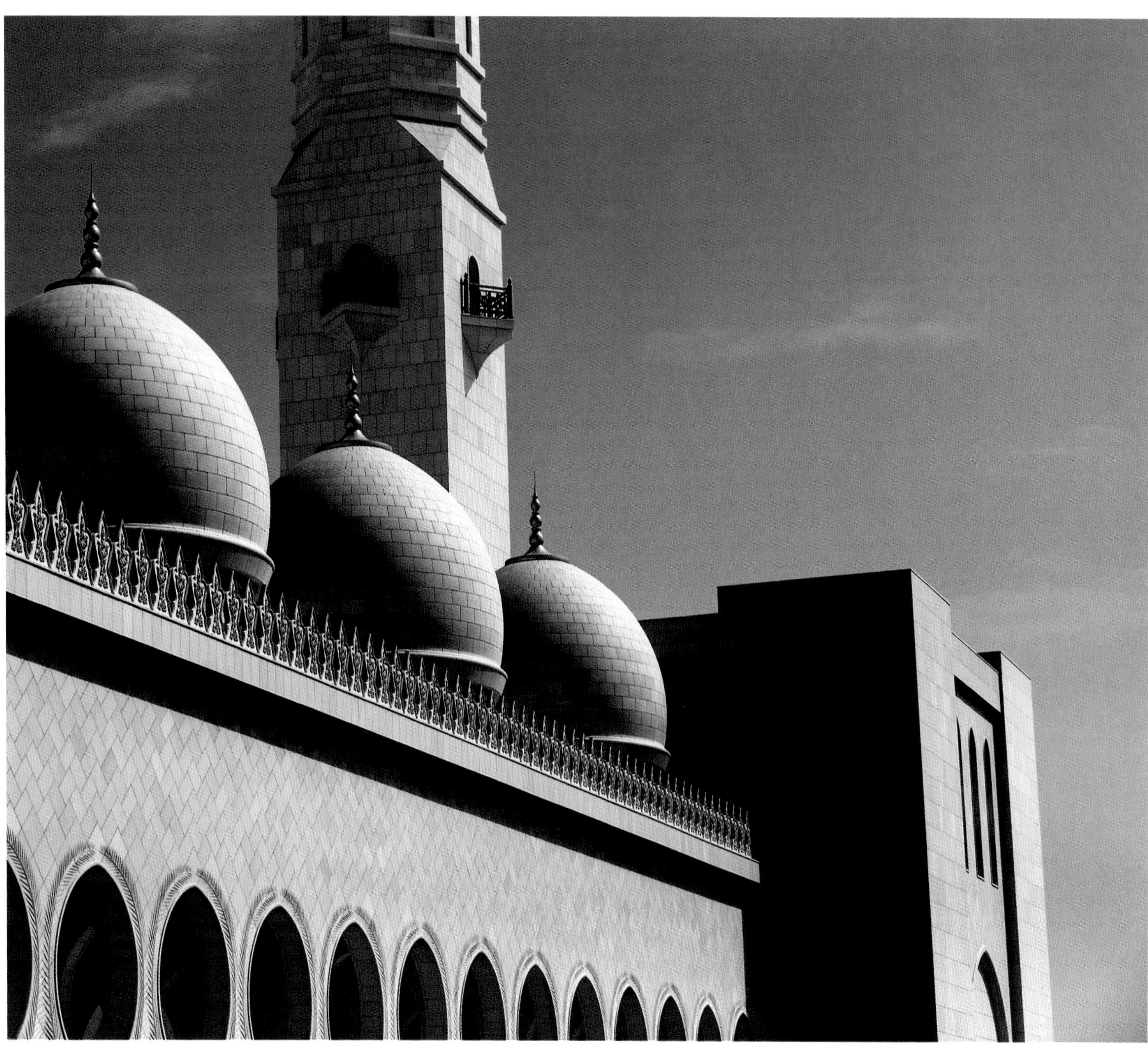

DIAGONAL LINES

A cousin of leading lines is diagonal lines because they also help lead the viewer's eye into the image. This is one of the easiest techniques to use from your composition toolbox because diagonal lines appear so often in scenes. Also, you can create diagonal lines from a straight line by either rotating your crop in post-production or by just rotating your camera to make a straight line diagonal. In the image here, I'm using the diagonal roof lines to lead the viewer into the image. Of course, the roof of the Sheikh Zayed Grand Mosque in Abu Dhabi is not diagonal. Those lines look diagonal because of where I'm standing—at an angle to the mosque that makes the lines diagonal—and this helps to not only add a leading line type of effect, but also gives the image more depth.

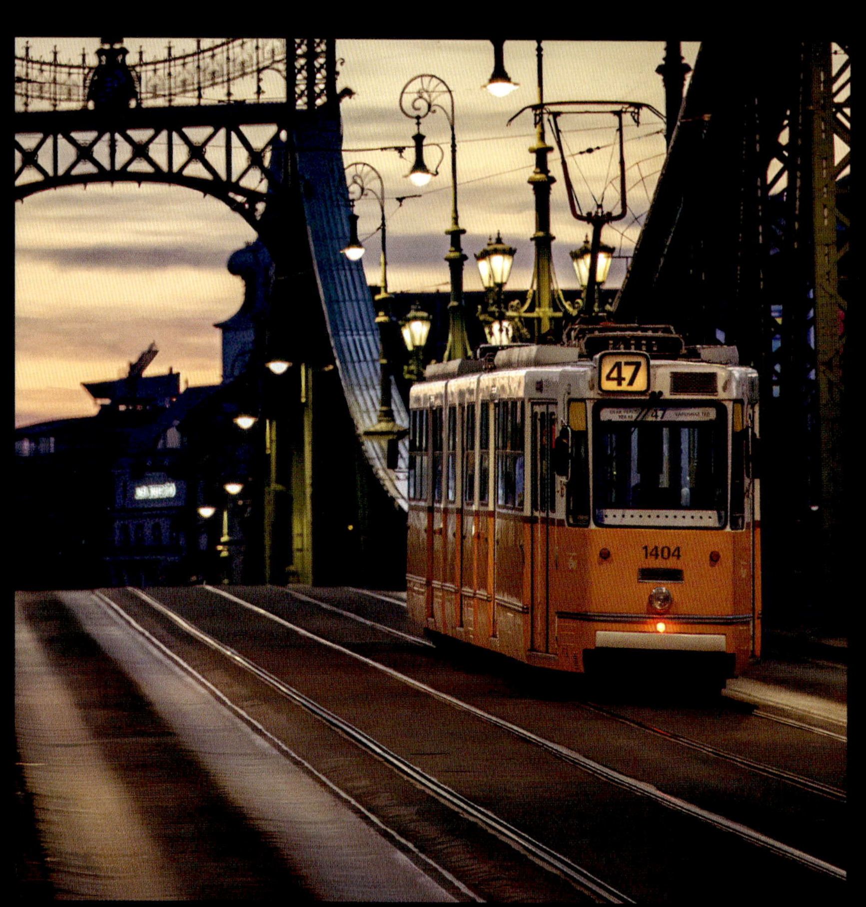

Chapter 12

THE NUMBERS
BEHIND THE PIXELS

Since this whole book is about the tools for creativity and vision, I thought it might be fun to include (in the very back of the book where nobody will be looking… well, maybe a few of us will) the EXIF data behind the images in the book. This is the information embedded into each image when it was taken, including the f-stop, shutter speed, and ISO. Boring stuff, unless you find numbers really interesting, in which case, this could easily be the most engaging chapter in the book (don't worry—it's not. That's why it's way back here). Just a quick reminder: the EXIF data you see on the following pages represents the settings I needed to use based on the lighting conditions in that location on that particular day, in that particular season, at that time of day, if it was outdoors or indoors with natural light, and the weather conditions outdoors on that day (was the light bright and sunny or was it a cloudy day, or raining, or snowing, etc.). So, even if you go to the same location where I was standing and you look down at the floor and see two carefully drawn Xs where you're supposed to put your feet, and my note written in chalk, which says "photographer stand here" with an arrow pointing between the two Xs, the settings I used will be pretty useless. Nevertheless, I included them here because we're photographers and we like stuff like this. Also, because we're weird. I like that about us.

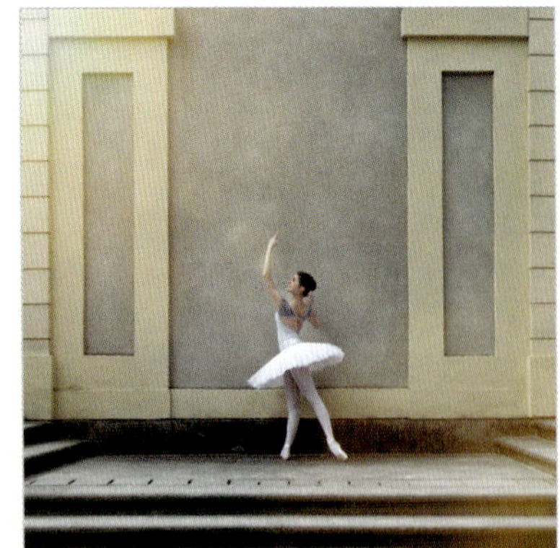

Cover

- Camera: Canon EOS R6
- Lens: 24–240mm f/4–6.3 @ 47mm
- Aperture Value: f/6.3
- Shutter Speed: 1/1250 sec
- ISO: 400

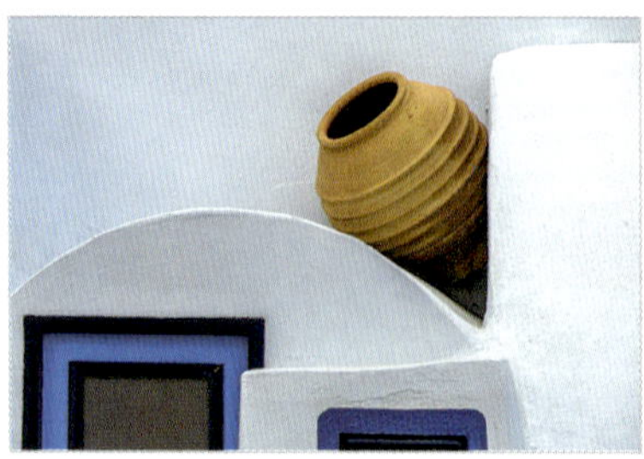

Page xii

- Camera: Canon EOS R6 Mark II
- Lens: 24–240mm f/4–6.3 @ 129mm
- Aperture Value: f/7.1
- Shutter Speed: 1/400 sec
- ISO: 200

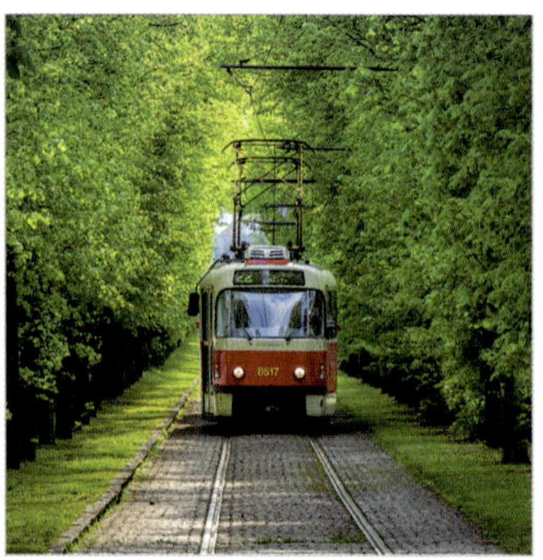

Page xiv

- Camera: Canon EOS R6
- Lens: 24–240mm f/4–6.3 @ 240mm
- Aperture Value: f/6.3
- Shutter Speed: 1/640 sec
- ISO: 1250

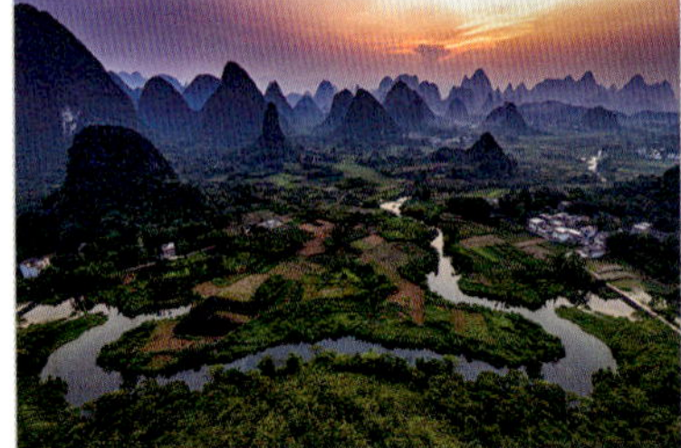

Page 02

- Camera: Canon EOS R
- Lens: 16–35mm f/4 @ 16mm
- Aperture Value: f/11
- Shutter Speed: 1/2 sec
- ISO: 100

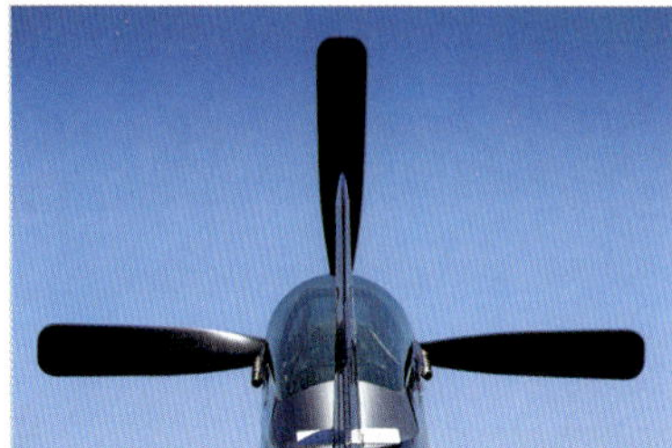

Page 04

- Camera: Canon EOS R6 Mark II
- Lens: 150–600mm f/5–6.3 @ 273mm
- Aperture Value: f/8
- Shutter Speed: 1/500 sec
- ISO: 100

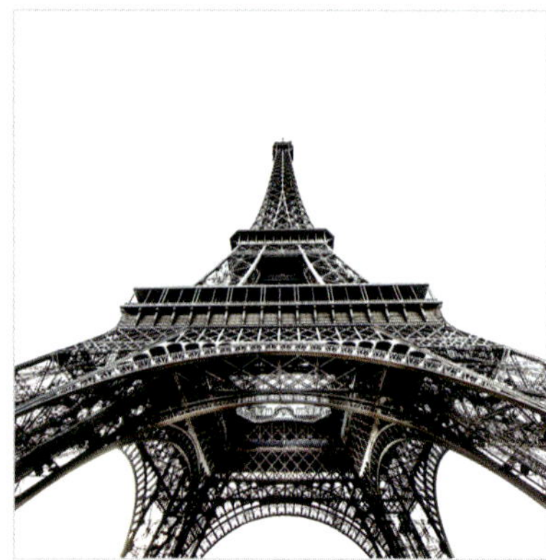

Page 06

- Camera: Nikon D700
- Lens: 14–24mm f/2.8 @ 14mm
- Aperture Value: f/6.3
- Shutter Speed: 1/25 sec
- ISO: 200

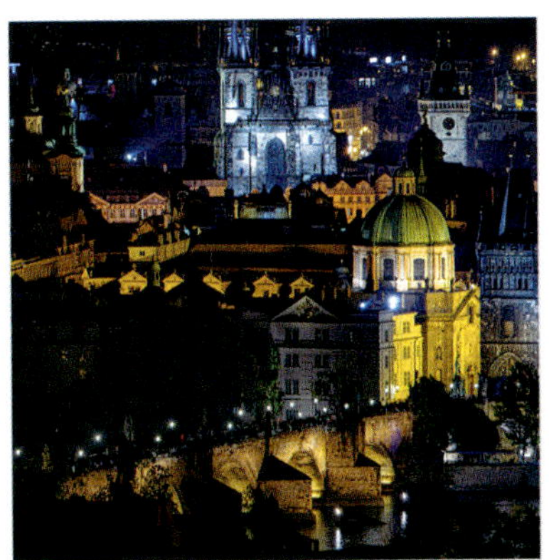

Page 08

- Camera: Canon EOS R6
- Lens: 100–400mm f/5.6-8 @ 270mm
- Aperture Value: *f*/8
- Shutter Speed: 1 sec
- ISO: 400

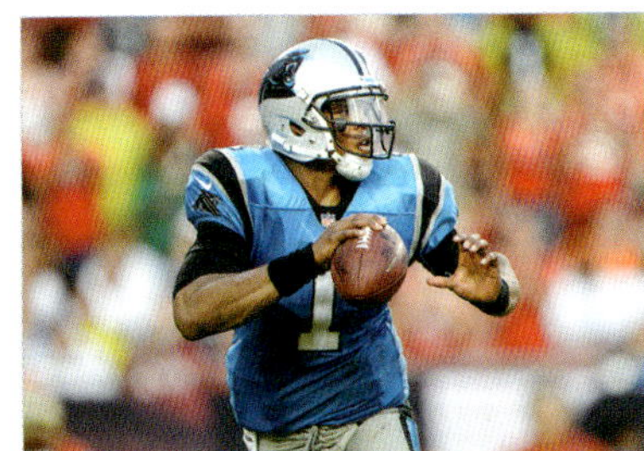

Page 10

- Camera: Nikon D4
- Lens: 400mm f/2.8 @ 400mm
- Aperture Value: *f*/2.8
- Shutter Speed: 1/1600 sec
- ISO: 1250

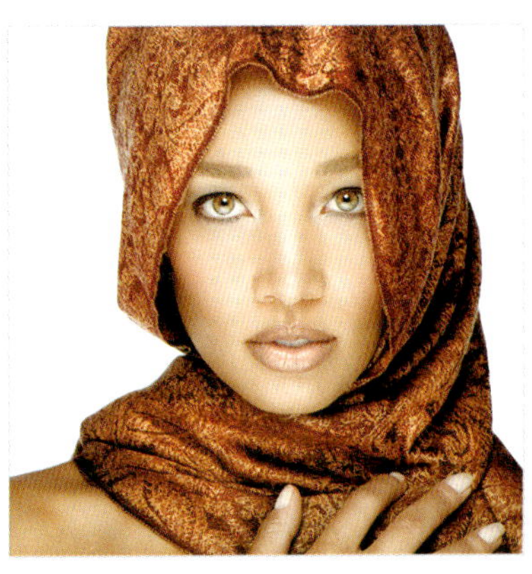

Page 12

- Camera: Nikon D3
- Lens: 70–200mm f/2.8 @ 200mm
- Aperture Value: *f*/10
- Shutter Speed: 1/160 sec
- ISO: 200

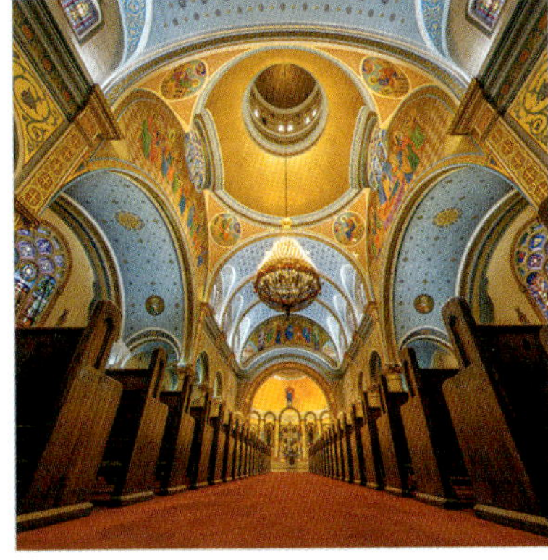

Page 14

- Camera: Canon EOS R
- Lens: 11–24mm f/4 @ 11mm
- Aperture Value: *f*/11
- Shutter Speed: 2/5 sec
- ISO: 100

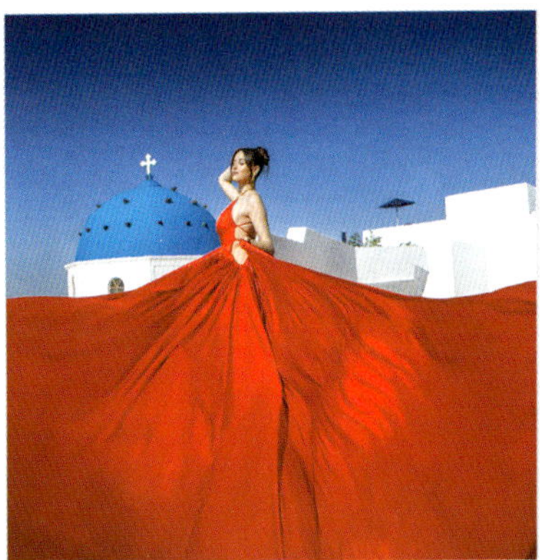

Page 16

- Camera: Canon EOS R6 Mark II
- Lens: 24–240mm f/4-6.3 @ 24mm
- Aperture Value: *f*/6.3
- Shutter Speed: 1/1000 sec
- ISO: 160

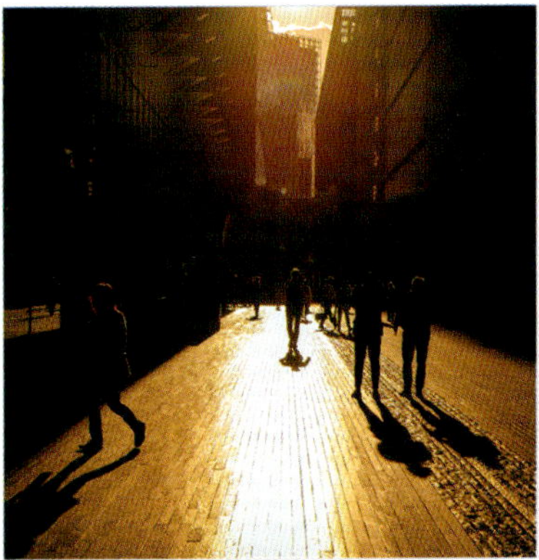

Page 18

- Camera: Canon EOS R6 Mark II
- Lens: 24–240mm f/4-6.3 @ 50mm
- Aperture Value: *f*/5
- Shutter Speed: 1/2000 sec
- ISO: 100

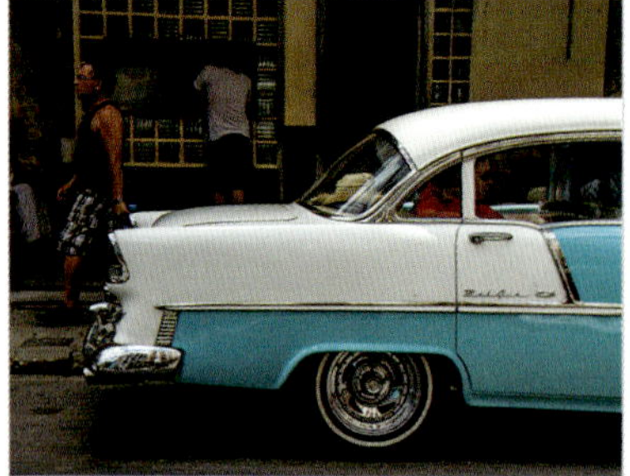

Page 20

Camera: Nikon D800

Lens: 28–300mm f/3.5–5.6 @ 78mm

Aperture Value: $f/8$

Shutter Speed: 1/1500 sec

ISO: 800

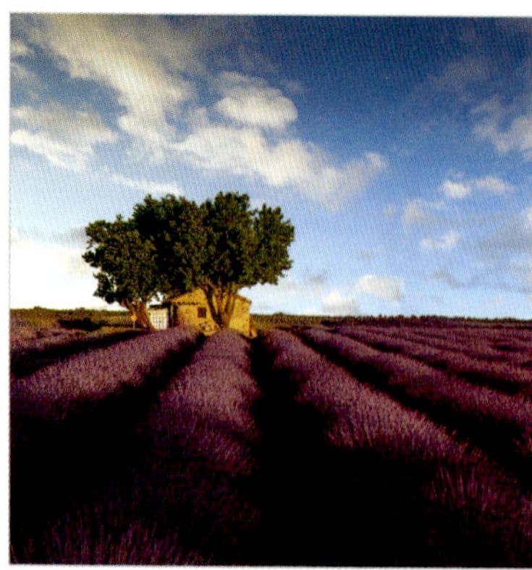

Page 22

Camera: Canon EOS R

Lens: 70–200mm f/2.8 @ 70mm

Aperture Value: $f/7.1$

Shutter Speed: 1/80 sec

ISO: 100

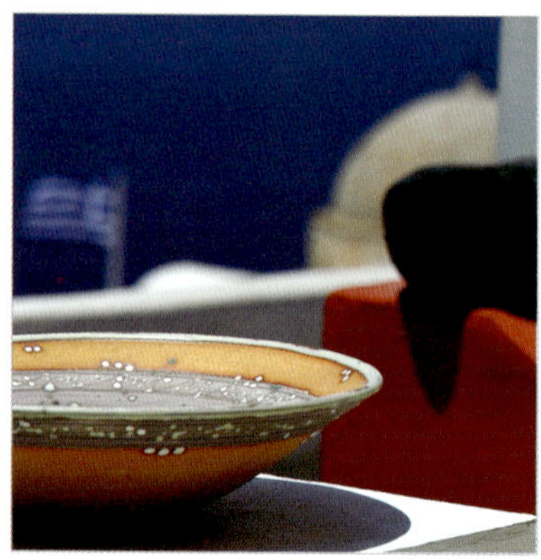

Page 24

Camera: Nikon D3S

Lens: 28–300mm f/3.5–5.6 @ 150mm

Aperture Value: $f/8$

Shutter Speed: 1/1600 sec

ISO: 200

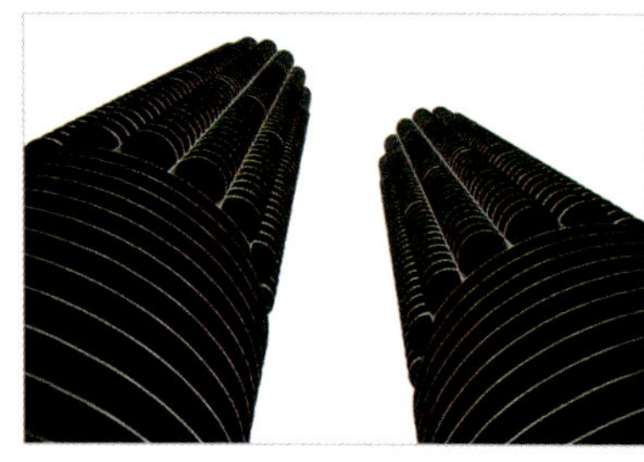

Page 26

Camera: Canon EOS R6

Lens: 24–240mm f/4–6.3 @ 24mm

Aperture Value: $f/4$

Shutter Speed: 1/4000 sec

ISO: 100

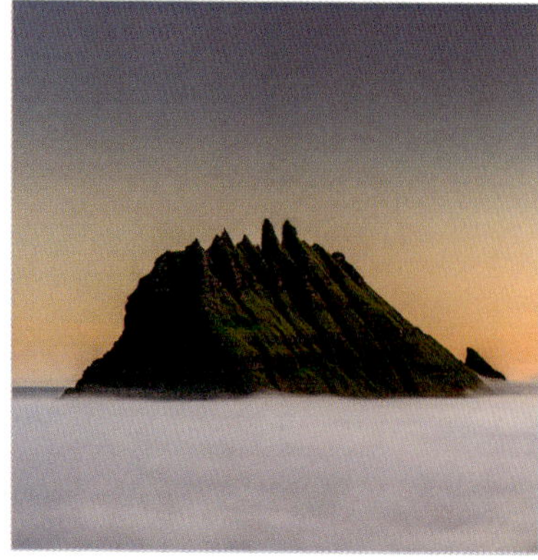

Page 28

Camera: Canon EOS R

Lens: 70–200mm f/2.8 @ 100mm

Aperture Value: $f/11$

Shutter Speed: 1/400 sec

ISO: 100

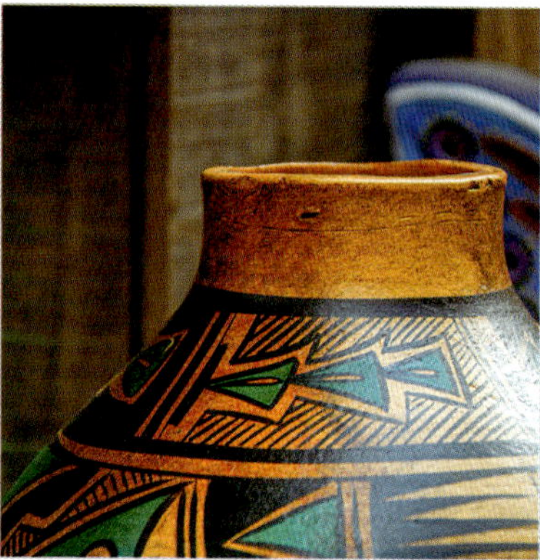

Page 30

Camera: Canon EOS-1D X

28–300mm f/3.5–5.6 @ 300mm

Aperture Value: $f/6.3$

Shutter Speed: 1/100 sec

ISO: 400

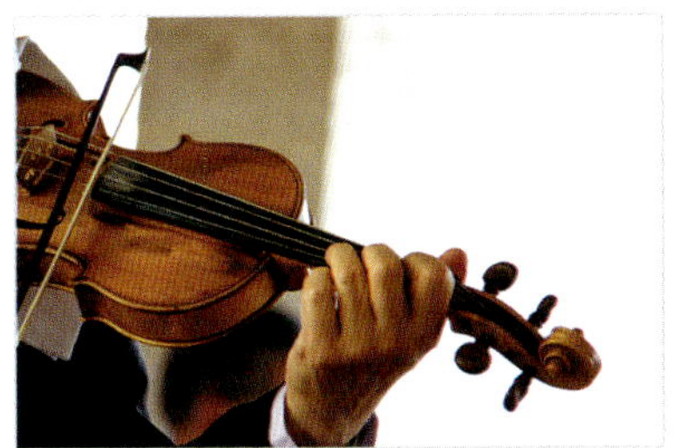

Page 32

Camera: Canon EOS 5D Mark III

Lens: 28–300mm @ 300mm

Aperture Value: f/6.3

Shutter Speed: 1/160 sec

ISO: 400

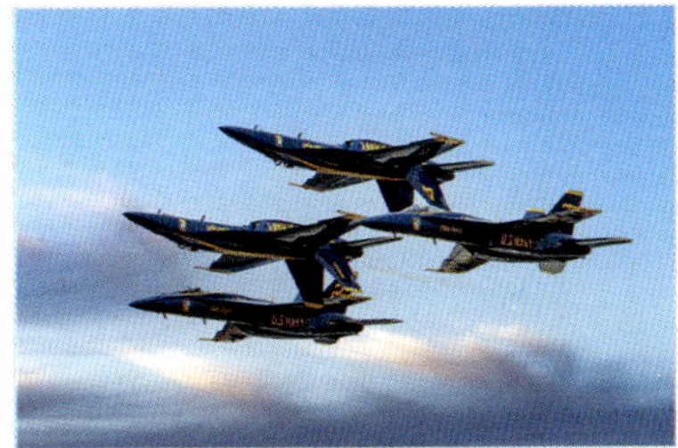

Page 34

Camera: Canon EOS R6

Lens: 150–600mm f/5–6.3 @ 483mm

Aperture Value: f/6.3

Shutter Speed: 1/1250 sec

ISO: 320

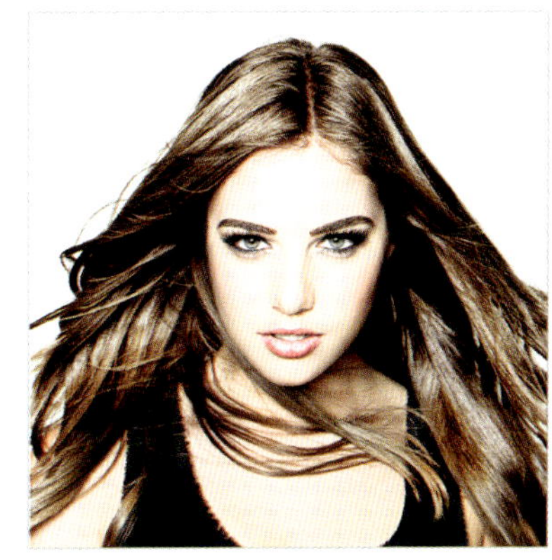

Page 36

Camera: Nikon D3S

Lens: 70–200mm f/2.8 @ 70mm

Aperture Value: f/10

Shutter Speed: 1/125 sec

ISO: 200

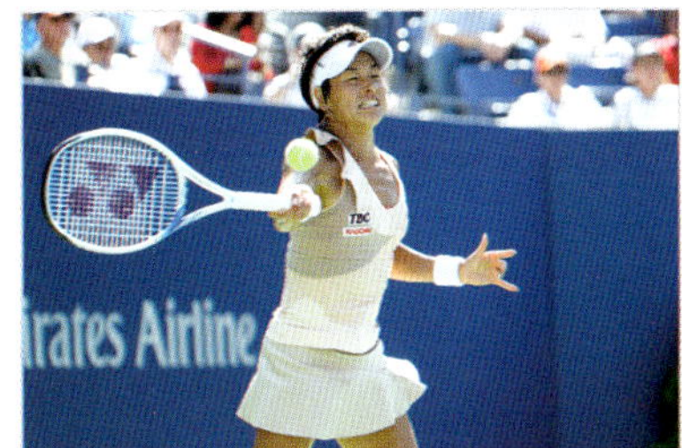

Page 38

Camera: Canon EOS-1D X

Lens: 200–400mm f/4 @ 200mm

Aperture Value: f/4

Shutter Speed: 1/2500 sec

ISO: 1600

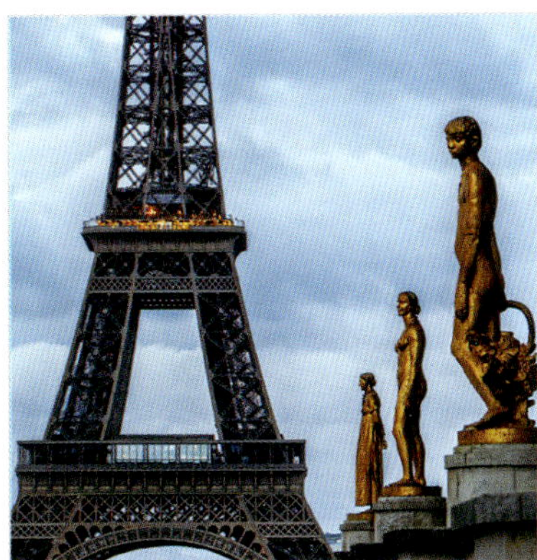

Page 40

Camera: Canon EOS R

Lens: 70–200mm f/2.8 @ 110mm

Aperture Value: f/11

Shutter Speed: 3/5 sec

ISO: 100

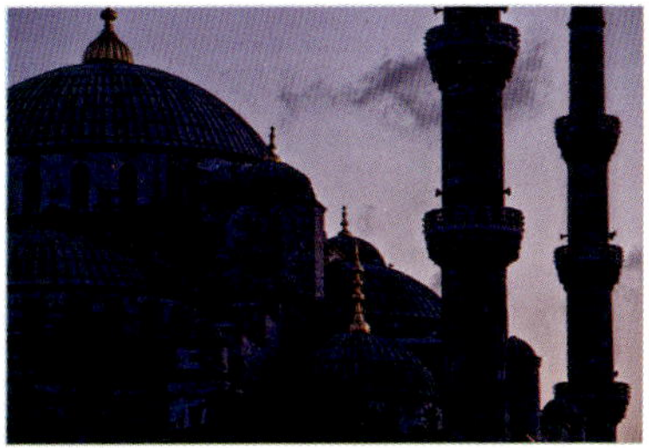

Page 42

Camera: Nikon D3

Lens: 70–200mm f/2.8 @ 170mm

Aperture Value: f/5.6

Shutter Speed: 1/15 sec

ISO: 200

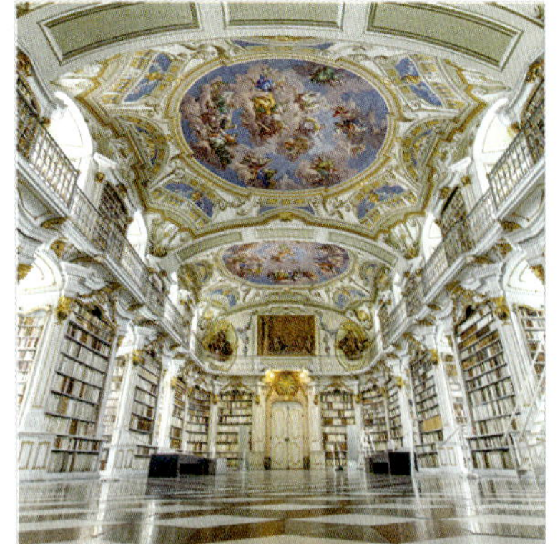

Page 44

Camera: Canon EOS R

Lens: 15–30mm f/2.8 @ 17mm

Aperture Value: $f/11$

Shutter Speed: 1/4 sec

ISO: 100

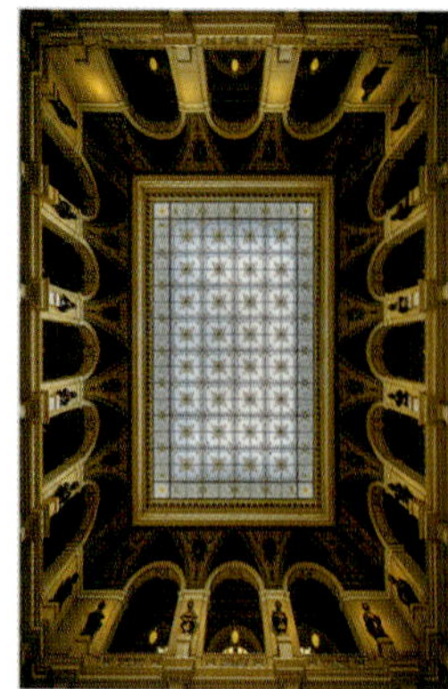

Page 46

Camera: Canon EOS R6

Lens: 11–24mm f/4 @ 11mm

Aperture Value: $f/4$

Shutter Speed: 1/1000 sec

ISO: 1600

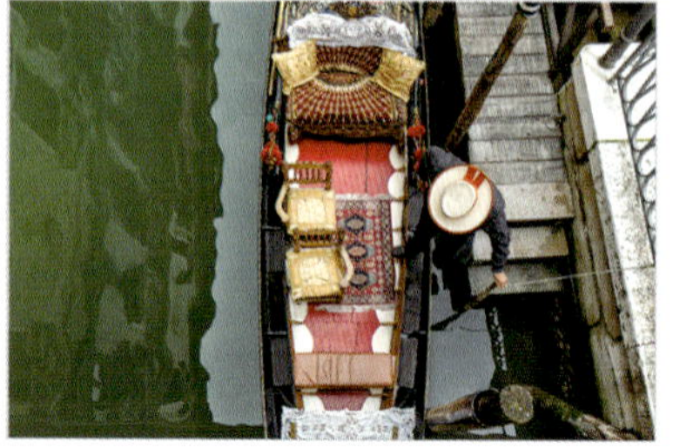

Page 48

Camera: Canon EOS 5D Mark IV

Lens: 16–35mm f/4 @ 22mm

Aperture Value: $f/5.6$

Shutter Speed: 1/100 sec

ISO: 1000

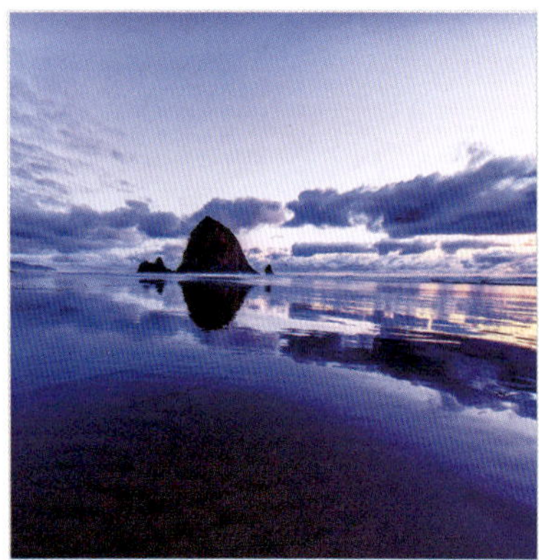

Page 50

Camera: Canon EOS 5D Mark III

Lens: 11–24mm f/4 @ 11mm

Aperture Value: $f/11$

Shutter Speed: 13/10 sec

ISO: 100

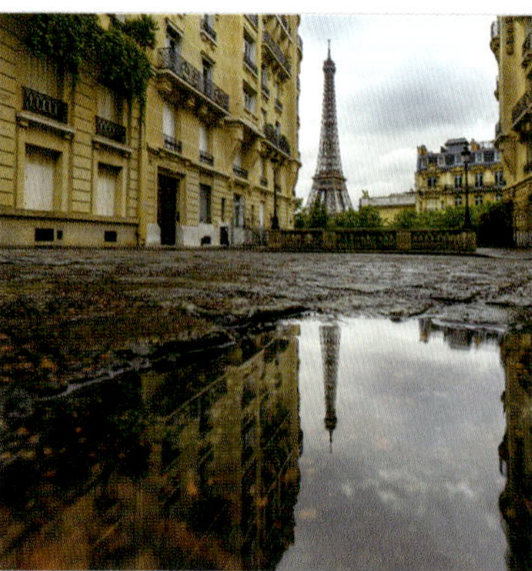

Page 52

Camera: Canon EOS R

Lens: 16–35mm f/4 @ 16mm

Aperture Value: $f/11$

Shutter Speed: 1/8 sec

ISO: 400

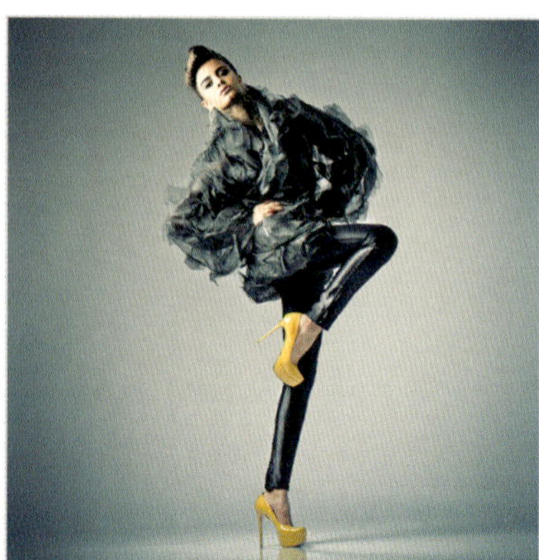

Page 54

Camera: Nikon D3

Lens: 70–200mm f/2.8 @ 95mm

Aperture Value: $f/11$

Shutter Speed: 1/125 sec

ISO: 200

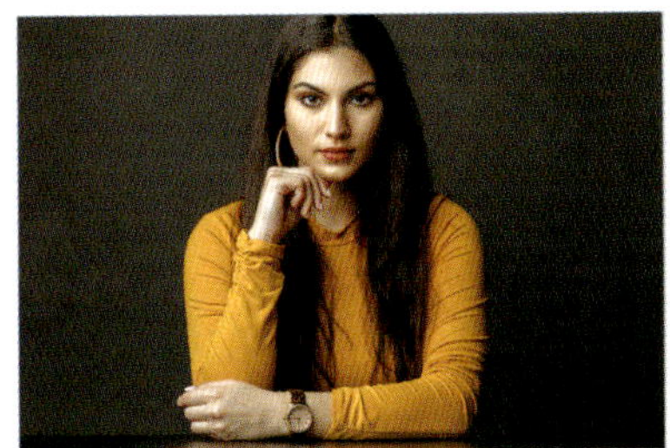

Page 56

Camera: Canon EOS 5D Mark IV

Lens: 70–200mm f/2.8 @ 155mm

Aperture Value: f/11

Shutter Speed: 1/125 sec

ISO: 100

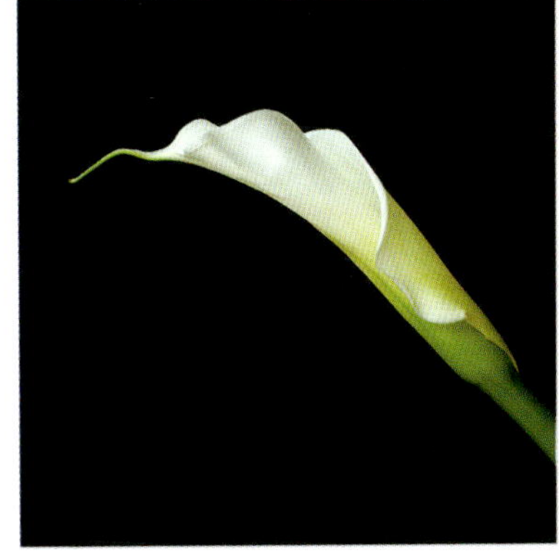

Page 58

Camera: Nikon D200

Lens: 70–180mm f/4.5–5.6 @ 70mm

Aperture Value: f/5.6

Shutter Speed: 1/160 sec

ISO: 800

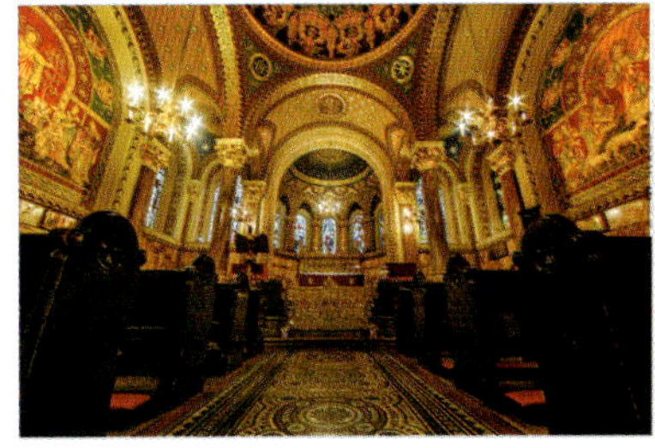

Page 60

Camera: Canon EOS 5D Mark III

Lens: 14mm f/2.8 @ 14mm

Aperture Value: f/11

Shutter Speed: 2/5 sec

ISO: 100

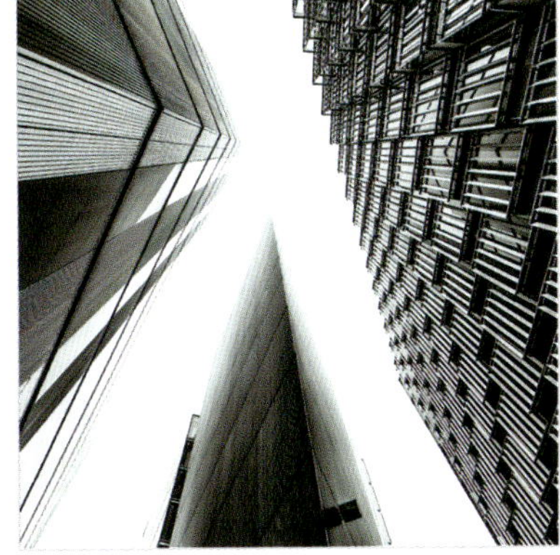

Page 62

Camera: Canon EOS 5D Mark III

Lens: 14mm f/2.8 @ 14mm

Aperture Value: f/5.6

Shutter Speed: 1/500 sec

ISO: 100

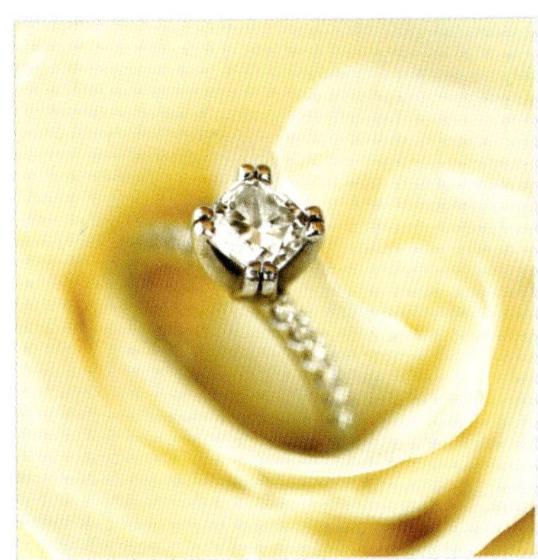

Page 64

Camera: Canon EOS-1D X

Lens: 100mm f/2.8 @ 100mm

Aperture Value: f/2.8

Shutter Speed: 1/320 sec

ISO: 100

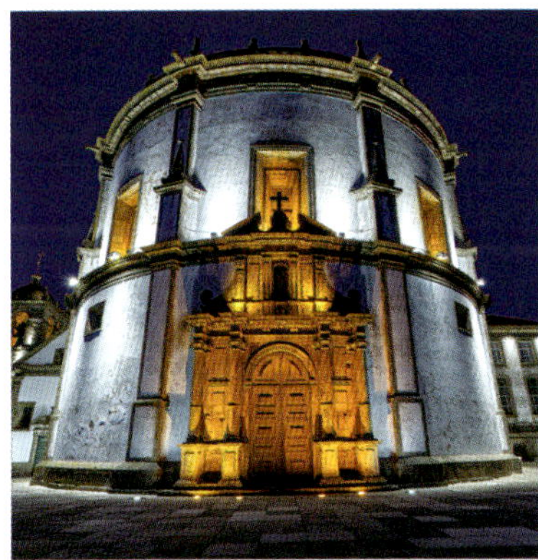

Page 66

Camera: Canon EOS R6 Mark II

Lens: 14–35mm f/4 @ 17mm

Aperture Value: f/11

Shutter Speed: 8/5 sec

ISO: 100

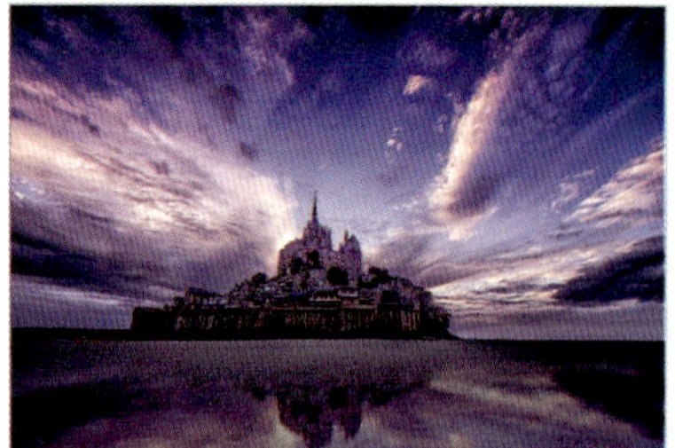

Page 68

Camera: Nikon D800

Lens: 14-24mm f/2.8 @ 14mm

Aperture Value: f/11

Shutter Speed: 1/30 sec

ISO: 100

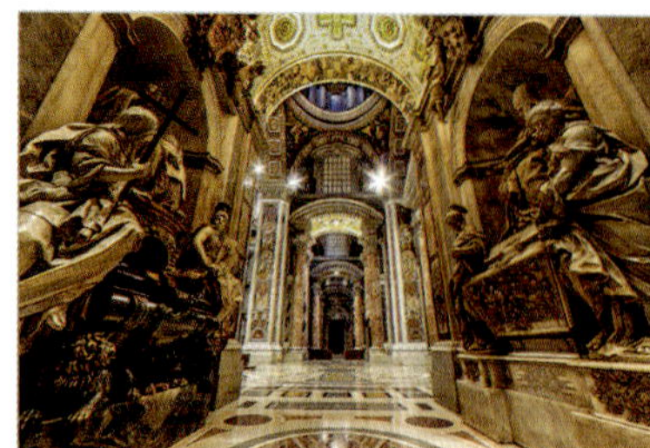

Page 70

Camera: Canon EOS R

Lens: 14mm f/2.8 @ 14mm

Aperture Value: f/9

Shutter Speed: 16/5 sec

ISO: 100

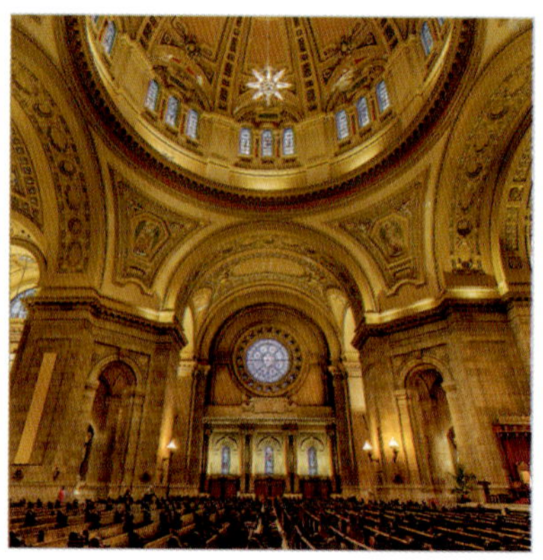

Page 72

Camera: Canon EOS 5D Mark IV

Lens: 16–35mm f/4 @ 16mm

Aperture Value: f/9

Shutter Speed: 3/5 sec

ISO: 100

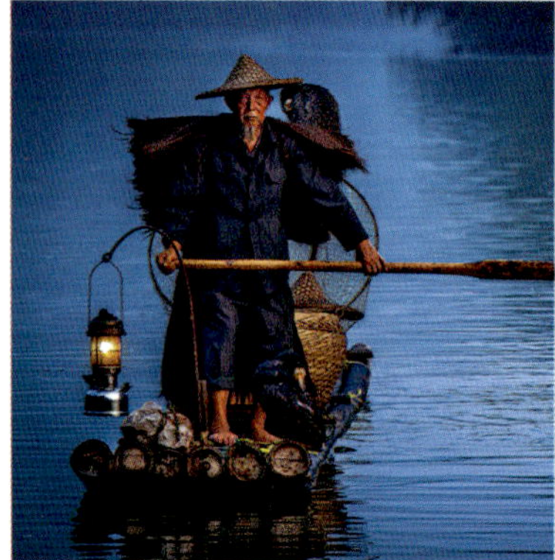

Page 74

Camera: Canon EOS R

Lens: 24-240mm f/4-6.3 @ 213mm

Aperture Value: f/6.3

Shutter Speed: 1/100 sec

ISO: 800

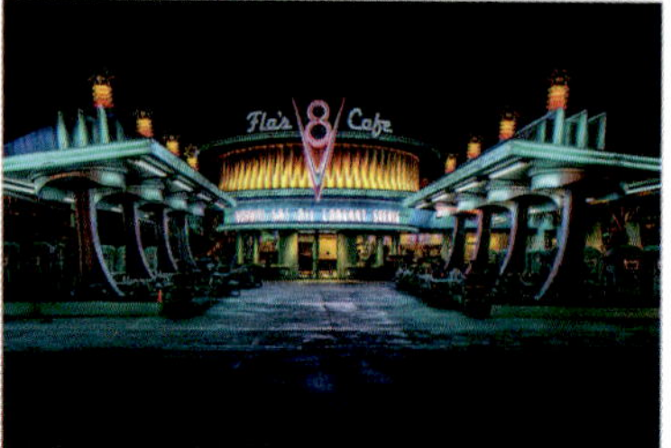

Page 76

Camera: Nikon D4

Lens: 28-300mm f/3.5-5.6 @ 28mm

Aperture Value: f/5

Shutter Speed: 1/60 sec

ISO: 1600

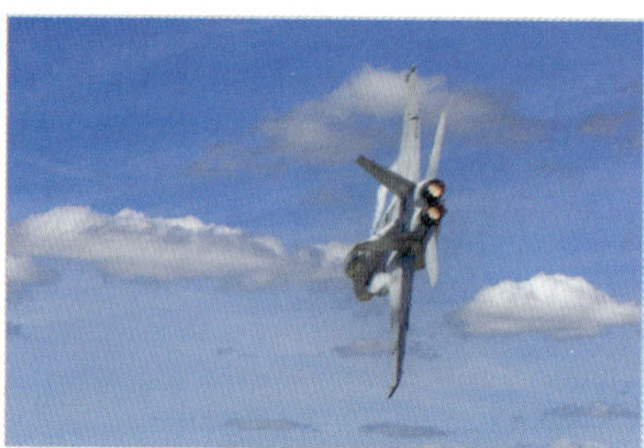

Page 78

Camera: Canon EOS R6 Mark II

Lens: 150-600mm f/5-6.3 @ 600mm

Aperture Value: f/6.3

Shutter Speed: 1/2000 sec

ISO: 500

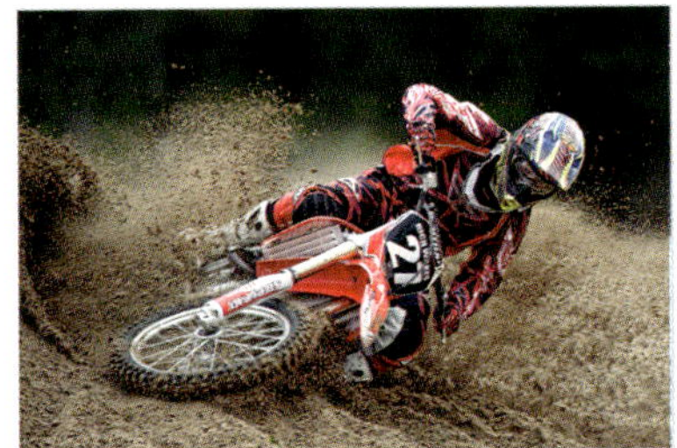

Page 80

Camera: Nikon D3

Lens: 300mm f/2.8 @ 300mm

Aperture Value: $f/2.8$

Shutter Speed: 1/320 sec

ISO: 1000

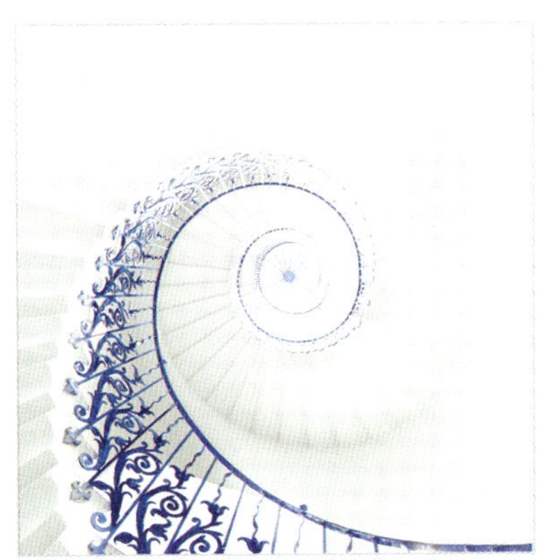

Page 82

Camera: Canon EOS R

Lens: 14mm f/2.8 @ 14mm

Aperture Value: $f/11$

Shutter Speed: 1/8 sec

ISO: 100

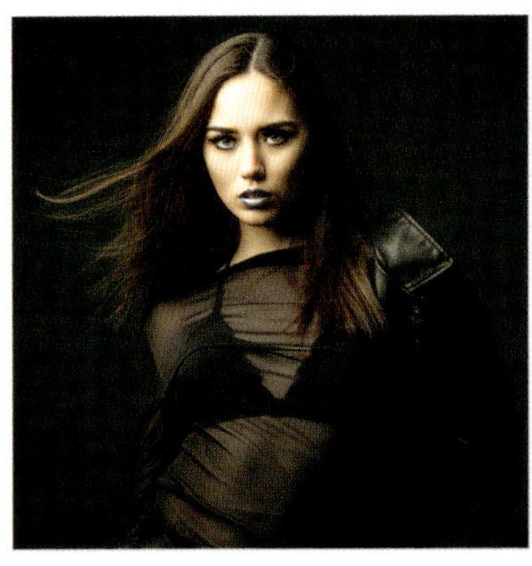

Page 84

Camera: Canon EOS R6 Mark II

Lens: 24–240mm f/4–6.3 @ 123mm

Aperture Value: $f/8$

Shutter Speed: 1/100 sec

ISO: 100

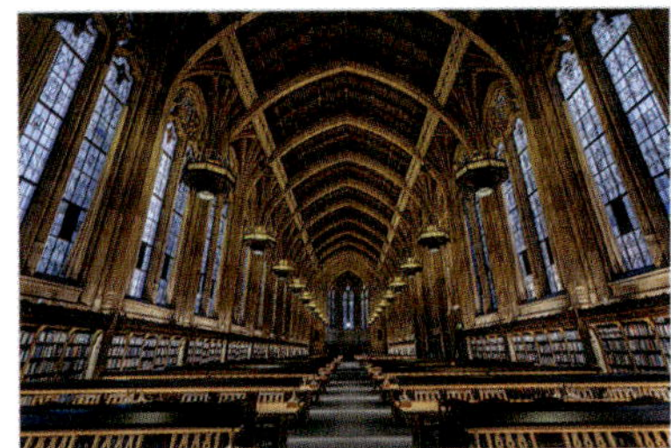

Page 86

Camera: Canon EOS R

Lens: 16–35mm f/4 @ 16mm

Aperture Value: $f/11$

Shutter Speed: 5/2 sec

ISO: 100

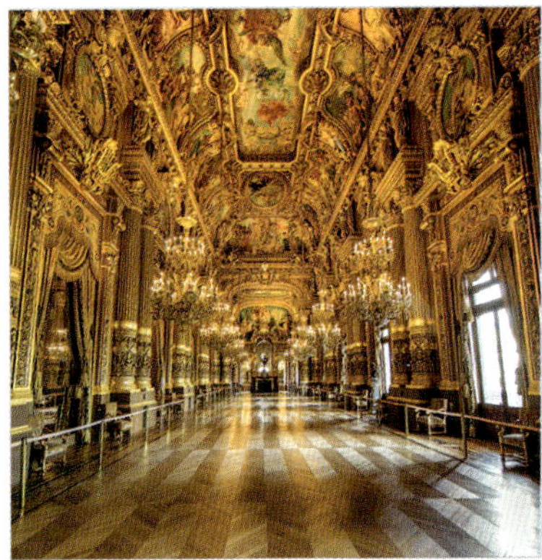

Page 88

Camera: Canon EOS-1D X

Lens: 11–24mm f/4 @ 11mm

Aperture Value: $f/4$

Shutter Speed: 1/25 sec

ISO: 800

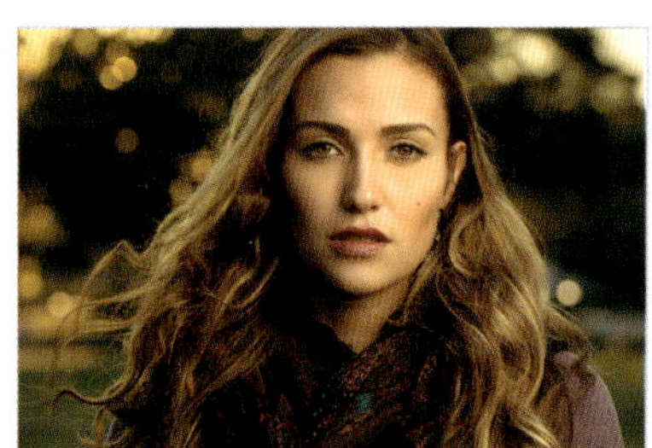

Page 90

Camera: Canon EOS 5D Mark III

Lens: 70–200mm f/2.8 @ 200mm

Aperture Value: $f/8$

Shutter Speed: 1/60 sec

ISO: 100

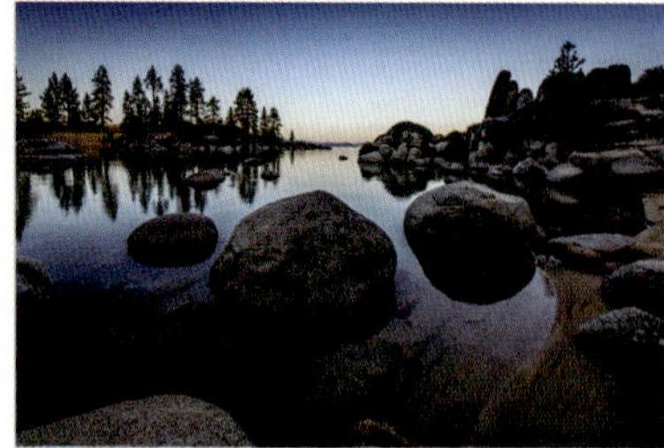

Page 92

Camera: Nikon D800

Lens: 14–24mm f/2.8 @ 14mm

Aperture Value: f/22

Shutter Speed: 1/2 sec

ISO: 100

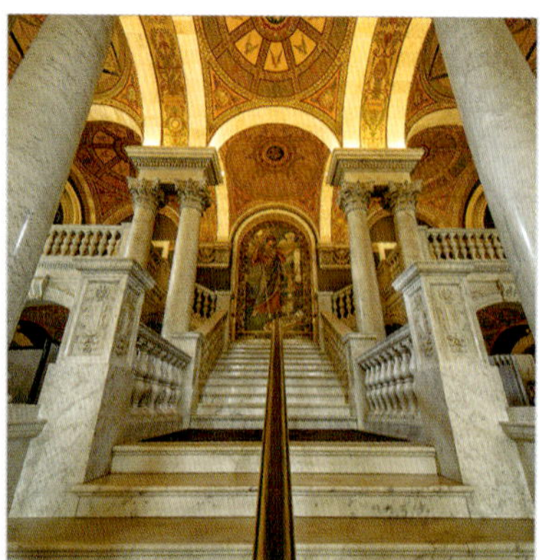

Page 94

Camera: Canon EOS 5D Mark IV

Lens: 11–24mm f/4 @ 13mm

Aperture Value: f/11

Shutter Speed: 1/2 sec

ISO: 100

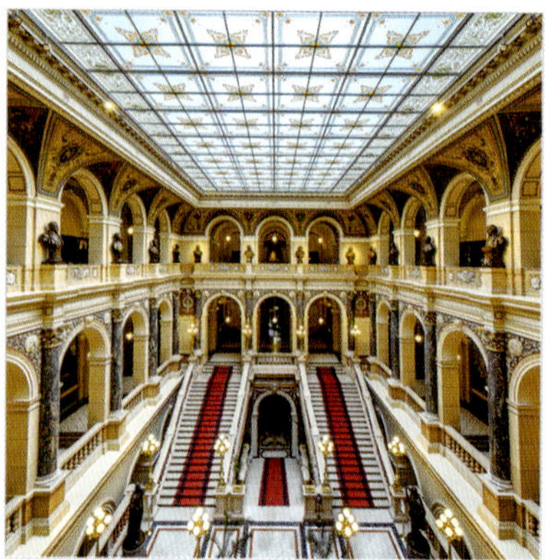

Page 96

Camera: Canon EOS R6

Lens: 11–24mm f/4 @ 11mm

Aperture Value: f/11

Shutter Speed: 1/13 sec

ISO: 100

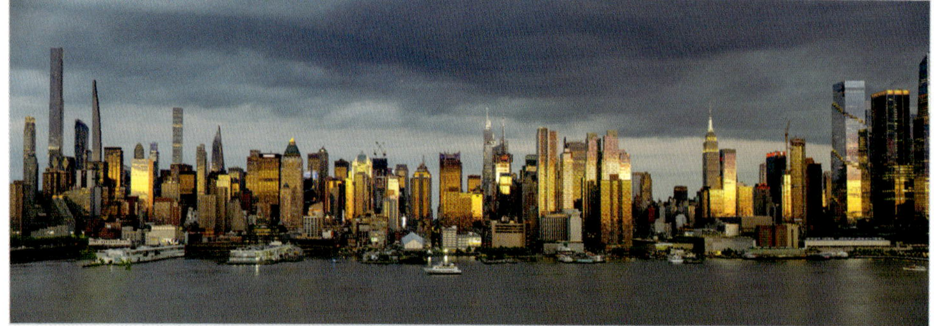

Page 98-99

Camera: Canon EOS R6 Mark II

Lens: 24–240mm f/4–6.3 @ 83mm

Aperture Value: f/6.3

Shutter Speed: 1/125 sec

ISO: 2000

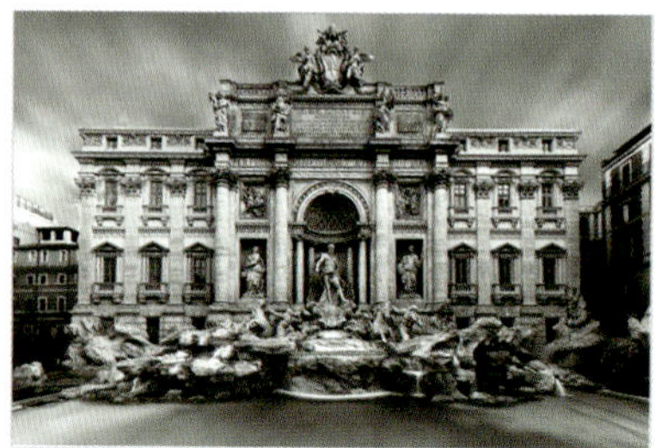

Page 100

Camera: Canon EOS R

Lens: 16–35mm f/4 @ 17mm

Aperture Value: f/16

Shutter Speed: 154 sec

ISO: 100

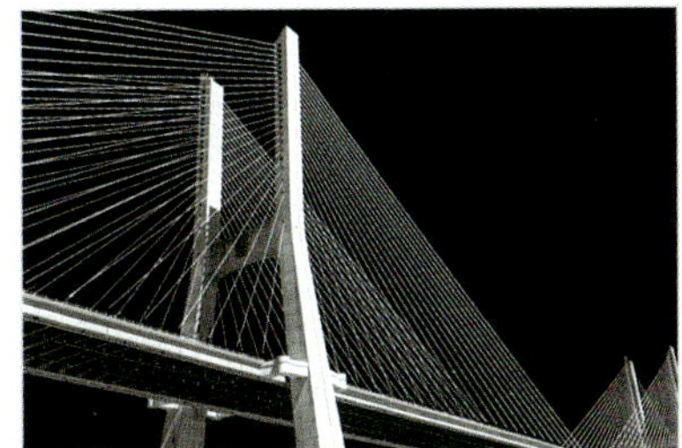

Page 102

Camera: Canon EOS R6 Mark II

Lens: 24–240mm f/4–6.3 @ 40mm

Aperture Value: f/4.5

Shutter Speed: 1/1000 sec

ISO: 100

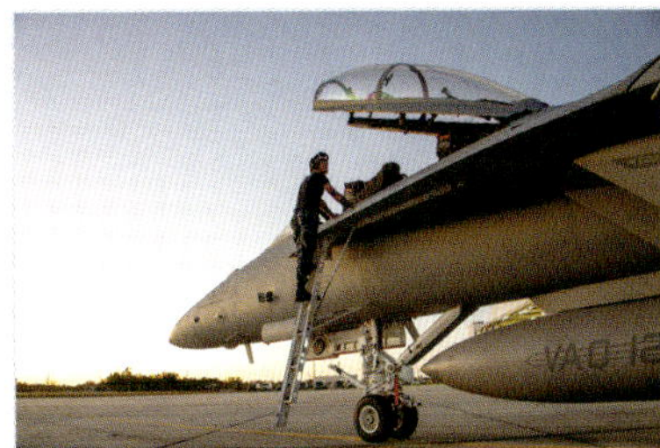

Page 104

Camera: Nikon D4

Lens: 28–300mm f/3.5–5.6 @ 28mm

Aperture Value: f/7.1

Shutter Speed: 4/5 sec

ISO: 400

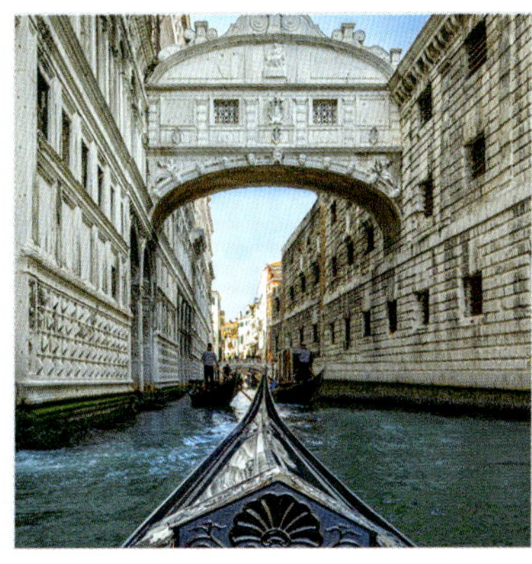

Page 106

Camera: Canon EOS 5D Mark IV

Lens: 16–35mm f/4 @ 30mm

Aperture Value: f/4

Shutter Speed: 1/320 sec

ISO: 100

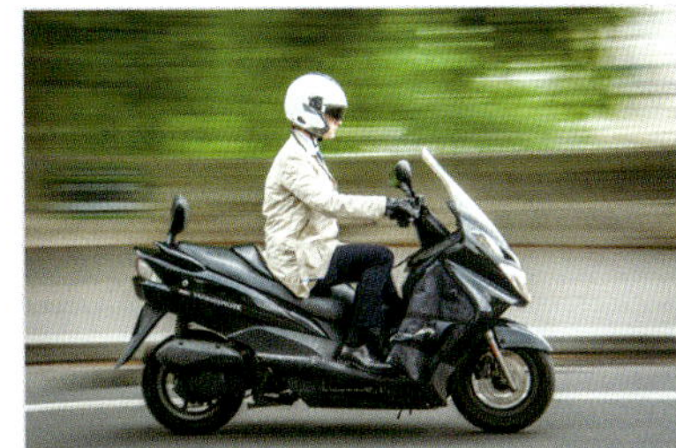

Page 108

Camera: Nikon D700

Lens: 28–300mm f/3.5–5.6 @ 100mm

Aperture Value: f/14

Shutter Speed: 1/15 sec

ISO: 200

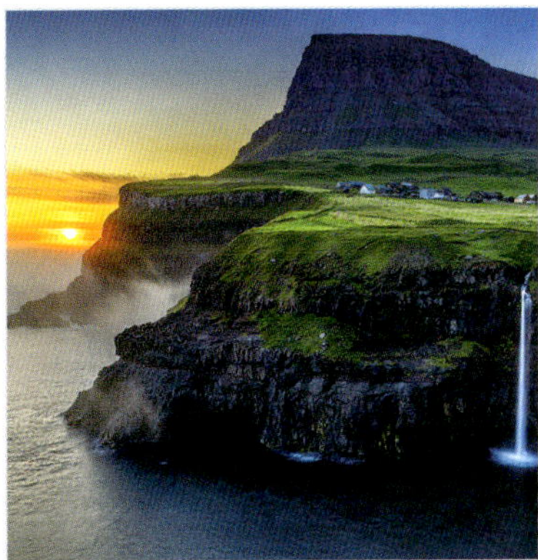

Page 110

Camera: Canon EOS R

Lens: 16–35mm f/4 @ 28mm

Aperture Value: f/11

Shutter Speed: 2/5 sec

ISO: 100

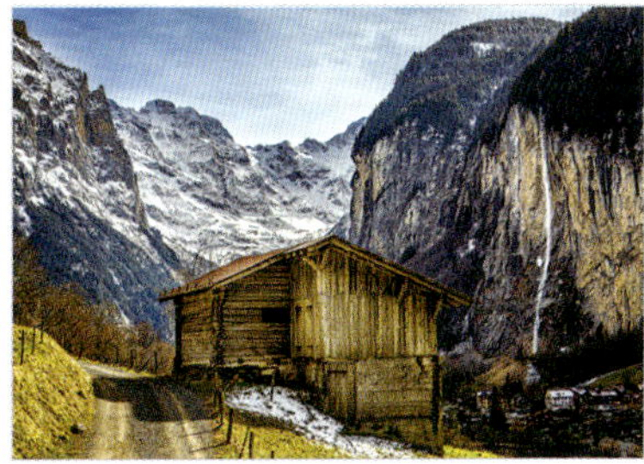

Page 112

Camera: Canon EOS R6 Mark II

Lens: 24–240mm f/4–6.3 @ 58mm

Aperture Value: f/8

Shutter Speed: 1/250 sec

ISO: 100

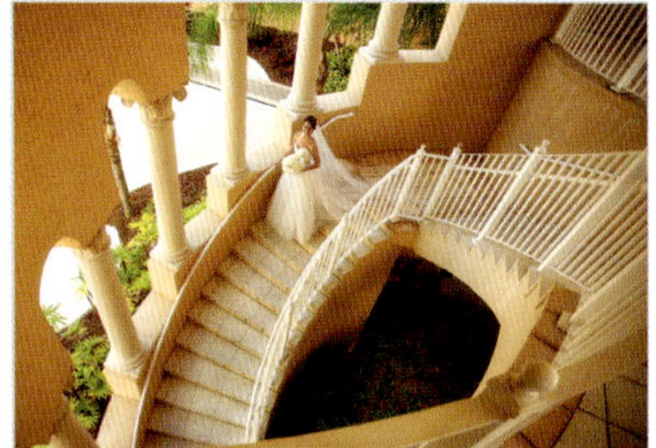

Page 114

Camera: Canon EOS-1D X

Lens: 16–35mm f/2.8 @ 16mm

Aperture Value: $f/2.8$

Shutter Speed: 1/125 sec

ISO: 100

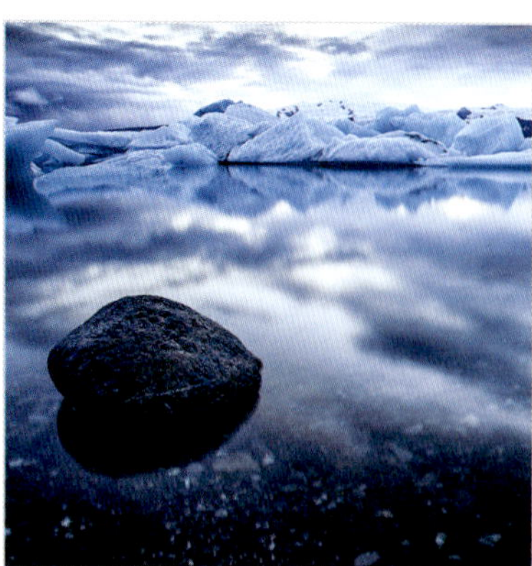

Page 116

Camera: Canon EOS 5D Mark IV

Lens: 24–70mm f/2.8 @ 24mm

Aperture Value: $f/22$

Shutter Speed: 30 sec

ISO: 100

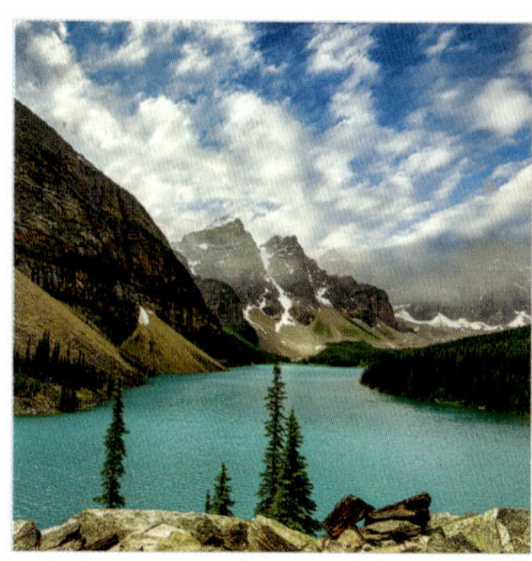

Page 118

Camera: Nikon D3S

Lens: 14–24mm f/2.8 @ 14mm

Aperture Value: $f/8$

Shutter Speed: 1/1000 sec

ISO: 200

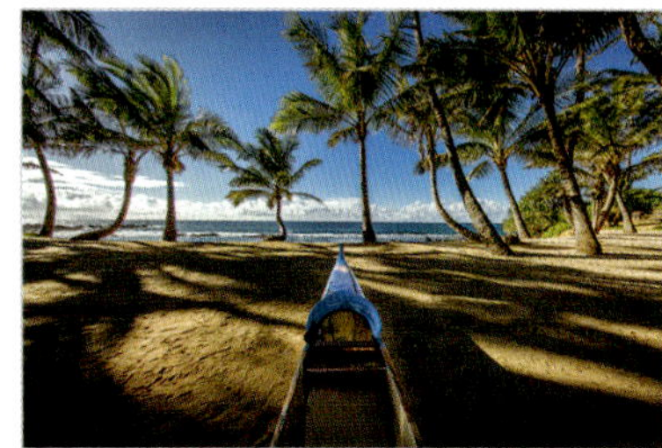

Page 120

Camera: Canon EOS 5DS

Lens: 11–24mm f/4 @ 11mm

Aperture Value: $f/7.1$

Shutter Speed: 1/250 sec

ISO: 100

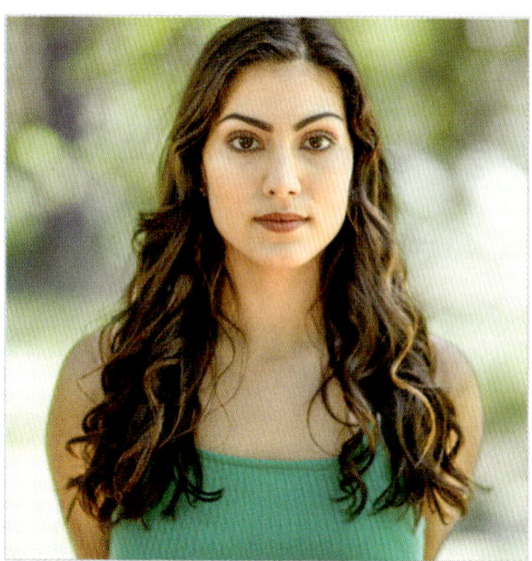

Page 122

Camera: Canon EOS 5D Mark IV

Lens: 70–200mm f/2.8 @ 200mm

Aperture Value: $f/2.8$

Shutter Speed: 1/160 sec

ISO: 100

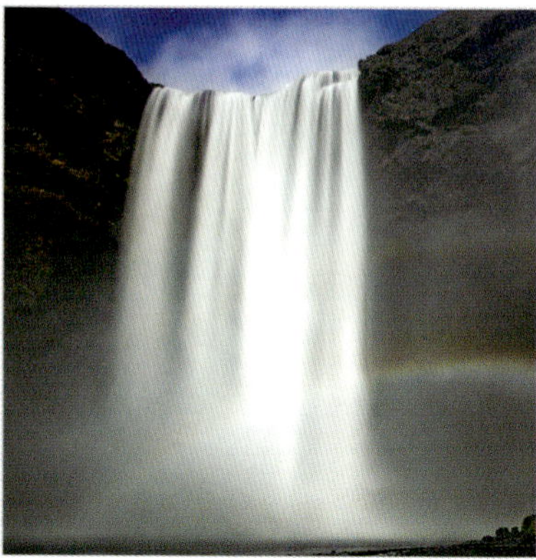

Page 124

Camera: Canon EOS 5D Mark IV

Lens: 24–70mm f/2.8 @ 24mm

Aperture Value: $f/18$

Shutter Speed: 13 sec

ISO: 100

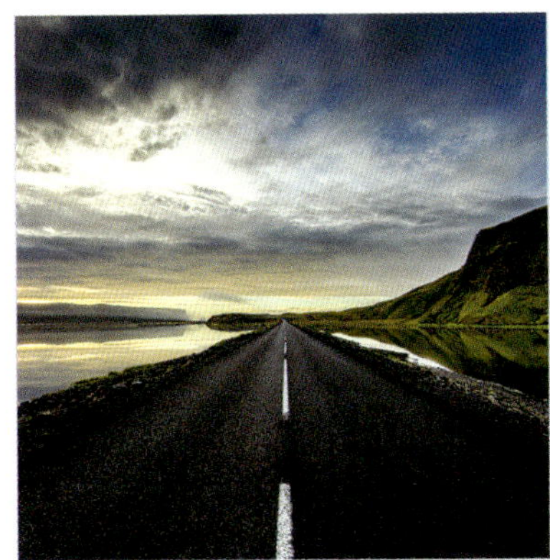

Page 126

- Camera: Canon EOS 5D Mark IV
- Lens: 14mm f/2.8 @ 14mm
- Aperture Value: f/11
- Shutter Speed: 1/320 sec
- ISO: 100

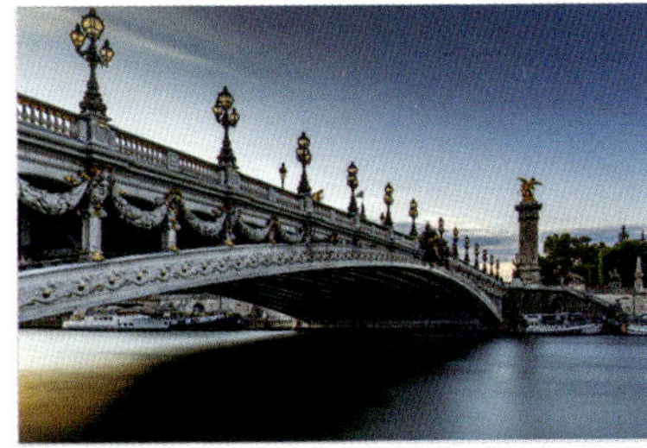

Page 128

- Camera: Canon EOS R
- Lens: 16–35mm f/4 @ 29mm
- Aperture Value: f/11
- Shutter Speed: 59 sec
- ISO: 100

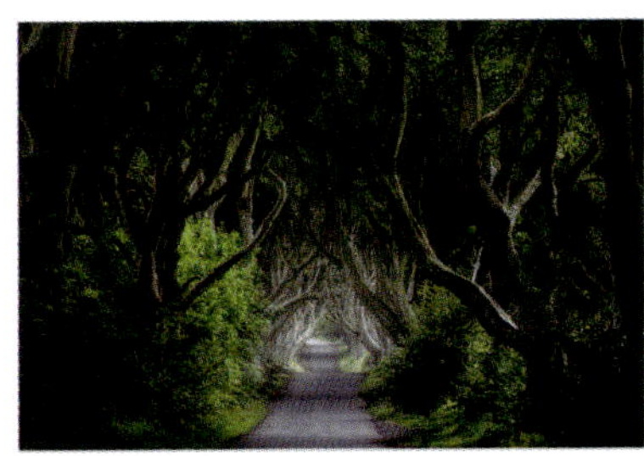

Page 130

- Camera: Canon EOS R
- Lens: 70–200mm f/2.8 @ 135mm
- Aperture Value: f/11
- Shutter Speed: 1/50 sec
- ISO: 100

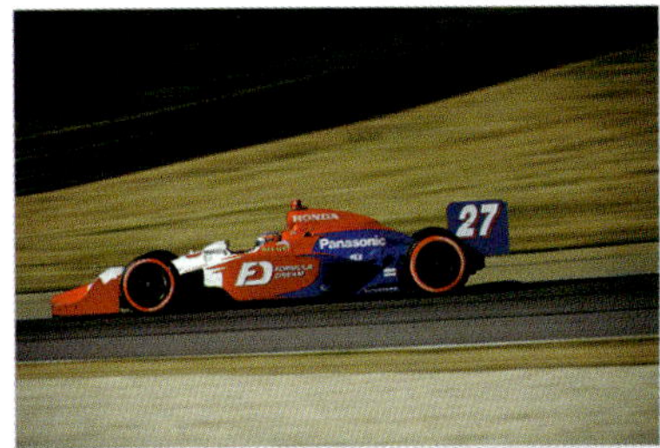

Page 132

- Camera: Nikon D3
- Lens: 200–400mm f/4 @ 200mm
- Aperture Value: f/4
- Shutter Speed: 1/8000 sec
- ISO: 400

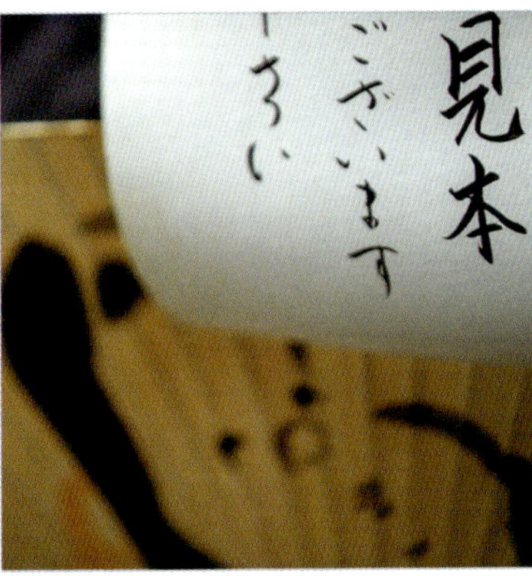

Page 134

- Camera: Canon EOS R
- Lens: 70–200mm f/2.8 @ 200mm
- Aperture Value: f/2.8
- Shutter Speed: 1/640 sec
- ISO: 100

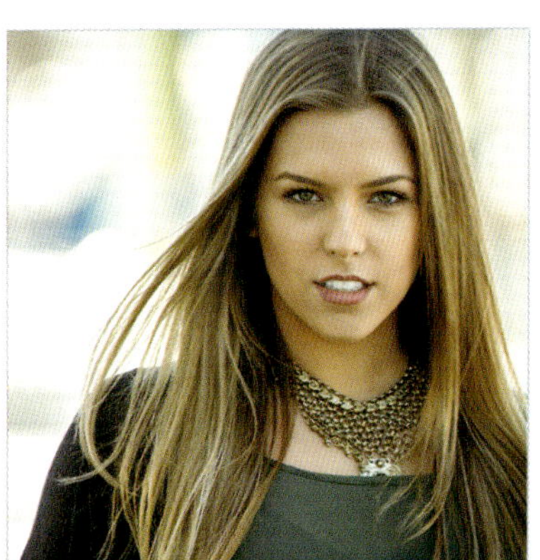

Page 136

- Camera: Canon EOS-1D X
- Lens: 70–200mm f/2.8 @ 200mm
- Aperture Value: f/2.8
- Shutter Speed: 1/160 sec
- ISO: 400

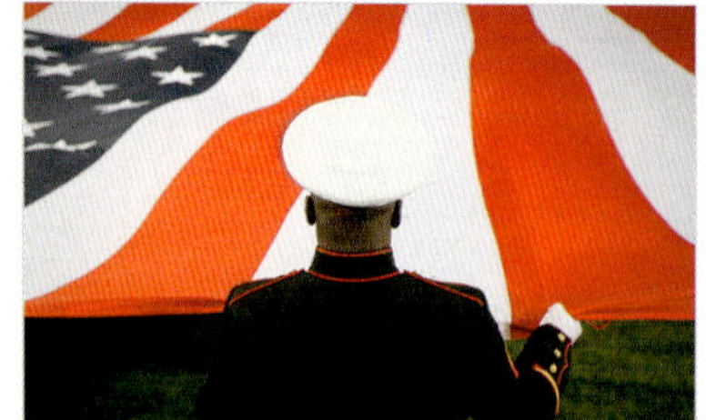

Page 138

Camera: Canon EOS-1D X

Lens: 16–35mm f/2.8 @ 35mm

Aperture Value: $f/2.8$

Shutter Speed: 1/6400 sec

ISO: 6400

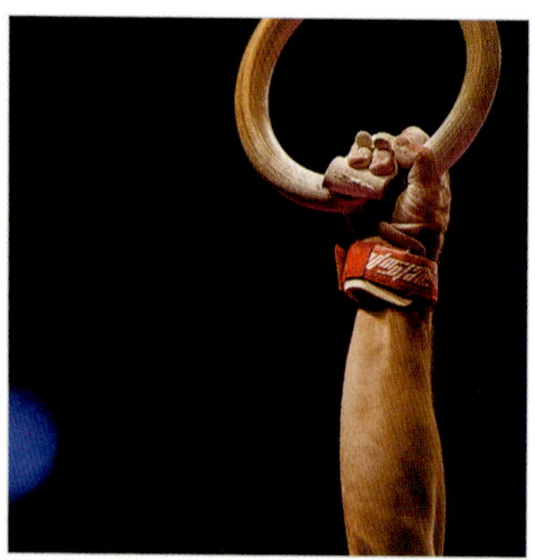

Page 140

Camera: Nikon 3DS

Lens: 200–400mm f/4 @ 400mm

Aperture Value: $f/4$

Shutter Speed: 1/2000 sec

ISO: 4000

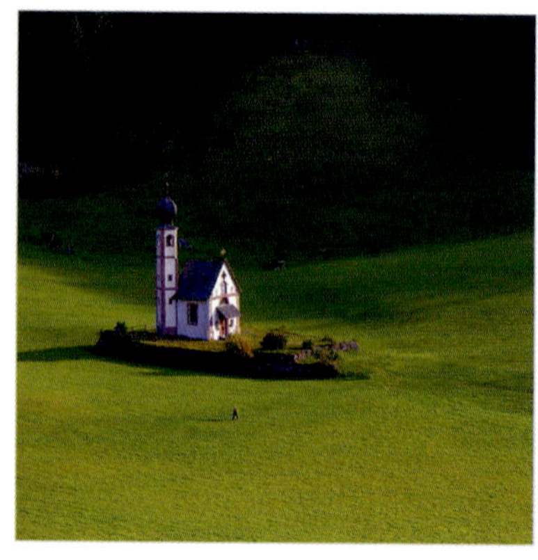

Page 142

Camera: Canon EOS 5D Mark IV

Lens: 70–200mm f/2.8 @ 180mm

Aperture Value: $f/7.1$

Shutter Speed: 1/100 sec

ISO: 100

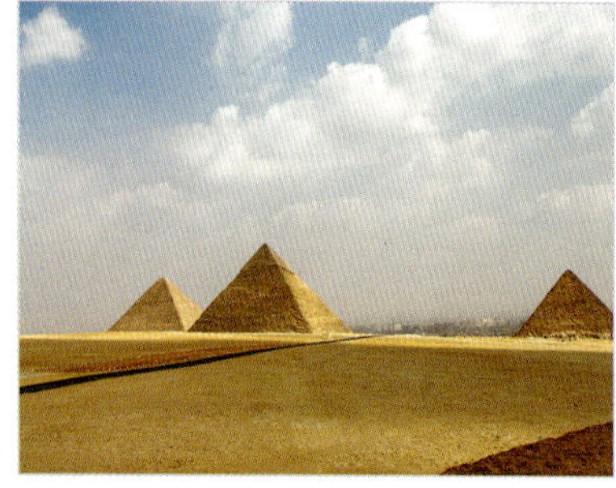

Page 144

Camera: Nikon D300

Lens: 18–200mm f/3.5–5.6 @ 18mm

Aperture Value: $f/8$

Shutter Speed: 1/1000 sec

ISO: 200

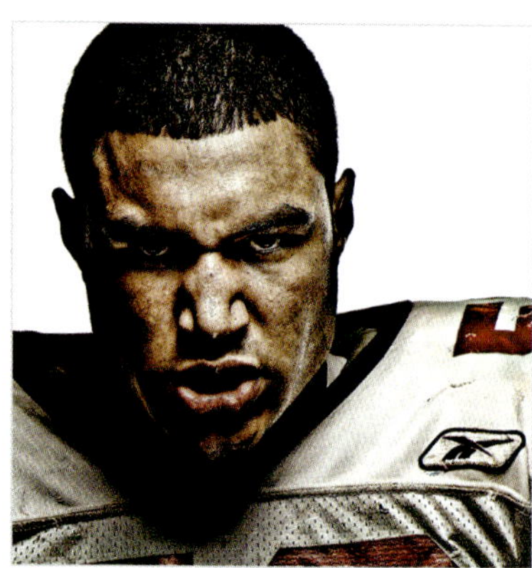

Page 146

Camera: Nikon D3

Lens: 70–200mm f/2.8 @ 200mm

Aperture Value: $f/13$

Shutter Speed: 1/200 sec

ISO: 200

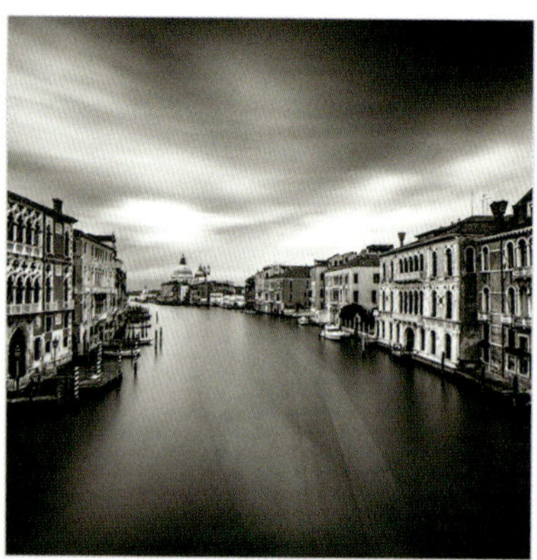

Page 148

Camera: Canon EOS 5D Mark IV

Lens: 12–24mm @ 12mm

Aperture Value: $f/16$

Shutter Speed: 241 sec

ISO: 100

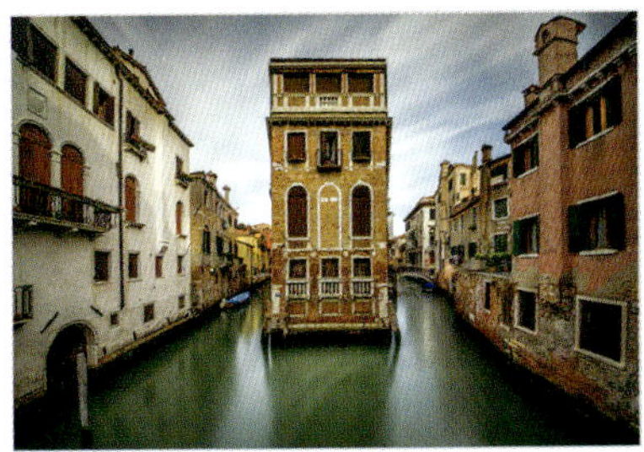

Page 150

Camera: Canon EOS 5D Mark IV

Lens: 12–24mm @ 13mm

Aperture Value: *f*/16

Shutter Speed: 130 sec

ISO: 100

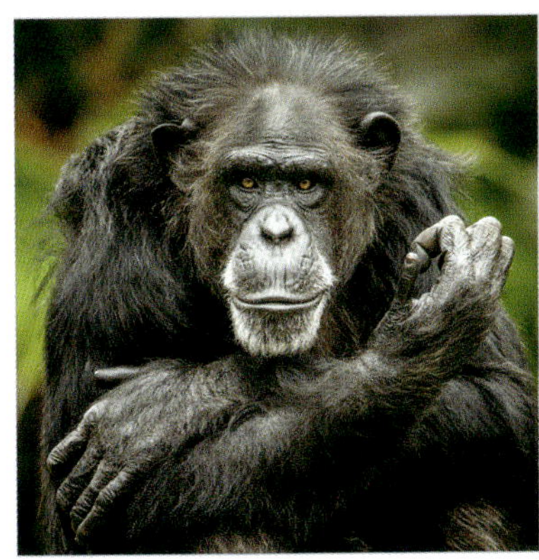

Page 152

Camera: Canon EOS-1D X

Lens: 200–400mm f/4 EXT @ 506mm

Aperture Value: *f*/5.6

Shutter Speed: 1/400 sec

ISO: 1250

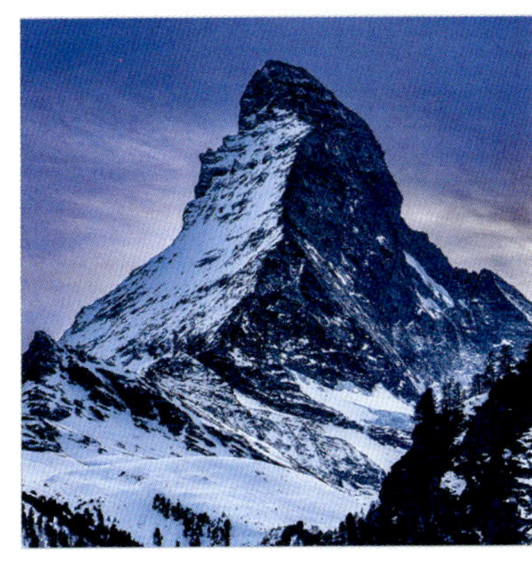

Page 154

Camera: Canon EOS R6 Mark II

Lens: 24–240mm f/4–6.3 @ 118mm

Aperture Value: *f*/6.3

Shutter Speed: 1/100 sec

ISO: 100

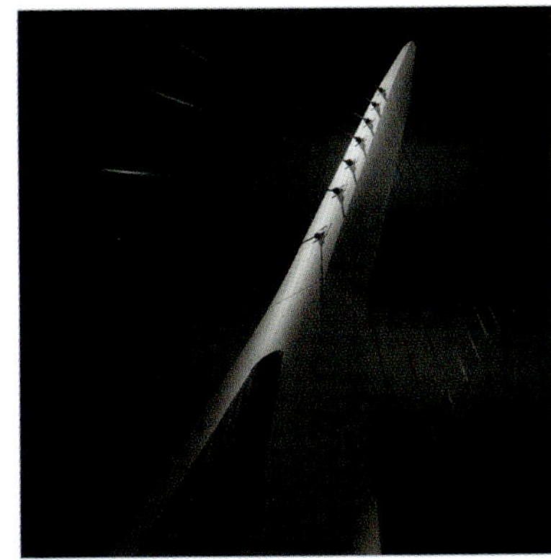

Page 156

Camera: Canon EOS R

Lens: 16–35mm f/4 @ 35mm

Aperture Value: *f*/11

Shutter Speed: 1/250 sec

ISO: 100

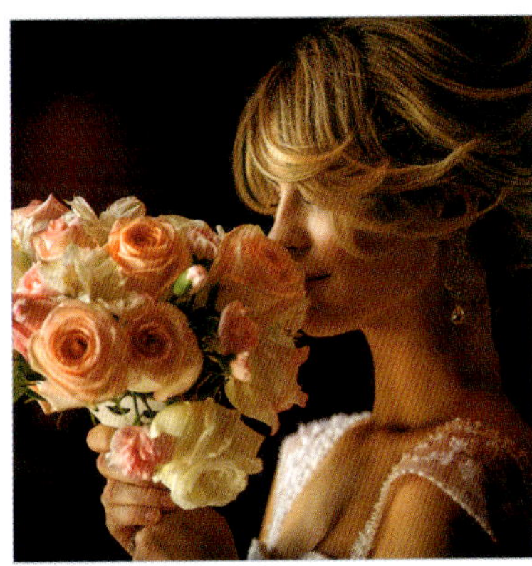

Page 158

Camera: Canon EOS 5D Mark III

Lens: 70–200mm f/2.8 @ 142mm

Aperture Value: *f*/2.8

Shutter Speed: 1/125 sec

ISO: 200

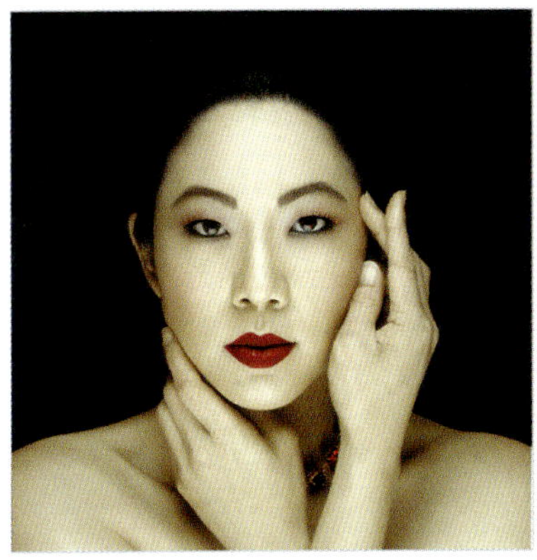

Page 160

Camera: Canon EOS 5D Mark III

Lens: 70–200mm f/2.8 @ 125mm

Aperture Value: *f*/8

Shutter Speed: 1/125 sec

ISO: 100

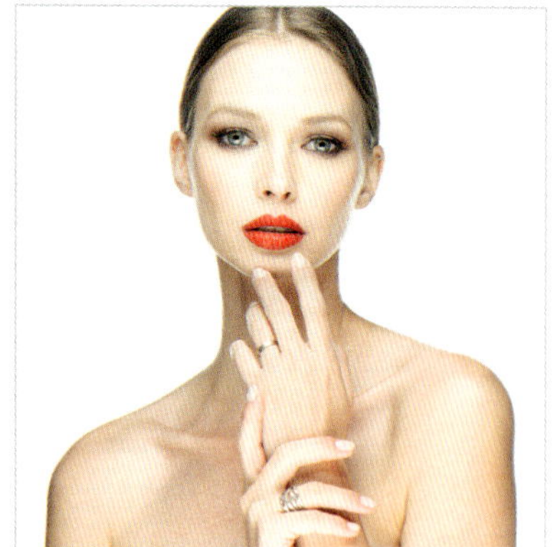

Page 162

Camera: Canon EOS 5D Mark IV

Lens: 70–200mm f/2.8 @ 155mm

Aperture Value: $f/5.6$

Shutter Speed: 1/125 sec

ISO: 100

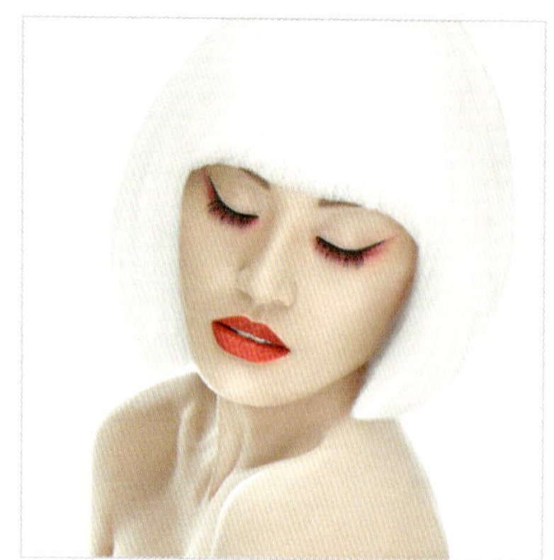

Page 164

Camera: Canon EOS-1D X

Lens: 70–200mm f/2.8 @ 130mm

Aperture Value: $f/13$

Shutter Speed: 1/125 sec

ISO: 100

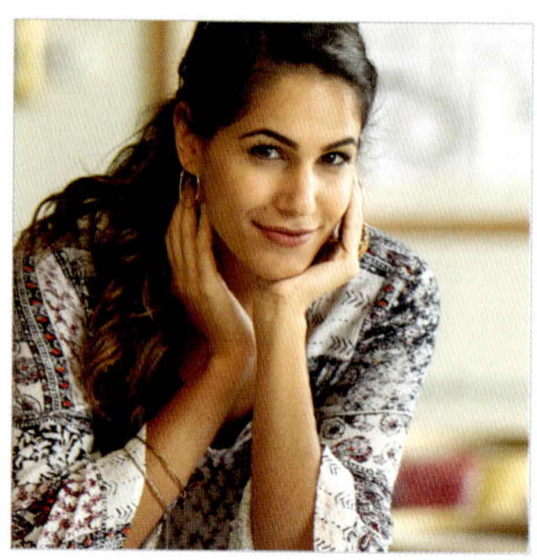

Page 166

Camera: Canon 5D Mark IV

Lens: 70–200mm f/2.8 @ 115mm

Aperture Value: $f/2.8$

Shutter Speed: 1/80 sec

ISO: 100

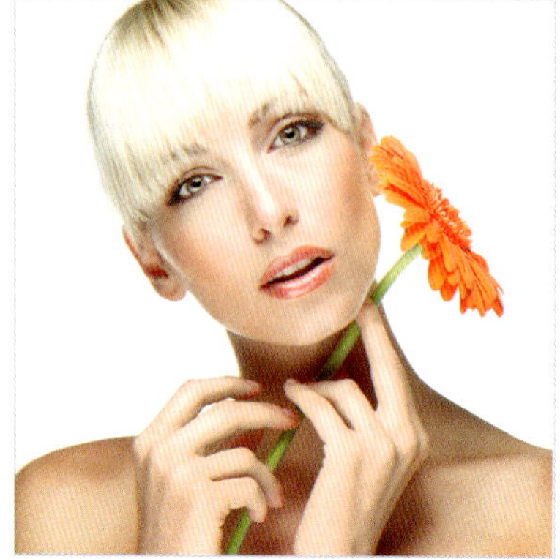

Page 168

Camera: Nikon D3S

Lens: 70–200mm f/2.8 @ 155mm

Aperture Value: $f/14$

Shutter Speed: 1/125 sec

ISO: 200

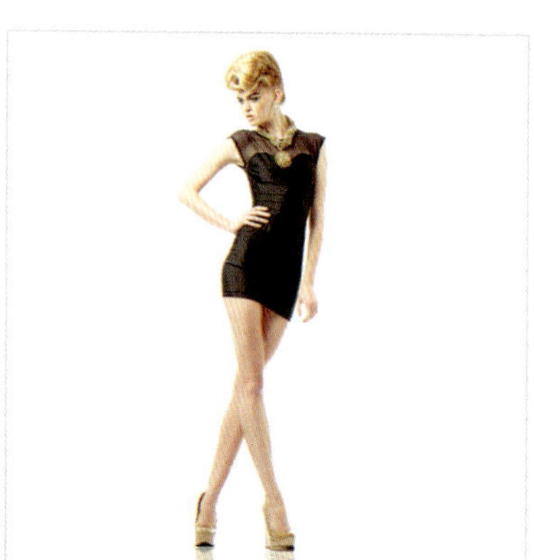

Page 170

Camera: Nikon D3S

Lens: 70–200mm f/2.8 @ 80mm

Aperture Value: $f/13$

Shutter Speed: 1/125 sec

ISO: 200

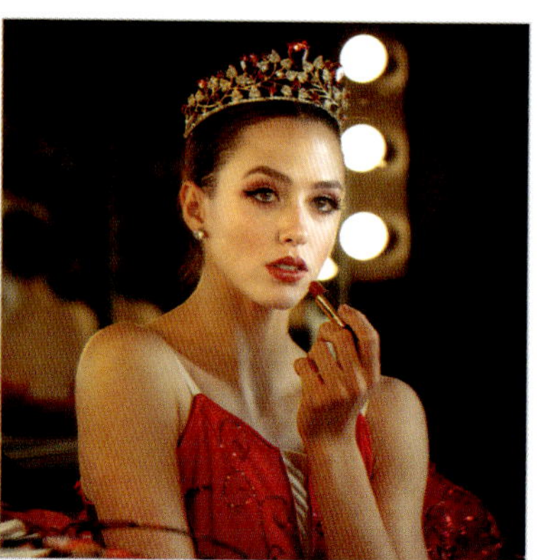

Page 172

Camera: Canon EOS 5DS

Lens: 70–200mm f/2.8 @ 100mm

Aperture Value: $f/4$

Shutter Speed: 1/100 sec

ISO: 200

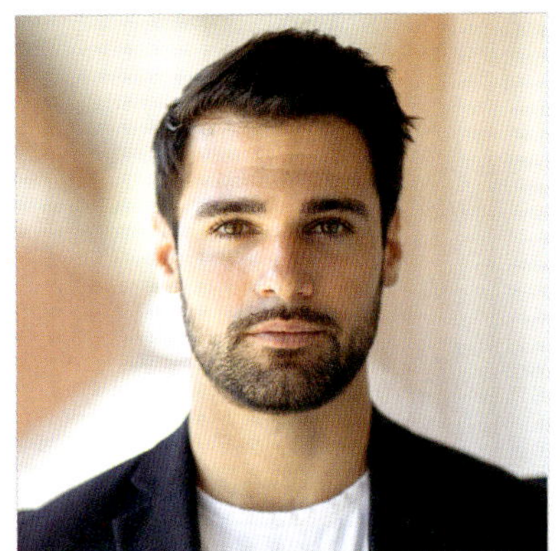

Page 174

Camera: Canon EOS R

Lens: 85mm f/1.2 @ 85mm

Aperture Value: f/1.8

Shutter Speed: 1/500 sec

ISO: 100

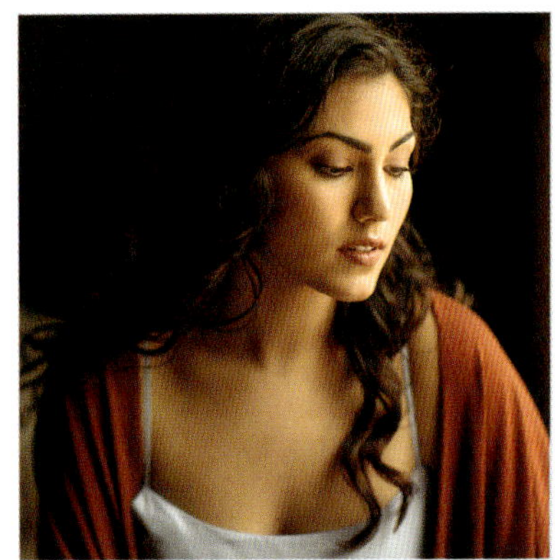

Page 176

Camera: Canon EOS 5D Mark IV

Lens: 85mm f/1.2 @ 85mm

Aperture Value: f/1.8

Shutter Speed: 1/160 sec

ISO: 100

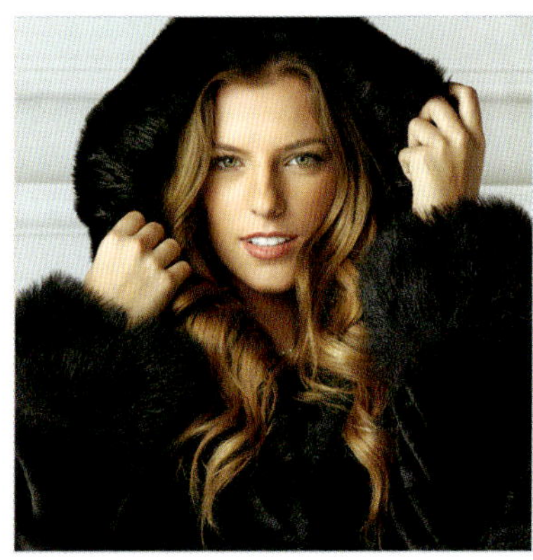

Page 178

Camera: Canon EOS-1D X

Lens: 70–200mm f/2.8 @ 123mm

Aperture Value: f/11

Shutter Speed: 1/100 sec

ISO: 100

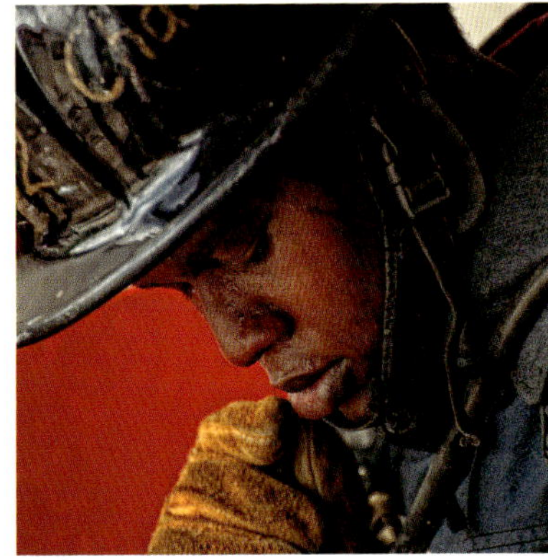

Page 180

Camera: Nikon D3

Lens: 70–300mm f/4.5–5.6 @ 270mm

Aperture Value: f/5.6

Shutter Speed: 1/125 sec

ISO: 200

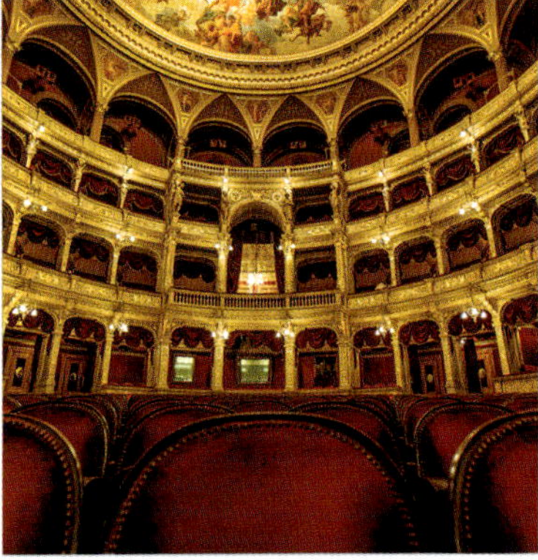

Page 182

Camera: Canon EOS 5D Mark III

Lens: 16–35mm f/2.8 @ 16mm

Aperture Value: f/2.8

Shutter Speed: 1/13 sec

ISO: 1600

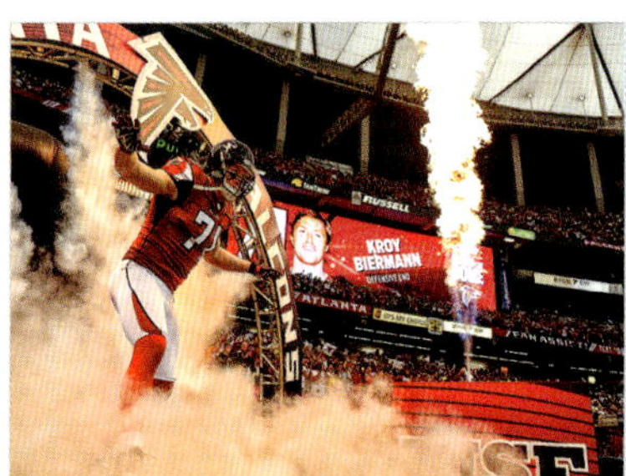

Page 184 Top Row

Camera: Nikon D3S

Lens: 24–120mm f/4 @ 24mm

Aperture Value: f/4

Shutter Speed: 1/800 sec

ISO: 2000

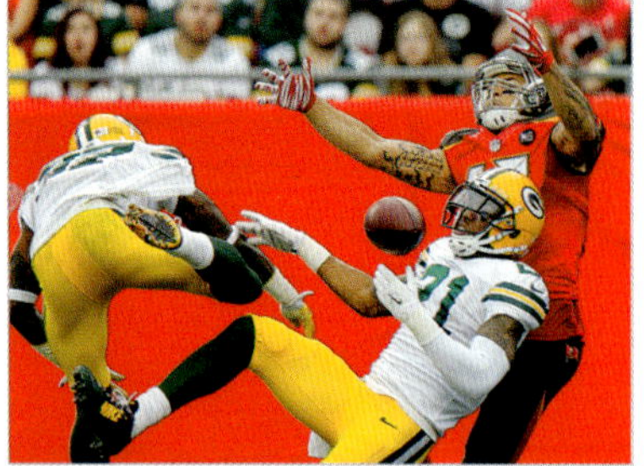

Page 184 Top Row

Camera: Canon EOS-1D X

Lens: 400mm f/2.8 @ 400mm

Aperture Value: f/2.8

Shutter Speed: 1/1250 sec

ISO: 500

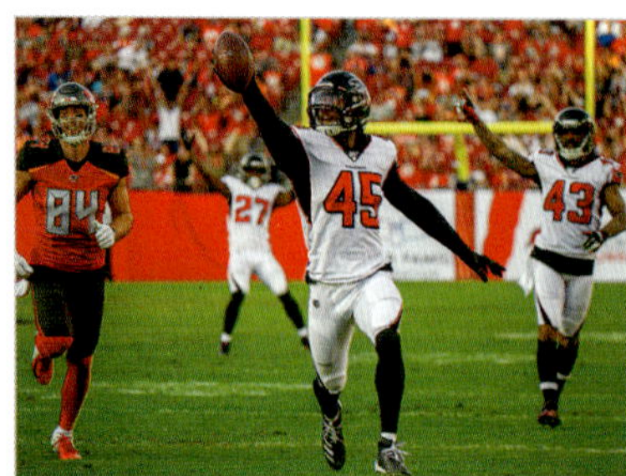

Page 184 Top Row

Camera: Canon EOS-1D X

Lens: 200–400mm f/4 @ 297mm

Aperture Value: f/5.6

Shutter Speed: 1/1250 sec

ISO: 800

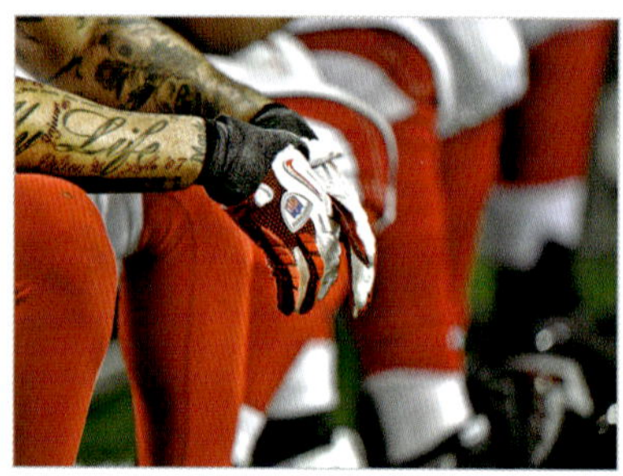

Page 184 Second Row (Also Page 224)

Camera: Nikon D3S

Lens: 400mm f/2.8 @ 400mm

Aperture Value: f/2.8

Shutter Speed: 1/320 sec

ISO: 2500

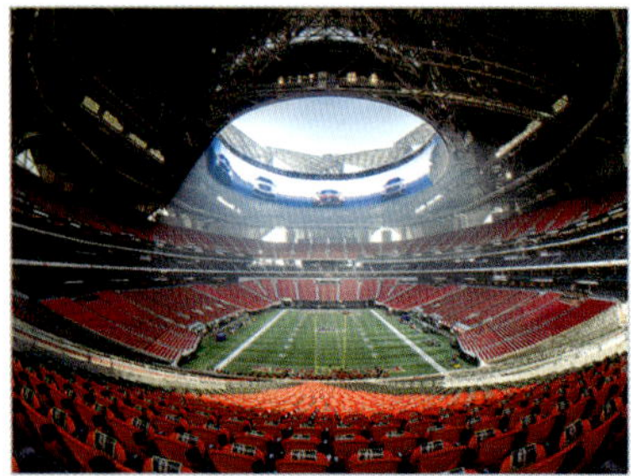

Page 184 Second Row

Camera: Canon EOS 5D Mark IV

Lens: 8–15mm f/4 @ 15mm

Aperture Value: f/11

Shutter Speed: 1/125 sec

ISO: 100

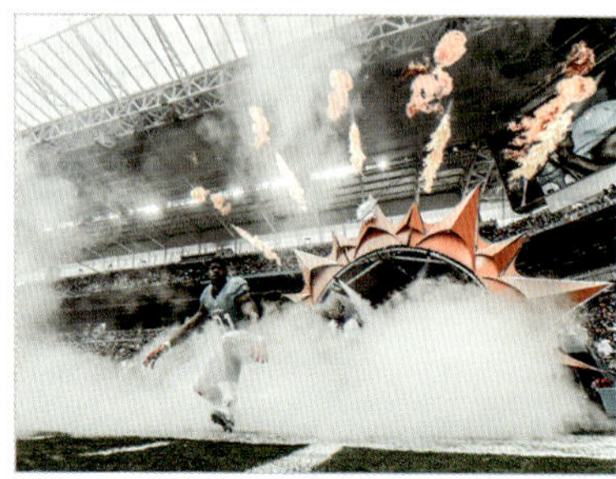

Page 184 Second Row

Camera: Canon EOS-1D X

Lens: 14mm f/2.8 @ 14mm

Aperture Value: f/5.6

Shutter Speed: 1/1000 sec

ISO: 160

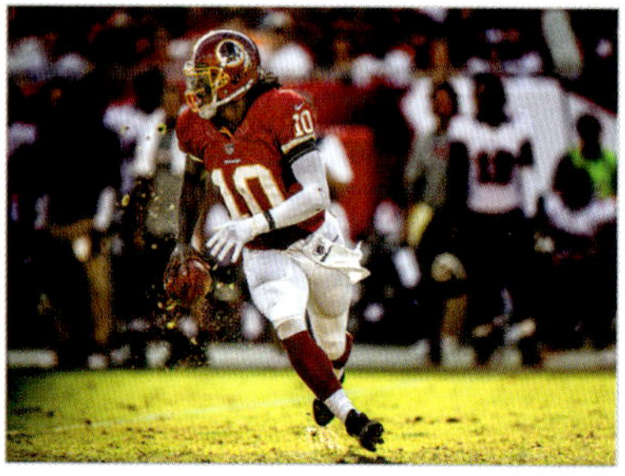

Page 184 Third Row

Camera: Nikon D4

Lens: 400mm f/2.8 @ 400mm

Aperture Value: f/2.8

Shutter Speed: 1/1600 sec

ISO: 200

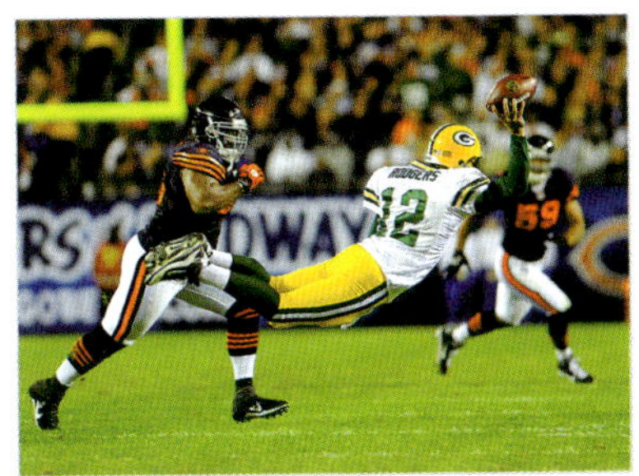

Page 184 Third Row

Camera: Nikon D3S

Lens: 300mm f/2.8 @ 300mm

Aperture Value: f/2.8

Shutter Speed: 1/1000 sec

ISO: 1600

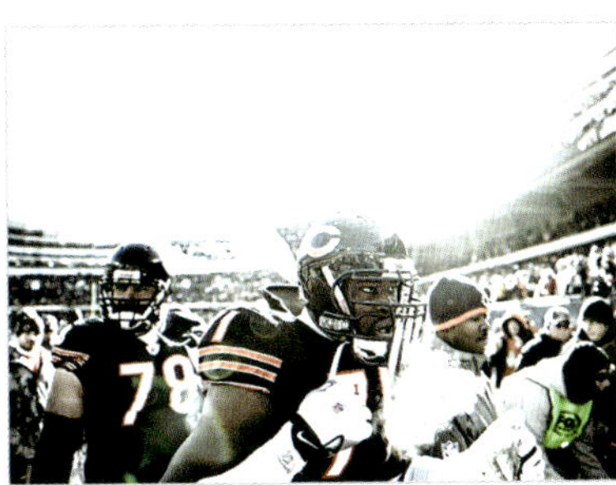

Page 184 Third Row

Camera: Nikon D3

Lens: 24–70mm f/2.8 @ 24mm

Aperture Value: f/2.8

Shutter Speed: 1/6400 sec

ISO: 200

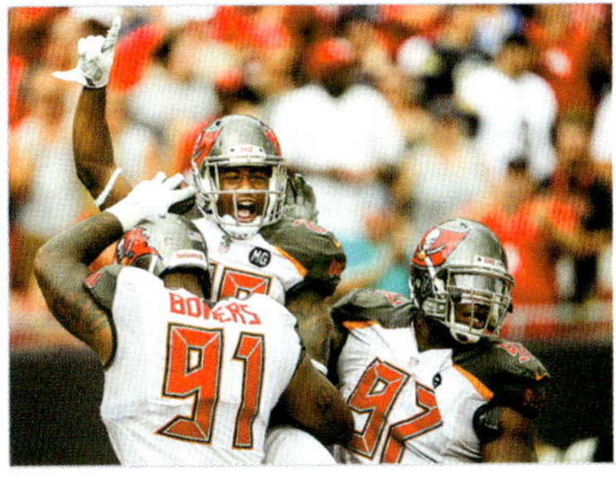

Page 184 Bottom Row

Camera: Canon EOS-1D X

Lens: 400mm f/2.8 + 1.4x @ 560mm

Aperture Value: f/4

Shutter Speed: 1/1250 sec

ISO: 320

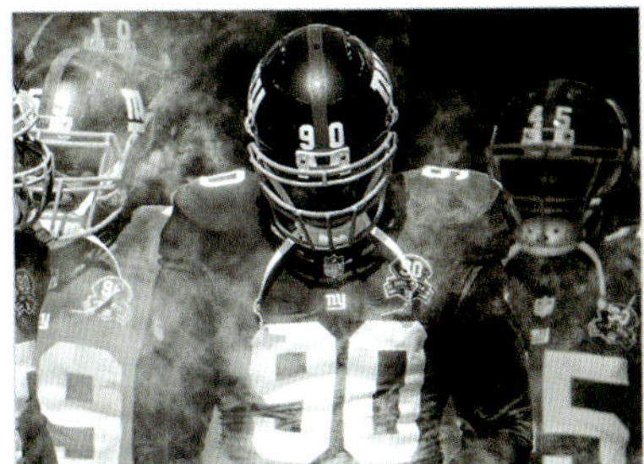

Page 184 Bottom Row

Camera: Canon EOS-1D X

Lens: 400mm f/2.8 @ 400mm

Aperture Value: f/2.8

Shutter Speed: 1/1000 sec

ISO: 100

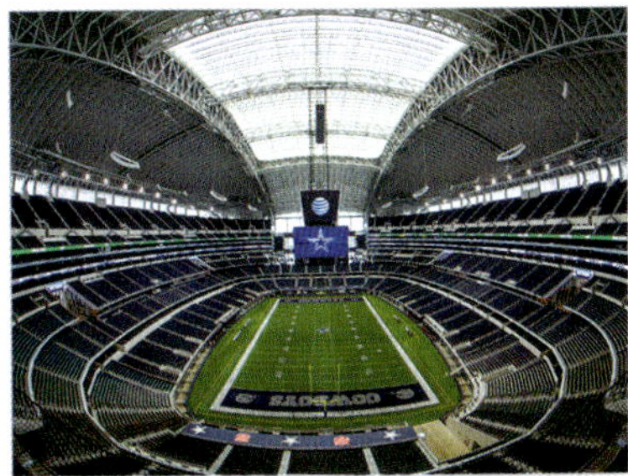

Page 184 Bottom Row

Camera: Canon EOS 5D Mark III

Lens: 8–15mm f/4 @ 14mm

Aperture Value: f/7.1

Shutter Speed: 1/100 sec

ISO: 800

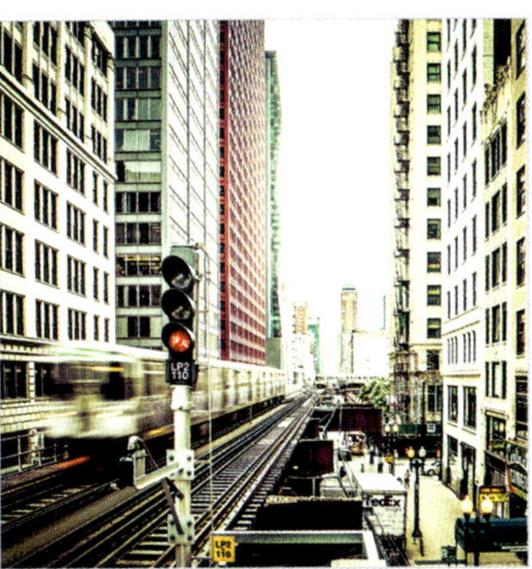

Page 186

Camera: Canon EOS R

Lens: 24–240mm f/4–6.3 @ 26mm

Aperture Value: f/22

Shutter Speed: 1/8 sec

ISO: 100

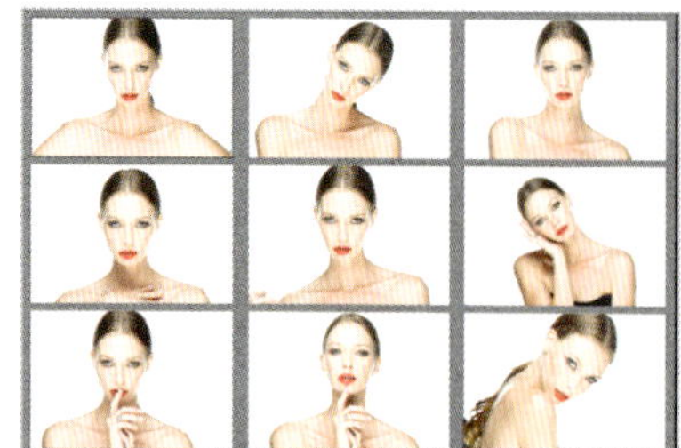

Page 188

Camera: Canon EOS 5D Mark IV

Lens: 70–200mm f/2.8 @ 155mm

Aperture Value: f/5.6

Shutter Speed: 1/125 sec

ISO: 100

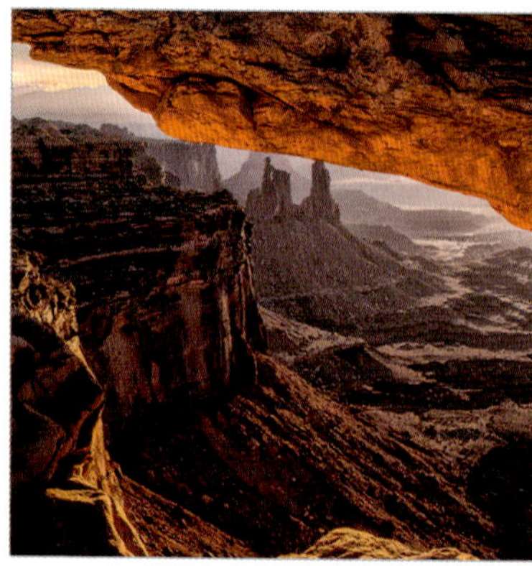

Page 190

Camera: Nikon D3

Lens: 24–70mm f/2.8 @ 28mm

Aperture Value: f/22

Shutter Speed: 3/10 sec

ISO: 200

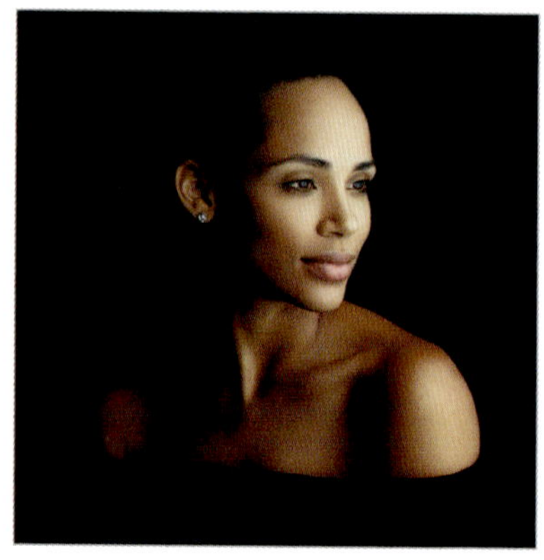

Page 192

Camera: Canon EOS 5D Mark III

Lens: 70–200mm f/2.8 @ 100mm

Aperture Value: f/9

Shutter Speed: 1/125 sec

ISO: 100

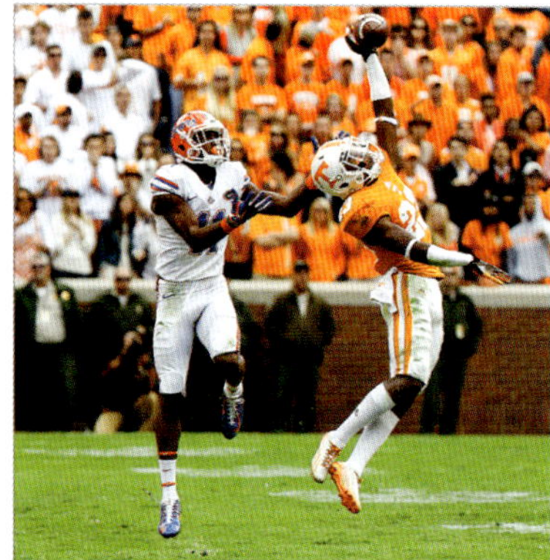

Page 194

Camera: Canon EOS 7D Mark III

Lens: 200–400mm f/4 @ 266mm

Aperture Value: f/4

Shutter Speed: 1/1250 sec

ISO: 320

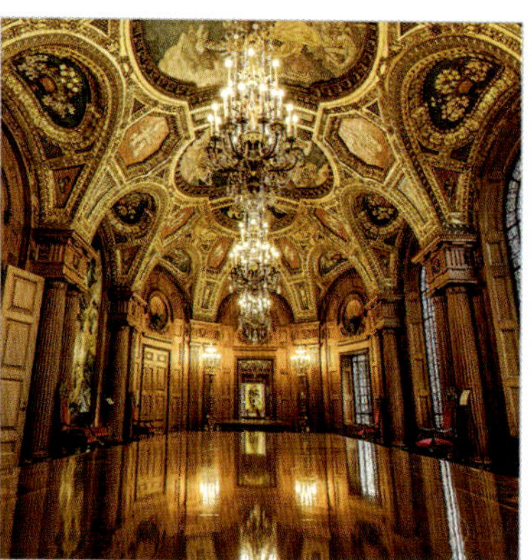

Page 196

Camera: Canon EOS R

Lens: 16–35mm f/4 @ 16mm

Aperture Value: f/11

Shutter Speed: 2/5 sec

ISO: 100

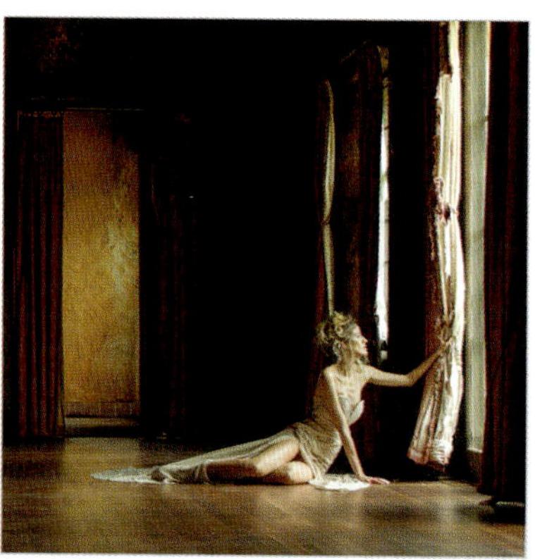

Page 198

Camera: Canon EOS-1D X

Lens: 70–200mm f/2.8 @ 70mm

Aperture Value: f/2.8

Shutter Speed: 1/50 sec

ISO: 200

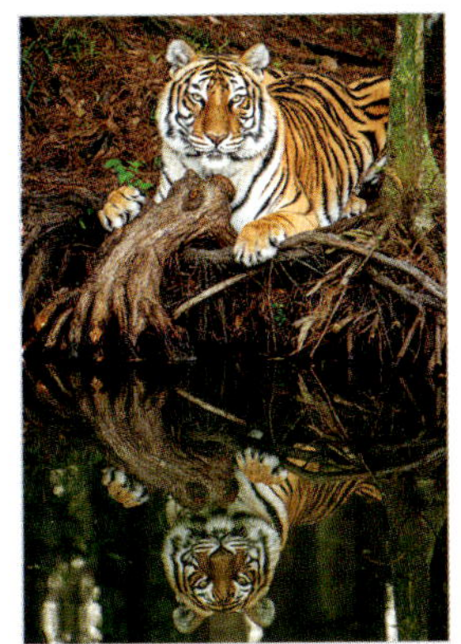

Page 200

Camera: Nikon D200

Lens: 70–200mm f/2.8 @ 220mm

Aperture Value: $f/4$

Shutter Speed: 1/20 sec

ISO: 400

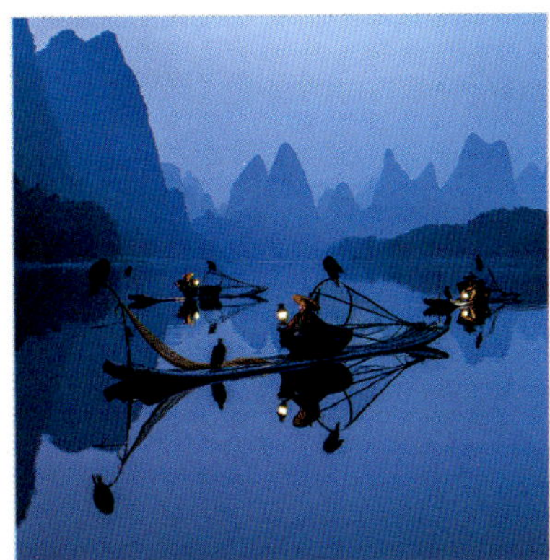

Page 202

Camera: Canon EOS R

Lens: 24–240mm f/4–6.3 @ 35mm

Aperture Value: $f/5.6$

Shutter Speed: 1/5 sec

ISO: 800

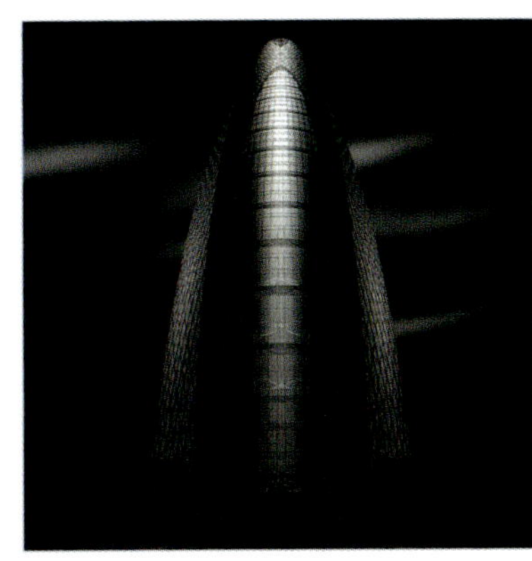

Page 204

Camera: Canon EOS R

Lens: 16–35mm f/4 @ 16mm

Aperture Value: $f/11$

Shutter Speed: 1/50 sec

ISO: 100

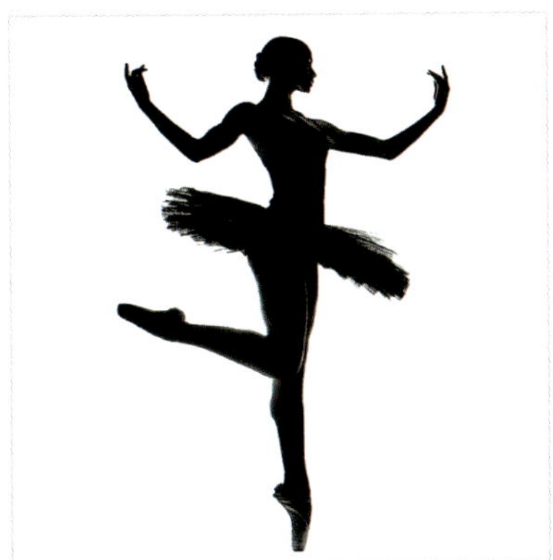

Page 206

Camera: Canon EOS 5DS

Lens: 16–35mm f/4 @ 35mm

Aperture Value: $f/5.6$

Shutter Speed: 1/125 sec

ISO: 100

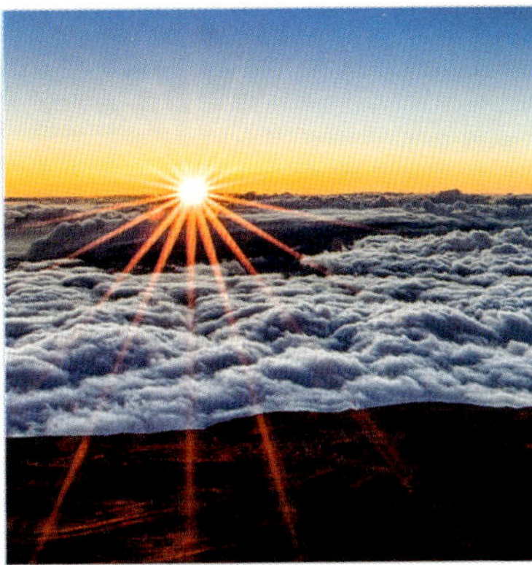

Page 208

Camera: Canon EOS 5DS

Lens: 11–24mm f/4 @ 11mm

Aperture Value: $f/22$

Shutter Speed: 1/25 sec

ISO: 100

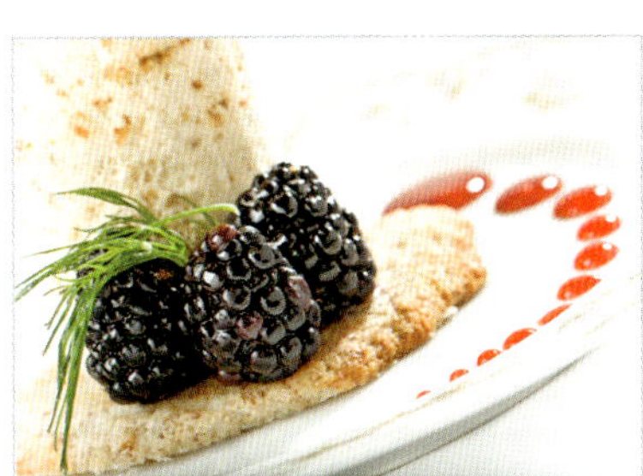

Page 210

Camera: Nikon D3

Lens: 70–180mm f/4.5–5.6 @ 170mm

Aperture Value: $f/14$

Shutter Speed: 1/250 sec

ISO: 100

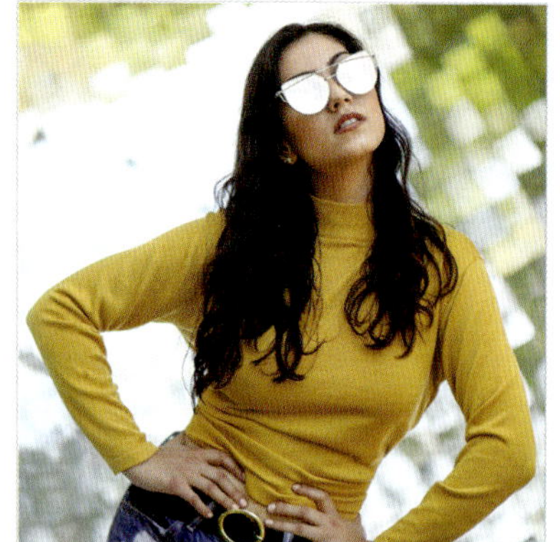

Page 212

Camera: Canon EOS 5D Mark IV

Lens: 85mm f/1.2 @ 85mm

Aperture Value: f/1.8

Shutter Speed: 1/2000 sec

ISO: 400

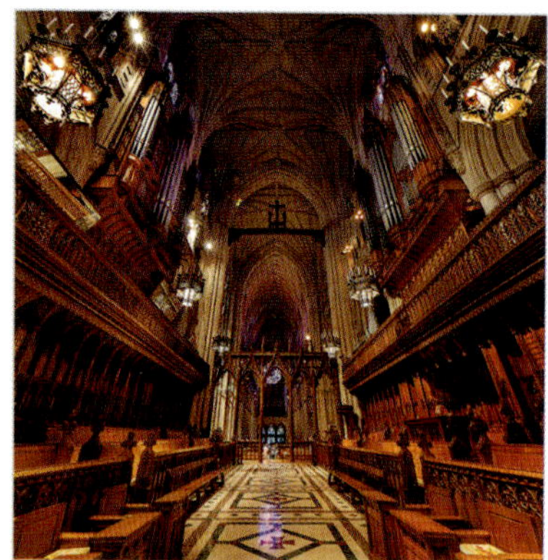

Page 214

Camera: Canon EOS 5D Mark IV

Lens: 11–24mm f/4 @ 11mm

Aperture Value: f/10

Shutter Speed: 9/5 sec

ISO: 100

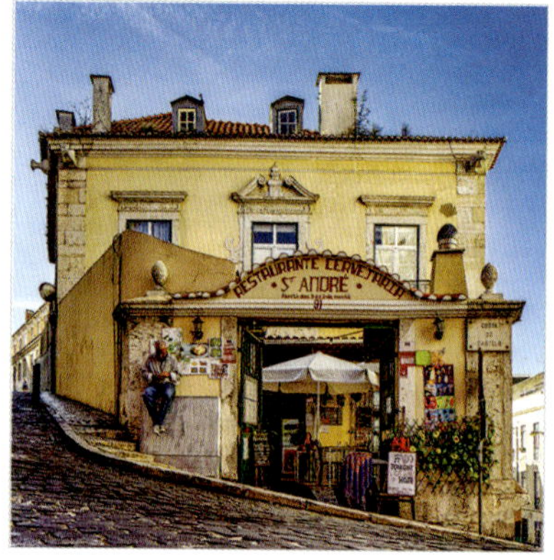

Page 216

Camera: Canon EOS R6 Mark II

Lens: 24–240mm f/4–6.3 @ 24mm

Aperture Value: f/5.6

Shutter Speed: 1/1250 sec

ISO: 400

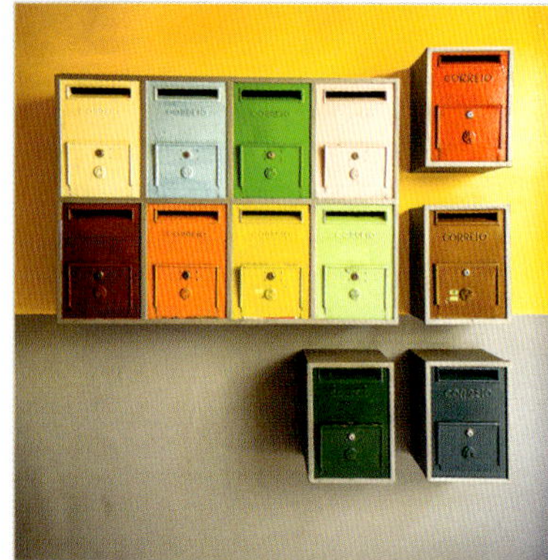

Page 218

Camera: Canon EOS R6 Mark II

Lens: 24–240mm f/4–6.3 @ 24mm

Aperture Value: f/4

Shutter Speed: 1/100 sec

ISO: 1600

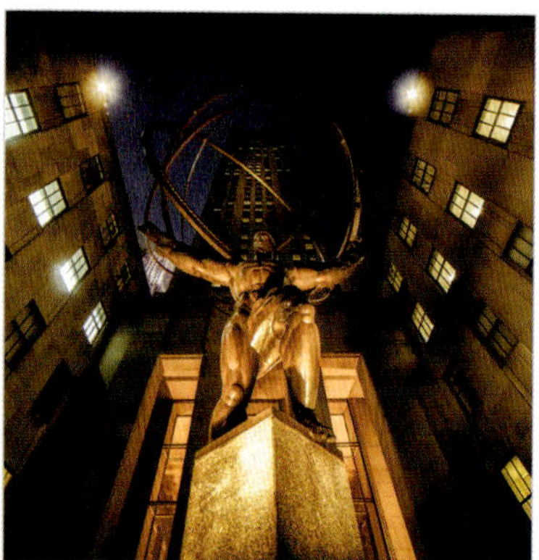

Page 220

Camera: Canon EOS 5D Mark IV

Lens: 14mm f/2.8 @ 14mm

Aperture Value: f/5.6

Shutter Speed: 1/50 sec

ISO: 12800

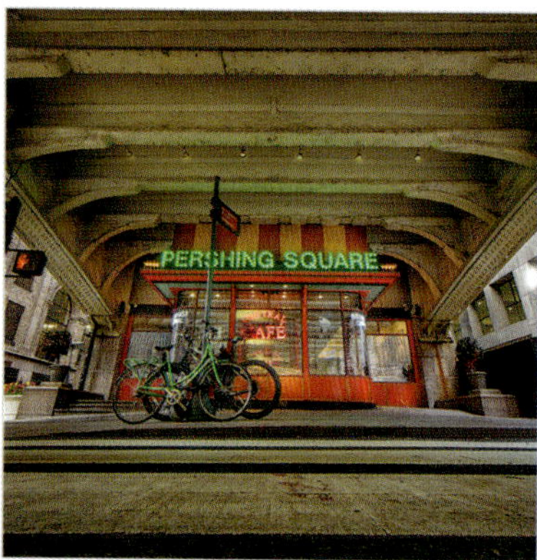

Page 222

Camera: Canon EOS 5D Mark IV

Lens: 14mm f/2.8 @ 14mm

Aperture Value: f/11

Shutter Speed: 3/10 sec

ISO: 100

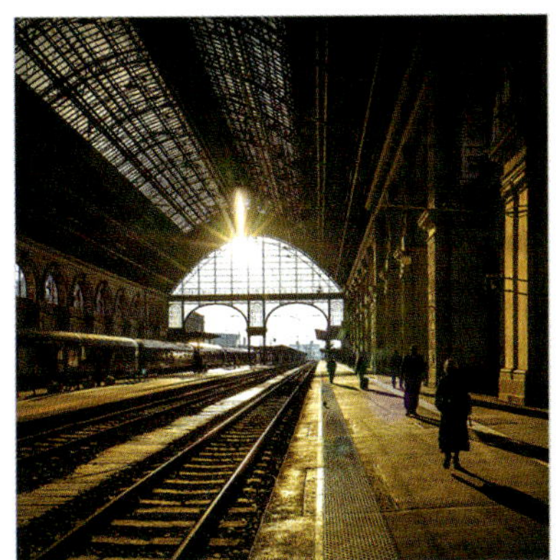

Page 226

Camera: Canon EOS R6 Mark II

Lens: 24–240mm f/4–6.3 @ 24mm

Aperture Value: f/8

Shutter Speed: 1/4000 sec

ISO: 200

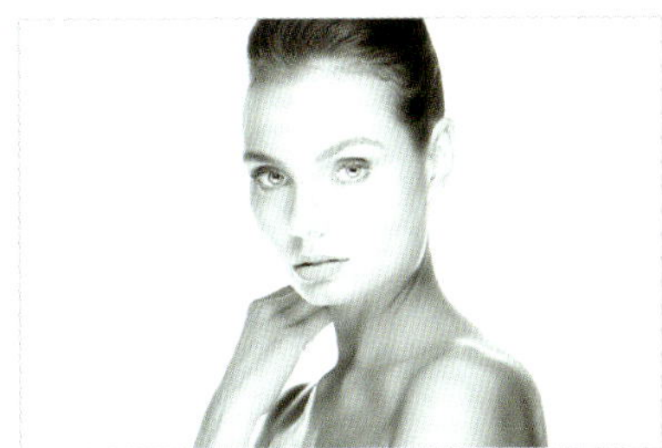

Page 228

Camera: Canon EOS-1D X

Lens: 70–200mm f/2.8 @ 168mm

Aperture Value: f/8

Shutter Speed: 1/125 sec

ISO: 100

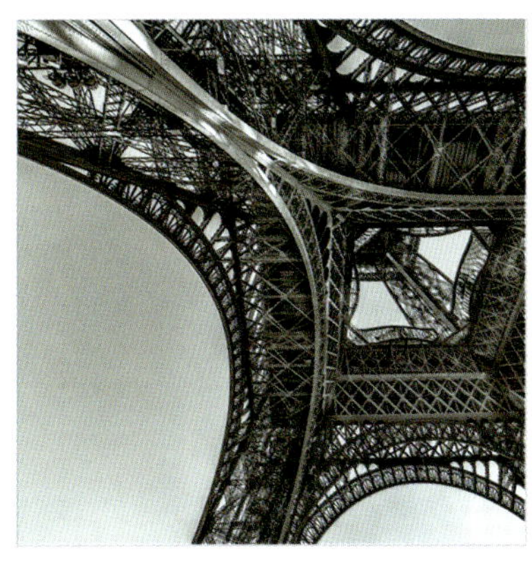

Page 230

Camera: Canon EOS-1D X

Lens: 11–24mm f/4 @ 12mm

Aperture Value: f/5.6

Shutter Speed: 1/125 sec

ISO: 100

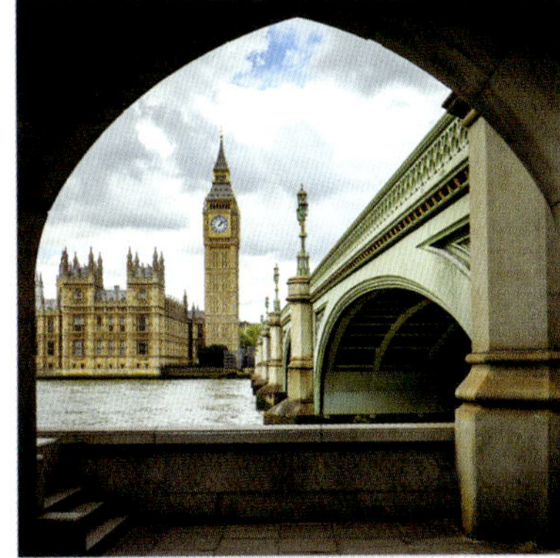

Page 232

Camera: Canon EOS R6 Mark II

Lens: 24–240mm f/4–6.3 @ 35mm

Aperture Value: f/5

Shutter Speed: 1/320 sec

ISO: 100

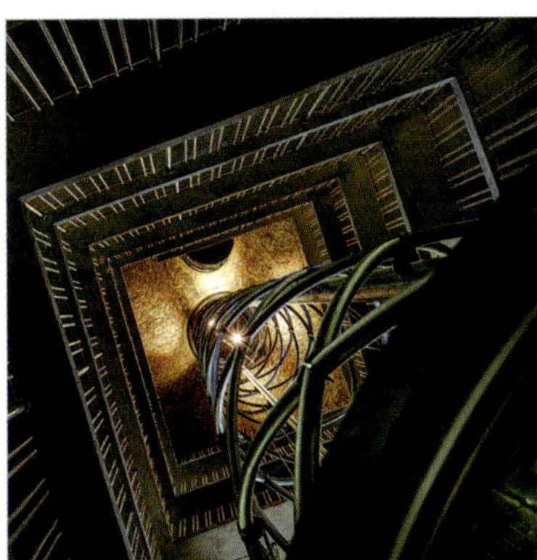

Page 234

Camera: Canon EOS 5D Mark III

Lens: 16–35mm f/2.8 @ 35mm

Aperture Value: f/6.4

Shutter Speed: 4/5 sec

ISO: 400

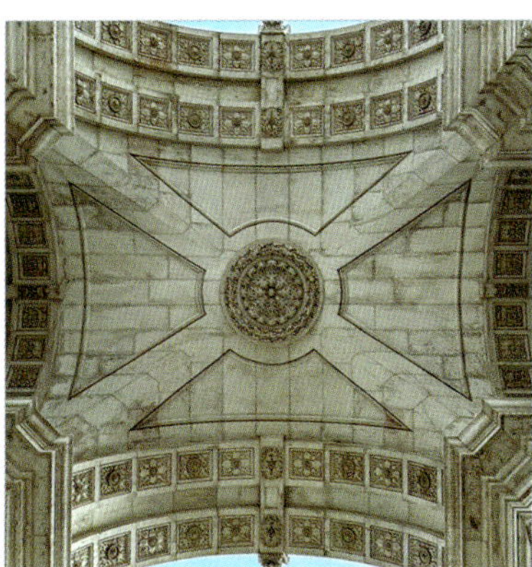

Page 236

Camera: Apple iPhone 14 Pro

Lens: @2.7 mm

Aperture Value: f/1.9

Shutter Speed: 1/25 sec

ISO: 400

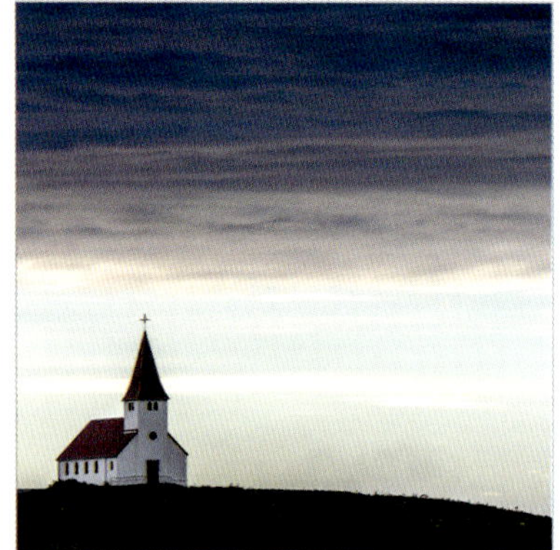

Page 238

Camera: Canon EOS 5D Mark IV

Lens: 70–200mm f/2.8 @ 200mm

Aperture Value: f/11

Shutter Speed: 1/160 sec

ISO: 100

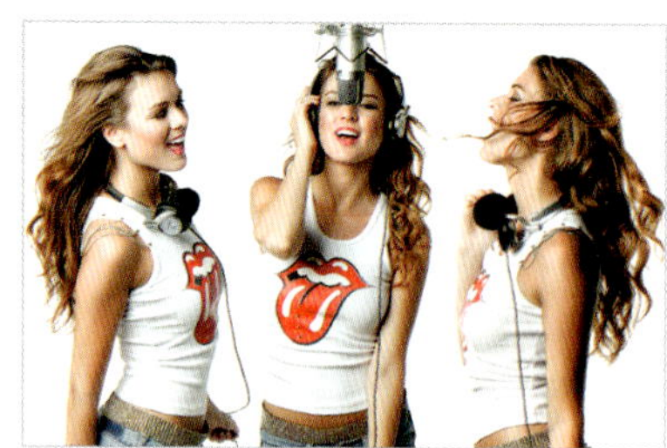

Page 240

Camera: Nikon D3

Lens: 70–200mm f/2.8 @ 82mm

Aperture Value: f/7.1

Shutter Speed: 1/160 sec

ISO: 200

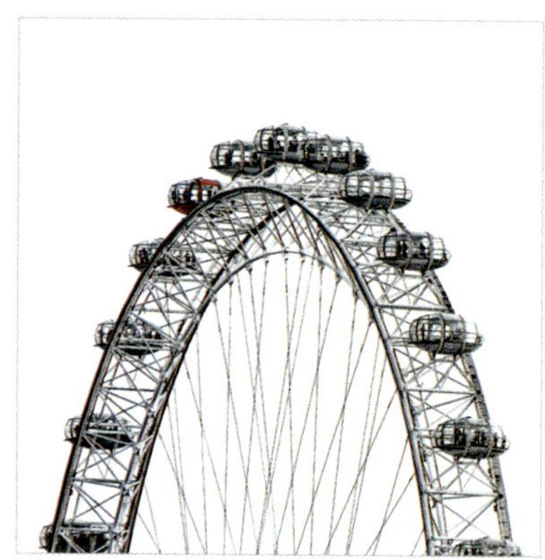

Page 242

Camera: Nikon D3

Lens: 28–300mm f/3.5–5.6 @ 300mm

Aperture Value: f/5.6

Shutter Speed: 1/1000 sec

ISO: 200

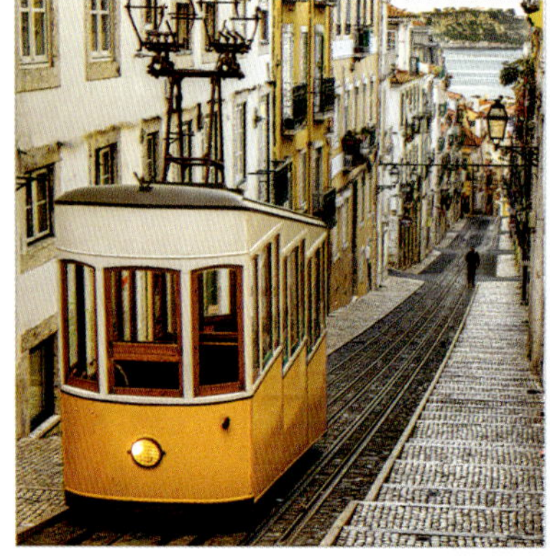

Page 244

Camera: Canon EOS R6 Mark II

Lens: 24–240mm f/4–6.3 @ 52mm

Aperture Value: f/5

Shutter Speed: 1/200 sec

ISO: 1600

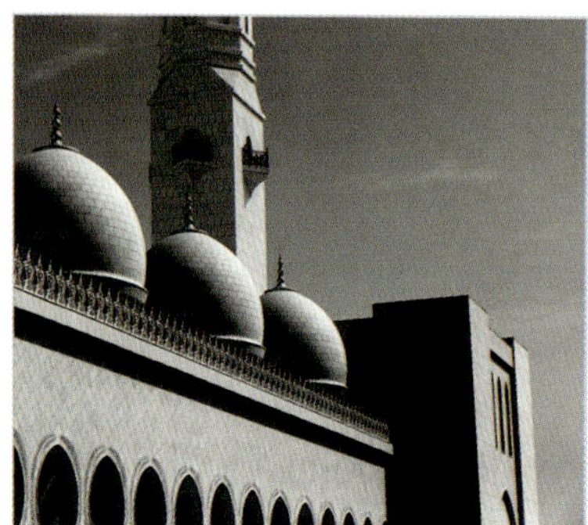

Page 246

Camera: Canon EOS-1D X

Lens: 70–200mm f/2.8 @ 70mm

Aperture Value: f/4

Shutter Speed: 1/4000 sec

ISO: 100

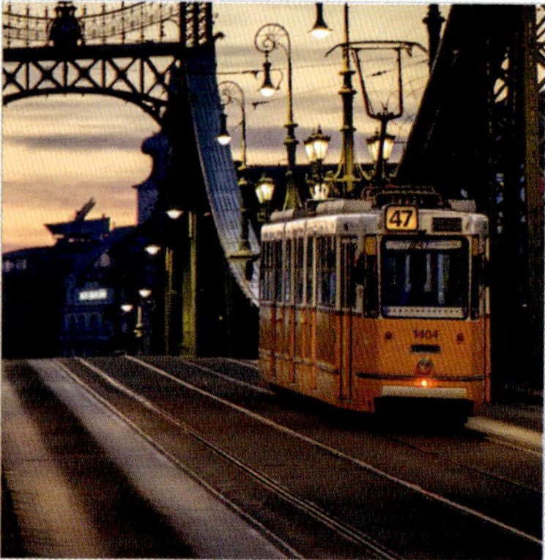

Page 248

Camera: Canon EOS R6 Mark II

Lens: 24–240mm f/4–6.3 @ 240mm

Aperture Value: f/6.3

Shutter Speed: 1/200 sec

ISO: 6400

INDEX